A GRAMMAR OF THE JEWISH ARABIC DIALECT OF GABES

A Grammar of the Jewish Arabic Dialect of Gabes

Wiktor Gębski

https://www.openbookpublishers.com

©2024 Wiktor Gębski

This work is licensed under an Attribution-NonCommercial 4.0 International (CC BY-NC 4.0). This license allows you to share, copy, distribute, and transmit the text; to adapt the text for non-commercial purposes of the text providing attribution is made to the authors (but not in any way that suggests that they endorse you or your use of the work). Attribution should include the following information:

Wiktor Gębski, *A Grammar of the Jewish Arabic Dialect of Gabes*. Cambridge, UK: Open Book Publishers, 2024, https://doi.org/10.11647/OBP.0394

Further details about CC BY-NC licenses are available at
http://creativecommons.org/licenses/by-nc/4.0/

All external links were active at the time of publication unless otherwise stated and have been archived via the Internet Archive Wayback Machine at
https://archive.org/web

Any digital material and resources associated with this volume will be available at https://doi.org/10.11647/OBP.0394#resources

Semitic Languages and Cultures, vol. 23

ISSN (print): 2632-6906
ISSN (digital): 2632-6914
ISBN Paperback: 978-1-80511-251-8
ISBN Hardback: 978-1-80511-252-5
ISBN Digital (PDF): 978-1-80511-253-2
DOI: 10.11647/OBP.0394

Cover image: Tunisia (2021), photo by Attila Janosi on Unsplash, https://unsplash.com/photos/green-palm-tree-near-brown-mountain-during-daytime-xlO4V1RRFIY

Cover design: Jeevanjot Kaur Nagpal

The main fonts used in this volume are Charis SIL, SBL Hebrew, Scheherazade New, and SBL Greek.

Nothing is ever really lost, or can be lost
No birth, identity, norm—no object of the world
Walt Whitman

ספר זה מוקדש לחיה, לאה ויוסף באהבה ובהערכה.

CONTENTS

Preface ix

List of Tables and Figures xiii

Abbreviations and Symbols xvii

1. Introduction 1

Part I: Phonology 23

   2. Phonology 25

Part II: Morphology 89

   3. Verbal Morphology 91

   4. Nominal Morphology 139

Part III: Diachronic and Comparative Studies in Syntax 203

   5. Syntax of Nouns 205

      1.0. Definiteness 205

      2.0. Genitive Constructions 229

      3.0. Grammatical Concord 243

6. Syntax of Verbs and Clauses 261
    1.0. Clausal Subordination 261
    2.0. Expressions of Tense and Aspect 320
    3.0. Word Order 365
7. Syntax of Pronouns 385
    1.0. Demonstrative Pronouns 385

8. Conclusion 401

Appendix: A Corpus of Selected Narratives
Quoted in the Volume 407
Bibliography 463
Index 491

PREFACE

This volume presents a linguistic study of the Arabic dialect spoken by the Jews of Gabes (Southern Tunisia)—a variety that belongs to the group of sedentary North African dialects and nowadays is spoken by a limited number of native speakers in Israel and France. As with virtually all modern varieties of Judaeo-Arabic and many other Jewish languages, Jewish Gabes faces imminent extinction. This study, therefore, aims at the documentation and the description of its major features while there are still reliable speakers alive.

The data for this study were collected during several stints of fieldwork in Israel and France between December 2018 and March 2022. Due to the COVID pandemic, the collection of data for the syntax chapter also involved the use of social media and other online methods of communication. The linguistic analysis is based on questionnaires and a corpus of transcribed tales and memories.

This project has attempted to answer some of the most immediate challenges posed by Maghrebi Arabic dialectology. In contradistinction to the eastern branch of Arabic, many North-African dialects have not received a thorough linguistic description, particularly those spoken outside large, historic towns. Even less studied are Jewish dialects, whose linguistic features and isoglosses remain *terra incognita*. A lack of text corpora and appropriate data, in turn, has caused an almost complete absence of syntactic studies in the field. The main objective of this volume is thus a detailed comparative analysis of Jewish Gabes, with a particular focus on syntax.

The volume comprises three main sections: phonology, morphology, and syntax. The first two sections follow a traditional grammatical model. Syntax has been approached from historical and typological points of view. In order to establish whether certain linguistic features are unique to Jewish Gabes, a comparison with other North African dialects has been applied throughout the study.

The publication of this volume was made possible thanks to the generous support of the Rothschild Foundation. A postdoctoral fellowship sponsored by the Rothschild Foundation enabled me to prepare the final manuscript of this book. I am also deeply grateful to the British Academy, which awarded me a travel grant (grant no. SRG2223\231603). Thanks to this, I was able to return to Israel after the pandemic and consult with my informants further.

The realisation of this project was extended over a period of a few years, during which a number of individuals showed me support and kindness. Firstly, I would like to express my deep gratitude to my friend Eylon Ben-Lulu, thanks to whom I became interested in modern Israel and in the cultural heritage of the Jewish communities of North Africa. His support and hospitality during my field trips to Israel have been invaluable.

I would like to thank all my informants, who agreed to participate in my study despite many difficult conditions. I am immensely grateful to Haya Mazouz, Tzivia Tobi, Yosef Maymon, and Mazliah and Sara Hakmoun for their patience and kindness.

A special thanks goes to Lea Maymon from Ramle, whose help during the COVID pandemic has made the completion of this project possible.

I am deeply grateful to my supervisor, Professor Geoffrey Khan, who made coming to Cambridge possible and guided me throughout my doctoral and postdoctoral research. I have greatly benefited from his knowledge, experience, and support. Discovering field linguistics and documenting an endangered language under his supervision have been a fascinating adventure indeed.

I would like to extend my gratitude to the editor of this book, Dr Anne Burberry, and Professor Aaron Hornkohl, who offered me a great deal of technical support during the preparation of this book. In addition, I would like to thank two anonymous reviewers, whose comments have greatly improved the quality of the volume.

I would like to thank my family for their love, care, and support.

LIST OF TABLES AND FIGURES

Tables

Table 1: Native speakers of Jewish Gabes participating in the study

Table 2: Transcription of Classical Arabic sounds used in this volume

Table 3: Consonantal inventory

Table 4: Minimal pairs involving sibilants in selected dialects of North Africa

Table 5: Directionality of emphasis spread in Jewish Gabes

Table 6: Emphasis spread scale

Table 7: Diphthongs in CA, Jewish Wad-Souf, and Jewish Gabes

Table 8: Syllable structure development in CA and Jewish Gabes

Table 9: Comparison of syllable structure in selected dialects of North-African Arabic

Table 10: Triliteral verb stems attested in Jewish Gabes

Table 11: Vocalic variants of the I stem in CA

Table 12: Formation of the passive in Berber (based on Kossmann 2002)

Table 13: Suffix conjugation

Table 14: Prefix conjugation

Table 15: Paradigm of *ḍrəb–yəḍrab* 'to hit' (strong root)

Table 16: Paradigm of *šədd–yšədd* 'to seize' (geminated root)

Table 17: Paradigm of *wṣəl* 'to arrive' (first radical semi-vowel /w/)

Table 18: Paradigm of *yəbəš* 'to dry' (first radical semi-vowel /i/)

Table 19: Paradigm of *qām–yqūm* 'to wake up' (pattern CāC–yəCūC)

Table 20: Paradigm of *žāb–yžīb* 'to bring' (pattern CāC–yəCīC)

Table 21: Paradigm of *xāf–yxāf* 'to be frightened' (pattern CāC–yəCāC)

Table 22: Paradigm of *ṛma–yəṛmi* 'to throw' (pattern CCa–yəCCi)

Table 23: Paradigm of *ṛḍa–yəṛḍa* 'to agree' (pattern CCa–yəCCa)

Table 24: Paradigm of *kla* 'to eat'

Table 25: Paradigm of *ufa* 'to stop' (pattern Iw + IIIy)

Table 26: Paradigm of *ža* 'to come'

Table 27: Paradigm of *ṛa* 'to see'

Table 28: Paradigm of *ṣaṛṛəf* 'to cash money' (strong root)

Table 29: Paradigm of *xammən* 'to think' (geminated root)

Table 30: Paradigm of *waṛṛa* 'to show' (weak third radical)

Table 31: Paradigm of *qābəl* 'to meet' (strong root)

Table 32: Paradigm of *ʕāwən* 'to help' (weak first radical)

Table 33: Paradigm of *nāda* 'to call, to warn' (weak third radical)

Table 34: Paradigm of *təktəb* 'to be written' (strong root)

Table 35: Paradigm of *tkalləm* 'to talk' (strong root)

Table 36: Paradigm of *txabba* 'to hide oneself' (weak third radical)

Table 37: Paradigm of *tʕāžəb* 'to be surprised' (strong root)

Table 38: Paradigm of *nədbaḥ* 'to be slaughtered' (strong root)

Table 39: Paradigm of *xṭāṛ* 'to choose' (weak second radical)

Table 40: Paradigm of *štaʕžəb* 'to be surprised' (strong root)

Table 41: Paradigm of *sthaqq* 'to be in need of' (geminated root)

Table 42: Paradigm of *štāhəl* 'to deserve' (weak first radical)

Table 43: Paradigm of *štaġna* 'to become rich' (weak third radical)
Table 44: Paradigm of *ḍʕāf* 'to lose weight'
Table 45: Gender divergence in Jewish Gabes as compared to CA
Table 46: Nouns with irregular gender formation
Table 47: Formation of the collective in Jewish Gabes
Table 48: Independent personal pronouns
Table 49: Pronominal suffixes
Table 50: Examples of nouns with pronominal suffixes
Table 51: *ṣḍəṛ* 'breast' with pronominal suffixes
Table 52: *livro* (Ital.) 'book' with possessive particle
Table 53: *nša* 'he forgot' and *žāt* 'she came' with pronominal suffixes
Table 54: Strong verb with pronominal suffixes
Table 55: Prefix conjugation with enclitic dative marker
Table 56: Suffix conjugation with enclitic dative marker
Table 57: Inflection of particle /rūḥ-/
Table 58: Inflection of particle /waḥd-/
Table 59: *mā-/ša-* + elative with pronominal suffixes
Table 60: Near demonstrative pronouns
Table 61: Far demonstrative pronouns
Table 62: Hopper and Thompson's parameters of transitivity
Table 63: Hierarchy of individuation based on Khan (1988)
Table 64: Points of divergence between the system of definiteness in Jewish Gabes and Moroccan Arabic
Table 65: Anthropomorphism in Text (7)
Table 66: Genitive exponents in selected dialects of Arabic
Table 67: Agreement patterns in Jewish Tunis (Cohen 1964)

Table 68: Vowel distribution in Eastern and Western dialects of Arabic

Figures

Figure 1: Mean qualities of the main phonemic vowels of Jewish Gabes
Figure 2: Qualities of /a/
Figure 3: Qualities of /ī/
Figure 4: Qualities of /ū/
Figure 5: Qualities of /ə/
Figure 6: An example of a thematical span

ABBREVIATIONS AND SYMBOLS

ACC	accusative
AUX	auxiliary
C	consonant
CA	Classical Arabic
coll.	collective
DEF	definite article
DU	dual
F	feminine
Fr.	French
GEN	genitive
Gr.	Greek
Heb.	Hebrew
INDF	indefinite article
Ital.	Italian
M	masculine
N/A	not attested
NEG	negation
P / PL	plural
PFX	prefix
PVPT	preverbal particle
REL	relative particle
SUB	subordinate particle
SFX	suffix
S / SG	singular
Sp.	Spanish
S, V, O	subject, verb, object

T–C	topic–comment
Turk.	Turkish
V	vowel
VOC	vocative
<	derives from
>	results in
*	ungrammatical or unattested form
[]	non-phonemic sounds, IPA transcription
//	phonemic sounds
ᴴᴱ_ᴴᴱ	Hebrew

1. INTRODUCTION

1.0. Historical Background of the Jewish Community of Gabes

Gabes (in the local Jewish dialect pronounced as Gābəš), alongside Tunis and Djerba, was one of the centres of Jewish life in Tunisia. It is hard to establish when exactly the Jews first settled down in this city, since sources about the beginning of the Jewish presence in the region are rather obscure. The Jewish community in Gabes started to prosper after the Muslim conquest in 670 (Saadoun 2006, 11) and significantly increased the number of its members after 1492 when many Jews were forced to leave Spain. The historical documents of the Cairo Genizah constitute an invaluable source of our knowledge of the day-to-day life of the Jewish community of Gabes. Among them are the responsa of the Babylonian Geonim to halakhic questions asked by the Jews of Gabes, which attest to robust trade networks, as well as a wide range of agricultural activities (Ben-Sasson 1982, 278). In the first half of the 20th century, the Jewish population of Tunisia was gradually increasing. According to official statistics, there were 48,436 Jews in Tunisia in 1921, whereas in 1946 this number increased to 70,900, and then rapidly dropped in 1956 to 57,543 (Saadoun 2006, 30). The population of the Jewish community of Gabes exhibits a similar tendency, reaching 3,210 members in 1946, then decreasing to 2,252 in 1956 and falling to its lowest point in 1976 with only 70 members. Currently, most of the speakers of Jewish Gabes live in France (Paris, Marseille), and Israel (Ashkelon, Ramle, Netivot, and others).

2.0. Linguistic Features of Jewish Gabes

The Jewish dialect of Gabes can be categorised as a sedentary, urban Maghrebi dialect and, like many other Jewish dialects, it differs in certain ways from Muslim dialects.[1] The linguistic features of this dialect have their origin in the first wave of Arab settlement in this region (7th–10th century), which was subsequently followed by an extensive invasion by the tribes of Banū Sulaym and Banū Hilāl. The latter event brought about a shift from the sedentary rural dialects to dialects of the Bedouin type (Palva 2011). In the present book, following a recently coined terminology, the terms 'pre-Hilālī' and 'first-wave' dialects will be used interchangeably.

The cultural and linguistic legacy of North African Jews faced the threat of disappearance after the foundation of the state of Israel in 1947. After massive migrations to Israel from Arabic countries, Jewish communities were immersed in a Hebrew-speaking environment, where their native Arabic tongue was perceived as second class by the local population and the immigrants alike. The generations born in Israel did not acquire the languages of their parents and grandparents and hence nowadays the only native speakers of Jewish Arabic dialects are people born between the 1930s and 1950s, i.e., those who grew up in an Arabic-speaking environment and whose first language is Arabic. It

---

[1] Considering the classification coined by Ph. Marçais, Jewish Gabes exhibits several isoglosses characteristic for *parlers citadins* (1957, 221).

is estimated, therefore, that all Jewish Arabic vernaculars will disappear within a generation (except for the Jewish dialect of Djerba, where a Jewish community still exists).

From a typological point of view, the dialect of Gabes shares many features with dialects of Libya, Algeria, and, naturally, other sedentary Tunisian dialects. In this study, therefore, the dialect of Jewish Gabes will be compared with Muslim and Jewish dialects of Libya, Tunisia, and Algeria. The data for the Jewish dialect of Wad-Souf (El-Oued) in eastern Algeria and Jewish Djerba have been collected by the author and are also analysed in the study.[2] The data for Muslim Gabes come primarily from Skik (1969) and from a recording of a male Muslim speaker from Gabes.[3] Due to the lack of sufficient data, the comparative study of the Jewish and Muslim dialects of Gabes is limited to phonology. Nevertheless, as will be demonstrated, phonological features indicate that these dialects are typologically distinct, with the Jewish variety being of a sedentary character, while the Muslim one exhibits numerous Hilālī features.[4] Occasionally, some references are made to Moroccan Arabic, which, however,

---

[2] Unless indicated as based on Behnstedt (1998; 1999), my observations of Jewish Djerba are based on my own recordings of 7 informants made in December 2022 in Israel.

[3] The speaker was recorded by Dr Maciej Klimiuk in 2016. I would like to extend my gratitude to Dr Klimiuk for sharing this recording with me.

[4] Indeed, William Marçais classifies the dialect of Gabes as Bedouin (1950, 207).

due to its complexity and distinct character, is beyond the comparative scope of this study. Finally, Classical Arabic serves as comparative material when discussing the historical development of selected forms in Jewish Gabes.

3.0. Previous Research on North African Arabic and its Challenges

In contradistinction to the eastern branch of Arabic (i.e., east of Egypt), North African Arabic is distinguished by a relative dearth of linguistic studies. Due to the vast distances involved and the geographic isolation of many communities, previous research has been mainly focused on large coastal cities, e.g., Algiers (Cohen 1912), Djidjelli (Marçais 1956), Tunis (Muslim Tunis: Singer 1984, Jewish Tunis: Cohen 1975), Jewish Tripoli (Yoda 2005), Benghazi (Benkato 2014), Oran (Guerrero 2015), and Dellys (Souag 2005). Lucienne Saada published a study on the west Tunisian dialect of Tozeur containing an extensive glossary (1984). In addition, Peter Behnstedt has made an important contribution to our knowledge of Tunisian Arabic by publishing two extensive articles on the dialects of Djerba, both the Muslim and Jewish ones (1998 grammar; 1999 texts). In recent years, there have also been some detailed studies of the Bedouin varieties, mostly from Tunisia (Ritt-Benmimoun 2011; 2014). It is worth noting, however, that the aforementioned works deal primarily with phonology and morphology. Syntax, on the other hand, remains heavily understudied. An exception to this rule is found in a detailed description of the syntax of Moroccan Arabic by Caubet (1993).

Modern varieties of spoken Judaeo-Arabic have started to attract significant scholarly attention in recent years. This has given birth to several valuable studies, like those of Bar-Moshe on Baghdadi Arabic (2019), Matsa on Damascene (2019), and Shachmon on Jewish Yemeni (2022), and numerous other books and articles. The Jewish dialects of North African Arabic have also sparked much interest, with most of the publications focusing on Moroccan (e.g., Heath & Bar-Asher 1982; Chetrit 2017; Sibony 2022) and more recently, on Libyan Arabic (D'Anna 2021). General overviews of the Jewish Maghrebi dialects have been offered by Chetrit (2014; 2015). Jewish varieties of Tunisian and particularly of Algerian Arabic, on the other hand, have received much less attention.[5] In fact, since Cohen's (1975) grammar of the Jewish dialect of Tunis, no major grammar of Tunisian Judaeo-Arabic has been published.

The field of spoken Judaeo-Arabic faces limitations due to socio-historical factors. Conducting fully-fledged fieldwork is increasingly difficult, as most of the informants are of advanced age. Moreover, the reliability of data is diminishing because of prolonged contact with the speakers' L2 languages, such as Hebrew or French. Currently, the only Jewish community in the Arab world where robust field research is still feasible is that of

---

[5] Lucienne Saada published two articles on spoken Tunisian Judaeo-Arabic, specifically the dialect of Sousa (1958) and a short description of the dialect of Djerba (1963). It is important to notice, however, that Behnstedt (1998; 1999), in his study of Djerba Arabic, notices some differences between Saada's data and his own. This highlights the need for more updated and comprehensive fieldwork.

Djerba. As mentioned before, Behnstedt (1998; 1999) has provided a preliminary description of this dialect, but a more extensive and in-depth study is still needed.

The field of North African dialectology suffers from three major defects: lack of sufficient primary data, lack of comparative studies, and lack of syntactic studies. Naturally, the last lacuna stems from the two previous ones, since syntactic phenomena can be ascertained only on the basis of text corpora. In addition, we still do not have a complete picture of the confessional and communal aspects of Maghrebi Arabic, presumably due to the difficulty of reaching both Jewish speakers in Israel, and their Muslim neighbours in their country of origin. On the other hand, the field of Jewish North African dialectology has its own challenges. One of them is undoubtedly a lack of a diachronic approach to both older forms of Judaeo-Arabic and its modern varieties, which currently exist as two separate entities. As a result, the historical development of Jewish Arabic as spoken in the Maghreb has been almost completely neglected in scholarship. Additionally, due to the age of the speakers, the modern varieties of Maghrebi Judaeo-Arabic face imminent extinction. Admirable efforts to document and preserve these dialects, and indeed many other Jewish languages, have been made in recent years by the Mother Tongue Project (Israel, directed by Yehudit Henshke). The final factor hindering thorough research on modern Jewish Arabic is extensive language contact with Hebrew, which causes serious erosion of original linguistic features and contributes to the loss of complexity. A scholar of Jewish North African Arabic therefore has to distinguish which forms and structures constitute the original layer of the language, and which have emerged under the influence of Israeli Hebrew.

4.0. Languages Spoken in North Africa Prior to the Arrival of Arabs: Historical Background[6]

As mentioned earlier, Jewish Gabes represents one of the so-called 'first-wave' dialects, which emerged at the onset of the Muslim presence in North Africa. The debate regarding the exact start of Jewish settlement in North Africa is yet to be concluded, but even the most stringent historical accounts suggest a Jewish presence in the region as early as the first century CE (Le Bohec 2021, 89).[7] Given the historical depth of these varieties, it is pertinent to provide a brief overview of the languages spoken in the Maghreb before the arrival of Arabs, as they are relevant to the formation of the first Arabic dialects.

---

[6] This section is a modified version of a part of my article 'The Development of Sibilant Harmony in Maghrebi Arabic from the Perspective of Language Contact in Pre-Islamic Africa' (Gębski 2023b).

[7] Some historians propose an even earlier dating. N. Slousch (1906) argues that the first Jewish settlements in North Africa were established during the Punic era. Le Bohec (2021, 19) rejects this assumption, calling into question the arguments presented by Slousch and claiming that the first Jews arrived in North Africa after the two Jewish uprisings against the Romans in the first century CE. Regardless of whether Jewish settlement in the Maghreb started before the common era or, as suggested in §4.2, at the beginning of it, Punic could have survived as a vernacular until the first half of the first millennium CE. It therefore seems reasonable to look for potential linguistic traits it could have left in first-wave dialects.

Synchronically, the linguistic landscape of North Africa is relatively homogenous compared to other parts of the Arab world, where Arabic dialects coexist with different language families. For example, in northern Iraq, apart from Arabic, there are spoken numerous varieties of Kurdish (Indo-Iranian) and dialects of Turkish (Turkic) as well as North-Eastern Neo-Aramaic dialects (Semitic; Khan 2018). However, this has not always been the case, and a diachronic study reveals that the linguistic situation in the Maghreb in the seventh century was much more diverse. Apart from different varieties of Berber, African Latin and Neo-Punic are believed to have been used to some extent in the region of present Libya and Tunisia on the eve of the advent of Islam (Adams 2007; Kossmann 2009, 194, 521; Whittaker 2009, 194). Sources about the active usage of these languages are naturally very scarce, and establishing precisely when they ceased to be used is therefore rather difficult. Nevertheless, one should not assume that a lack of textual sources after a certain point in time necessarily implies the complete extinction of a language. It is entirely possible that both African Latin and Neo-Punic went on being spoken in the first decades of the Arab presence in the Maghreb. Although the expansion of Arabic as an official language was undoubtedly rapid, its adoption in rural and remote areas by speakers of Berber, Latin, and Neo-Punic was rather a gradual process. The multi-linguistic reality of pre-Islamic North Africa should therefore not be omitted in the reconstruction of the processes that led to the formation of the present-day Maghrebi dialectal group.

4.1. Berber

Berber is the only family of languages that has remained in permanent contact with Arabic in this region up until the present day. The mutual influences between Arabic and Berber have been the subject of numerous studies (Diem 1979; El Aissati 2006; Kossmann 2013; Souag 2017). As one would expect, the influence of Arabic on Berber is significantly more prominent than that of Berber on Arabic. After the Islamic conquest of the Maghreb, Arabic started functioning as the *lingua franca* of the region, and, as a prestigious language of administration and trade, it naturally triggered contact-induced changes in Berber. Nevertheless, it is plausible to assume that the prolonged contact between the two languages on the one hand, and their genetic proximity (both of them belong to the Afro-Asiatic family) on the other, could also have furnished linguistic developments in Arabic. These two factors should not be omitted in studies on Maghrebi Arabic and Berber, as they could potentially cast light on some of the phenomena that distinguish North African Arabic from its eastern-branch counterparts.

Due to cultural and political reasons, Berber was in the weaker position in the language-contact situation from the get-go. The Arab conquest of the Maghreb led to the spread of Islam in the region, and Arabic naturally became the language of the transmission of Islamic teaching and communication (Chtatou 1997, 103). Thus, the religious and linguistic domination imposed by the Arabs on the region inevitably situated Berber in the position of the recipient, rather than the donor, of linguistic borrowing. Nevertheless, there are local fluctuations in Arabic that can be attributed to Berber influence.

Investigation of Berber-induced changes in Arabic presents two major obstacles. Firstly, due to the fact that both linguistic families have been in permanent contact for over 1300 years, it is rather difficult to establish whether certain phenomena in Arabic developed under the influence of Berber, or whether they result from internal language development. Moreover, in cases where both families demonstrate some innovations, the direction of the borrowing is very often uncertain. Another factor weakening any diachronic argumentation is that, since both Maghrebi Arabic and Berber are mainly spoken languages and only limited written sources are available, the history of the language contact between them is always burdened with a high level of vagueness. Therefore, scholars tend to disagree on the nature of many borrowings, often presenting contradictory opinions.

There are several studies available on linguistic borrowings from Berber to Arabic, mainly Moroccan Arabic (Chtatou 1997; El Aissati 2011; Aguadé 2018). Although in the case of lexical borrowings and morphological change there is not much dispute between scholars, explanations of phonological peculiarities of Maghrebi Arabic that involve Berber influence are often met by radically different opinions. Aguadé lists several morphosyntactic phenomena in Moroccan and Algerian Arabic where the influence of Berber is evident (Aguadé 2018, 36). This includes *inter alia* a shift in gender of some nouns, e.g., the originally masculine *lḥam* 'meat' and *ṣūf* 'wool' become feminine since they are feminine in Berber. Certain varieties of Maghrebi Arabic grammaticalise the noun *rāṣ* 'head' instead of *nəfs* 'soul' as a reflexive marker. In addition, Aguadé argues that comparative sentences with *ʕal* instead of *mən* are a calque from Berber. Other morphosyntactic developments are more controversial. El Aissati adduces instances of verb serialisation consisting of two verbal forms, in which the first verb loses its inflection. Although the same phenomenon is attested in Berber, several other varieties of spoken Arabic (Egyptian, Lebanese, Iraqi) also employ this strategy (El Aissati 2011). This evidence, therefore, calls into question the idea of Berber influence and points rather to an internal innovation of spoken Arabic.

As has previously been mentioned, the influence of Berber on the phonology of Maghrebi Arabic is less evident, and many cases of language change in North African Arabic fall within the 'grey zone', i.e., their occurrence cannot be unequivocally accounted for by either internal or external factors. This is the case, for instance, with the loss of the glottal stop in Maghrebi Arabic. Chtatou (1997, 107) has argued that the disappearance of [ʔ] in Moroccan Arabic was caused by the lack of a corresponding sound in Berber. This view was criticised by Aguadé (2018, 35), who points out numerous dialects where [ʔ] is retained, and argues that it is rather a matter of internal innovation. Similar controversies surround the development of the Maghrebi Arabic vowel system, which is noticeably reduced in comparison to its eastern counterparts. Although both Chtatou (1997) and El Aissati (2011) point with a high degree of certainty to Berber influence, Kossmann (2013, 173) expresses a more moderate view. He argues that the present vowel inventory in both Maghrebi Arabic and Berber is a result of innovation and, since we do not have sufficient knowledge of the diachronic development in Berber, it is impossible to establish the starting point of the vowel system reduction.

The examples of language change described above cannot be unequivocally explained either by contact with Berber or by internal innovation of Maghrebi Arabic. Nevertheless, the presence of similar or parallel developments in Berber, considered together with the lack of these phenomena in the eastern branches of Arabic, allows us to tentatively propose that Berber could be what provoked them, or at least not to preclude its role.

4.2. Late Punic

Punic is a term designating a Phoenician language spoken in the western Mediterranean. Following an extensive expansion in the whole basin of the Mediterranean, by the ninth century BCE, the Phoenicians had established a number of colonies with prominent urban centres across North Africa, e.g., Carthage in present-day Tunisia. They had at the same time developed a chain of harbours located on the North-African coast, which facilitated their trade and settlement (Segert 1976, 25). The Phoenician language in North Africa, due to its disconnection from the mainland, soon evolved and developed its distinct features. Our knowledge about vernacular Punic is very limited. We should assume some level of both historical and linguistic discrepancy between the spoken and the written forms of Punic. With regards to the latter, the available inscriptions attest to a shift that took place in approximately the first century CE whereby the Neo-Punic script was replaced by Latino-Punic, namely Punic written in Latin script.

Did the first Arab warriors and their families settling down in North Africa get to hear Punic? The presence of Punic in the Maghreb is well documented up until the fourth century CE. However, similarly to African Latin, it is unknown when exactly it ceased to be actively used as a vernacular. The main source of our knowledge of Late Punic is inscriptions, whose absence does not imply the extinction of a spoken language. The population that used Punic was not limited only to cities. Numerous words in Punic are of Libyco-Berber provenance and attest to widespread usage of this language also across rural areas, where we should assume some level of bilingualism among both Berbers and native speakers of African Latin. As pointed out by Jongeling (2005, 4), the last attestations of vernacular Punic come from St Augustine, who knew this language himself to some extent. We can infer from his works that Punic was still very much alive in his times, i.e., in the late fourth and early fifth centuries CE. Interestingly, in one of his letters, he makes mention of rural parishes where Punic was the dominant language (Ep. 66.2). The following passage (Ep. 209.3, CSEL 57, 348; Adams 2003, 238) also confirms this assumption:

> *quod ut fieret, aptum loco illi congruumque requirebam, qui et Punica lingua esset instructus, et habebam, de quo cogitabam, paratum presbyterum.*

> Fussala, a fortified, settlement of Augustine's diocese, had been a scene of violence between Donatists and Catholics. Because of its distance from Hippo, Augustine decided to

appoint a bishop for the place. One of the requirements was that he must know Punic, and Augustine had a presbyter who was thus prepared.

This and other passages from Augustine seem to indicate that, although Latin enjoyed the status of prestige language, Punic remained the vernacular of the ordinary people across North Africa (Jongeling 2005, 4). Its extinction, therefore, despite the lack of historical evidence, might have taken place much later, and one cannot exclude the possibility that, in rural areas, some portions of the population shifted directly from Punic to Arabic.[8]

4.3. African Latin

We can assume with a great degree of certainty that, upon the arrival of the first Arab colonisers in North Africa, some sort of Romance language was spoken across the region. There is a debate about whether it was Latin or some other vernacular derived therefrom (Kossmann 2009, 195). Adams presents a number of arguments suggesting that 'African Latin' was a vernacular, possessing phonological and syntactic features that set it apart from Roman Latin (Adams 2007, 259). Indeed, certain indirect attestations, including passages from St Augustine and Statius, imply that African speakers of Latin had different pronunciations, which could be perceived by speakers in Italy (Adams 2007,

---

[8] Cf. Jongeling (2005, 5): "Based on what we know of the Vandal period and the following Byzantine reconquest, there is no reason to suppose a dramatic decline in Punic culture.... Romanization in the [sic] North Africa was but minimal and indigenous culture seems to have continued to flourish under Roman suzerainty."

193). A hint as to how this variety of Latin might have sounded is provided by a passage from Jerome, who tells a story of a student who imitated the manner of speaking of his African teacher (Adams 2007, 269):

> A certain person had an African teacher of grammar at Rome, a most learned man, and [yet] he thought that he was emulating his teacher if he reproduced the hissing of his speech and merely the vices of his pronunciation.

This fragment seems to suggest that the peculiarity of African Latin pronunciation to some extent involved sibilants, as the teacher's speech is described as 'hissing'.

Naturally, the central question in the investigation of the language contact between African Latin and Arabic is whether, and for how long, this variety was in use after the Arab invasion of the Maghreb. Was it replaced rapidly by Arabic, or was the adoption of Arabic rather a gradual process, during which Latin continued to be spoken in provincial and rural areas? Unfortunately, there are no attestations of African Latin being actively used in the sixth or the seventh century CE. This does not mean, however, that it was in that period already extinct. Heath (2002, 3) rightly points out that the same lack of sources for vernacular Latin is true for Europe, where Classical Latin was used as a means of official communication. Indeed, a relatively slow process of conversion of the Romanised communities in the Maghreb from Christianity to Islam probably paralleled the communal shift from African Latin to Arabic (Bulliet 1979). Rushworth (2004, 94) even suggests that African Latin, termed *al-lisan al-latini al-Afariq* by al-Idrisi in the twelfth century CE, was spoken up until the fourteenth century CE. Another indirect piece of evidence for the prolonged use of African Latin is provided by numerous linguistic traces that this language has left in Arabic itself.

The Latin substrate in North African Arabic has been discussed by several scholars. One of the most vocal supporters of this theory is Heath, who manages to make a strong case regarding Moroccan Arabic by presenting compelling historical arguments (Heath 2002, 2). In the realm of morphology, the Latin influence on Arabic is particularly conspicuous in some northern dialects of Morocco, which adopted the plural morpheme -əš / -oš (Colin 1926, 65). As observed by Aguadé (2018, 34), this morpheme can be agglutinated to both Latin loanwords and original Arabic items alike. Another morphological feature that is pointed out by some scholars as a possible Latin influence is a merger of gender marking. As argued by Corriente (2012, 142), in Andalusi Arabic, as well as in some Maghrebi dialects and in Maltese, the distinction between 2FS and 2MS has disappeared, both in personal pronouns and in verbs. This isogloss, according to Corriente, must have emerged due to the Romance substrate. Finally, there is a significant number of lexical items which have been borrowed from Latin into Maghrebi Arabic. Most of the loanwords are related to fauna, flora, and agriculture. There exist numerous studies on this topic and it is therefore superfluous to deal with it here in detail.[9]

---

[9] For the Romance verbs adopted in the Arabic spoken in Susa, Sfax, and Tunis, see Talmoudi (1986).

As can be inferred from the above paragraph, the Latin/Romance substrate in North African Arabic is most obvious in lexicon and morphology. The fate of phonology, on the other hand, is much more obscure and little is known as to the extent to which the development of vowels and consonants in North Africa was conditioned by Late Latin. Nevertheless, considering the political and cultural influence of the Roman Empire on the entire region of North Africa, as well as the vast proportion of the population using Latin, we cannot exclude the possibility that the receding Latin would have left some sort of traces in the newly adopted Arabic in the realm of phonology also.

5.0. Aims of the Study

The present volume aims to address some of the challenges outlined above. Firstly, one of its major aims is a comprehensive linguistic study of Jewish Gabes from a comparative perspective. To this end, data from both sedentary and rural dialects have been utilised in order to understand better the typological status of the dialect in question and place it within a wider dialectological framework. Secondly, it attempts to cast some light on the historical development of the Jewish varieties of North African Arabic in general, particularly in the field of phonology and syntax of the verb. A special interest has been taken in notions of language contact and substrate. Finally, a significant part of the volume is devoted to the study of syntax from a cross-linguistic, as well as a Semitic, perspective.

6.0. Methodology and Transcription

The data utilised in this study were obtained during several stints of fieldwork undertaken in Israel and in France between December 2018 and March 2022, and comprise recordings of a total running time of 42 hours.[10] The total number of native speakers of Jewish Gabes that participated in the research is eight. Out of four men and four women, seven have completed basic secondary education, while one of them has obtained a higher academic degree.

Table 1: Native speakers of Jewish Gabes participating in the study

Gender	Age when recorded	Location
F	81	Ramle, Israel
F	72	Rehovot, Israel
F	76	Ramle, Israel
F	79	Beer Sheva, Israel
M	81	Marseille, France
M	92	Ashkelon, Israel
M	87	Beer Sheva, Israel
M	70 (?)	Haifa, Israel

My text corpus of Jewish Gabes included in this volume represents the traditional oral culture of the informants, primarily folktales. For practical reasons, some transcriptions could not be included in the corpus. In addition, for the purpose of grammatical clarification, some examples were elicited. When an example quoted in the volume has been excerpted from the corpus, its location is indicated by two numbers: the first marks the number

---

[10] This includes portions of free speech, as well as elicitations and questionnaires.

of the text, the second one the number of the passage. Otherwise, when no location is indicated, an example has been excerpted from the data not included in the corpus. Other recordings, not included in the appendix, include personal memoirs, dialogues, and narratives about day-to-day life in Gabes.[11] The division of passages has been made according to the natural prosodic pauses applied by the speakers.

In the course of my search for potential informants, I encountered numerous speakers who were introducing Hebrew words and expressions into their Arabic. These speakers were not included in the study due to the high level of contamination of the dialect with Hebrew words, which, in turn, calls into question the reliability of the data obtained from such informants. The genuine Hebrew component in Jewish Gabes, which does not stem from the extensive language contact with Israeli Hebrew but constitutes an integral part of Arabic spoken by Jews, has not been studied due to the lack of sufficient data. In general, the focus of this study is primarily grammatical and not lexical.

The system of transcription used in this volume is mostly phonemic, but some elements of phonetics have been included as well, as explained in the following. The transcription of vowels is generally phonemic, i.e., only the following phonemic vowels are rendered: long vowels: /ī/, /ā/, /ū/, short vowels: /a/, /o/

---

[11] The transcription of the recordings not included in this volume, together with texts from other undocumented Jewish dialects of Algeria and Tunisia, will hopefully be published in the future in a separate book.

and /ə/. The only exception to this rule is the reflex of the historical short vowels /u/ and /i/, which are retained in certain contexts. Thus, /u/ is preserved in certain verbs, e.g., *yuṣkur* 'to thank', and the determiner *kull* 'all'.[12] In this case, /u/ is not an allophonic realisation of /ə/ conditioned by the consonantal environment, and although short /u/ is not phonemic, it has been transcribed as such in places where it is relevant for linguistic discussion. Similarly, although short /i/ is generally non-phonemic, it is retained in the preposition *fi* when followed by a noun starting with a non-emphatic consonant.[13] It has therefore been transcribed as such. For practical reasons, different qualities of vowels are not represented in the transcription. As a general rule, short vowels are not permitted in open syllables in Jewish Gabes. The long vowels are marked by a macron, while the short ones are unmarked. The final vowels are presumed to be long by default and therefore they are not marked as such. The only exception to this rule is verbal forms and prepositions ending with a vowel followed by a 3MS personal pronoun, in which the final vowel is significantly prolonged, and is therefore marked by a macron, i.e., *qərqru* 'they dragged', *qərqrū* 'they dragged him'; *fi* 'in', *fī* 'in him'. Stress is generally not marked, except for cases where its placement is not obvious. On the other hand, the transcription of the consonants is more phonetic, in order to render some of the characteristic traits of Jewish Gabes. Thus, I strove

---

[12] Both *kull* and *kəll* variants have been attested. They are transcribed accordingly.

[13] As opposed to a noun starting with an emphatic consonant. In this case, /i/ shifts to /ə/, i.e., *fi-l-bīt* 'in the room', but *fə-ḍ-ḍāṛ* 'in the house'.

to render some secondary processes like emphasis spread. Naturally, it is not feasible to precisely establish the exact range of the spread in every word, and it was therefore marked only in the most explicit cases. In addition, the occasional gemination of final consonants attested in Jewish Gabes has also been marked in transcription, e.g., *ḍrəbb* < *ḍrəb* 'he hit'. Preverbal particles, the definite article, and the prepositions *lə-* 'to' and *fi-* 'in' are followed by a hyphen. The prepositions that in Classical Arabic are not attached to the noun are written separately.

The table below demonstrates the transcription of Classical Arabic sounds used in this volume:[14]

Table 2: Transcription of Classical Arabic sounds used in this volume

أ	ب	ج	د	ه	و	ز	ح	ط	ي	ك	ل	م	ن
ʔ	b	j	d	h	w	z	ḥ	ṭ	y	k	l	m	n

ش	غ	ع	ف	ض	ق	ر	س	ت	ث	خ	ذ	ظ	ص
š	ġ	ʕ	f	ḍ	q	r	s	t	ṯ	x	ḏ	ẓ	ṣ

7.0. Structure of the Volume

The volume consists of three main sections: phonology (part I), morphology (part II), and syntax (part III). The first two sections follow a traditional grammatical model. Syntax has been approached from historical and cross-linguistic points of view. Chapter 2, on phonology, is broadly divided into two subsections: analysis of the sounds inventory (§§2.0–4.0), and phonotactics

---

[14] A table containing all the consonants found in Jewish Gabes and used in the transcription of the dialectal words is presented in chapter 2, §2.0 (Table 3).

(§5.0), which includes a description of the syllable structure and the epenthesis patterns. The section on morphology consists of chapter 3, on verbal morphology, and chapter 4, on nominal, including pronominal, morphology. Finally, the section on syntax (chapters 5–7) includes a number of subsections devoted to various syntactic phenomena: definiteness, genitive constructions, grammatical agreement, subordination, expressions of tense and aspect, syntax and pronouns, and sentence typology. The grammar is followed by an appendix containing a corpus of selected folktales that have been quoted in the earlier sections of the volume.

In order to ascertain whether certain linguistic features are unique to Jewish Gabes, a comparison with other North African dialects has been applied throughout the study.

PART I
PHONOLOGY

2. PHONOLOGY

1.0. Introduction[1]

This chapter presents a phonological analysis of the Arabic dialect of the Jews of Gabes, combined with a comparative examination of various phonological phenomena in the Muslim variety of Gabes and in selected Arabic dialects of the region. The primary aim of the study is to establish the features that distinguish Jewish Gabes from other Jewish North African dialects, and, since no south Tunisian Jewish dialect has been studied to date, to produce a thorough analysis of the sound system of this variety.[2] Special attention is paid to the distribution of sibilants in the region, which is tentatively explained by a substrate theory. Moreover, this survey constitutes the first attempt at acoustic analysis of the emphatics and vowels in North African Arabic. Based on data obtained by means of the software Praat, it has been shown that the emphatic consonants in Jewish Gabes have different levels of spreadability.

---

[1] This chapter is a revised and updated version of my paper titled 'The Phonology of the Judaeo-Arabic Dialect of Gabes' (2023a). Several changes have been implemented in comparison to the original article, primarily due to improved data accessibility after the pandemic. This facilitated additional verifications and validations, which were impossible during lockdown.

[2] Some remarks on the phonology and morphology of the Jewish dialect of Djerba have been mentioned in Behnstedt (1998).

Apart from the works of Saada (1964) and Behnstedt (1998) on Jewish Djerba, no systematic phonological description of any Jewish dialect of southern Tunisia has been undertaken so far. Moreover, no acoustic analyses of any Maghrebi dialects are known to me. It is therefore not surprising that, for instance, the phenomenon of emphasis spread, which has received much treatment in the eastern branch of Arabic (Watson 1999 for Yemeni; Omani and Jaber 2019 for Jordanian; Altairi et al. 2017 for Egyptian, Palestinian, Saudi, and Yemeni), in North Africa is almost entirely unexplored.[3] Against this background, this chapter has two principal aims. Firstly, it investigates the peculiarities of the Jewish Gabes phonological system in contrast with neighbouring dialects, and it attempts to cast light on the distribution of the sibilants within the region. Secondly, by providing an acoustic analysis of emphatics and vowels, it endeavours to fill the aforementioned lacuna in the study of the phonology of North African Arabic.

2.0. Overview of the Consonants

As Table 3 below shows, the consonantal system of Jewish Gabes is considerably different from that of Classical Arabic (henceforth: CA), and of Muslim dialects of the region. The set of consonants has undergone both reduction and enrichment compared to CA and, as a result, although some groups of sounds have disappeared, new sounds have emerged as well. This phenomenon

---

[3] The only study known to me on emphasis in North African Arabic is that of Marçais (1948).

is observed in many Maghrebi dialects (Cohen 1912, 19). Similarly to other Jewish dialects of the North African group, the interdentals are completely non-existent in Jewish Gabes. On the other hand, a series of new emphatic consonants have emerged: [ṃ], [ṇ], [ḷ],[4] /ḅ/ and /ṛ/. However, compared to some neighbouring dialects, Jewish Gabes does retain some CA sounds. For instance, in Jewish Algiers, /q/ is pronounced as a glottal stop (Cohen 1912, 29), while /h/, similarly to in Jewish Tripoli (Yoda 2005, 75) and Jewish Tunis (Cohen 1975, 35), has almost completely disappeared. Contrary to this, in Jewish Gabes both of these sounds are stable, although, as will be argued, the realisation of /q/ is not uniform. In the following section (§3.0), I describe selected consonants that are characteristic of Jewish Gabes, or whose realisation differs from CA and the neighbouring dialects.

---

[4] In the transcription, phonemes are placed between two slashes, whereas allophones and consonants that do not possess phonemic status are marked by square brackets.

Table 3: Consonantal inventory

	Labial	Dental / Alveolar	Palato-alveolar	Velar	Uvular	Pharyngeal	Laryngeal
Stop							
Unvoiced	[p]	t		k	q		
Voiced	b	d		g			
Emphatic	ḅ	ḍ ṭ					
Affricate							
Unvoiced							
Voiced							
Fricative							
Unvoiced	f	[s]	š	x		ḥ	h
Voiced		[z]	ž	ġ		ʕ	
Emphatic	[ḟ]	ṣ ẓ					
Nasal							
Plain	m	n					
Emphatic	[ṃ]	[ṇ]					
Lateral							
Plain		l					
Emphatic		[ḷ]					
Rhotic							
Trill			r				
Emphatic			ṛ				
Approximant	w	y					

3.0. Remarks on Realisation of Consonants

3.1. Bilabials

3.1.1. /b/–/ḅ/

CA ب is preserved as a plosive bilabial voiced consonant. Its realisation can change depending on its position in a word. When /b/ is at the beginning of a word and is followed by an unvoiced consonant, it turns into a devoiced allophone [p], e.g., *bḥar* [pḥar] 'sea'. When, however, the same sequence is preceded by a vowel, /b/ has its regular plosive realisation, e.g., *yəbkīw* 'they cry'. On the other hand, in word-final position, especially in monosyllabic words containing a short vowel, /b/ tends to be geminated, e.g., *rkəb[b]* 'he rode'. In these cases, the air stream pressing on the mouth very often gives an impression that /b/ is emphatic, since emphasis consists of pharyngealisation and labialisation.[5]

/b/ has an emphatic counterpart /ḅ/, which occurs either as an independent phoneme or as a result of emphasis spread in the vicinity of an emphatic consonant. Its phonemic status, contrary to Muslim Gabes, is not certain (Skik 1969, 85). The following minimal pair potentially proves the phonemic character of

---

[5] Gemination of a consonant at the end of a word is also attested in Jewish Algiers; see Cohen (1912, 66).

/ḅ/: bāba 'her door' : ḅāḅa 'father'.⁶ The minimal pair that proves the phonemic status of /ḅ/ in Jewish Tripoli, i.e., rəbbi 'rabbi' : ṛəḅḅi 'God', is not valid in Jewish Gabes, as the two words differ both in terms of emphaticity and vowel quality, i.e., rəbbi 'rabbi' : ṛaḅḅi 'God'.⁷ However, in words like yəṭlaḅ 'he asks', /ḅ/ results from rightward extension of the emphasis rooted in originally emphatic /ṭ/. In most cases /ḅ/ has a clearly plosive character, and in certain words it is followed by reduced, short epenthetic /u/ and hence has a labial vocalic release, e.g., ḍrəḅᵘha 'he hit her', ʕaṛḅᵘi 'Arabic'. A similar phenomenon is attested in Jewish Algiers (Cohen 1912, 57).⁸ One of the possible explanations for this "semi-vocalic complement," as Cohen refers to it, is related

---

⁶ The 3FS pronominal suffix in bāba 'her door' is unstable. I have recorded utterances where the etymological /h/ is clearly audible, but it is lost in the stream of fast speech. The minimal pair in question should therefore be taken with a pinch of salt, as it involves an allophonic realisation.

⁷ It is important to notice, however, that the quality of /r/ in rəbbi 'rabbi' is unstable and the consonant occasionally tends to be emphaticised. The second formant of the segment /ra/ pronounced by the same male informant had on one occasion a value of 1938 Hz, i.e., it clearly was not emphatic, but on another occasion dropped to 1681 Hz, i.e., closer to the emphatic region. Indeed, in fast speech, these two words are more easily distinguished by the vowel quality.

⁸ Paradoxically, this phenomenon is not attested in Jewish Tunis, in which /b/ is explicitly plosive (Cohen 1975, 15) and, contrary to some other Maghrebi dialects, does not bear any traces of spirantisation.

to the realisation of the emphatic consonants, which usually involves some level of lip-rounding, i.e., retraction of the dorsum simultaneously brings about a slight rounding of the lips.

Similarly to /b/, /ḅ/ undergoes the same process of devoicing when followed by a voiceless plosive or fricative and shifts to emphatic /ṗ/, e.g. ṗṭən [ḅṭən] 'belly'. From an etymological point of view, the /ḅ/ phoneme occurs in many loans from other languages and essentially corresponds to /p/, /b/, and /v/, e.g., ḅḷāṣa 'place, building' (Ital. *palazzo*), ḅīḅāṣ 'Christian priest' (Gr. *papas* > Turk. *papaz*), ḅrīma 'well' (Ital. *prima*), ḅāḅūr 'boat' (Ital. *vapore*).[9]

3.1.2. /m/–[ṃ]

/m/ occurs in two realisations, i.e., a plain nasal bilabial, and an emphatic one, which in Jewish Gabes is not a phoneme. The emphaticisation of /m/ is similar to that of /b/. Similarly to Jewish Tripoli, when [ṃ] is followed by /əy/ or /i/, it becomes labialised, e.g., əṃṃʷi 'my mother' (Yoda 2005, 27). In addition, in some words, the initial /m/, which should normally be followed by /w/, shifts to geminated [ṃ], whereby /w/ is fully assimilated. This phenomenon, ubiquitous in Jewish Tunis, is in Gabes only partially operational, and one can therefore find forms with /w/ retained alongside those with geminated [ṃ], e.g., mwākəl–ṃṃākəl 'food' (Cohen 1975, 18).

---

[9] In Jewish Tripoli, Italian /v/ and /p/ shifted into /ḅ/, i.e., ḅaḅur (Yoda 2005, 318), while in Jewish Algiers they shifted into /p/, i.e., papōr (Cohen 1912, 58).

3.2. Labiodentals

3.2.1. /f/–[ḟ]

ف in Jewish Gabes is realised as a labiodental voiceless fricative /f/. It has its emphatic counterpart *ḟ*, which often stems from emphasis spread, e.g., *ṭḟər* 'nail'. In addition, as in the case of geminated [ṃ], emphatic [ḟ] emerges due to a shift from /fw/ to geminated /ḟ/, e.g. *ḟḟām* < **fwām* 'mouths'. Interestingly, this shift is also attested in the Bedouin dialect of the region of Douz (Ritt-Benmimoun 2014, 51). As far as I could establish, [ḟ] is not phonemic in Jewish Gabes.

3.3. Dentals

3.3.1. /t/

The /t/ sound in Jewish Gabes represents two CA consonants, namely, ت and ث. The post-dental realisation of the latter CA interdental fricative ث can be found in words like: *tlāta* 'three', *təlž* 'snow', or *tūm* 'garlic'. Contrary to this, Muslim dialects do distinguish between them; both Muslim Gabes (Skik 1969, 86), Tunis (Cohen 1975, 19), and Muslim Algiers (Cohen 1912, 21) have preserved the interdental /ṯ/. In addition, in Jewish Gabes, /t/ is also the result of the devoicing of /d/, e.g., *tqīqa* 'minute' (< *daqīqa*).[10] Similarly, /t/ reflects, in some cases, a historical

---

[10] In the present chapter, the '<' sign represents correspondence to an item in CA and does not signify direct descendance of the dialectal forms from CA.

CA /ḏ/ that has undergone devoicing, e.g., ḏakar > tkər 'masculine'.

The loss of interdental consonants in North Africa is considered to be a feature of some Jewish urban dialects, while in the second-layer dialects, both rural and Muslim urban, they are generally preserved.[11] In the Jewish dialects, being mostly of the urban, pre-Hilālī type, one observes a strong tendency towards the plosive realisation of /ṯ/ and /ḏ/. To the best of my knowledge, among the Jewish varieties of the central Maghreb, only speakers from Wad-Souf (El-Oued) preserve the interdentals (Gębski, forthcoming a).

3.3.2. /ṭ/

The emphatic counterpart of /t/, as in CA, is an independent phoneme. This can be proved by minimal pairs: ṭāb 'he cured' : tāb 'he admitted, he pleaded guilty', šəṭṭ 'coast' : šədd 'he seized', ṭār 'he flew' : ḍār 'house'. The origin of this consonant in Jewish Gabes is more complex. It reflects CA ط e.g., ḥaṭṭ (< CA ḥaṭṭa) 'he put', as well as ظ in words like ṭfər (< CA ḍufur) 'nail'. In addition, in some numerals, due to emphasis spread, /t/ shifts to /ṭ/, e.g., ṭləṭṭāš (< CA ṯalāṯat ʕašar) 'thirteen'.

3.3.3. /d/

In Jewish Gabes, both CA dental د and interdental ذ have the reflex of the same consonant /d/, e.g., rədd (< CA radda) 'he replied', dhəbb (< CA ḏahab) 'gold'. It tends to be geminated at

---

[11] It has recently been suggested that the preservation of interdentals might be a trait of some pre-Hilālī dialects (Guerrero, 2021).

the end of the word by strong pressure of the tongue on the front teeth, e.g., *ḥadd* 'someone'. In some words, however, it reflects an original /t/ consonant that has undergone voicing, especially when followed by a voiced consonant, e.g., *tžī > džī* 'you come'.

3.3.4. /ḍ/

The occurrence of /ḍ/ follows a similar pattern to that of /ṭ/. Its phonemic status can be demonstrated on the basis of minimal pairs such as *ḍāq* 'he became narrow' : *dāq* 'he tasted'. The Jewish Gabes /ḍ/ represents several CA consonants, as well as some foreign sounds. First of all, it reflects the following Arabic consonants: emphatic ض as in *ḍrəb* 'he hit' (< CA *ḍaraba*), interdental emphatic ظ as in *nəḍḍəf* 'he cleaned' (< CA *naḍafa*), plosive /d/ as in *ẓḍəm* 'he attacked' (< CA *ṣadama*), and emphatic /ṭ/ as in *ẓḍaḍ* 'he hunted' (< CA *ʔiṣṭāda*). In addition, emphatic /ḍ/ represents some foreign elements, e.g., *ṣəḍḍūṛ* 'prayer book' from Hebrew סידור.

3.3.5. /n/–[ṇ]

The Classical ن is represented by a nasal consonant, which in the vicinity of the emphatics becomes emphaticised, e.g., *ṇəẓḍəm* 'I attack'. In Jewish Gabes, similarly to Jewish Tunis, emphatic [ṇ] is very frequent (Cohen 1975, 20). Remarkably, while the prefix of the first person is fairly regularly emphaticised, it is almost never emphaticised in the suffix of the first person plural, e.g., *ṇəṭləb* 'I/we ask', but *ṭləbna* 'we asked'. In turn, when /n/ is followed by a velar consonant, its pronunciation shifts to a velar nasal, e.g., *zəŋqa* 'blind alley'.

3.4. Alveolars and Postalveolars

3.4.1. [s]–/ṣ/

Due to the processes of emphasis spread and palatalisation, the occurrence of the /s/ consonant in Jewish Gabes is considerably limited. Yoda (2006) claims that Jewish Gabes has lost its /s/ and /z/ altogether, arguing that, in items containing emphatic consonants, CA /s/ shifts regularly to /ṣ/. My data, however, suggest that the situation of /s/ in Jewish Gabes is more complex. Indeed, in many cases, CA /s/ has shifted in Jewish Gabes to /ṣ/ due to assimilation in emphaticity, e.g., ṣəlṭān 'sultan' (< CA sulṭān), rāṣ 'head' (< CA raʔs). Nevertheless, the emphatic property of /ṣ/ is often dropped and a plain /s/ emerges, even in words with etymological /ṣ/. An acoustic study of the second formant (F2) of selected occurrences of /ṣ/ reveals that its emphatic realisation is unstable, e.g., the F2 of segment /ṣə/ in yāṣər 'a lot' has in one speaker a value of 1745.57 Hz, and in another a value of 2036.18 Hz. Both of these speakers are female and of similar age. Meanwhile, loss of emphasis takes place also in items with etymological /ṣ/. For example, in bṣəl 'onion', the frequency of the segment /ṣə/ is 2984.77 Hz, while that of /ṣa/ in ṣānʕa 'servant' is 2630.96 Hz. Against this background, /ṣ/ in ṣābūn 'soap' has a middle-height frequency of 1993.16 Hz, while the same consonant in ma rqāwāṣ 'they did not find her' is as low as 1363.15 Hz. Such a wide span of F2 suggests that, in certain lexical items, speakers tend to de-emphasise /ṣ/, presumably due to language contact with Modern Hebrew, which does not possess emphatic consonants. This, in turn, seems to indicate that /s/ as a sound does exist in Jewish Gabes, although its phonemic status remains ambiguous.

3.4.2. /š/

In Jewish Gabes, in lexical items not containing emphatic consonants, CA /s/ has shifted to /š/, e.g., /š/, e.g., *šīd* 'master' (< CA *sayyid*), *xmīš* 'fifth' (< CA *xāmis*). The realisation of postalveolar /š/ in Jewish Gabes depends on the age of the speaker. Those of the older generations tend to pronounce this consonant as a palatal, younger speakers as a postalveolar. In his study of Jewish Algiers, Marcel Cohen (1912, 24) also points out that a great number of speakers of that dialect tend to realise /š/ in the frontal part of the palate, creating an impression of an affricated articulation, i.e., [ɕ] in IPA. He calls this realisation 'lisping' (Fr. *zézaiement*) and notes that it is one of the distinctive features of Maghrebi Jewish dialects in general.

In Table 4 below one can find minimal pairs involving /s/, /ṣ/, and /š/ in five dialects of the region. As can be seen, Jewish Gabes and Jewish Tunis are the only dialects with no minimal pair involving s : š. This, in turn, points to an extensive weakening of this phoneme caused by a gradual shift from a plain realisation to palatalised and emphasised ones. On the other hand, the Muslim dialect of Gabes distinguishes phonemically between /s/ and /š/ (Skik 1969, 88).

Table 4: Minimal pairs involving sibilants in selected dialects of North Africa

Dialect	s : š	ṣ : š	s : ṣ
Jewish Gabes	-	ṣīf 'summer' : šīf 'sword'	-
Muslim Gabes[12]	sadd 'he moved' : šadd 'he grasped'		sūm 'price proposal' : ṣūm 'fast!'
Muslim Tunis[13]	sæbb 'he insulted' : šæbb 'alum'	-	sbōʕ 'week' : ṣbōʕ 'finger'
Jewish Tripoli	nsa 'women' : nša 'starch'	ṣur 'wall' : šur 'months'	sif 'sword' : ṣif 'summer'
Jewish Tunis	-	ṣif 'summer' : šif 'sword'	-
Jewish Algiers	-	-	sif 'sword' : ṣif 'summer'

3.4.3. [z]–/ẓ/–/ž/

CA /z/ is retained only in a limited number of items, where it is followed by a non-emphatic /r/, e.g., əzri 'run!'. According to Yoda (2006, 15), the plain /z/, like the plain /s/, does not exist in Jewish Gabes. However, as is the case with /s/, analysis of F2 demonstrates that the high value of the second formant in some items containing /ẓ/ does not permit us simply to classify it as emphatic. For instance, the frequency of the segment /əz/ in əzri 'run!' is 2002.95 Hz, as opposed to the 1302.35 Hz of /ẓə/ in

---

[12] Sources: Muslim Gabes—Skik (1969, 89); Muslim Tunis—Singer (1984, 51); Jewish Tripoli—Yoda (2005, 18), Jewish Tunis—Cohen (1975, 25), Jewish Algiers—Cohen (1912, 122, 206).

[13] The items are quoted according to their original transcription in the grammar book they were borrowed from.

ṛāẓəl 'man', or the 1228.67 Hz of /əz/ in əzṛāṛa 'rope'. We should assume, therefore, that the rule known from Jewish Tunis, by which the plain /z/ is retained before a non-emphatic /r/, is to some extent also valid in Jewish Gabes.

Emphatic [ẓ] in Jewish Gabes does not have any direct ancestor in CA and reflects either original /z/ which was emphaticised in the vicinity of emphatics, e.g., ẓlaq 'he slipped' (<CA zaliqa), əẓṛaq 'blue' (<CA ʔazraq); or original /j/, which had shifted to /z/ and was subsequently emphaticised due to its proximity to emphatics, e.g., jār > *zāṛ > ẓāṛ 'neighbour'. In addition, it reflects CA /ṣ/, as in ẓġīr 'small' (< CA ṣaġīr).

/ž/ in Jewish Gabes is a retroflex fricative sibilant and, like /š/, is palatalised amongst older speakers to [ẓ]. Essentially, it reflects two CA consonants: /j/, e.g., ʕažūža 'elderly woman' (< CA ʕajūza), žbəl 'mountain' (< CA jabal); or /z/, e.g., žūž 'pair' (< CA zawj), žītūn 'olives' (< CA zaytūn).

In lexical items containing an alveolar and an alveopalatal sibilant, we observe an assimilation of the former by which sibilant harmony is formed, e.g., CA šams > šəmš.[14] In addition, it is worth mentioning that Jewish Gabes exhibits a certain level of exchangeability of emphatics and palatalised sibilants in items containing only one sibilant, e.g., ṛāžəl has been attested alongside ṛāẓəl 'man', and similarly šxən alongside ṣxən 'he warmed himself'. This development is presumably rooted in the linguistic landscape of North Africa before the first wave of Islamisation of the region (Gębski, 2023b).

---

[14] The phenomenon of sibilant harmony in North African Arabic is discussed in greater detail in Gębski (2023b).

3.5. Laterals

3.5.1. /l/–[ḷ]

This is a lateral liquid, which undergoes emphaticisation in the vicinity of an emphatic consonant, e.g., ṣḷa 'synagogue'. The emphatic realisation occurs also in some words of foreign origin, e.g., ḫḷāṣa 'place, building' (Ital. *palazzo*), ḷāḇəṣ 'pencil' (Ital. *lapis*). As far as I have observed, [ḷ] in Jewish Gabes is not an independent phoneme.[15]

3.6. Trills

3.6.1. /r/–/ṛ/

There are two types of non-emphatic /r/ that can be distinguished in Jewish Gabes. The first, which occurs more frequently, is an alveolar trill produced by an intensive vibration of the tip of the tongue above the alveolar ridge. When /r/ is preceded by a vowel, the vibration tends to be considerably reduced. The second variant is a uvular fricative [ʁ] which, according to Cohen (1975, 26), occurred in Jewish Tunis due to the influence of French and is audible mostly among younger speakers. In Jewish Gabes, the fricative realisation seems to be conditioned by the phonetic environment, i.e., when an emphatic /ṛ/ is preceded by a vowel, it tends to shift to a uvular fricative. It is worth noting,

---

[15] It seems that /l/ in Jewish Tripoli is an independent phoneme given the following minimal pair: *wəlla* 'or' : *wəḷḷa* 'by God' (Yoda 2005, 20). Similarly in Muslim Gabes, *xalli* 'lead' : *xaḷḷi* 'my vinegar' (Skik 1969, 90).

however, that this is not a fixed rule and, in certain cases, even when preceded by a vowel, /r/ is realised as a trill.[16] In Jewish Tripoli and Jewish Benghazi, on the other hand, /r/ is a back continuant regardless of the phonetic environment, e.g., ʕarūsa [ʕaʁōsa] 'fiancé', rāḥ [ʁāh], 'he went', kbīra [kbīʁa] 'big (FS)'. The same realisation is found in words of Hebrew origin, e.g., paraša [paʁaša] 'weekly Torah portion'.[17]

As has already been mentioned, /r/ has its emphatic counterpart /ṛ/. In contradistinction to Muslim Gabes and other dialects of the region, where this consonant is phonemic, in Jewish Gabes its phonemic status is unclear (Skik 1969, 90).[18] Two minimal pairs have been found where the emphatic feature of /ṛ/ seems to be phonemic, i.e., kra 'he rented' : kṛa 'he hated',[19] zra 'he ran' : ẓṛa 'it happened'. The F2 of the /ra/ segment in the latter pair is respectively 1610 Hz and 1310 Hz. This clearly indicates that /r/ has different levels of emphaticity in these words.

---

[16] One cannot exclude the possibility that this realisation emerged due to the influence of Israeli Hebrew, in which /r/ is pronounced by younger generations as a velar or uvular fricative.

[17] This has been established based on recordings of native speakers of Jewish Tripoli and Jewish Benghazi uploaded on the website of the Mother Tongue project: https://www.lashon.org/1/taxonomy/term/132, accessed 15 November 2023.

[18] The phonemic status of /ṛ/ is attested in both Jewish and Muslim Tunis (Cohen 1975, 27; Singer 1984, 47), Jewish Algiers (Cohen 1912, 53), and Jewish Tripoli (Yoda 2005, 59).

[19] This minimal pair is somewhat dubious, as I recorded also kṛah 'he hated', where /h/ is preserved in a slow speech. The allophonic realisation kṛa has been attested in a fast stream of speech.

Although in many cases, /r̞/ has developed through emphasis spread from a nearby emphatic consonant, e.g., *m̞r̞īḍ* 'sick' (< CA *mariḍ*), in numerous words, /r̞/ is the only emphatic, e.g., *mar̞r̞a* 'time'. At times, the /i/ vowel has prevented the emphaticisation of /r/ to /r̞/, e.g., *fār̞* 'mouse'–*fīrān* 'mice', *ẓār̞* 'neighbour'–*žīrān* 'neighbours'.[20] The same phenomenon is attested in the Bedouin dialect of Douz (Ritt-Benmimoun 2014, 15). In addition, one can observe that /r̞/ does not occur in certain consonantal environments, namely, when it occurs after or before the following consonants:

- velar plosive /k/ and /g/, e.g., *drək* 'he was in a hurry', *rkəb* 'he rode', *škər* 'he got drunk';
- uvular fricative /x/ and /ġ/, e.g., *xrəž* 'he went out', *waxxər* 'he was late', *rġab* 'he begged', *ġarbān* 'strainer';
- pharyngeal /ḥ/, e.g., *rḥātu* 'she grinded him', *rtāḥ* 'he rested', *xrəb* 'he ruined';
- palato-alveolar sibilants /ž/ and /š/, e.g., *kərši* 'chair', *frəš* 'bed', *ržaʕ* 'he returned'.

It is worth noting, however, that in many words where the occurrence of /r̞/ is conditioned by emphasis spread, its emphatic character is not stable and, in some cases, /r/ is audible instead of the expected /r̞/. This phenomenon has already been identified in Jewish Tunis, where the distribution of /r̞/ is very often related to a social group or neighbourhood. Cohen (1975, 29) remarks

---

[20] A more comprehensive analysis of this phenomenon can be found in §3.13.

that, in the Ḥāṛa of Tunis, most speakers tend to pronounce /r/ as emphatic, whereas elsewhere it is pronounced plain.

3.7. Uvulars

3.7.1. /q/

Even though /q/ has been classified here as a uvular consonant, its realisation is very often more frontal, as palato-velar /k/. This is also attested in Jewish Tunis (Cohen 1975, 31), whereas in Jewish Algiers, CA ق has weakened to the extent that it is realised as /ʔ/ (Cohen 1912, 43).[21] Fronting of /q/ to /k/ is one of the characteristic traits of sedentary Jewish dialects in North Africa (Aguadé 2018, 45).[22]

3.7.2. /ġ/

In Jewish Gabes, the realisation of /ġ/ is as a uvular fricative, and no cases of trill realisation are attested. In Jewish Tripoli both realisations exist, and Yoda (2005, 11) reports that /ġ/ has the same phonetic value as /ṛ/.

---

[21] Cohen (1912, 44) points out that the realisation of /q/ is unstable among Jewish speakers and men tend to pronounce it as a uvular, while women prefer the weakened realisation /ʔ/. This can be explained by the fact that women were less exposed to contact with Muslim speakers, who pronounce /q/ as a uvular.

[22] It is worth noting that, in some Arabic dialects of the eastern branch, a further fronting takes place, which also involves palatalisation, i.e., /k/ > /č/, e.g., *samak* > *samač* in Muslim Baghdadi (based on my own recordings).

The phonemes /q/ and /ġ/ display in some words a certain degree of labialisation. A parallel phenomenon is attested in Berber, where velars and uvulars are labialised due to the historical process of the loss of short /u/, which subsequently brought about a rounding of the adjacent consonantal element (Kossmann 2013, 172).

3.8. Velar Plosives

3.8.1. /k/

CA ك is realised as a velar plosive /k/, by raising the back of the tongue towards the palate. It occurs in aspirated and unaspirated variants. The former is the default realisation, e.g., *kān* 'he was', while the latter occurs due to the de-pharyngealisation of /q/, e.g., *ka-yəmši* 'he is/was going'. The distinct character of the two variants of /k/ is confirmed both by their F2 and by their voice onset time (VOT) value.[23] Thus, while the F2 of /k/ in *ka-truḥ* 'she is going' is 1277.06 Hz, the F2 of /k/ in *kādu* 'it hurt him' is much higher at 1863.47 Hz. Additionally, the aspirated /k/ has a much longer VOT: the VOT of /k/ in *kādu* is 36ms, but in *ka-truḥ* is only 15ms.

3.8.2. /g/

The shift of /q/ > /g/ is a well-known feature that characterises Bedouin dialects across the Arabic-speaking world. In both the Muslim and the Jewish dialect of Gabes, this sound is phonemic,

---

[23] Voice onset time is the time interval between the release of the stop burst and the onset of voicing.

although its distribution in the former is undoubtedly much higher (Skik 1096, 95).[24] I have found only one minimal pair in Jewish Gabes where the opposition q/g is phonemic, namely, *yqərqər* 'he drags' : *ygərgər* 'he gargles, he talks a lot'. The minimal pair provided by Cohen (1975, 31) for Jewish Tunis, i.e., *kād* 'it was a pity for him' : *gād* 'he led an animal', is not valid in Jewish Gabes, as the form of the latter verb is *gəyyəd*. In a similar vein, the opposition between /g/ and /x/ found in Jewish Tripoli, i.e., *gdəm* 'he bit' : *xdəm* 'he worked', is not attested in Jewish Gabes, as the former verb is not used in this dialect (*ʕāḍ* is used instead). Indeed, the occurrences of the /g/ sound in Jewish Gabes are much more limited and usually either stem from a sound change or are found in a lexical borrowing. For example, when the voiceless velar /k/ is followed by a voiced consonant, it shifts to /g/, e.g., *gdəb* 'he told a lie' (< CA *kaḏaba*). In some words, however, it represents CA *qāf*, which is also pronounced as /g/ in Bedouin dialects. In Jewish Gabes, most of the words containing /g/ are related to agriculture, natural phenomena, or animals, e.g., *bagra* 'cow', *gumra* 'moon', *nāga* 'female camel'. The geographically closest Bedouin dialect to Jewish Gabes is the dialect of El-

---

[24] In neighboring Muslim and Bedouin dialects, one finds more minimal pairs of /q/:/g/. For instance, in the Abadite Djerba dialect (Behnstedt 1998, 57), as well as in Jewish Wad-Souf (Gebski, forthcoming a), the phonemic status of /g/ is proved by the pair *grīb* 'near': *qrīb* 'relative'. In Jewish Gabes, both words are rendered as *qrīb*.

Ḥāmma, in which the shift from /q/ to /g/ is almost a rule (Cantineau 1960, 208).[25] It is thus reasonable to assume that, in Jewish Gabes, this consonant has emerged through contact with Bedouin dialects, specifically by borrowing lexical items containing /g/. In addition, it is worth noting that the shift from CA /q/ to /g/ is also present in some rural dialects of Algeria, as well as in Jewish Algiers to a limited extent. Marcel Cohen (1912, 46) claims that plosive post-palatal realisation of /q/ is, similarly to in Jewish Gabes, audible in "objets venus de la campagne ou qu'on ne connaît qu'à la campagne." Interestingly, a close examination of some contemporary recordings of native speakers of Jewish Algerian Arabic from Wad-Souf reveals that, unlike in other Jewish dialects of the Maghreb, /g/ is found not only in words related to agriculture, such as *gəmaḥ* 'wheat', but also in high-occurrence verbs of everyday use: *ḥatt yərgud* 'until he fell asleep', *gūm!* 'wake up!', *gəltlu* 'I told him'.

3.9. Velar Fricative

3.9.1. /x/

The Classical consonant خ is represented by a velar fricative /x/. Its original realisation involves the raising of the back part of the tongue towards the furthest part of the soft palate. As a result, a uvular sound can very often be heard. Among the older speakers of Jewish Gabes, however, the place of articulation of this consonant is moved forward to the region of the hard palate, and hence

---

[25] As pointed out by Cantineau (1960, 208), /q/ in the dialect of El-Ḥāmma has been preserved only in lexical items borrowed from CA.

the uvula does not take part in the articulation. On the other hand, younger speakers, who grew up in a Hebrew-speaking environment, articulate /x/ by pressing the root of the tongue towards the soft palate. This realisation is therefore probably conditioned by the influence of Hebrew. A parallel discrepancy has been observed by Marcel Cohen (1912, 30) in Algiers, where Muslim speakers pronounce /x/ in the region of the uvula, while the place of articulation among Jews is on the hard palate.[26] The velar realisation of /x/ is not attested in Jewish Tunis (Cohen 1975, 32).

3.10. Pharyngeals

3.10.1. /ḥ/

CA ح is represented by a pharyngeal fricative /ḥ/. The realisation of this consonant involves pulling the root of the tongue towards the back wall of the upper pharynx (Ladefoged 1982, 171; Watson 2002, 18). Apart from etymological ح, occurrences of /ḥ/ are produced by a sound shift of /ʕ/ followed by /h/ (see §3.16.2).

3.10.2. /ʕ/

The pharyngeal fricative /ʕ/ reflects the Classical ʕayn. This consonant is well preserved, and its realisation is stable among both male and female speakers.[27]

---

[26] Cohen transcribes the former as /ḫ/ and the latter as /x/.

[27] As pointed out by Cohen (1912, 31), /ʕ/ in Jewish Algiers is articulated more strongly by men than by women, who tend to weaken its realisation.

3.11. Laryngeal

3.11.1. /h/

The fricative voiced laryngeal /h/ corresponds to CA ه, in which language it had a phonemic status. In Jewish Gabes, as far as I can establish, /h/ retains its phonemic status, e.g., šhər 'month' : škər 'he got drunk'. Nevertheless, it is important to notice that, although speakers are aware of the etymological /h/ and tend to articulate it in regular-tempo speech, its articulation is less audible in fast speech.

The weakening of /h/ is a phenomenon widely attested in several Jewish Maghrebi dialects. According to Yoda (2005, 75), despite the fact that many speakers of Jewish Tripoli are aware of the etymological existence of /h/, it is essentially absent in this dialect. Marcel Cohen (1975, 34) points out that even though CA ه is generally well preserved in modern Arabic dialects, among the Jews of Algiers, its realisation is weakened to the extent that it is almost completely inaudible. Similarly, in Jewish Tunis, one can find only vestiges of /h/, which in the majority of cases has been reduced to zero. The elimination of /h/ has two possible outcomes, namely, either the gemination of an adjacent consonant, or the compensatory lengthening of a vowel around the elided /h/ (Yoda 2005, 75).

Despite the general tendency towards the weakening of /h/ among the North African dialects, some Muslim dialects have preserved the original realisation of /h/, as can be found in both Muslim Tunis (Singer 1984, 60), Muslim Algiers (Cohen 1912, 32), and the Bedouin dialect of Douz (Ritt-Benmimoun 2014, 14).

Surprisingly, in respect of this feature, Jewish Gabes aligns with the Muslim dialects.

Below are presented the cases in which /h/ is retained; words in round brackets represent Jewish Tunis (Cohen 1975, 36):

- initial:
    - hābəl 'mad' (cf. abāl), hbūṭ 'unit of measure' (cf. abūṭ), ḥḍaṛ 'he talked' (cf. aḍaṛ[r]), hṛab 'he fled' (cf. aṛab[ḅ]), hrəd 'he has been destroyed' (cf. arəd[d]), hažž 'he raised' (cf. ažž), hməll 'he got lost' (cf. aməl[l]);

- medial:
    - hV: šūha 'scandal' (cf. šūwa), žīha 'side' (cf. žīya), yəhūdi 'Jew' (cf. yūdi), mənhum 'from them', dhəbb 'gold';
    - hC: mahbūl 'crazy' (cf. mabūl), mahrūd 'rotten' (cf. marūd), qahwa 'coffee' (cf. qāwa), šahwa 'desire' (cf. šāwa);

- final (in a fast stream of speech, the final /h/ is occasionally assimilated to /a/):
    - nādātha / nādāta 'she called her', ḍharha / ḍhāra 'her back', mʕāha 'with her', uṃha / uṃṃa 'her mother', ṛāẓəlha 'her husband', yḥabbūha 'they love her'.

As can be inferred from the above examples, in Jewish Gabes, /h/ is retained in the initial, medial, and final positions.

However, its realisation is weakened in monosyllabic words in which /h/ is in the initial position, e.g., *(h)āk* 'that'.

3.12. Treatment of *hamza*

CA *hamza* has disappeared from virtually all Jewish dialects of Tunisia.[28] In Jewish Gabes also, the glottal stop is completely absent and, depending on the position of *hamza* in the word, some compensatory processes can be observed.[29]

The elimination of *hamza* in word-initial position usually gives rise to a short vowel whose quality depends on the following consonant, e.g., CA *ʔuktub* > *əktəb* 'write!', CA *ʔummi* > *ummi* 'my mother', CA *ʔarḍ* > *arḍ* 'earth', CA *ʔaḥmar* > *aḥmaṛ* 'red'. As can be seen, a bilabial consonant conditions the occurrence of a rounded /u/ vowel, while a pharyngeal fricative or emphatic /ṛ/ is preceded by a low vowel /a/. In addition, verbs with first radical *hamza* have developed a sort of semi-vowel which substitutes for the elided glottal stop, e.g., *waxxər* 'he was late', *wakkəl* 'he fed'. However, in a limited number of words, *hamza* disappears along with the following vowel. This occurs in nouns of frequent use, e.g., CA *ʔabū* > *ḫu* 'father', CA *ʔaxū* > *xu* 'brother'; and in

---

[28] As pointed out by Y. Henshke (2007, 18), the realisation of /ʔ/ in the reading tradition of Hebrew among the Jews of Tunisia is essentially limited to two words, namely *nəboʔa* 'prophecy' and *šənʔa* 'hatred'.

[29] In Muslim Gabes, the glottal stop has been retained in word-initial position before a vowel, e.g., *ʔism* 'name', *ʔaṣl* 'origin'. Skik (1969, 97) points out, however, that the glottal stop in these words can be dropped without affecting the meaning of the item. A similar tendency to preserve the glottal stop at the beginning of a word is observed in Bedouin Douz (Ritt-Benmimoun 2014, 13).

verbs of the tenth stem, e.g., CA *ʔistaḥaqq* > *stḥaqq* 'he was in need of'.[30]

The disappearance of *hamza* in word-medial position brought about a wide range of processes. To begin with, in some words, it is simply eliminated, and no compensation occurs, e.g., CA *ʔimarʔah* > *mṛa* 'woman'. On the other hand, sometimes the loss of *hamza* results in lengthening of the adjacent vowel, e.g., CA *diʔb* > *dīb* 'jackal', CA *raʔs* > *ṛāṣ* 'head', CA *yaʔxuḏ* > *yāxəd* 'he takes'; or in the emergence of /w/ and /i/, e.g., CA *muʔaxxar* > *mwaxxəṛ* 'late', CA *miʔah* > *mīya* 'hundred'.

In word-final position, *hamza* is usually elided without leaving any trace, e.g., CA *samāʔ* > *šma* 'heaven', CA *badaʔ* > *bda* 'he began'. In a few cases, it brings about gemination of the preceding consonant, e.g., CA *ḏawʔ* > *ḍuww* 'light'.

3.13. Emphasis and Emphaticisation: A Cross-Dialectal Perspective

The emphatic consonants have two places of articulation, namely, the primary coronal obstruction and the secondary tongue root retraction towards the back wall of the pharynx (Ladefoged 1982, 171; Davis 1995, 465). As pointed out by Cohen (1975, 14), the emphasis in many cases does not have any particular significance from the phonological point of view and

---

[30] This phenomenon is widely attested in Jewish Tripoli. According to Yoda (2005, 84), the drop of the initial syllable was brought about by the stress shift from paroxytone to oxytone due to frequent use of the construct state with pronominal suffixes, e.g., CA *ʔabūna* 'our father', CA *ʔabūka* 'your father', etc.

is optional, but has an emotional and expressive function and therefore often occurs in words designating members of the family, taboo words, or words of foreign origin. Nonetheless, a high occurrence of emphatic consonants is among the characteristic features of Jewish Tunisian dialects and therefore deserves close examination within Jewish Gabes. Cohen (1975, 14) notes that, when Muslim residents of Tunis tried to imitate the Arabic of their Jewish neighbours, they would use exaggerated emphasis.

One of the properties of this group of consonants is that they can affect their phonetic environment through spread of the pharyngealisation to adjacent consonants and vowels, which become rounded and deeper. This phenomenon is widely attested in many Semitic languages, such as Hebrew—where, for instance, in the *hitpaʕel* stem, an emphatic first radical turns the plain /t/ of the stem's prefix into emphatic /ṭ/—and North-Eastern Neo-Aramaic dialects (Napiorkowska 2015, 46). Arabic dialects present differences in the directionality and the extent of emphasis spread. In some, such as Cairene, emphasis usually extends over the entire phonological word, while in others, such as the Abha dialect spoken in Saudi Arabia, emphasis does not usually spread beyond an adjacent vowel (Bukshaisha 1985, 217–19). In terms of directionality, in some dialects, emphasis is bidirectional and unbounded, while in others, such as some Palestinian dialects, only leftward spread is unbounded, while rightward spread is blocked by a several opaque elements. A similar tendency has been observed by Cohen (1975, 14) in Jewish Tunis, where the assimilatory influence of the emphasis spreads in both directions, but leftward spread is much more frequent than rightward spread. Arabic dialects also tend to differ in terms of the opaque elements that block emphasis spread; for example, Heath (1987) reports that, in one of the dialects of Moroccan Arabic, high non-back phonemes—i.e., /y/, /š/ and /ž/—block rightward spread, whereas in a Libyan dialect discussed by Ghazali (1977; quoted in Davis 1995, 494), only the front vowels /i/ and /e/ are opaque to rightward emphasis spread. Some elements can also block leftward emphasis spread. For instance, in a Palestinian dialect studied by Hoberman (1989, 73–97), the same type of phonemes—namely, /i/, /y/, and /š/—are opaque to both leftward and rightward spread. On the other hand, Ghazali (1977) has found that some southern Tunisian dialects lack any phonemes that are opaque to emphasis spread.

Despite the remarks above, the phenomenon of emphasis spread in the North African dialects has not yet been thoroughly studied. In particular, compared to other dialect groups, Maghrebi Arabic lacks comprehensive acoustic analyses. Some scholars, such as David Cohen (1975, 14), mention the capacity for emphasis to spread, but this is not supported by quantitative data. Therefore, the acoustic analysis of emphasis spread in Jewish Gabes that is presented in the following sections (§§3.14–3.15) is of importance both for elucidating the phonology of this language and its typological status, and for understanding emphasis spread in Maghrebi Arabic more generally.

3.14. Acoustic Data

The following study has been conducted using the software Praat. The criterion taken into consideration in establishing whether a certain sound is produced with a retracted tongue root, abbreviated as [RTR],[31] is the second formant F2, which decreases in the case of pharyngealised consonants. The data presented in Table 5 below include measurements of the frequencies of the emphatic consonants, compared to their plain counterparts. The given frequencies correspond to the syllables in bold.

The data presented in Table 5 is divided into two categories, according to the direction of the spread of pharyngealisation. There is one emphatic consonant in each of the words, which is either historically emphatic, as in ḍrəbha 'he hit her', or has acquired an emphatic nature as a result of a secondary process, e.g., ḥraḅ > CA haraba 'he fled'. Thus, in the first column are presented lexical items that possess a pharyngealised segment (hence +RTR), while the second column comprises items with corresponding plain segments (hence -RTR). The main aim of the study was to detect the direction of the spread, whether there are any elements that are opaque to the spread, and whether emphasis is anchored in every pharyngeal consonant identically or whether some pharyngeal consonants bring about a spread of emphasis beyond an adjacent sound.

---

[31] This is within the framework of the theory of grounded phonology proposed by Archangeli and Pulleybank (1994).

Table 5: Directionality of emphasis spread in Jewish Gabes

1. Leftward spread

	[+RTR]	[-RTR]
/q/ 1.	(1) tərqa 1250.66026 Hz (2) tərqa 1342.43292 Hz (3) zənqa 1165.66389 Hz	kān 1800.81868 Hz təšbaḥ 2225.83514 Hz rāzəlha 1787.56570 Hz
/ḍ/ 2.	(1) abyaḍ 1089.41890 Hz (2) ḫāḫāha 1140.60608 Hz	žāb 1570.77986 Hz
/ṛ/ 3.	kabṛat 1089.28449 Hz	nḥabbha 1607.00414 Hz
/ṭ/ 4.	(1) əṣ-ṣəlṭān 1488.24324 Hz (2) yxayyəṭ 1598.02826 Hz (3) yxayyəṭ 2244.11668 Hz	səzra 2043.50565 Hz təšbaḥ 2225.83514 Hz xarraž 1537.04294 Hz
/ṣ/ 5.	wəṣlu 820.50536	wəžžha 1284.4205 Hz

2. Rightward spread

	[+RTR]	[-RTR]
/ṭ/ 6.	(1) ṭṭəyybi 1378.20092 Hz (2) yəṭlab 1089.42714 Hz	bī 2186.87534 Hz nḥabba 1607.00414 Hz
/ṛ/ 7.	hraḫ - 978.36830 Hz	žāb – 1570.77986 Hz
/ṣ/ 8.	ṣbāḥa 1270.75092 Hz	bāš 2652.70550 Hz
/ḍ/ 9.	dṛəbha 1281.23549 Hz	nḥabba 1607.00414 Hz
/q/ 10.	(1) qāltəlha 1553.06365 Hz (2) qāltəlha 1839.09118 Hz (3) qāltəlha 1929.96698 Hz	kān 1800.81868 Hz bālək 1967.83617 Hz təšbaḥ 2225.83514 Hz

3.15. Data Analysis

The following conclusions can be drawn from the study presented in Table 5, discussed by section number:

3.15.1. Leftward Spread

§1.1. /q/ involves a certain degree of lowering of pitch: the frequency of the syllable /qa/ is 600 Hz lower than that of the syllable /ka/ containing the plain counterpart of /q/. The low pitch of the first segment of example (1), *tərqa* 'you/she find(s)', is not necessarily the result of emphasis spread, but could be due to the consonant /r/. It is, furthermore, rather difficult to determine the status of /r/ in this word, as its low pitch could be either anchored in the adjacent /q/, or, equally, caused by the general tendency of /r/ in Jewish Gabes to become pharyngealised. Similarly, the low frequency F2 of /zə/ in *zənqa* in example (3) is either owing to the shift of plain /z/ to /ẓ/ or /ž/, or, alternatively, due to the following /n/, which involves lowering of the tongue root.

§1.2. An interesting phenomenon can be observed with the word *abyaḍ* 'white', where the emphasis originally anchored in /ḍ/ spreads over a high /y/ sound and affects the first syllable /ab/. In this word in other dialects, such as Abha Saudi Arabic, emphasis spread stops beyond the second /a/ and leaves the first syllable unaffected (Watson 1999, 293). For the sake of comparison, the marked syllable in example (2) has a similar frequency to that of *abyaḍ*, even though it does not contain any emphatic consonant. It can be assumed that it is an example of the 'emotional' emphasis mentioned by Cohen (1975, 14).

§1.3. The /r̩/ in *kab̲rat* brings about a lowering of the pitch of the first syllable, and /r/ should therefore be recognised as the source of the emphasis spread.

§1.4. As the examples show, the leftward spread of /ṭ/ is rather unbounded. In example (1), *əṣ-ṣəlṭān*, it affects the entire segment located to its left. Contrary to this, examples (2) and (3) demonstrate that final /ṭ/ does not bring about emphasis spread beyond an adjacent vowel. This fact constitutes a strong piece of evidence for the existence of opaque elements in Jewish Gabes; specifically, it can be assumed that high front /y/ is opaque to emphasis spread caused by /ṭ/. Interestingly, the same word *yxayyəṭ* 'he saws' in both northern and southern Palestinian Arabic demonstrates a lack of opacity (Davis 1995, 473).

§1.5. /ṣ/ causes a clear downswing in the F2 of the preceding segment /wə/, as demonstrated in the example *wəṣlu* 'they arrived'. One can expect low pitch when the approximant /w/ is followed by the back vowel /ə/, but if one compares a word which does not contain any emphatic consonant, like *wəžžha* 'her face', the F2 is much higher, by more than 400 Hz.

3.15.2. Rightward Spread

§2.6. The emphasis anchored in /ṭ/ in example (1), *ṭṭəyybi* 'you (FS) cook', spreads over the entire phonological word and brings about a drop of the F2 of the last syllable. This downswing is significant, taking into consideration the frequency of an identical segment in a non-pharyngealised word: the difference between /bi/ in *ṭṭəyybi* 'you (FS) cook' and the same segment occurring as an independent word *bī* 'in' is more than 800 Hz. This token provides strong evidence that, in Jewish Gabes, the high consonant /y/ does not block the rightward emphasis spread of /ṭ/. Similarly, in example (2), /ab/ is strongly affected by the emphatic character of /ṭ/. However, the measurement of the F2 of the syllable /yə/ preceding the emphatic /ṭ/ in *yəṭlab* 'he asks' demonstrates that it remains unaffected by emphasis (/yə/ F2: 2779.35477 Hz); this rather surprising finding can be explained by the fact that the segment in question is not part of the stem, although it is a part of the phonological word. The relationship between emphasis spread and morphology has already been mentioned by Younes (1993); in the Palestinian dialect he examined, the leftward spread of emphasis into prefixes was unstable, while the rightward spread into suffixes was obligatory. Davis (1995, 474) confirms these findings and suggests that this discrepancy is related to some sociolinguistic factors that need to be further examined. The examples that I examined in the present study indicate that, in Jewish Gabes, inflectional prefixes remain unaffected by emphasis spread.

§§2.7.–2.9. The consonants /ṣ/, /ḍ/, and /ṛ/ all display a clear tendency to lower the F2 of the preceding segments. It seems, however, that /ṣ/ causes a much deeper downswing, as demonstrated by the difference between the pharyngealised and the plain /ba/ being more than 1200 Hz (in the case of /ṛ/, the difference is approximately 600 Hz).

§2.10. The F2 of the first syllable in *qāltəlha* suggests that /q/ involves some lowering of the pharynx, but, compared to other clearly emphatic consonants, it is rather insignificant. This is demonstrated in the analysis in that there is no drop in the F2 of the two following syllables.

3.15.3. Summary of Findings

The findings presented above suggest that Jewish Gabes exhibits an asymmetry in the direction of emphasis spread, though no unambiguous conclusions can be drawn regarding the nature of each of the examined phonemes. It would have been possible to infer that, in the dialect in question, both the leftward and the rightward spread of pharyngealisation are unbounded. However, examples (2) and (3) in §1.4. prove that for /ṭ/, the element /y/ is opaque, blocking leftward spread, though simultaneously, the same element /y/ does not block the spread of emphasis from /ḍ/ (§1.2). This phenomenon by which different emphatic consonants are unequal in their potential for causing emphasis spread is not undocumented. In Moroccan Arabic, for example, even the same phoneme can have different degrees of emphatic potential. In that dialect, as has been noted by Heath (1987, 309), emphasis spreads from /ṛ/ onto adjacent coronal consonants in most cases, e.g., ḍrəṣ 'study', but there are several examples in which /ṛ/ does not bring about the emphaticisation of an adjacent coronal, e.g., ṭrab 'dirt'. It should be stressed that /t/ remains unchanged in this example even though it occurs directly to the left of /ṛ/, where one would expect unblocked emphasis spread.

Therefore, in light of what has previously been said, an alternative classification should be offered. Following Napiorkowska (2015, 70), who applied Ladefoged's (1971) approach based on the assumption that the features of sounds are gradable and not distinctive, we can classify the emphatic consonants in a descending scale, where (3) conveys the strongest type of emphasis in terms of spreading into an adjacent consonant, while (0) conveys the weakest one:

Table 6: Emphasis spread scale

3	2	1	0
/ḍ/	/ṣ/, /ṛ/	/ṭ/	/q/

3.16. Assimilation

In this section, I will discuss partial and total assimilation.

3.16.1. Partial Assimilation

The notion of partial assimilation in fact comprises several other phonological phenomena, such as voicing, devoicing, and nasalisation, due to which a sound change occurs. As pointed out by Cohen (1975, 44), the assimilation in Jewish Tunis is mostly regressive, i.e., it affects consonants preceding the sound that is the trigger of the assimilation. Below one can find some of the most common examples of assimilation in Jewish Gabes:

a) voicing: may occur when a voiceless fricative is followed by a voiced plosive, e.g., *iẓdaḍ* 'he hunts' (<CA *iṣṭād*), *gdəb* 'he lied' (<CA *kadaba*);

b) devoicing: is prone to take place when a voiceless plosive or fricative is preceded by a voiced plosive: *txəl* 'he entered' (<CA *daxala*), *tkər* 'masculine' (<CA *ḏakar*), *pḥər* 'sea' (<CA *bḥar*);

c) place assimilation (in the velar environment): a consonant preceding a velar/uvular plosive phoneme receives its velarised allophone, e.g., zəŋqa 'blind alley' (< zənqa), ŋkətbu 'we write' (< nkətbu), yəŋqaṣṣ 'it is cut off' (< yənqaṣṣ);

d) labialisation: can take place when /m/, /ṃ/, or /ḅ/ precedes /ey/ or /i/, e.g., əmmʷi 'my mother', ṃʷəyya 'water', təṣrḅʷi 'you (FS) drink'.

3.16.2. Total Assimilation

Similarly to partial assimilation, the total kind is also conditioned by a certain phonetic environment. Below are listed the most common cases of total assimilation in Jewish Gabes:

a) ln > nn; there are numerous cases of the assimilation of /l/ to /n/, e.g., ma ʕmənna šəy 'we did not do anything' (< ʕməlna), ʕṭāwənna 'they gave her to us' (< ʕṭāwəlna);

b) nl > ll; contrary to the previous case, when /n/ is followed by /l/, it gives rise to doubled /ll/, e.g., willʕabu? 'where did they play?' (< wīn lʕabu);

c) nr > rr, e.g., məṛṛāžəl 'from man' (< mən ṛāžəl);

d) nm > mm, e.g., kāmma 'if not' (< kān ma); elision of /n/ and subsequent gemination of the following /m/ is particularly common on the border between two phonological segments;

e) qk > qq, e.g., fūqqəm 'above you (PL)' (< fūqkəm);

f) ʕh > ḥḥ, e.g., ntāʕha > ntāḥḥa 'her'.

4.0. Vowels

4.1. General Characteristics

One of the most conspicuous characteristics of the phonology of North African Arabic dialects is the relatively poor inventory of vowel phonemes.[32] This has already been mentioned by Cohen (1975, 46) in his description of Jewish Tunis, though he simultaneously points out that, compared to other Maghrebi dialects, the vowels in that dialect demonstrate a fairly high level of diversity. The study presented here attempts to establish the phonemic vowel inventory of Jewish Gabes as opposed to other Maghrebi dialects, as well as to outline some challenges in the examination of vowels in modern Arabic dialects.

Among the most significant parameters in the investigation of vowels is the opposition between short and long vowels. In this respect, several modern Maghrebi dialects display a considerable reduction of the short vowels inventory, resulting in the existence of a single phonemic short vowel /ə/. Yoda (2005, 31) notes that this development has so far been attested in Jewish Tripoli, Jewish Algiers, Djidjelli, and Jewish Constantine. In addition, according to Behnstedt (1998, 60), Jewish Djerba also features only one phonemic vowel /ə/. D'Anna (2021, 17) also reports only one phonemic short vowel in Jewish Yefren (Libya). Moroccan Arabic presents rather a similar system of long vowels to the above-mentioned dialects, which Heath (1987, 23) terms 'full', but only two

---

[32] In this respect, Maghrebi Arabic demonstrates similarity to Berber (Kossmann 2013, 174).

phonemic short vowels, namely /ə/ and /u/. From the perspective of language contact, the same reduction of vowel inventory is also found outside Arabic in the Maghrebi Arabic speech region, namely, among all the northern dialects of Berber (Kossmann 2013, 171).

Jewish Gabes distinguishes between three phonemic long vowels: /ī/, /ā/, /ū/, and three phonemic short vowels: /a/, /o/ and /ə/.[33] Its phonemic inventory is therefore more diverse than that of Jewish Tripoli and resembles the phonemic vowels of Jewish Tunis. However, it is important to note that the /ə/ vowel has multiple qualities which, in turn, depend on the consonantal environment. Kossmann (2013, 174) observes that the flexibility of /ə/ in terms of its quality is among the parallels between Maghrebi Arabic and northern Berber.

Establishing the quality of /ə/ accurately is rather challenging for several reasons. First of all, the quality of /ə/ does not depend purely on adjacent consonants, but may also sometimes be influenced by remote elements found in non-adjacent syllables. In addition, one needs to bear in mind that the realisation of a vowel which does not possess phonemic status can vary from speaker to speaker and is prone to reflect the individual's physical formation of the speech organs, level of education, usage of other languages, etc. An attempt to precisely determine the allophones of the short vowel in Jewish Tripoli has been presented by Yoda (2005, 32), who establishes 10 allophones. As the classification of these allophones is rather abstract and tentative, in

---

[33] However, the phonemic status of /o/, as will be demonstrated, is uncertain.

the present study of Jewish Gabes I have opted, instead, to analyse the major phonemic vowels of the dialect (/o/ has been excluded from this analysis due to its limited occurrence), which are presented in the form of plots within various consonantal environments.

4.2. Long Vowels

From a cross-dialectal perspective, the North African dialects can be divided into two groups with respect to their inventory of long vowels, namely, dialects with three long vowels: /ī/, /ā/, and /ū/, and dialects with five long vowels: /ī/, /ā/, /ū/, /ē/, and /ō/. This discrepancy stems from the different development of the diphthongs /aw/ and /ay/, which in the first group shifted respectively to /ū/ and /ī/, but in the second one to /ō/ and /ē/ (Yoda 2005, 32; Ritt-Benmimoun 2014, 25). Almost all the sedentary dialects belong to the group with three long vowels, and the Bedouin ones to the group with five. One would expect, therefore, that the long vowel inventory of Jewish Gabes, as a dialect of the sedentary type, will consist of three vowels. The Muslim dialect of Gabes, on the other hand, features a set of five phonemic long vowels (Skik 1969, 98). Jewish Gabes does indeed have three long phonemic vowels, as can be established by the following minimal pairs:

- Phoneme /ū/:
    - /ū/ : /ə/
      ẓūṛna 'visit (MS) us!' : *ẓəṛna* 'we visited';
    - /ū/ : /ā/
      fūq 'above' : *fāq* 'he woke up';

- Phoneme /ā/:
    - /ā/ : /a/
      kbār 'big (PL)' : *kbar* 'he grew up';
    - /ā/ : /ī/
      žāt 'she came' : *žīt* 'I came';
- Phoneme /ī/:
    - /ī/ : /a/
      kbīr 'big (MS)' : *kbar* 'he grew up'.

Long /ī/ in the vicinity of /ḥ/ and /x/ tends to be lowered to /ē/, e.g., [xētˤ] 'thread'. In addition, when /ī/ is followed by an emphatic consonant, a secondary diphthongisation is produced, namely /ī/ > [əy], e.g., [sˤəyf] 'summer'. Similarly, long /ū/, when found between two emphatic or uvular consonants, occasionally shifts to long /ō/, e.g., * *ṣūṭ* > *ṣōṭ* 'voice' (cf. §4.4).

4.3. Short Vowels

Based on interviews with informants, it has been established that there are three phonemic short vowels in Jewish Gabes: /a/, /o/ and /ə/. Cohen (1975, 50) reports the same set of phonemic short vowels in Jewish Tunis. The /u/ vowel appears not to be phonemic. Lucienne Saada (1963) claims that /u/ is phonemic in Jewish Djerba and adduces the following minimal pair, *rəkba* 'riding' : *rukba* 'knee', but in Jewish Gabes, these words are homonymic.[34] Behnstedt (1998, 60), on the other hand, argues that

---

[34] It is important to notice that Behnstedt (1998, 60), in an article written 35 years after Saada's work, reported an absence of the phonemic

short /i/, /u/, and /a/ in Jewish Djerba have merged into a single phoneme /ə/.[35] Muslim Gabes, similarly to Jewish Gabes, has a set of three phonemic short vowels: /a/, /o/, and /i/ (Skik 1969, 100). In places where Muslim Gabes has /i/, Jewish Gabes usually has /ə/, e.g., the minimal pair in the Muslim dialect, *midda* 'give her!' : *modda* 'period', is rendered in the Jewish one as *məddha* and *mədda* respectively. Below one can find minimal pairs that prove the phonemic status of all three short vowels:

/a/ : /o/[36]
  ḥabb 'he loved' : *ḥobb* 'love';
/ə/ : /a/
  məktūb 'written, destiny' : *maktūb* 'wallet';
/ə/ : /ā/
  žməl 'camel' : *žmāl* 'camels';
/ə/ : /ū/
  šxən 'he warmed himself up' : *šxūn* 'hot'.

It has previously been mentioned that /ə/ can admit different qualities depending on its consonantal environment. In what follows, I will briefly present the allophones of /ə/ as compared to the three basic non-phonemic qualities: [e], [u], and [i]. I will

---

/u/ in Jewish Djerba. He records that, similarly to in Jewish Gabes, both 'riding' and 'knee' have the same form *rəkba*.

[35] This is not the case, however, in the Malekite Arabic of Djerba, which typologically belongs to the Hilālī group (Behnstedt 1998, 60).

[36] As far as I could establish, this is the only minimal pair where short /o/ appears to differentiate the meaning. Similarly to emphatic /ṛ/, therefore, its phonemic status is uncertain.

give a general outline of the consonantal environment that each of the allophones prefers.

4.3.1. /ə/ with the quality of [e]

[e] reflecting a historical [a] quality is audible when /ə/ occurs in the vicinity of an emphatic or plain consonant, e.g., ṭəlʕat [ṭélʕat] 'she went out', ḍrəbtu [ḍrébtu] 'she hit him', ṣəlli [ṣélli] 'pray!', kəbru [kébru] 'they grew up'.

4.3.2. /ə/ with the quality of [u]

This realisation usually occurs when /ə/ is followed or preceded by a labial consonant, /r/–/ṛ/,[37] /w/, or /q/, e.g., fəmm [fumm] 'mouth', rəbṭūha [rubṭūha] 'they tied her', məṛtu [muṛtu] 'his wife', wəld [wuld] 'child', wəžžəʕat [wužžəʕat] 'I swam', qəmt [qumt] 'I/you (MS) woke up'. The /u/ vowel is also present in several items where it reflects the historical short /u/ vowel, as exemplified by yəškut 'he is silent', yuškur 'he thanks', and kull 'all, every'. Furthermore, the short /u/ vowel is observable in loanwords, as seen in examples such as gumra 'moon' (borrowing from a Bedouin-type variety) and šurrīya 'shirt'.

4.3.3. /ə/ with the quality of [i]

This realisation occurs when /ə/ is followed by /y/, e.g., bəyyət [biyyət] 'he spent a night', məyyət [miyyət] 'dead', gəyyəd [giyyəd] 'he led an animal', šəyyəbha [šiyyəbha] 'he left her'.

---

[37] In Jewish Tripoli, the occurrence of /r/ or /ṛ/ brings about a quality of [e]; see Yoda (2005, 36).

4.3.4. The Distribution of /o/

It must be noticed that, although there exists one minimal pair where the /o/ quality is phonemic, the distribution of /o/ in Jewish Gabes is more limited than in Muslim Gabes or Jewish Tunis. As previously mentioned, in many lexical items containing /o/ in Muslim Gabes, its Jewish counterpart has /ə/, e.g., *modda–mədda* 'period'.[38] In addition, in Jewish Tunis, verbs of this group have a long /ā/ vowel in the 3MS form of the suffix conjugation, which shifts to short /o/ when the 2MS suffix is added, e.g., *ṭār–ṭorṭ*[39] 'to fly away', *tāq–toqt* 'to support', *ḍāʕ–ḍoʕt* 'to get lost', *fāq–foqt* 'to wake up' (Cohen 1975, 103). The [o] quality in these verbs occurs usually in the environment of emphatics and labials. In the parallel forms in Jewish Gabes, /o/ tends to interchange with /u/ and /a/, e.g., *ḍāṛ–ḍoṛt / ḍuṛt* 'to roam, to go around', *ṣām–ṣomt / ṣamt* 'to fast'. Moreover, there exists a group of I-stem strong root verbs where we observe interchangeability in both the prefix and the thematic vowel, e.g., *yədxəl / yədxul* 'to enter', *yəmṛaḍ / yumṛaḍ* 'to get sick'. It can be established, therefore, that there exists in Jewish Gabes some level of vowel interchangeability in certain morphological environments, by which /ə/ and other phonemic and non-phonemic vowels can occur in the same form, often uttered by the same speaker. As demonstrated above by the example *ḍāṛ–ḍoṛt / ḍuṛt* 'to roam, to go around', this is

---

[38] Jewish Wad-Souf has preserved the historical /u/ vowel in this item, i.e., *mudda*.

[39] Cohen (1975, 48) utilises in his system of transcription various qualities of vowels. In the present study, however, when quoting examples from his grammar, I will limit myself to the basic vowel quality.

particularly the case with /ə/ and /o/–/u/ in verbs of stem I with second radical /w/ or /y/. The occurrence of the short /u/ can potentially be explained as a reflex of the historical /u/ vowel.[40]

4.3.5. Sounds Reflecting Hebrew Vocalisation Signs

Apart from the aforementioned set of three long vowels and three short ones, there are also numerous allophonic realisations of /e/ that reflect the Hebrew vocalisation signs *ṣere* and *segol* in lexical items of Hebrew origin. *Ṣere*, as pointed out by Henshke (2007, 53), is rendered as either /e/ or /i/. In the northern communities /e/ prevails, while in the south, especially in Djerba, /i/ is predominant, e.g. *yušif* (< יוֹסֵף *yosēp̄*) 'Joseph'. In the vicinity of emphatic consonants, however, *ṣere* is realised in the southern communities as /e/, e.g., *zaqen* (< זָקֵן *zaqēn*) 'old'. The realisation of *segol* is not fixed either, but rather demonstrates various tendencies. In segolate nouns, the first *segol* is usually pronounced as /i/ or /e/, while the second *segol* is as a rule reduced to /ə/, e.g., *kibəš* (< כֶּבֶשׂ *keḇeś*) 'lamb'. The realisation of *hateph-segol* is not regular either and it can be represented by either /e/ or /i/, e.g., *emona* (< אֱמוּנָה *ĕmūna*) 'faith', *imit* (< אֱמֶת *ĕmēt*) 'truth' (Henshke 2009, 55). Another sound that does not exist in spoken Tunisian Arabic but can be heard among Jews is /o/ which represents the Hebrew *ḥolem*. It is realised at times as /u/, but in the vicinity of emphatics and pharyngeals /o/ is preferred, e.g., *xaššof* (> כִּישׁוּף *kiššūp̄*) 'magic' (Henshke 2009, 55).

---

[40] This problem will be discussed in greater detail in chapter 3, §3.1.1.

4.4. Acoustic Analysis of Vowels

The following chart presents a mean plot representing the mean of all the individual tokens of the four main vowels in Jewish Gabes. Both long and short vowels have been taken into account. Formant values were obtained by means of the acoustic software Praat, which provides an acoustic analysis of speech. The horizontal axis represents the front-back quality, while the vertical axis defines the height of the vowel, i.e., the higher the value on the *x* axis, the more frontal the vowel, and the higher the value on the *y* axis, the lower the vowel. The numerical values that follow the chart are the averages calculated for each of the vowels based on fifteen allophone tokens taken from recordings of the speakers participating in the study. Below, one can find the acoustic variation of each of the vowel phonemes along with the examples. As noted in §4.1, /o/ has not been included in the analysis of the acoustic scatter of vowels due to its limited occurrence.

Figure 1: Mean qualities of the main phonemic vowels of Jewish Gabes

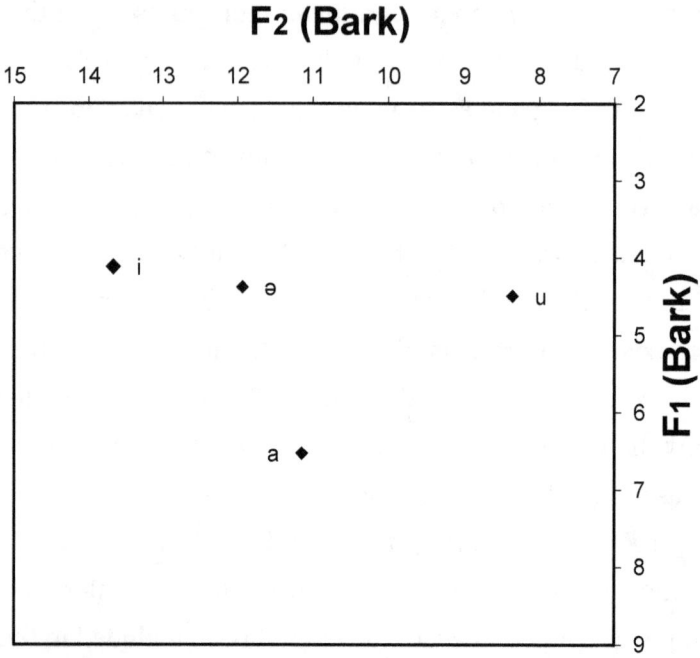

/ā, a/ 718 : 1489 Hz
/ī/ 430 : 2184 Hz
/ū/ 472 : 977 Hz
/ə/ 459 : 1674 Hz

Figure 2: Qualities of /a/

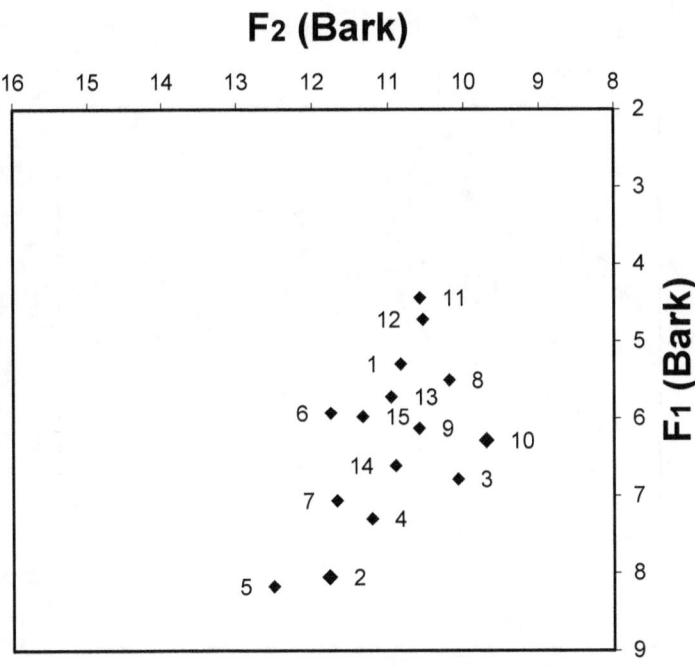

1. *āna* 'I'
2. *aġnī* 'make him rich!'
3. *yəṭlab* 'he asks'
4. *ḍār* 'house'
5. *xadma* 'work'
6. *ṣəlṭān* 'sultan'
7. *ʕažīža* 'dear (FS)'
8. *mra* 'woman'
9. *ṣanaʕ* 'maidservant'
10. *qatla* 'she told her'
11. *raqdət* 'she fell asleep'
12. *ttabbaṣ* 'you (MS) / she bend(s)'
13. *bāba* 'father'
14. *ṭār* 'it flew away'
15. *qṣar* 'castle'

As the chart demonstrates, the lowest realisations of /a/ occur in short vowels following velar or uvular consonants (5, 2), and the highest in short vowels occurring after plain consonants (11, 12). In terms of the back-front opposition, most of the back realisations appear in short vowels after emphatics (10, 8, 3).

Figure 3: Qualities of /ī/

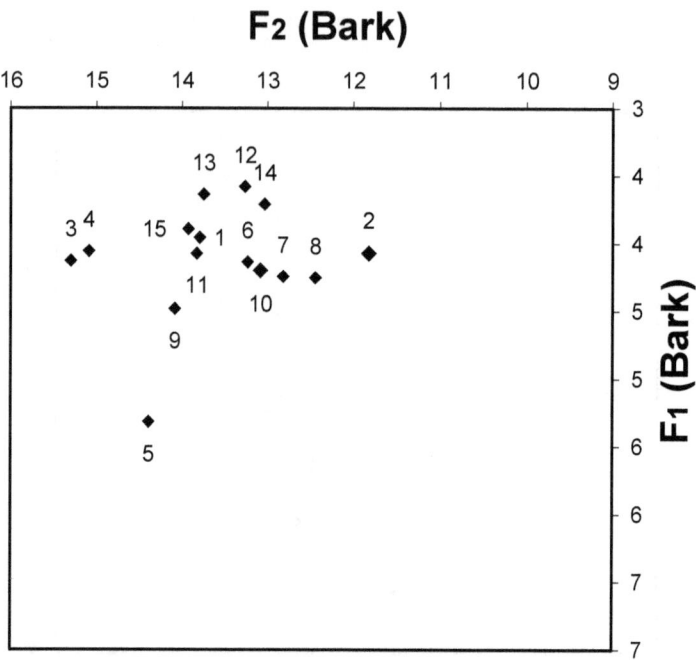

1. bīt 'room'
2. kbīra 'big (FS)'
3. aḥyī 'make him alive!'
4. ʕažīž 'dear'
5. xlīqa 'figure'
6. xīr 'better'
7. brīma 'fine'
8. xdīt 'I took'
9. žīb 'bring! (MS)'
10. kīf 'when'
11. ḍārī 'my house'
12. rāžlī 'my man'
13. šīd 'lord'
14. rabbī 'God'
15. hādī 'this (FS)'

Compared to the plot of /a/ in the chart above, the scatter of the allophones of /i/ is wide with respect to the front-back opposition. The allophones with the highest values on the x axis are those which occur in the vicinity of the semi-vowel /y/ and the sibilants (3, 4). On the opposite side of the scale are allophones occurring next to /x/ and /ṛ/, i.e., 2 and 8, which possess a back quality due to the retraction of the tongue root required for the realisation of these consonants.

Figure 4: Qualities of /ū/

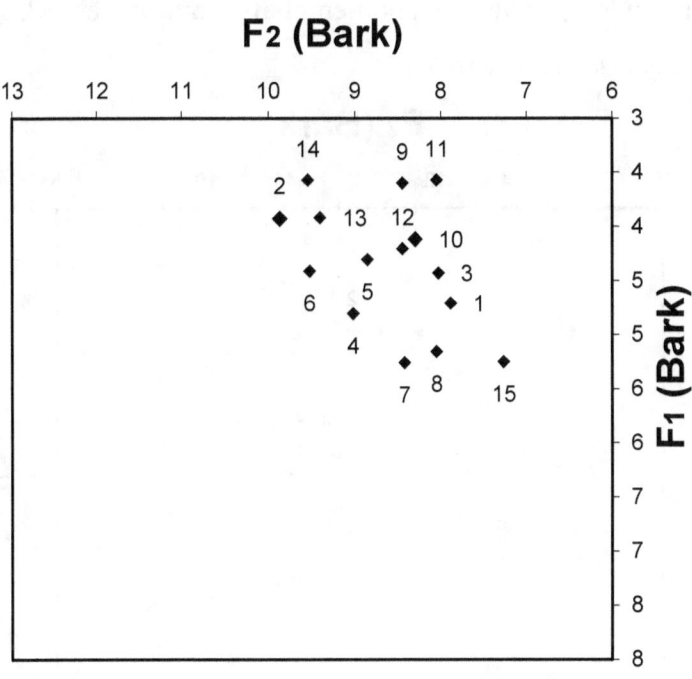

1. *farḥu* 'they rejoiced'
2. *yaʕmlū* 'they make it'
3. *škūn* 'who'
4. *qāllu* 'he told him'
5. *tūqaf* 'you (MS) stop'
6. *yšūfu* 'they look'
7. *nəqrāwu* 'we read it'
8. *fūq* 'above'
9. *yūžən* 'he weighs'
10. *mā rqāwūṣ* 'they did not find it'
11. *ʕandu* 'he has'
12. *kūl* 'eat!'
13. *flūš* 'money'
14. *lūla* 'first (FS)'
15. *yqūllu* 'he tells him'

The realisations of /u/ have a very wide scatter in terms of the high-low relationship. The highest tokens occur in long vowels following plain consonants (14, 9, 11). On the other hand, the lowest realisations of /u/ are observed in the vicinity of /q/ or /r/. The back allophones of /u/ occur after pharyngeal and laryngeal consonants (15, 1), while the front realisation is found mostly in long vowels in a non-emphatic environment (2, 14, 6).

Figure 5: Qualities of /ə/

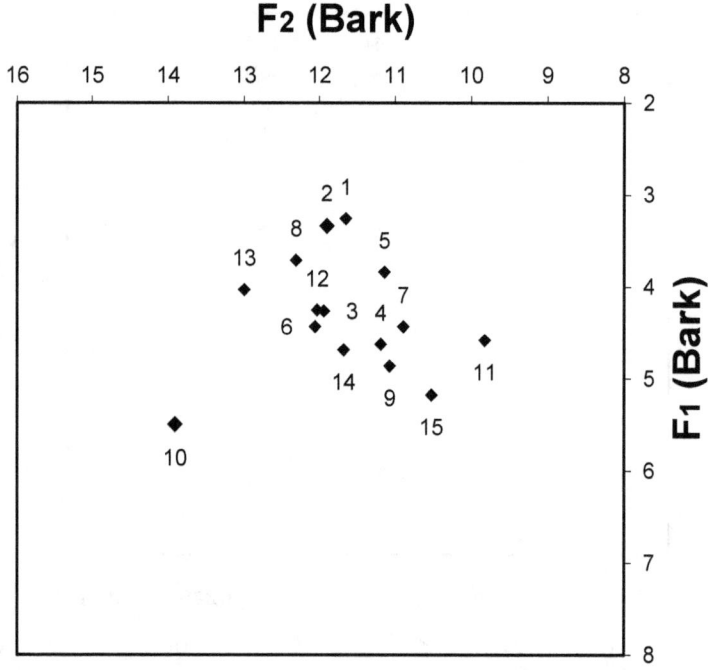

1. ṣəlṭān 'sultan'
2. bənt 'daughter'
3. mərtu 'his wife'
4. təṭlaʕ 'you (MS)/she will go out'
5. šəmš 'sun'
6. qṭəlha 'he killed her'
7. raqdət 'she fell asleep'
8. kəlbək 'your dog'
9. qəlbək 'your heart'
10. ləqmi 'date wine'
11. kəbrət 'she grew up'
12. baʕtəthəm 'she sent them'
13. aʕməlli 'make for me'
14. tāxəd 'you (MS)/she will take'
15. təḍrbu 'you (MS)/she will hit him'

The data presented in the chart above indicates that, even though the allophones of /ə/ have a broad scatter, the majority are realised between mid-close central unrounded [ᵊ] and close-mid central rounded [ɵ]. Some allophones occurring in the vicinity of pharyngeal consonants (10, 15) possess the quality of low-mid central unrounded [ɜ]. Additionally, some variants occurring next to /q/ or pharyngealised /ṛ/ or /ḍ/ demonstrate back realisation (11, 15). It is worth noting that, in Jewish Djerba, /ə/ has a much shorter realisation, often creating an impression of a consonant cluster, e.g., Jewish Gabes: bərša, Jewish Djerba: bᵊrša 'a lot'.

4.5. Diphthongs

As has been mentioned in §4.1, many CA diphthongs have been contracted in Jewish Gabes to a single long vowel. This, however, is not the case in all other dialects of the region, and the distribution of diphthongs within the Maghrebi dialects seems to be more complex. According to the general tendency, the shift /ay/ > /ī/ and /aw/ > /ū/ is a trait of sedentary dialects, while that resulting respectively in /ō/ and /ē/ characterises the Bedouin varieties (D'Anna 2021, 17). Cohen (1975, 65), on the other hand, notes that preservation of the diphthongs is one of the characteristic traits of some Jewish Tunisian dialects, and he adduces numerous examples of lexemes containing diphthongs in Jewish Tunis which seemingly confirm this claim. However, the data from Jewish Gabes and Jewish Djerba indicate that, in contrast to Jewish Tunis, in these Jewish dialects from southern Tunisia, the diphthongs are contracted. Table 7 below demonstrates the aforementioned development of the CA diphthongs in Jewish

Gabes as compared to the Bedouin dialect of Wad-Souf from eastern Algeria, which exhibits numerous Bedouin features:

Table 7: Diphthongs in CA, Jewish Wad-Souf, and Jewish Gabes

CA	Jewish Wad-Souf	Jewish Gabes	
etymological diphthong /ay/			
dayn	dēn	dīn	debt
xayṭ	xēṭ	xīṭ	thread
xayr	xēr	xīr	better
zayn	zēn	žīn	beauty
zaytun	zītūn	žītūn	olives
ṣayf	ṣēf	ṣīf	summer
layla	lēla	līla	night
etymological diphthong /aw/			
xawx	xōx	xūx	peaches
fawq	fōg	fūq	above
lawz	lōz	lūž	almonds
mawt	mōt	mūt	death
ṣawṭ	ṣōṭ	ṣūṭ	voice
zawj	zōz	žūž	pair
lawṭa	lōṭa	lūṭa	beneath

As can be seen, the shift of /aw/ > /ū/ and of /ay/ to /ī/ is very regular in Jewish Gabes. Nevertheless, a secondary process is observed when long /ī/ is placed between two guttural or emphatic consonants, in which case it tends to be diphthongised with an additional /ə/ sound, e.g., ṣayf > ṣīf > ṣᵊyf 'summer'. Examples of diphthong contraction from Jewish Djerba include the following items: žūž (Jewish Tunis: žawž) 'pair', žīt (Jewish Tunis: žayt) 'oil', žītūn (Jewish Tunis: žaytūn) 'olives'. It can be established, therefore, that the reduction of diphthongs is one of the hallmarks of the southern Jewish dialects, in contrast to Jewish Tunis, where they tend to be preserved.

5.0. Phonotactics

5.1. Syllabic Patterns

The following syllabic patterns are attested in Jewish Gabes:

a) Open syllables:

 - CV̄: **žā.bu** 'they brought';
 - CCV̄: **mši**.na 'we went';

b) Closed syllables:

 - əC: **əš**.maʕ! 'listen!';
 - CəC: **təb**.ki 'you (MS) cry';
 - CCəCC: **ktəbt** 'I wrote';
 - CəCC: **kənt** 'I was';
 - CCCəCC: **stḥəmm** 'he warmed up';
 - CV̄C: **qāl** 'he said';
 - CCV̄C: **tžīb**.lu 'you (MS) bring him'.

5.2. The Syllable Structure of Jewish Gabes as Compared to CA

In order to establish the distribution of short and long vowels in Jewish Gabes, one needs to take into consideration the diachronic development of the syllable structure of CA. In this study, I will utilise the rules of the distribution of vowels developed by Marcel Cohen (1912, 14) in his work on Jewish Algiers, and subsequently repeated by David Cohen (1975, 72) in Jewish Tunis.

Table 8: Syllable structure development in CA and Jewish Gabes

No.	Rule	CA	Jewish Gabes
1.	No short vowel is permitted in an open syllable.[1]	jabal 'mountain'	žbəl
2.	Short vowels in closed syllables of CA are represented by a reduced vowel or zero vowel.	qālat 'she said'	qālət
3.	When a word contains two short vowels in open syllables, the second one is elided in order to form one closed syllable.	raqadat 'she fell asleep'	raqdət

5.3. Epenthetic Vowel

As has previously been mentioned, modern Arabic dialects, and particularly the Maghrebi varieties, have undergone a considerable reduction of vowel inventory compared to CA. This resulted in new types of syllables and various consonant clusters that violate fixed prosodic structures attested in CA. Therefore, in order to prevent the occurrence of some sequences of consonants, an epenthetic vowel is inserted. Modern Arabic dialects deal in different ways with the insertion of an auxiliary vowel; a comparative cross-dialectal study will follow in §5.5. Below I will analyse the strategies by means of which consonant clusters are broken in Jewish Gabes.

---

[1] The exception to this rule is plural and singular feminine forms of the imperative of stem I, e.g., ášəṛbi 'drink! (FS)', áxəržu 'get out! (PL)'. As pointed out by Yoda (2005, 103), the same rule is operational in Jewish Tripoli, where, however, there exist more cases of /ə/ in open syllables due to the weakening of /h/.

5.3.1. Word Initial

a) CCV-

A cluster of two consonants at the beginning of a word is generally permitted in Jewish Gabes, e.g., *tžīb* 'you (MS) / she will bring', *ḍrəb* 'he hit', *ẓdəm* 'he attacked', *tbəddəl* 'he changed', *ẓġār* 'children', *nxāfu* 'we are scared'.

b) CCCV

This sequence is attested only in *stḥaqt* 'I was in need of' and *stḥəmm* 'he warmed up'.

5.3.2. In the Middle of the Word

a) CCC

Consonant clusters in the middle of a word are prone to appear when a pronominal suffix is added to a verbal form, e.g., *ḥšəmt* 'she put to shame' + /-ni/ 'me' = **ḥšəmtni* 'she put me to shame'. The cluster is resolved by means of a two-stage process. First of all, the stem short vowel is moved back between /ḥ/ and /š/, and then subsequently an auxiliary vowel is inserted after the first consonant of the cluster, i.e., *ḥašmətni* 'she put me to shame'. On the other hand, the consonant cluster that occurs in 3PL prefix forms, e.g., *yəktbu* 'they will write', is usually tolerable in Jewish Gabes, unless the first radical is a guttural consonant. In this case, an epenthetic vowel is usually inserted, e.g., *yəxəržu* 'they go out', *yaʕarfu* 'they know'. In Jewish Djerba, an epenthetic vowel tends to appear after the first radical regardless of its place of articulation, e.g., *yəkətbu* [yəkítbu] 'they write'. The timbre of this vowel is probably an effect of assimilation to the quality of the prefix semi-consonant /y/. The same strategy can be observed in Jewish Tripoli, i.e., *ykətbu* (Yoda 2005, 159).

b) CC

The same reciprocal movement of the schwa exemplified by *ḥašmətni* 'she put me to shame' is observable when a vocalic suffix is added to a verbal form terminating with a consonant, e.g., *ḍrəb* 'he hit' + /-u/ 'him'. The expected form is **ḍrəbu*; however, in that case, the syllabic division would be *ḍrə.bu*, with a short vowel in an open syllable. As a general rule, short vowels cannot exist in an open syllable and therefore the actual form is *ḍər.bu*. Another way of preventing the emergence of an open syllable containing a short vowel is by gemination of the consonant of the inflectional suffix, as in, e.g., **ḍərbətəm* 'she hit them'. In this case the middle /ə/ is in an open syllable, hence the /t/ is geminated in order to close the syllable, i.e., *ḍər.bət.təm*.

The above examples present the process of restructuring the syllable when a vocalic suffix is agglutinated. However, when a suffix beginning with a consonant is added, no change is observed and a cluster of CCC is tolerable, e.g., *qtəlt* + /-kəm/ = *qtəltkəm* 'I killed them', since this sequence does not violate the general rule of avoiding short vowels in open syllables. Similarly, the pronoun /lə/ when added does not bring about any fluctuation in terms of syllable structure, e.g., *yərbṭu* + /lu/ > *yərbṭūlu* 'they sew him'; there is, however, a shift of the stress onto the suffix vowel of the verb.

5.3.3. Word Final

A cluster of three consonants in word-final position usually occurs when a verbal form contains both the /-t/ suffix and the negation particle /-š/. In these cases, an auxiliary vowel is not mandatory, but sometimes it is inserted, e.g., *ma xəftš ~ ma xəfətš* 'I did not fear'. However, clusters of three consonants in monosyllabic words are consistently resolved. The strategy in nouns differs from the strategy in verbs, namely, in verbs, an auxiliary vowel is inserted after the second radical, e.g., *gdəb* 'he lied', while in nouns, it is usually placed after the first radical, e.g., *kəlb* 'dog'.

5.4. Syllable Structure in the Perspective of Sonority

The theory of sonority states that the formulation of syllables and words in a language is motivated by a scale of sound 'strength', which places the loudest sounds in the centre of a word (nucleus) and the least audible ones either at the beginning (onset) or at the end (coda). Based on this view, the sonority sequencing principle has been developed, according to which a vowel constitutes the sonority peak in a word and consonants are organised in decreasing order. Usually, the hierarchy of sounds is as follows: vowels, liquids, fricatives, and plosives. This scale, however, differs from language to language (Ohala 1992).

In the field of the Maghrebi dialects, the theory of sonority has been used by several scholars, e.g., Philippe Marçais (1956, 112) and Marcel Cohen (1912, 140). However, the term used in French is *pouvoir ouvrant*, and their main focus is therefore not on the level of sonority of the consonants, but rather on the principles governing their placement in the word. David Cohen (1975, 79) has developed a provisional 'sonority' hierarchy for Jewish Tunis, considering the impact it has on the syllable structure. Additionally, he points out that, compared to Muslim Tunis, the Jewish dialect is much more tolerant of consonant clusters. Below I will present a few examples from Jewish Gabes, utilising Cohen's findings.

In Jewish Tunis, liquids, pharyngeals, and labials have a strong tendency to be placed at the end of the word. Cohen (1975, 80) remarks, however, that the situation where a word terminates with a consonant cluster and the last consonant is liquid is not tolerated. Therefore, a vowel is placed between them in order to prevent the sequence of less sonorous consonants followed by more sonorous ones in the coda of a word. Jewish Gabes utilises the same strategy, disjoining clusters from CA, e.g., CA *baḥr* > *bḥaṛ* 'sea', CA *ḥabl* > *ḥbəl* 'rope', CA *laḥm* > *lḥam* 'meat'. Also, in words which in CA have two short vowels, due to the process of reduction, the short vowel is retained only between the second and the third radical, e.g., *jamal* > *žməl* 'camel'. The consonant /ʕ/ has the same disjunctive effect, since it must be preceded by a vowel, e.g., CA *dabuʕ* > *ḍbaʕ* 'hyena'. Also, in some cases /b/ brings about the insertion of the vowel, e.g., *žanb* > *žnəb*. Contrary to this, /ḥ/ can easily be found in the sequence CVCC as the third radical, e.g., *qamḥ* 'wheat'.

Word-initial clusters, in turn, are much more frequent, and even combinations of consonants that, when found in the second and the third radicals, would normally be disjointed, are permitted, e.g., *žamal* > *žməl* 'camel'. However, one can find several examples of disjunction when the second radical is a liquid, e.g., *malak* > *məlk* 'king'.

Another strategy for preventing a consonant cluster in word-initial position is insertion of the prosthetic, ultra-short vowel, which principally takes place when the first consonant is a liquid, e.g., *ᵊrḍa* 'he agreed', *ᵊrqāw* 'they found', *ᵊntāy* 'mine', *ᵊmġarfa* 'spoon'.

However, as has been noticed by Cohen (1975, 82), there are numerous cases when the aforementioned rules are suspended due to morphological reasons. The position of the disjunctive vowel can disambiguate between a verb and a verbal noun, e.g., *ṣəṛb* 'drinking' as opposed to *ṣṛəb* 'he drank'.

5.5. The Syllabic Typology of Jewish Gabes in a Cross-Dialectal Perspective

Kiparsky (2003) has divided the dialects of Arabic into three main groups in terms of the resolving of a consonant cluster by an epenthetic vowel, namely, VC dialects (CVCC), CC dialects (CCC) and CV dialects (CCVC). Seemingly, this division does not, as shown above, apply to all dialects, and Jewish Gabes cannot be unambiguously classified as one or other of them, since there are multiple examples of all three patterns of syllabification.

Kiparsky (2003) reasons that the VC and CC dialects are different from the CV dialects in terms of the treatment of unsyllabified consonants, since, prosodically, these are affiliated directly to the word node as a semisyllable possessing the status of a mora (Watson 2007, 337). There are, however, dialects that share some features of both of the groups. Below I will present examples from several Maghrebi dialects in order to establish their typology.

Table 9: Comparison of syllable structure in selected dialects of North-African Arabic

Dialect	Example	Classification
Jewish Gabes	qālətla 'she told her'	VC
	qāltlo 'she told him'	CC
	nədfnūha 'we bury her'	CC
Jewish Tunis[2]	nšədtni 'you asked me'	CC
	yarḥmu 'may he [God] have mercy upon him'	CC
	yəxᵊržu 'they go out' (> yəxrež)	VC
	nəfšna 'our soul'	CC
	aṣalkəm 'your origin'	VC
Jewish Algiers[3]	kəlbna 'our dog'	CC
	marṣtna 'our port'	CC
	mākəlti 'my food'	VC
	bġórti 'my cow'	VC
Jewish Tripoli	kčəbtləm 'you wrote them'	CC
	kčəbčələm 'you wrote them'	CV
	qaltla 'she said'	CC
	yənqətlu 'they will be killed'	VC
Bedouin Douz[4]	šⁱbaḥᵊtni 'you saw me'	VC
	gⁱtalᵊtni 'you killed me'	VC
	xubᵊzti 'my bread'	VC
	mākilti 'my food'	VC
	nⁱhār iž-žᵊmōʕa 'Friday'	CV
Muslim Tunis[5]	qalbha 'her heart'	CC
	žābəlkum 'he brought you (PL)'	VC
	žābəthāli 'she brought her to me'	VC

[2] The examples are borrowed from Cohen (1964).
[3] See Cohen (1912, 327).
[4] See Ritt-Benmimoun (2011, 282; 2014, 76–79).
[5] See Singer (1984, 253).

As can be seen, the dialects in question represent all three types of syllable structure. Watson (2003, 340), elaborating on Kiparsky's theory, classifies Iraqi Arabic as a VC dialect, giving the example of *gilitla* 'she told her', while Moroccan Arabic is categorised as CC dialect based on the example of *qiltlu* 'I told him'. She proposes the following syllabification of the last lexical item: *qil.(t)lu*. According to this scheme, the first syllable consists of two moras, i.e., /i/ and /l/, while /q/ is perceived as a non-moraic onset. The second syllable is formed by /l/ and /u/, but only the latter has a mora. Interestingly, /t/ is analysed as an extrasyllabic element, albeit possessing a moraic status. This analysis draws from Kiparsky's (2003) theory, according to which consonants can form semisyllables. Similarly, in the first and second items from Jewish Gabes listed in Table 9 above, i.e., *qālǝtla* 'she told her', and *qāltlo* 'she told him', /t/ should be analysed as a semisyllable: (qal).(t).(la). The epenthetic vowel is omitted in the analysis, as its occurrence is optional.

Based on the examples provided above, it should be concluded that Jewish Gabes shares features of other Maghrebi dialects in terms of the syllable structure. Typologically, the North-African group cannot be unambiguously classified as CC dialects, as there are numerous cases of epenthesis on the left of the unsyllabified consonant, and occasionally on the right.

6.0. Stress

The placement of the stress in an isolated word in Jewish Gabes does not differ from other Maghrebi dialects. Nonetheless, as has been observed by Cohen (1975, 84), there is a conspicuous discrepancy between the Jewish and Muslim dialects of Tunis, where Muslim speakers pronounce much stronger stress than Jewish speakers, the stress in the latter case being hardly audible. It is worth noting that the stress in Jewish Gabes, as in other North African dialects of Arabic, is mobile, namely, it can change its position in a word when the syllable structure is changed due to an agglutination of affixes or the negation particle, e.g., *mā́tət* 'she died' > *mā mātə́tš* 'she did not die'.

The rules established by Cohen (1975, 85) regarding the stress in an isolated word in Jewish Tunis are also relevant to Jewish Gabes. According to these rules, the ultimate syllable is stressed either when it contains a long vowel and is closed by a single consonant, or when it is closed by a cluster of two consonants, e.g., *xabbā́ž* 'baker', *ma ʕarfə́tš* 'she did not understand', *wṣə́lt* 'I arrived'. In turn, the penultimate syllable is stressed in all other cases, namely, both when the ultimate syllable is open, e.g., *kə́lba* 'bitch', and when it is closed, e.g., *tə́kməl* 'she finishes'.

The placement of stress can have a twofold effect. As has been observed by Cohen (1975, 88), it has an impact on both the vowels and the consonants. It is well known that stress prolongs the vowel length, as a natural consequence of the prominence given to the stressed syllable (Cruttenden 1997, 13). Interestingly, both in Jewish Tunis and in Jewish Gabes, stress can also affect consonants, when found in a monosyllabic word or in word-final position, by giving them an additional reinforcement, and in the case of labial consonants, gemination can be observed, e.g., *wəld* > *wulədd* 'child', *hbaṭ* > *hbaṭṭ* 'he went down'.

7.0. Conclusions

This chapter has described the phonology of Jewish Gabes and its place within the Tunisian varieties of Arabic, especially the Jewish ones. As I have demonstrated, there are significant differences between the Muslim and Jewish dialects of Gabes in terms of the realisation of certain consonants. The Muslim variety aligns with Bedouin-type dialects in terms of phonological traits, while the Jewish dialect exhibits typically sedentary isoglosses. Moreover, I have demonstrated the development of diphthongs in Jewish Gabes, where /ay/ generally shifted to /ī/, and /aw/ to /ū/. This was compared to the Bedouin-type Jewish Wad-Souf dialect, where the shift is that of /ay/ to /ē/ and /aw/ to /ō/, and to Jewish Tunis, where the diphthongs are preserved. In the discussion on consonants, I have paid special attention to the development of sibilants in the region. Moreover, I have demonstrated that, in contradistinction to many dialects of the region, /h/ is generally retained in Jewish Gabes. In §§3.13–3.15, I studied emphasis spread in Jewish Gabes. The preliminary results of this analysis prove, firstly, that the pharyngealised character of /q/ is weak, and secondly, that the emphatic consonants in the dialect in question have different degrees of spreadability. In terms of the vowel inventory, I have demonstrated that Jewish Gabes has three long phonemic vowels: /ī/, /ā/, /ū/, and three short phonemic vowels: /a/, /ə/, and /o/. I have pointed out three non-phonemic qualities of /ə/, depending on the consonantal environment. My findings prove that, although the vowel inventory of Jewish Gabes is similar to that of Jewish Tunis, the distribution of /o/ in the former is much more limited. Finally, I have shown that David Cohen's (1975, 65) argument about the tendency towards the preservation of diphthongs among Jewish dialects of Tunisian Arabic is not valid for southern Tunisian dialects, which reflect a strong contractive tendency.

PART II
MORPHOLOGY

3. VERBAL MORPHOLOGY

1.0. General Characteristics of the Verbal System of Jewish Gabes

The verbal morphology of Jewish Gabes shares many features with other sedentary Maghrebi dialects. Like most of the modern varieties of Arabic, Jewish Gabes does not have reflexes of any of the three moods of CA, nor the inner passive. The dual, as well as gender distinction in 2PL p-stem forms, is completely absent. However, contrary to the Jewish and Muslim dialects of Tunis, it does differentiate morphologically between 2MS and 2FS in both suffix and prefix stems.[1] This distinction has been also attested in Jewish Djerba (Behnstedt 1998, 66). The distinction between active and passive participles of the derived forms known from CA has completely disappeared. The distribution and the aspectual value of the I-stem active participle—not only in Jewish Gabes, but in many Jewish North African Arabic dialects in general—constitutes one of the major factors that sets them apart from their Muslim counterparts.[2]

2.0. Stem Patterns of the Verbal System

When it comes to the distribution of the verbal forms, IV and IX forms are absent. As a result, some of the verbs that originally

---

[1] The Jewish dialect of Tripoli has preserved this distinction in the imperfect conjugation as well; see Yoda (2005, 140).

[2] I will discuss this topic in greater detail in chapter 4, §5.0.

occured in those forms in CA have been transferred to other stems. For instance, verbs with passive meaning in form VII that have active counterparts in form I, have been transferred to the /t-/ passive form (according to the scheme presented below), or form the passive in a descriptive way.[3] In addition, a purely dialectal stem has emerged with a prefixed /t-/, presumably by analogy to CA stems V and VI. Like other North African dialects of Arabic, Jewish Gabes possesses the XI stem, which corresponds to the IX stem in the eastern group (Ritt-Benmimoun 2014, 383). As pointed out by Yoda (2005, 143), this stem has in fact substituted for the ninth form of CA. Consequently, ten verbal forms have been attested in Jewish Gabes, each of the forms possessing a regular form ($C^1C^2C^3$); a second radical geminated form ($C^1C^2C^2$); and forms with a first radical semi-vowel (w/y C^2C^3), second radical semi-vowel (C^1 w/y C^3), and third radical semi-vowel (C^1C^2 w/y). Thus, the system of the verbal forms of the Jewish Gabes dialect can be represented as follows:[4]

Table 10: Triliteral verb stems attested in Jewish Gabes

Form I	$C^1C^2əC^3$	Form VI	$TC^1āC^2əC^3$
Form II	$C^1əC^2C^2əC^3$	[Form VII	$nəC^1C^2əC^3$][5]
Form III	$C^1āC^2əC^3$	[Form VIII	$C^1TəC^2C^3$]
t-passive	$təC^1C^2əC^3$	Form X	$štaC^1C^2əC^3$
Form V	$TC^1əC^2C^2əC^3$	Form XI	$C^1C^2āC^3$

---

[3] For the development of the IV stem in Moroccan Arabic, see Aguadé (2012).

[4] The list includes only perfect forms of the strong verb.

[5] The square brackets denote forms which are vestigial or restricted locally. Their distribution is discussed in greater detail in §§3.2.6–3.2.7.

2.1. Basic Form

In CA, as well as in many modern dialects, the basic form appears in three vowel sub-groups, each of which includes verbs with a certain meaning (Fischer 2002, 98).

Table 11: Vocalic variants of the I stem in CA

S-stem	P-stem	Meaning
CaCaCa	yaCCa/i/uCu	Transitive and intransitive action, e.g., *qatala–yaqtulu* 'to kill'
CaCiCa	yaCCaCu	Non action verbs and attributes, e.g., *baliha–yablahu*, 'to be simple-minded'
CaCuCa	yaCCuCu	Qualities and attributes, e.g., *ʕamuqa–yaʕmuqu*, 'to be deep'

This diversity has been reduced in the Jewish Gabes dialect to only one short vowel phoneme, which, depending on the phonetic environment, can be either /ə/ or /a/. Thus, instead of CA *kabura*, one finds *kbər* 'he grew big'; instead of *kataba*, *ktəb* 'he wrote'; and instead of *barida*, *brəd* 'he was cold'. Laryngeal and pharyngeal consonants bring about an /a/ quality, e.g., *dbaḥ* 'he slaughtered', *lʕab* 'he played'. It is worth mentioning that the same process of unification of the vowel classes in the first stem took place also in other Jewish dialects, like Tunis and Tripoli. In the dialect of Tripoli, the reduction was even more radical, since the short epenthetic vowel /ə/ remained stable in proximity to the gutturals (Yoda 2004, 142). In the Jewish Tunis dialect, as pointed out by Cohen (1975, 96), the distribution of /ə/ and /a/ is determined by the neighbouring consonants. Contrary to this, the Muslim dialect of Tunis preserved all three short vowels of the s-stem conjugation, which subsequently gave rise to six derivative forms of the p-stem (Singer 1984, 331).

An interesting dichotomy in the vowel distribution of the s-stem and the p-stem can be observed in another Tunisian dialect, namely, the Bedouin dialect of Marāzīg (Ritt-Benmimoun 2014, 289). The 3MS has only two variants in the suffix stem, namely, fʕal and ᵊfʕil, while in the prefix stem one can find as many as five forms, namely, yafʕal, yifʕil, yufʕil, yufʕul and yafʕal.[6] Moreover, the 3FS has three variants in the suffix stem, namely, fiʕˡlat, fuʕᵘlat, and fiʕlat. The two aforementioned dialects, therefore, are much more conservative in the preservation of the stem vowels present in CA than the Jewish dialects, which display a strong tendency towards reduction, and consequently unification of the sub-groups of the first stem.

The phenomenon described above has a serious impact on the semantic structure of the verbal system, particularly the second form, since, in CA, the distinction between the 3MS suffix stem and imperative SG is based on the different vowel qualities. Hence, when all the short vowels have been reduced, there is no possibility of expressing such a differentiation. In the Jewish Gabes dialect, therefore, the aforementioned forms are the same, e.g., ṣarraf 'he cashed' and 'cash!'. In Jewish Tripoli Arabic, this problem of ambiguity has been resolved by differentiation of the stress position: in suffix forms, the stress falls on the penultimate syllable, while in imperative ones, it falls on the ultimate, e.g., ʕə́lləm 'he taught', but ʕəllə́m 'teach!' (Yoda 2005, 142). The dialect of Marāzīg, on the other hand, seems to preserve the original /i/ vowel of the imperative, e.g., baṭṭal 'he stopped', but baṭṭil

---

[6] Transcription according to the source.

'stop!' (Ritt-Benmimoun 2014, 333). Other dialects, like the Muslim dialect of Tunis and the dialect of Sūsa, choose not to distinguish the perfect stem from the imperative by inserting a vowel with a different quality, even though they do possess a set of three short vowels (Talmoudi 1980, 99; Singer 1984, 368).

2.2. Development of the Passive[7]

Some verb stems that occur in CA are scarcely attested in the Maghrebi dialects, while others have uneven geographical distribution. This is particularly the case with stems expressing passivity and reflexivity. Depending on the region, the passive voice of stem I is realised either through the /n-/ prefix, i.e., nəC^{1}C^{2}əC^3, or the /t-/ prefix, i.e., təC^{1}C^{2}əC^3.[8] In a number of dialects, both stems exist and are used interchangeably, while in others, the two competing forms fulfil different pragmatic functions. Moreover, as will be demonstrated, in Jewish Gabes and in other dialects of the region, a secondary process takes place that attests to an analogical change. In the present section, I argue that the replacement of the Old Arabic /n-/ stem by a dialectal t-stem passive took place in analogy to stems V and VI, which form the passive

---

[7] This section is a part of my article 'Between Analogy and Language Contact: A Case Study of Grammatical Change in Maghrebi Judaeo-Arabic Dialects' (Gębski, forthcoming b).

[8] The syllabic structure of the /n-/ stem is not uniform across the region. While in both Jewish Tripoli (Yoda 2005, 177) and Jewish Gabes the schwa is placed after the /n-/ prefix, in the dialect of Douz the vowel is placed after the first radical and the initial consonantal cluster is resolved by an epenthetic vowel, e.g., ʾnfṭam 'he was weaned' (Ritt-Benmimoun 2014, 361).

of forms II and III respectively. The /t-/ prefix in these dialects is reanalysed as a marker of passivity, opening a pathway to its extension over stem VII. In the following paragraphs, I will first describe the distribution of the two stems across North Africa, and then propose a reconstruction of the analogical process that led to the emergence of the /t-/ stem.

Let us first discuss the distribution of the /n-/ and the /t-/ stems in selected dialects of Libya, Tunisia, and Algeria. Within the Libyan dialectological landscape, the passive stem with an /n-/ prefix prevails. Indeed, it occurs in Jewish Tripoli, although the /t-/ stem seems to be sporadically employed to express passivity too (Yoda 2005, 177). The /n/- stem is well attested and stable in the Muslim dialect of Tripoli (Pereira 2008, 109). In the Muslim dialect of Benghazi, the /n-/ stem is dominant, but a limited number of verbs form the passive voice with an infixed /t-/ (Benkato 2014, 79). Overall, Libyan Arabic seems to exhibit a preference towards the /n-/ stem.

The Tunisian varieties seem to be more heterogenous in terms of their expressions of the passive. Within the Bedouin varieties of Tunisian Arabic, the central and northern dialects employ the /t-/ type passive, while the southern ones utilise the /n-/ type (Marçais 1950, 215).[9] The /n-/ stem is attested, among others, in the Bedouin dialect of Douz (Ritt-Benmimoun 2014, 361).[10] In terms of sedentary dialects, according to D. Cohen

---

[9] Marçais (1950, 209) also argues that the /t-/ passive is an isogloss of the sedentary dialects in Tunisia.

[10] Bin Murad reports that the formerly Bedouin population inhabiting the region of Nifzāwa (southern Tunisia) used the VII and the VIII forms

(1975, 125), some vestiges of this conjugation can be found also in the Jewish dialect of Tunis. Nevertheless, this prefix seems to be perceived as unusual and artificial, since speakers tend to use a hybrid prefix /tən-/ consisting of a combination of the /n-/ prefix and the morpheme /tə-/, which are naturally associated with passivity and reflexivity. As a result, one can find forms like *təndrab* 'he was hit' (Cohen 1975, 124). The /n-/ prefix has completely disappeared from both the Muslim dialect of Sūsa, in which the reflexive-passive function was acquired subsequently by the pattern *tifʕal* (Talmoudi 1980, 103), and the Muslim dialect of Tunis (Cohen 1975, 125). In these dialects, the function of the Old Arabic form VII was inherited by the conjugation with the prefix /t-/.[11] Marcel Cohen (1912, 227) points out that this type of prefix in the passive conjugation historically precedes the infixation present in form VIII and is typical of Tunisian dialects. On the other hand, the dialects of Djerba feature both the /n-/ stem and the /t-/ stem. The Ibadite variety demonstrates a preference for the /t-/ variant, while the Malakite one favours the /n-/ stem. In addition, the Malakite variety of Ababsa has developed an alternative /l-/ prefix, which is presumably a phonetic variant of /n-/. The /n-/ variant is also attested in the Jewish

---

interchangeably in order to encode the passive voice of stem I, while in the rural community dwelling in the north of the same region, the /t-/ passive form prevails (Ritt-Benmimoun 2014, 360).

[11] As has been observed by D. Cohen (1975, 124), the use of the ungeminated /t-/ prefix is one of the characteristics of the Eastern Maghrebi dialects, since both Moroccan and Algerian dialects tend to use a geminated prefix /tt-/, e.g., *ttaʕmal* 'to be done' (Cohen 1912, 228).

variety of Djerba Arabic (Behnstedt 1998, 69). In Jewish Gabes, the use of passive stems is generally limited, with both the /n-/ and the /t-/ stem being only scarcely attested.

Within the Algerian dialects, the /n-/ stem is very well attested in the Bedouin dialect of Oulad Brahim of Saida, as well as in the sedentary dialects of Tlemcen (Marçais 1908, 99) and Oran (Guerrero 2015, 226), where the /n-/ stem has eclipsed the /t-/ form as the main device for expressing passivity. However, Marçais (1908, 99) points out that, in some dialects spoken east of Oran (Mazouna, Mostaganem), it is the /t-/ stem that has prevailed. Similarly, the /n-/ stem serves as the principal way of encoding the passive in Jewish Algiers, where the /t-/ prefix has mostly intensive meaning (Cohen 1912, 218). On the other hand, in Jewish Wad-Souf, the /n-/ stem is non-existent, and the /t-/ stem serves as the sole means of expressing the passive, e.g., *l-māʕž əddəbḥu* (by assimilation of the /t-/ to /d̪/) 'the goats have been slaughtered', *hūwa təḍṛə́b* 'he has been beaten', *əl-sod təkšə́f* 'the secret was revealed'. The situation is similar in the north of Constantine and in Djidjelli (Marçais 1956, 193). Grand'Henry (1976, 56) reports the prevalence of the /t-/ stem in the Arabic spoken in the region of Mzab.

This brief comparison suggests that neither Tunisian nor Algerian Arabic can be unequivocally classified as /t-/ or /n-/ dialects, as the distribution of these forms is uneven and diverse. It is important to notice that the state of affairs in Morocco is similar. In virtually all non-Saharan Muslim varieties of Moroccan Arabic, both variants coexist. In some Jewish dialects, like Debdou, Ksar Es-Souk, and Oujda, as well as in the urban belt

Rabat-Meknes-Fes, the /n-/ stem is the only option. In the Western dialects of Jewish Moroccan Arabic, the two forms in question have different grammatical functions, namely, the /n-/ stem is usually used with human referents, while the /t-/ stem refers to non-human nouns. Heath (2002, 355) has attested several examples of the hybrid /tn-/ and /nt-/ passives.

In the Jewish dialect of Gabes, the dominant strategy for expressing the passive is different from the binary system described above. Besides the monopartite /n-/ stem, which is attested only scarcely, speakers often choose an active verb with an impersonal subject, followed by a direct object, e.g., *qətlū* 'they killed him', instead of the anticipated *nəqtəl* or *təqtəl*. This development, involving a bipartite construction, i.e., a verb and a personal pronoun, conforms to Kuryłowicz's (1947) first law of analogy, stating that bipartite (complex) markers tend to replace monopartite (simple) ones. This is exemplified, among others, by the periphrastic future in spoken French (*je vais voyager* instead of *je voyagerai* 'I am going to travel') and some varieties of Spanish (*voy a cantar* instead of *cantaré* 'I am going to sing'), which often comes to replace the monopartite future tense form. As pointed out by McMahon (1994, 77), the analogical change from single to double marking is motivated by disambiguation. This explains why, in Jewish Gabes, the 3MS form of the VII stem, *nəqtəl*, which can also be interpreted as the 1SG form of the p-stem, is replaced by the more overtly marked form *qətlū*.

In those dialects where the /t-/ stem is attested, the /t-/ morpheme of stems V, VI, and VIII, analysed as a marker of passivity, has been extended analogically onto the formation of the passive of form I. From the point of view of analogical reasoning, the 'irregular' and non-/t-/ Old Arabic /n-/ stem has been fully or partially eradicated, since it did not match the mirror-like system of verbal stems. Thus, the analogical development which took place in some dialects of Maghrebi Arabic can be summarised as follows:

if: stem II $C_1\partial C_2C_2\partial C_3$ (active) + /t/ = stem V $tC_1\partial C_2C_2\partial C_3$ (passive)

and: stem III $C_1\bar{a}C_2\partial C_3$ (active) + /t/ = stem VI $tC_1\bar{a}C_2\partial C_3$ (passive)

then: stem I $C_1C_2\partial C_3$ (active) + /t/ = stem IV $tC_1C_2\partial C_3$ (passive)

The survey presented above shows that the distribution of the /n-/ and the /t-/ passive variants is conditioned neither geographically nor communally. The sole regularity that can be observed is the absence of the form /t-/ in virtually all Libyan dialects. If we accept a hypothesis that the prefixed /t-/ stem was not part of the verbal system imported from the Arabian Peninsula in the seventh century CE, but rather emerged regionally at a later stage through analogical extension of the /-t/ prefix of stems V and VI, the question naturally arises as to where this innovation started. Since the /t-/ stem is poorly attested in Libya, and its distribution in Algeria and in Tunisia seems to be rather random, we could suppose that its diffusion is related to nomadic movements across the region. According to Catherine Taine-Cheikh (1983, 76), the occurrence of the /t-/ stem is much higher in the western dialects than in the eastern ones, where we still find traces of the internal vocalic passive. One should therefore not exclude the possibility that the analogical extension of this prefix was stimulated by language contact with Berber, where the /t-/ prefix functions as a marker of the passive in many dialects. Indeed, Heath (2002, 356) has suggested that the shift from infixed to prefixed /t-/ passives was probably influenced by the similar prefixed /t-/ passives of Berber. Below one can find several examples of the /t-/ passive in Berber:

Table 12: Formation of the passive in Berber (based on Kossmann 2002)

Dialect	Active	Passive
Awjila (eastern Libya)	ămt 'to bury'	ittemt 'to be buried'
Touareg of Iwellemmeden	elmed 'to learn'	tălmăd 'to be learnt'
Kabyle	gzem 'to cut'	ttegzem 'to be cut'
Chleuh	šš 'to eat'	ttš 'to be eaten'
Figuig (eastern Morocco)	sek 'to build'	ttwasek 'to be built'

Indeed, the /t-/ prefix is a common marker of passivity in many varieties of Berber. Although language contact and analogy tend to be perceived in linguistics as two separate phenomena, cases like this form ground to conceive of an intersection of those two factors: when a target form of an analogical change is similar to a form found in a language in contact, the latter can act synergetically as an additional factor contributing to a language change. In the case of the /t-/ prefix, it is plausible that, since there had existed within Arabic potential for the analogical extension of the /t-/ passive marker, the language contact with Berber stimulated and accelerated this development, triggering the loss of stem VII in some varieties. It is worth noting that the emergence of the /t-/ passive stem is not limited only to the Maghreb. We also observe the loss of the /n-/ stem in some dialects of Upper Egypt and the Levant, where the Berber influence is not expected (Nishio 1995, 209). It is rather difficult to establish whether we are dealing here with two independent phenomena, or there exists some sort of historical continuum between these dialectal families.[12]

2.3. Development of Form IV

The CA form IV conveying causative and declarative meaning is absent in the Jewish dialect of Gabes (Fischer 2002, 99). Its properties have been transferred to form II, similarly to in the dialect of Sūsa (Talmoudi 1980, 100). According to Talmoudi (1980, 100), this stem has disappeared from all North African dialects, although, as shown by Aguadé (2012), its vestiges can be found in Moroccan Arabic. Indeed, most of the dialects found other ways to express causativity; however, vestiges of form IV can be identified in the verbal systems of some of them. As pointed out by M. Cohen (1912, 211), in the Jewish dialect of Algiers, some characteristics of the stem with prosthetic *aleph* survived in forms conveying active meaning, as well as in verbs with a second or third radical semi-vowel /u/, in which the imperative is always vocalised with /i/. In addition, some traces of form IV can be found in the dialect of Tripoli, namely, the noun *məsləm*, which morphologically is the active participle of the IV-stem verb

---

[12] The emergence of the /t-/ stem in the eastern dialects might have been stimulated by the passive verb forms with the /t-/ prefix in Aramaic (Bunis 2018, 185). One can imagine a situation where, during the Arabisation of North Africa, this form spread westwards and was further promoted by a parallel form in Berber.

ʔaslam, and the imperfect form of the verb tfa, which instead of yətfa is yətfi (Yoda 2005, 143).

2.4. Vestiges of Form VIII

Compared to how it appears in other dialects, form VIII is attested in Jewish Gabes only obsoletely. In fact, there is no strong root attested in this stem, just as is also the case in Jewish Tunis (Cohen 1975, 126). However, according to Cohen (1975, 126), the first /ḍ/ of the form ṣḍāḍ represents the infixed /-t-/, which has been assimilated to the next consonant. A root with a high frequency of use in both dialects is xṭār 'to choose'. A similar situation can be observed in the Muslim dialect of Tunis. As pointed out by Singer (1984, 365), most of the roots from the CA form VIII have transferred to other stems. In the dialect of Sūsa, on the contrary, form VIII is stable and well attested (Talmoudi 1980, 106); the same is true in the dialect of Douz (Ritt-Benmimoun 2014, 370).

2.5. Reflex of Form IX

As has already been mentioned, in all Maghrebi dialects, form IX was replaced by a form with a long /a/ vowel after the second radical, which resembles the CA pattern $ʔiC^1C^2āC^3C^3$. Due to a historical development, the initial *alif* was elided, and the third radical lost its gemination. This form is abundantly represented in both the dialect of Gabes and the Jewish dialect of Tunis (Cohen 1975, 122). In most cases, roots occurring in this form derive from adjectives and convey the meaning of becoming and acquiring a certain property, e.g., *šāyəb* 'old', *šyāb* 'to become old'; *bnīn* 'tasty', *bnān* 'to become tasty'.

3.0. Inflection

A verb in the suffix conjugation consists of a verb root and a conjugational suffix.

Table 13: Suffix conjugation

	Singular	Plural
3M	-/-	-u
3F	-ət	
2M	-t	-tu
2F	-ti	
1	-t	-na

The prefix conjugation is formed by adding a prefix (and a suffix) to the verbal stem.

Table 14: Prefix conjugation

	Singular	Plural
3M	y(ə)	y(ə)...-u
3F	t(ə)	
2M	t(ə)	t(ə)...-u
2F	t(ə)...-i	
1	n(ə)	n(ə)...-u

3.1. Stem I

3.1.1. Strong Roots

Table 15: Paradigm of *ḍrəb–yəḍrab* 'to hit' (strong root)

	S-stem	P-stem	Imperative
3MS	ḍrəb	yəḍrab	
3FS	ḍərbət	təḍrab	
2MS	ḍrəbt	təḍrab	aḍrəb
2FS	ḍrəbti	təḍrbi	aḍrbi
1SG	ḍrəbt	nəḍrab	
3PL	ḍərbu	yəḍrbu	
2PL	ḍrəbtu	təḍrbu	aḍrbu
1PL	ḍrəbna	nəḍrbu	

Active participle: *ḍārəb, ḍārba, ḍārbīn*
Passive participle: *məḍrūb, məḍrūba, məḍrūbīn*

Suffix Stem

The Jewish dialect of Gabes distinguishes morphologically between 2FS and 2MS. Compared to other dialects of the region, this gender differentiation in 2S is rare, since, in many of them, morphological distinction of gender has disappeared. The Muslim dialect of Sūsa (Talmoudi 1980, 78), Jewish Tunis (Cohen 1975, 94), and the Muslim dialect of Tunis (Singer 1984, 338) tend to use only the historically masculine form for both genders. The Jewish dialect of Algiers follows the same pattern; however, as pointed out by Cohen (1912, 182), Muslim speakers of Algiers use both forms. Gender distinction exists also in the dialect of Douz (Ritt-Benmimoun 2014, 295).

The quality of the theme vowel in the Jewish Gabes dialect is in principle fixed and in most cases is /ə/. In the environment of guttural and emphatic consonants, however, it is lowered to /a/, e.g., *dbaḥ* 'he slaughtered', *zlaq* 'he slipped'. There exists a small group of verbs whose thematic vowel is /u/, e.g., *škut* 'he was silent'. The Jewish dialect of Tunis exhibits the same tendency, even though, as pointed out by Cohen (1975, 95), the two vowels have a wide range of timbres and, in certain environments, the vowel /o/ can occur. Nonetheless, the fact remains that in this dialect, as in the Jewish dialects of Gabes and Algiers (Cohen 1912, 184), the theme vowel of the suffix conjugation is in most cases /ə/ or /a/. The situation seems to be radically different in the Muslim dialect of Tunis, where one can find as many as five vowel subgroups (Singer 1984, 323).

Prefix Stem

The basic prefix vowel of the imperfective conjugation in the dialect of Gabes is /ə/, but when the first consonant of the stem is velar or laryngeal, /a/ occurs instead, e.g., *yaġməž* 'he hints'. Similarly, when the last consonant is emphatic or guttural, the thematic vowel is /a/, e.g., *yəṣraq* 'he steals'. However, it is worth noting that the first phenomenon is a tendency rather than a fixed rule, since there are numerous cases in which /ə/ occurs in a place where one would expect /a/, e.g., *yəxnəb* 'he steals'. Unlike in the dialect of Sūsa or Jewish Wad-Souf, the prefix vowel does not undergo any modification due to harmonisation with the thematic vowel (Talmoudi 1980, 79; Gębski, forthcoming a). An agreement between the prefix and the stem vowel occurs also in the dialect of Marāzīg, where, apart from one group, it seems to be a general rule (Ritt-Benmimoun 2014, 296).

3. Verbal Morphology

The data presented below confirms that Jewish Gabes has only two variants of the thematic vowel, i.e., the default /ə/ and /a/, which is triggered by emphatic, laryngeal, and pharyngeal sounds. In two verbs, we observe an /u/ vowel, presumably reflecting the CA short /u/, i.e., *yuṣkur* 'he thanks', *yəškut* 'to be silent'. The following combinations of prefix and theme vowels in the p-stem have been attested:

/ə/–/ə/: *lbəṣ–yəlbəṣ* 'to get dressed', *rkəb–yərkəb* 'to ride', *dfən–yədfən* 'to bury', *žbəd–yəžbəd* 'to pull', *nzəl–yənzəl* 'to go down', *nšəd–yənšəd* 'to ask', *ršəq–yəršəq* 'to stick', *škər–yəškər* 'to get drunk' *šmən–yəšmən* 'to get fat', *fṣəd–yəfṣəd* 'to lose, to get off', *kbər–yəkbər* 'to grow up', *ktər–yəktər* 'to multiply', *ktəb–yəktəb* 'to write', *rqəd–yərqəd* 'to sleep', *xṭəb–yəxṭəb* 'to propose to someone', *qtəl–yəqtəl* 'to kill', *škən–yəškən* 'to reside';

/a/–/a/: *ẓlaq–yaẓlaq* 'to slide, to slip', *xlaq–yaxlaq* 'to create', *hrab–yahrab* 'to escape', *ḥdar–yaḥdar* 'to be present', *ʕaṣar–yaʕṣar* 'to squeeze';

/ə/–/a/: *fham–yəfham* 'to understand', *qrab–yəqrab* 'to get closer', *qlaq–yəqlaq* 'to bother, to be fed up with', *ṭlab–yəṭlab* 'to ask', *ṣraf–yəṣraf* 'to support oneself', *ṣbaġ–yəṣbaġ* 'to paint', *ḍrəb–yəḍrab* 'to hit', *rqaṣ–yərqaṣ* 'to dance', *ḍlam–yəḍlam* 'to betray', *mḍaġ–yəmḍaġ* 'to chew', *nfax–yənfax* 'to blow', *ṣrab–yəṣrab* 'to drink', *nqaṣ–yənqaṣ* 'to reduce', *ṣhar–yəṣhar* 'to stay up until late', *ḍḥak–yəḍḥak* 'to laugh', *ržaʕ–yəržaʕ* 'to return', *ẓraʕ–yəẓraʕ* 'to sow', *ṭlaʕ–yəṭlaʕ* 'to go up', *ḍhar–yəḍhar* 'to transpire, to turn out', *mšaḥ–yəmšaḥ* 'to wipe', *dbaḥ–yədbaḥ* 'to slaughter', lʕab–yəlʕab 'to play', ṣraḥ–yəṣraḥ 'to herd', qtaʕ–yəqtaʕ 'to cut', mnaʕ–yəmnaʕ 'to prohibit', tʕab–yətʕab 'to get tired', šmaʕ–yəšmaʕ 'to listen', ṣbaḥ–yəṣbaḥ 'to get up early', šbaʕ–yəšbaʕ 'to eat one's fill', fraḥ–yəfraḥ 'to rejoice';

/a/–/ə/: ġləb–yaġləb 'to defeat', xdəm–yaxdəm 'to work', qṣəm–yaqṣəm 'to divide', xmər–yaxmər 'to ferment, to go rotten', hfar–yahfər 'to dig', ḥšəb–yaḥšəb 'to count', ḥbəš–yaḥbəš 'to arrest', ḥləb–yaḥləb 'to milk', ḥləm–yaḥləm 'to dream', ʕarəf–yaʕarəf 'to know', hbəṭ–yahbəṭ 'to go down, to descend', qbəl–yaqbəl 'to agree', ġšəl–yaġšəl 'to wash', ʕṭəṣ–yaʕṭəṣ 'to be thirsty';

/ə/–/u/: škut–yəškut 'to be silent';

/u/–/u/: ṣkər–yuṣkur 'to thank';

Mixed type, i.e., two variations have been attested: xrəž–yəxrəž / yaxrəž 'to go out', dxəl–yədxəl / yədxul 'to enter', mraḍ–yəmraḍ / yumraḍ 'to get sick', ftər–yəftər / yəftar 'to have breakfast'.

Active and Passive Participles

Apart from the three basic verbal forms, there exist in Jewish Gabes also active and passive participles. As has been mentioned in the introduction (§1.0), the distinction between them has been retained only in stem I, while in the remainder of the stems we observe a merger of these forms. The occurrence of the *fāʕəl* pattern in Jewish Gabes is highly irregular, occurring only in a limited number of verbs. As will be argued in chapter 6, §2.7.4, their common denominator is presumably their day-to-day usage.

Even less frequently attested is the passive participle, which, similarly to the passive verb stems, has been replaced by analytic constructions involving active verbs.

Active participle: *qāʕəd, qāʕda, qāʕdīn*
Passive participle: *məktūb, məktūba, məktūbīn*

3.1.2. Geminated Roots

Table 16: Paradigm of *šədd–yšədd* 'to seize' (geminated root)

	S-stem	P-stem	Imperative
3MS	*šədd*	*yšədd*	
3FS	*šəddət*	*tšədd*	
2MS	*šəddīt*	*tšədd*	*šədd*
2FS	*šəddīti*	*tšəddi*	*šəddi*
1SG	*šəddīt*	*nšədd*	
3PL	*šəddu*	*yšəddu*	
2PL	*šəddītu*	*tšəddu*	*šəddu*
1PL	*šəddīna*	*nšəddu*	

Active participle: *šādd, šādda, šāddīn*
Passive participle: *məšdūd, məšdūda, məšdūdīn*

Suffix Stem

In CA, the geminated consonants are separated by a vowel when a form has a consonantal ending, e.g., *radda* 'he returned', but *radadtu* 'I returned'. This phenomenon exists neither in the Jewish dialect of Gabes, nor in other neighbouring dialects.[13] Instead,

---

[13] This development is attested in all dialects of Arabic, with the only exception being the dialects of the Arabian Peninsula (Ferguson 1959; Ratcliffe 2011). Nonetheless, in contravention of this claim, the dialect

in forms with a consonantal ending, a linking long vowel /ī/ is inserted. As pointed out by Yoda (2005, 147), in many modern and medieval dialects, a linking diphthong /-ay/ is attested in these forms, which, following its contraction, gave rise to the aforementioned vowel. It can be assumed, therefore, that it was adopted by analogy to verbs with III /y/. The default quality of the suffix-stem thematic vowel is /ə/, which shifts to /a/ in the vicinity of guttural and emphatic consonants.

Prefix Stem

The prefix vowel in the imperfect forms starting with /t-/ and /n-/ morphemes has been completely elided. As a result, a cluster of two consonants emerges. It is worth noting that, in the case of clusters consisting of a plosive alveolar and a postalveolar fricative, a new sound emerges, namely, a palatal fricative. Thus, in the case of prefix forms of the verb *šədd* starting with /t/, the initial consonant is palatalised, and therefore the phonetic transcription of the 2MS form in IPA would be: [çədd]. The disappearance of the prefix vowel in this environment is a general tendency in the dialects examined here. As pointed out by Cohen (1912, 185), however, in the dialect of Algiers, in the 3SG and 3PL forms, the vowel of the prefix is preserved. In imperative forms, no auxiliary vowel is added, since the stem syllable has structure CvCC and therefore no consonant cluster occurs at the onset of the syllable. The stress in the prefix forms is placed on

---

of Mekka follows the same pattern, e.g., *ḥabbēt* 'I liked' (based on an interview with an informant).

the ultimate syllable. The thematic vowel of the prefix stem falls into two main groups:

- Thematic vowel /ə/: ʕašš–yʕəšš 'to live', gədd–ygədd 'to be able', ləmm–yləmm 'to collect', mədd–ymədd 'to bring', məšš–yməšš 'to touch', məll–yməll 'to get tired';
- Thematic vowel /a/: ʕaḍḍ–yʕaḍḍ 'to bite', ḍarr–yḍarr 'to harm', ḥašš–yḥašš 'to feel', ḥaṭṭ–yḥaṭṭ 'to put';
- Variation between /ə/ and /a/: qaṣṣ–yqaṣṣ / yqəṣṣ 'to cut', radd–yradd / yrədd 'to return', raṣṣ–yraṣṣ / yrəṣṣ 'to pressure'.

3.1.3. Weak First Radical

Table 17: Paradigm of wṣəl 'to arrive' (first radical semi-vowel /w/)

	S-stem	P-stem	Imperative
3MS	wṣəl	yūṣəl	
3FS	waṣlət	tūṣəl	
2MS	wṣəlt	tūṣəl	wṣəl
2FS	wṣəlti	tūṣli	waṣli
1SG	wṣəlt	nūṣəl	
3PL	waṣlu	yūṣlu	
2PL	wṣəltu	tūṣlu	waṣlu
1PL	wṣəlna	nūṣlu	

Active participle: wāṣəl, wāṣla, wāṣlīn

Table 18: Paradigm of *yəbəš* 'to dry' (first radical semi-vowel /i/)

	S-stem	P-stem	Imperative
3MS	ybəš(š)	yībəš	
3FS	yəbšat	tyībəš	
2MS	ybəšt	tyībəš	yībəš
2FS	ybəšti	tyībši	yībši
1SG	ybəšt	nyībəš	
3PL	yəbšu	yībšu	
2PL	ybəštu	tyībšu	yībšu
1PL	ybəšna	nyībšu	

Active participle: *yābəš, yābša, yābšīn*
Passive participle: not attested

Suffix Stem

The initial semi-vowel /w/ in the suffix conjugation is stable. In other dialects, for example in the Jewish dialect of Algiers and the Muslim dialect of Tunis, the initial semi-vowel was replaced by the vowel /u/ (Cohen 1912, 188; Singer 1984, 355). An interesting phenomenon can be observed in the dialect of Sūsa, where /w/ is realised as /w/ by the older generations, but young speakers tend to pronounce it as /u/ (Talmoudi 1980, 83). In the Jewish dialect of Tunis, on the other hand, the realisation of /w/ is conditioned by the phonetic environment, namely, /w/ is pronounced as /w/ only when followed by a vowel, e.g., *wəžnət* 'she weighed' but *užən* 'he weighed'. The dialect of Douz preserves the initial /w/, but no additional vowel is inserted afterwards, e.g., *wṣil* he arrived'. In the 3FS, 3FP, and 3MP forms, the theme vowel moves position to between the first and second radicals, but its quality remains unchanged, e.g., *wildu* 'they gave birth to' (Ritt-Benmimoun 2014, 307). In the dialect of Sūsa, both vowels occur, namely, the stem vowel is /u/, but in the 3FS and 3FP forms the retracted vowel is /i/, e.g., *wsul*, but *wislit* (Talmoudi 1985, 82).

The verb *ybəš* is the only verb with first radical /y/ that is attested in Jewish Gabes. The /y/ consonant is preserved throughout the conjugation and is followed by a long /ī/ vowel. In the 3MS suffix form, the last consonant is geminated.

Prefix Stem

In the prefix-stem forms of verbs with the first radical /w/ in CA, the initial semi-vowel disappears without leaving any trace, e.g., *yaṣilu* 'he will arrive'. However, it seems that, in the Jewish dialect of Gabes, as well as in many other neighbouring dialects, the long /u/ following the prefix vowel should be treated as a vestige of the radical /w/. Presumably, the long vowel emerged as a result of a contraction of the original diphthong /aw/, and thus the original form can be reconstructed as **yawṣil*. In the dialect of Douz, the assimilated /w/ gives rise to vowels of different quality, e.g., *wṣil–yūṣil* 'to arrive', *wlid–yilid* 'to give birth', *wḥil–yōḥal* 'to be stuck'. In addition, as pointed out by Ritt-Benmimoun (2014, 306), in forms with imperfect theme vowel /o/, this vowel interchanges with /u/, e.g., *tūḥli–tōḥli*.

In the Jewish dialect of Gabes, first-radical /y/ is stable and can be easily heard throughout the conjugation. In other dialects, this consonant is either replaced by a short vowel /i/ or, as in the dialect of Sūsa, gives rise to a lengthened /i/ vowel, e.g., *tībis* 'she will dry' (Talmoudi 1980, 83). A short /i/ vowel is attested, among others, in the Jewish dialect of Tripoli (Yoda 2004, 161). It is also recorded by one of the first grammar books of Tunisian

Arabic (Stumme 1896, 17). In the imperative, however, in the dialect of Gabes, the first radical /y/ is reduced to a short, stressed vowel /i/. In the dialect of Sūsa, on the other hand, the long /i/ vowel is retained even in the imperative.

3.1.4. Weak Second Radical

Depending on the vowel of the prefix conjugation, verbs with a weak second radical can be divided into three groups, as given below, i.e., with long /ū/, /ī/, and /ā/. The suffix-stem vowel alternates between long /ā/ in forms with suffixes starting with a vowel, and a short vowel of varying quality in forms with suffixes starting with a consonant. In order to exemplify these interchanges, the data below has been presented in the following manner: 3MS (s-stem)–1SG (s-stem)–3MS (p-stem):

Table 19: Paradigm of *qām–yqūm* 'to wake up' (pattern CāC–yəCūC)

	S-stem	P-stem	Imperative
3MS	qām	yqūm	
3FS	qāmət	tqūm	
2MS	qəmt	tqūm	qūm
2FS	qəmti	tqūmi	qūmi
1SG	qəmt	nqūm	
3PL	qāmu	yqūmu	
2PL	qəmtu	tqūmu	qūmu
1PL	qəmna	nqūmu	

Active participle: ṣāyəm, ṣāyma, ṣāymīn 'to fast'[14]

Passive participle: not attested

---

[14] In paradigms where participles are not attested, forms from different verbs are provided.

Also in this form: ʕām–ʕamt–yʕūm 'to swim', ḍāṛ–ḍoṛt / ḍuṛt–yḍūṛ 'to roam, to go around', bāš–bəšt–ybūš 'to kiss', ṣām–ṣamt / ṣomt–yṣūm 'to fast', dām–dəmt–ydūm 'to last', ẓāṛ–ẓaṛt–yẓūṛ 'to visit', lām–ləmt–ylūm 'to accuse', fāž–fəžt–yfūž 'to win', māt–mətt–ymūt 'to die', šāf–šəft–yšūf 'to see'.

Table 20: Paradigm of žāb–yžīb 'to bring' (pattern CāC–yəCīC)

	S-stem	P-stem	Imperative
3MS	žāb	yžīb	
3FS	žābət	tžīb	
2MS	žəbt	tžīb	žīb
2FS	žəbti	tžībi (džībi)	žībi
1SG	žəbt	nžīb	
3PL	žābu	yžību	
2PL	žəbtu	tžību	žību
1PL	žəbna	nžību	

Active participle: ṭāyəḥ, ṭāyḥa, ṭāyḥīn
Passive participle: not attested

Also in this form: žād–žədət[15]–yžīd 'to add', ʕāš–ʕašt–yʕīš 'to live', ʕāf–ʕaft–yʕīf 'to be fed up with', ṣāṛ–ṣəṛt–yṣīr 'to happen', ṭāḥ–ṭaḥt–yṭīḥ 'to fall', ṭāṛ–ṭaṛt–yṭīr 'to fly', rād–rādət–yrīd 'to desire, to want', ṭāb–ṭabət–yṭīb 'to be cooked', ġāb–ġabt–yġīb 'to disappear', fāq–faqt–yfīq 'to wake up'.

---

[15] In verbs where the third radical is /d/, /b/, or /t/, 1SG and 2MS forms tend to have an ultrashort epenthetic vowel between the last radical and the /t/ suffix to facilitate pronunciation.

Table 21: Paradigm of *xāf–yxāf* 'to be frightened' (pattern CāC–yəCāC)

	S-stem	P-stem	Imperative
3MS	xāf	yxāf	
3FS	xāfət	txāf	
2MS	xəft	txāf	xāf
2FS	xəfti	txāfi	xāfi
1SG	xəft	nxāf	
3PL	xāfu	yxāfu	
2PL	xəftu	txāfu	xāfu
1PL	xəfna	nxāfu	

Active participle: *xāyəf, xāyfa, xayfīn*

Also in this form: *bān–bənt–ybān* 'to appear, to look like', *bāt–bətət–ybāt* 'to spend the night'.

In CA, the suffix stem of verbs with second radical liquid /y/ or /w/ demonstrates interchanges between long and short vowels in their theme. Namely, the suffix-stem base of these verbs exhibits alternations of long /ā/ and short /u/ or /i/, which, in turn, reflect the quality of the medial weak consonant, e.g., *qāmat–qumt* (second radical /w/) 'she stood up'–'you stood up', *ṣāra–ṣirtu* (second radical /y/) 'he became'–'I became' (Fischer 2002, 131). As the data indicate, this rule is not applicable in Jewish Gabes, where the theme vowel of the suffix stem seems to be conditioned by the consonantal environment of this vowel. The default /ə/ vowel is lowered to /a/ when found adjacent to emphatic and guttural sounds, e.g., *ṭaḥt* 'I/you (MS) fell'. In two verbs, an /o/ vowel has been attested, namely *ḍoṛt* 'I roamed' alongside *ḍuṛt*, and *ṣomt* 'I fasted' alongside *ṣamt*. Importantly, however, almost no reflex of the historical /u/ vowel has been attested in verbs with second radical /w/. The only exception is *ḍuṛt*, where, in any case, /u/ tends to interchange with /o/.

Against this background, numerous dialects of the region do exhibit some vocalic vestiges of the elided weak radical in forms with consonantal suffixes. This is particularly noticeable in verbs with second radical /w/, where the thematic suffix-conjugation vowel is /u/. Since, in many dialects, short /i/ is not phonemic, verbs with second radical /y/ tend to feature /ə/ or /e/ instead of /i/. In the Muslim dialect of Tunis, one can find the following alternations:[16] /ā/–/u/: *qām–qumt* 'to stand up', /ā/–/o/: *ḥāz–ḥozt* 'to gain', /ā/–/ə/: *žāb–žəbt* 'to bring', /ā/–/e/: *ġāb–ġebt* 'to be absent' (Singer 1984, 358–59). The Muslim dialect of Sūsa has preserved most of the original theme vowels found in CA, shifting locally from long /ā/ to /o/ in forms with second radical /w/, e.g., *qāl–qolt* 'to say'.[17] Similarly, in forms with second radical /y/, which in CA have long /ā/, when a suffix starts with a vowel, a half open front vowel occurs, which subsequently shifts to /i/ in forms with consonantal suffixes, e.g., *mɛːl* 'he inclined', but *miltu* 'you (PL) inclined' (Talmoudi 1980, 84). In the dialect of Douz (southern Tunisia), depending on the consonantal environement of the root, the theme vowel of the past form can be /i/ or /u/: *māt–miťt* 'to die', *dām–dumt* 'to be over' (Ritt-

---

[16] All the following pairs designate respectively 3MS and 1SG.

[17] As pointed out by Talmoudi (1980, 85), in the Muslim dialect of Sūsa, weak verbs with second radical semi-vowel in the imperfect conjugation always have the same stem vowel as in CA, the only exception being the verb *ybaːt*.

Benmimoun 2014, 316). In another Bedouin dialect from southern Tunisia, namely the dialect of El-Hamma, the following alternations have been attested: /ā/–/u/: *gām–gumt* 'to wake up', /ā/–/o/: *rāḥ–roḥt* 'to go', and /ā/–/i/: *žāb–žibt* 'to bring' (Cantineau 1960, 220). The Jewish dialect of Wad-Souf, which exhibits numerous Bedouin traits, also demonstrates reflexes of the historical /w/: *lām–lumt* 'to accuse, to blame', *fāz–fuzt* 'to win', *ṣām–ṣumt* 'to fast', *bās–bust* 'to kiss'.

As the data indicate, the Jewish dialect of Gabes follows a different pattern, and the rule according to which the quality of the suffix-stem vowel depends on the second radical is less operative. In forms with consonantal suffixes, the long /ā/ vowel is reduced by default to /ə/ and conditionally to /a/, regardless of the quality of the second radical. This is also the case in Jewish Tripoli (Yoda 2014, 160), and the Jewish dialect of Tunis, where, as Cohen (1975, 102) points out, the quality of the thematic vowel of the perfect conjugation is conditioned by the consonantal environment. In a similar fashion, in Jewish Algiers, as pointed out by M. Cohen (1912, 190), short vowels of the first and the second persons of the suffix conjugation are regularly represented by /ə/.

The comparison presented above could potentially indicate that the Muslim dialects are more conservative in terms of the preservation of the CA stem vowels in forms with consonantal inflectional suffixes. Jewish dialects, on the other hand, tend to reduce short vowels in close stressed syllables to /ə/, which is prone to be assimilated to the adjacent consonants.

3.1.5. Weak Third Radical

Table 22: Paradigm of *r̥ma–yər̥mi* 'to throw' (pattern CCa–yəCCi)

	S-stem	P-stem	Imperative
3MS	r̥ma	yər̥mi	
3FS	r̥māt	tər̥mi	
2MS	r̥mīt	tər̥mi	ar̥mi
2FS	r̥mīti	tər̥məy	ar̥mīy
1SG	r̥mīt	nər̥mi	
3PL	r̥māw	yər̥mīw	
2PL	r̥mītu	tər̥mīw	ar̥mīw
1PL	r̥mīna	nər̥mīw	

Active participle: *bāni, bānya, baniyīn*
Passive participle: *məbni, məbnya, məbnyīn*

Also in this form: *ʕṭa–yaʕṭi* 'to give', *bna–yəbni* 'to build', *bka–yəbki* 'to cry', *mša–yəmši* 'to go', *šra–yəšri* 'to build', *žra / zra–yəžri / yəzri* 'to run'.

Table 23: Paradigm of *r̥ḍa–yər̥ḍa* 'to agree' (pattern CCa–yəCCa)

	S-stem	P-stem	Imperative
3MS	r̥ḍa	yər̥ḍa	
3FS	r̥ḍāt	tər̥ḍa	
2MS	r̥ḍīt	tər̥ḍa	ar̥ḍa
2FS	r̥ḍīti	tər̥ḍāy	ar̥ḍāy
1SG	r̥ḍīt	nər̥ḍa	
3PL	r̥ḍāw	yər̥ḍāw	
2PL	r̥ḍītu	tər̥ḍāw	ar̥ḍāw
1PL	r̥ḍīna	nər̥ḍāw	

Active participle: *r̥āḍi, r̥āḍya, r̥āḍyīn*
Passive participle: *mənši, mənšya, mənšyīn*

Also in this form: *bda–yəbda* 'to start',[18] *bqa–yəbqa* 'to stay', *nša–yənša* 'to forget'.

---

[18] I have recorded also a variant *bda–yəbdi*.

In the Jewish dialect of Gabes, as in the vast majority of neighbouring dialects, the group with etymological third radical /w/ was integrated into the group with third radical /y/. The vestiges of /w/ can be found only in some isolated verbs, e.g., the only verb preserving original /u/ in the p-stem conjugation that is attested in the Jewish and the Muslim dialect of Tunis is ḥba–yaḥbu 'to crawl (of a baby)' (Cohen 1975, 104; Singer 1984, 360).[19] The prefix conjugation exhibits one of the isoglosses of the sedentary dialects, namely the /-āw/ suffix in the plural forms of the prefix conjugation, e.g., yənšāw 'they will forget'. Contrary to this, Bedouin-type dialects feature the /-u/ suffix, e.g., nansu 'we will forget' (Ritt-Benmimoun 2014, 324).

3.1.6. Verbs kla 'to eat' and xda 'to take'

Table 24: Paradigm of kla 'to eat'

	S-stem	P-stem	Imperative
3MS	kla	yākəl	
3FS	klāt	tākəl	
2MS	klīt	tākəl	kūl
2FS	klīti	tākli	kūli
1SG	klīt	nākəl	
3PL	klāw	yāklu	
2PL	klītu	tāklu	kūlu
1PL	klīna	nāklu	

Active participle: wākəl, wākla, wāklīn

---

[19] The dialect of Djidjelli, on the other hand, has preserved also other verbs with third radical /w/, including, among others, ʕfa–yoʕfu 'to forgive', kba–yəkbu 'to drowse', žġa–yəžġu 'to wail'; see Marçais (1956, 171).

To this category belong verbs that in CA are classified as first radical *hamza*. There are only two roots attested: *kla* 'to eat' and *xda* 'to take'. As noticed by Cohen (1975, 109), the conjugation of this subgroup follows two different patterns, namely, the s-stem conjugates according to the pattern of forms with a weak third radical, whereas the imperative is formed according to the pattern of forms with a weak second radical.

3.1.7. Two Weak Radicals

Table 25: Paradigm of *ufa* 'to stop' (pattern Iw + IIIy)

	S-stem	P-stem	Imperative
3MS	ufa	yūfa	
3FS	ufāt	tūfa	
2MS	ufīt	tūfa	ūfa
2FS	ufīti	tufāy	ūfāy
1SG	ufīt	nūfa	
3PL	ufāw	yūfāw	
2PL	ufītu	tūfāw	ufāw
1PL	ufīna	nūfāw	

The verb *ufa* is the only root attested for this paradigm. It contains the first radical /w/ and the third one /y/. Thus, its conjugation follows two patterns simultaneously. As can be observed, /w/ in this verb in the s-stem does not have a consonantal character and is realised as /u/, even though in the regular I-w paradigm it is preserved as /w/. The long /ū/ in the p-stem has presumably emerged due to contraction of the /aw/ diphthong.

3.1.8. Irregular Forms

Table 26: Paradigm of ža 'to come'

	S-stem	P-stem	Imperative
3MS	ža	yži	
3FS	žāt	tži	
2MS	žīt	tži	iža
2FS	žīti	tžīy	ižīy
1SG	žīt	tži	
3PL	žāw	yžīw	
2PL	žītu	tžīw	ižīw
1PL	žīna	nžīw	

Table 27: Paradigm of ṛa 'to see'

	S-stem	P-stem	Imperative
3MS	ṛa	yṛa	
3FS	ṛāt	tṛa	
2MS	ṛīt	tṛa	N/A
2FS	ṛīti	tṛāy	N/A
1SG	ṛīt	nṛa	
3PL	ṛāw	yṛāw	
2PL	ṛītu	tṛāw	N/A
1PL	ṛīna	nṛāw	

These two verbs have been categorised in a separate section, since they cannot be assigned to any of the patterns discussed above. They correspond to the CA forms *jāʔa* and *ṛāʔa*. As has already been mentioned before, *hamza* has completely disappeared from the dialect of Gabes and consequently, both verbs possess only one strong radical. The verb *ṛa* is a unique case, since despite the existence of its prefix-conjugation forms as included in the table, most speakers use forms of the verb *šāf* instead. As noted by D. Cohen (1975, 106), this dichotomy can be observed in other Maghrebi dialects as well. The same scholar notes also that, in the Jewish dialect of Tunis, the s-stem conjugation of *ṛa* preserves the Classical diphthong /ay/, i.e., *ṛayt* 'I saw'. In the dialect of Gabes, this diphthong underwent a process of contraction, and thus the form *ṛīt* emerged.

3.2. Derived Stems

3.2.1. Stem II

Table 28: Paradigm of *ṣarrəf* 'to cash money' (strong root)

	S-stem	P-stem	Imperative
3MS	ṣarrəf	yṣarrəf	
3FS	ṣarrfət	tṣarrəf	
2MS	ṣarrəft	tṣarrəf	ṣarrəf
2FS	ṣarrəfti	tṣar(r)fi	ṣar(r)fi
1SG	ṣarrəft	nṣarrəf	
3PL	ṣarrfu	yṣar(r)fu	
2PL	ṣarraftu	tṣar(r)fu	ṣar(r)fu
1PL	ṣarrafna	nṣar(r)fu	

Participle: *mbəddəl, mbədla, mbədlīn*

Also in this form: *ʕalləm–yʕalləm* 'to teach', *ʕayyəṭ–yʕayyəṭ* 'to scream', *bəddəl–ybəddəl* 'to change', *ṭallaq–yṭallaq* 'to divorce', *daxxəl–ydaxxəl* 'to make something enter', *ḥaddəd–yḥaddəd* 'to iron', *nəžžəm–ynəžžəm* 'to be able', *naggəẓ–ynaggəẓ* 'to jump', *ražžaʕ–yražžaʕ* 'to return (trans.)', *qayyəd–yqayyəd* 'to register', *ṭallaʕ–yəṭllaʕ* 'to take out', *ṭayyəb–yṭayyəb* 'to cook', *xarrəf–yxarrəf* 'to tell a tale', *xayyəṭ–yxayyəṭ* 'to sew'.

Table 29: Paradigm of *xamməm* 'to think' (geminated root)

	S-stem	P-stem	Imperative
3MS	xamməm	yxamməm	
3FS	xamm(əm)ət	txamməm	
2MS	xamməmt	txamməm	xamməm
2FS	xamməmti	txamm(əm)i	xamm(əm)i
1SG	xamməmt	nxamməm	
3PL	xamm(əm)u	yxamm(əm)u	
2PL	xamməmtu	txamm(əm)u	xamm(əm)u
1PL	xamməmna	nxamm(əm)u	

Participle: *mdəlləl, mdəlləla, mdəlləlīn*

Also in this form: *dəlləl–ydəlləl* 'to spoil'.

Table 30: Paradigm of *waṛṛa* 'to show' (weak third radical)

	S-stem	P-stem	Imperative
3MS	wəṛṛa	ywəṛṛi	
3FS	wəṛṛāt	twəṛṛi	
2MS	wəṛṛīt	twəṛṛi	wəṛṛi
2FS	wəṛṛīti	twəṛṛiy	wəṛṛiy
1SG	wəṛṛīt	nwəṛṛi	
3PL	wṛṛāw	ywəṛṛiw	
2PL	wəṛṛitu	twəṛṛiw	wəṛṛiw
1PL	wəṛṛina	nwəṛṛiw	

Participle: *mʕabbi, mʕabbya, mʕabbyīn*

Also in this form: *ʕabba–yʕabbi* 'to fill'.

The most characteristic feature of stem II is the geminated middle consonant of the root. In regular roots, both vowels in s-stem forms are /ə/; however, when the doubled consonant is guttural or emphatic, the first vowel is /a/. The same tendency appears in the p-stem conjugation, i.e., instead of *yḥəḍḍəṛ* one finds *yḥaḍḍəṛ* 'he will prepare'. In p-stem forms ending with a vowel, the gemination of the middle consonant is hardly audible. The same phenomenon is attested in the dialect of Sūsa (Talmoudi 1985, 99). In the Jewish dialect of Gabes, the first vowel of the p-stem forms is stable and never undergoes elision. Contrary to this, in the Jewish dialect of Algiers, this vowel tends to be reduced and, as a result, a cluster of three consonants emerges (Cohen 1912, 200).

Verbs with a weak first radical do not exhibit any fluctuations and inflect as a regular verb. However, verbs with identical second and third radicals have a strong tendency to reduce the last consonant in forms with vocalic suffixes. The same phenomenon is attested, among others, in the dialect of Tripoli (Yoda 2005, 168) and the Jewish dialect of Tunis (Cohen 1975, 116). In addition, verbs with a weak second radical adjust their first vowel according to the quality of the following consonant, i.e., when *w* is geminated, the vowel is usually /u/, whereas forms with /y/ have /i/, e.g., *əḍuwwaq* 'he lets taste', *tbīyyət* 'she passes a night'.

3.2.2. Stem III

Table 31: Paradigm of *qābəl* 'to meet' (strong root)

	S-stem	P-stem	Imperative
3MS	qābəl	yqābəl	
3FS	qāblət	tqābəl	
2MS	qabəlt	tqābəl	qābəl
2FS	qabəlti	tqābli	qābli
1SG	qabəlt	nqābəl	
3PL	qāblu	yqāblu	
2PL	qabəltu	tqāblu	qāblu
1PL	qabəlna	nqāblu	

Table 32: Paradigm of ʕāwən 'to help' (weak first radical)

	S-stem	P-stem	Imperative
3MS	ʕāwən	yʕāwən	
3FS	ʕāwnət	tʕāwən	
2MS	ʕawənt	tʕāwən	ʕāwən
2FS	ʕawənti	tʕāwni	ʕāwni
1SG	ʕawənt	nʕāwən	
3PL	ʕāwnu	yʕāwnu	
2PL	ʕawəntu	tʕāwnu	ʕāwnu
1PL	ʕawənna	nʕāwnu	

Also in in this stem: ʕāwəḍ–yʕāwəḍ 'to repeat', ṣāwər–yṣāwər 'to consult'.

Table 33: Paradigm of nāda 'to call, to warn' (weak third radical)

	S-stem	P-stem	Imperative
3MS	nāda	ynādi	
3FS	nadāt	tnādi	
2MS	nadīt	tnādi	nādi
2FS	nadīti	tnadīy	nadīy
1SG	nadīt	nnādi	
3PL	nadāw	ynadīw	
2PL	nadītu	tnadīw	nadīw
1PL	nadīna	nnadīw	

The characteristic feature of stem III is a long /ā/ vowel after the first radical. However, as the above paradigm shows, contrary to CA, this vowel tends to be shortened in forms with a vocalic ending, in both the p-stem and the s-stem. Similarly to stem II, verbs with a first radical semivowel are not subject to any fluctuations. In addition, a second radical semivowel does not bring about any shift of the vowel, i.e., /a/ remains stable, even though its length can vary.

The length of the stem vowel differs in various dialects. In some dialects, like the dialect of Douz (Ritt-Benmimoun 2014, 347) or the dialect of Algiers (Cohen 1912, 208), long /ā/ is retained throughout the whole conjugation. The Jewish dialect of Tunis, similarly to the Jewish dialect of Gabes, exhibits a tendency to shorten the vowel in the suffix conjugation (Cohen 1975, 119). On the other hand, the dialect of Tlemcen presents exactly the opposite tendency, that is, it retains long /ā/ in s-stem forms with a consonantal ending and an epenthetic vowel after the second radical, i.e., Jewish Gabes: ʕāwən–ʕawənt 'to help'; Tlemcen: rakeb–rākəbt 'to ride' (Marçais 1902, 75).

3.2.3. The /t-/ Passive Stem

Table 34: Paradigm of təktəb 'to be written' (strong root)

	S-stem	P-stem	Imperative
3MS	təktə́b	yətəktəb	
3FS	təktəbt	əttəktə́b	
2MS	N/A	N/A	N/A
2FS	N/A	N/A	N/A
1SG	N/A	N/A	
3PL	əttəktbu	yətəktbu	
2PL	N/A	N/A	N/A
1PL	N/A	N/A	

Also in this stem: əttəxnəb 'to be stolen', ətləmm 'to gather' (cf. Bedouin Douz ltām).

As has been pointed out in §2.2, numerous roots in stem I form their passive voice in the purely dialectal /t-/ passive stem. In the 3PL form of the s-stem and the 3FS form of the p-stem, the /t-/ prefix tends to be geminated and preceded by an epenthetic vowel.

3.2.4. Stem V

Table 35: Paradigm of *tkəlləm* 'to talk' (strong root)

	S-stem	P-stem	Imperative
3MS	tkəlləm	yətkəlləm	
3FS	tkəl(l)mət	tətkəlləm	
2MS	tkəlləmt	tətkəlləm	ətkəlləm
2FS	tkəlləmti	tətkəl(l)mi	ətkəl(l)mi
1SG	tkəlləmt	ntkəlləm	
3PL	tkəl(l)mu	yətkəl(l)mu	
2PL	tkəlləmtu	tətkəllmu	ətkəl(l)mu
1PL	tkəlləmna	nətkəlmu	

Also in this stem: *tkaṣṣər* 'to be broken', *tfakkər* 'to remember', *tġaššəš* 'to get upset'.

Table 36: Paradigm of *txabba* 'to hide oneself' (weak third radical)

	S-stem	P-stem	Imperative
3MS	txabba	yətxabba	
3FS	txabbāt	tətxabba	
2MS	txabbīt	tətxabba	txabba
2FS	txabbīti	tətxabbāy	txabbāy
1SG	txabbīt	nətxabba	
3PL	txabbāw	yətxabāw	
2PL	txabbītu	tətxabāw	txabbāw
1PL	txabbīna	nətxabāw	

Participle: *mətxabbi, mətxabbya, mətxabbyīn*

Stem V is reflexive-passive in relation to stem II, e.g., *kaṣṣər* 'to break'–*tkaṣṣər* 'to be broken'. In addition, this stem includes some verbs inherited directly from CA which have active meaning, e.g., *tʕalləm* 'to learn'. The characteristic feature of stem V is the /t-/ prefix and doubled second radical. In the dialect of Gabes, the /t-/ prefix of the stem is stable and does not undergo any assimilation. On the contrary, in the dialect of Djidjelli, as pointed out by Marçais (1956, 188), /t/ tends to be assimilated to the first radical, e.g., *tṣarrəf–ṣṣarrəf* 'to manage'. A similar phenomenon can be observed in the dialect of Marāzīg, in which the prefix is assimilated to the first radical when it is an alveolar or postalveolar fricative, e.g., *ᵊzzayyan* 'he prepared' (Ritt-Benmimoun 2014, 351). A form with a doubled first radical is preceded by an epenthetic vowel that prevents a consonantal cluster at the beginning of the word. This occurs also in the dialect of Sūsa, where a prosthetic vowel is added to a form with a radical dental stop, e.g., *itdarraq* 'he hid himself' (Talmoudi 1985, 101). As argued by Talmoudi, the function of this epenthetic vowel is to create a syllable boundary separating the prefix from the first radical.

3.2.5. Stem VI

Table 37: Paradigm of *tʕāžəb* 'to be surprised' (strong root)

	S-stem	P-stem	Imperative
3MS	tʕāžəb	yətʕāžəb	
3FS	tʕāžbət	tətʕāžəb	
2MS	tʕažəbt	tətʕāžəb	ətʕāžəb
2FS	tʕažəbti	tətʕāžbi	ətʕāžbi
1SG	tʕažəbt	nətʕāžəb	
3PL	tʕāžbu	yətʕāžbu	
2PL	tʕažəbtu	tətʕāžbu	ətʕāžbu
1PL	tʕažəbna	nətʕāžbu	

Also in this form: *tʕārək* 'to dispute, to have an argument', *tqābəl* 'to meet with someone'.

The basic meaning of this form, as in CA, is reciprocity (Fischer 202, 99). Most of the verbs in this pattern have their active counterparts in form III. Verbs with weak first or second radical do not exhibit any variations, e.g., *ytʕāwnu* 'they help each other'. The length of the stem vowel /a/ in the suffix conjugation depends on the character of the ending, i.e., only the vocalic suffix preserves the long /ā/, whereas in the rest of the forms it is shortened. The same long vowel is retained throughout the whole p-stem and s-stem conjugations in the dialect of Douz (Ritt-Benmimoun 2014, 357).

3.2.6. Stem VII

Table 38: Paradigm of *nədbaḥ* 'to be slaughtered' (strong root)

	S-stem	P-stem	Imperative
3MS	nədbáḥ	N/A	
3FS	ndəbaḥt	N/A	
2MS	N/A	N/A	N/A
2FS	N/A	N/A	N/A
1SG	N/A	N/A	
3PL	ndəbḥu	N/A	
2PL	N/A	N/A	N/A
1PL	N/A	N/A	

The /n-/ prefix form in Jewish Gabes is attested only in the 3SG and 3PL. From a cross-dialectal perspective, stems expressing passivity and reflexivity, depending on the region, have developed either in the direction of the /n-/ stem, i.e., $nəC^1C^2əC^3$, or the /t-/ stem, i.e., $tC^1əC^2əC^3$. Moreover, as will be shown in the following paragraphs, in Jewish Gabes, a secondary process takes place that attests to an analogical change.

3.2.7. Stem VIII

Table 39: Paradigm of *xṭāṛ* 'to choose' (weak second radical)

	S-stem	P-stem	Imperative
3MS	xṭāṛ	yəxṭāṛ	
3FS	xṭāṛət	təxṭāṛ	
2MS	xṭart	təxṭāṛ	axṭāṛ
2FS	xṭaṛti	təxṭāṛi	axṭāṛi
1SG	xṭart	nəxṭāṛ	
3PL	xṭāṛu	yəxṭāṛu	
2PL	xṭaṛtu	təxṭāṛu	axṭāṛu
1PL	xṭaṛna	nəxṭāṛu	

Participle: *məxṭāṛ, məxṭāṛa, məxṭāṛīn*

Also in this form: *rtāḥ–yərtāḥ* 'to rest', *ḥtāž–yəḥtāž* 'to need'.

Form VIII is reflexive in character, and its distinctive feature is the /-t-/ inserted after the first radical. The form known from modern dialects was, in CA, preceded by a prosthetic vowel, i.e., *ʔiftaʕala* (Fischer 202, 100). The stem vowel /a/ in the p-stem is invariably long, while in the dialect of Wad-Souf, it tends to be shortened, and the stress tends to be placed on the prefix, i.e., *yúxṭar*.

The stem in question is poorly attested in Jewish Gabes and no sound roots have been attested in this stem. This is primarily due to the movement of the infixed /-t-/ to the prefixal position, presumably due to the influence of the /t-/ passive stem, e.g., *ltām* 'to gather' in Maṛāzīg is rendered in Jewish Gabes as *tləmm* (Ritt-Benmimoun 2014, 373). In the Jewish and also the Muslim dialect of Tunis, there exist only some vestiges of this pattern. As pointed out by Cohen (1975, 126), one of the most frequent verbs of this form in the Jewish dialect of Tunis is *ṣḍāḍ* 'he hunted', in which the first /ḍ/ represents the assimilated /t/. In addition, there is no strong root in stem VIII in this dialect. Also, in the Jewish dialect of Algiers, most of the reflexive verbs with active counterparts in the first stem belong instead to patterns with prefixes /t-/ and /n-/ (Cohen 1912, 222). Nonetheless, it seems that this form is much more frequently attested in Muslim dialects than in Jewish ones. In the dialect of Douz, one finds a wide variety of regular and irregular verbs in stem VIII (Ritt-Benmimoun 2014, 368–74). Forms of the suffix conjugation are preceded by a short epenthetic vowel /ə/, which presumably resembles the CA prosthetic vowel, e.g., ʾntaḥḥ 'he was removed'. In the dialect of Cherchell, as in other Algerian dialects (Djidjelli, Tlemcen), pattern VIII is no longer morphologically operative (Grand'Henry 1972, 63). Despite this, several archaic forms have been preserved in these dialects, most of them having weak roots (Marçais 1956, 196).

3.2.8. Stem X

Table 40: Paradigm of *štaʕžəb* 'to be surprised' (strong root)

	S-stem	P-stem	Imperative
3MS	štaʕžəb	yəštaʕžəb	
3FS	štaʕžbət	təštaʕžəb	
2MS	štaʕžəbt	təštaʕžəb	əštaʕžəb
2FS	štaʕžəbti	təštaʕžbi	əštaʕžbi
1SG	štaʕžəbt	nəštaʕžəb	
3PL	štaʕžbu	yəštaʕžbu	
2PL	štaʕažəbtu	təštaʕžbu	əštaʕžbu
1PL	štaʕžəbna	nəštaʕžbu	

Participle: *məštaʕžəb, məštaʕžba, məštaʕžbin*

Table 41: Paradigm of ṣtḥaqq 'to be in need of' (geminated root)

	S-stem	P-stem	Imperative
3MS	ṣtḥaqq	yəṣtḥaqq	
3FS	ṣtḥaq(q)ət	təṣtḥaqq	
2MS	ṣtḥaqəqt	təṣtḥaqq	əṣtḥaqq
2FS	ṣtḥaqəqti	təṣtḥaqqi	əṣtḥaqqi
1SG	ṣtḥaqaqt	nəṣtḥaqq	
3PL	ṣtḥaqaqu	yəṣtḥaqqu	
2PL	ṣtḥaqaqtu	təṣtḥaqqu	əṣtḥaqqu
1PL	ṣtḥaqaqna	nəṣtḥaqqu	

Participle: məṣtḥaqq, məṣtḥaqqa, məṣtḥaqqīn

Table 42: Paradigm of štāhəl 'to deserve' (weak first radical)

	S-stem	P-stem	Imperative
3MS	štāhəl	yəštāhəl	
3FS	štāhlət	təštāhəl	
2MS	štāhəlt	təštāhəl	N/A
2FS	štāhəlti	təštāhli	N/A
1SG	štāhəlt	nəštāhəl	
3PL	štāhlu	yəštāhlu	
2PL	štāhəltu	təštāhlu	N/A
1PL	štāhəlna	nəštāhlu	

Table 43: Paradigm of štaġna 'to become rich' (weak third radical)

	S-stem	P-stem	Imperative
3MS	štaġna	yəštaġna	
3FS	štaġnət	təštaġən	
2MS	štaġnīt	təštaġən	N/A
2FS	štaġnīti	təštaġni	N/A
1SG	štaġnīt	nəštaġən	
3PL	štaġnu	yəštaġnu	
2PL	štaġnītu	təštaġnu	N/A
1PL	štaġnīna	nəštaġnu	

Participle: məštaġni, məštaġnya, məštaġnyīn

Stem X corresponds to the CA pattern *ʔistafʕala*. However, as in the case of stem VIII, the initial vowel has been reduced, and thus this verb stem, in the dialect of Gabes, begins with /št-/. The prefix has a few variations within the Maghrebi dialects. The Jewish dialect of Tripoli (Yoda 2005, 181), Jewish Algiers (Cohen 1912, 232), and the dialect of Cherchell (Grand'Henry 1972, 65) tend to substitute /št-/ with /st-/, e.g., *stəxbor* 'he was informed'. On the other hand, in the dialects of Djidjelli (Marçais 1956, 197) and Tlemcen (Marçais 1902, 83), the prefix /t-/ has been assimilated to the preceding /s/, giving rise to a cluster of two identical consonants, e.g., *ssoxbaṛ* 'he asked for news'. In the dialect of Douz, the stem X prefix is preceded by a short epenthetic vowel /ə/, e.g., *ʾstⁱwadd* 'to wish, to desire' (Ritt-Benmimoun 2014, 377).

The vowel between the second and third radicals in the root *ḥqq* is stable, as opposed to in Jewish Tunis, where one finds the development *ṣtḥaqqīt* 'you needed'. The suffix of this form is characteristic of verbs of the geminated pattern, and thus the type of inflection found in the Jewish dialect of Gabes is unexpected. In the dialect of Algiers, in turn, in the aforementioned form, the stem vowel was also reduced, and consequently, a monosyllabic word with an initial consonantal cluster emerged, e.g., *stḥqīt* (Cohen 1912, 233). When it comes to the p-stem forms of the geminated verb, in the dialect of Gabes, second and third radicals are separated by a short epenthetic vowel /ə/, as in the regular verb. On the contrary, in most of the neighbouring dialects, no vowel is inserted between them.

3.2.9. Stem XI

Table 44: Paradigm of *ḍʕāf* 'to lose weight'

	S-stem	P-stem	Imperative
3MS	ḍʕāf	yəḍʕāf	
3FS	ḍʕāfət	təḍʕāf	
2MS	ḍʕāfīt	təḍʕāf	N/A
2FS	ḍʕāfīti	təḍʕāfi	N/A
1SG	ḍʕāfīt	nəḍʕāf	
3PL	ḍʕāfu	yəḍʕāfu	
2PL	ḍʕāfītu	təḍʕāfu	N/A
1PL	ḍʕāfīna	nəḍʕāf	

Participles: *məžyān, məžyāna, məžyānīn*

Stem XI corresponds to the CA pattern *(ʔi)fʕālla* and, as argued by Yoda (2005, 143), it replaces stem IX.[20] It retained a long /ā/ vowel after the second radical with simultaneous loss of gemination. The basic meaning of stem XI is the acquisition of a certain property, e.g., *ṭwāl* 'he became long', *žyān* 'he became beautiful' (Cohen 1975, 122).

When it comes to the inflection of the XI pattern in Jewish Gabes, there exist two parallel variants. On the one hand, there is the one presented above, where the original /ā/ vowel is preserved in the suffix conjugation, while the suffix presents an unexpected development, namely, forms with a consonantal suffix have a linking vowel /ī/, which is usually characteristic of verbs with a semi-vowel third radical. The same tendency is attested in

---

[20] As observed by Singer (1984, 392), the occurrence of the XI form is a characteristic feature of western dialects of Arabic, since in eastern dialects, form IX replaced XI.

the Jewish dialect of Algiers (Cohen 1912, 236), the Jewish dialect of Tripoli (Yoda 2005, 183), and the dialect of Tlemcen (Marçais 1902, 85). On the other hand, there exists also another variant, where no linking vowel appears, while long /ā/ is shortened in forms with consonantal suffixes, i.e., ḍʕaft. The Jewish dialect of Tunis exhibits this tendency, e.g., ḍʕaft 'you lost weight' (Cohen 1975, 121).

An interesting development of pattern XI is attested in the dialect of Marāzīg, where the long stem vowel /ā/, in forms with consonantal suffixes, interchanges with short /i/, e.g., ʾṭwāḷ 'he became long', ʾṭwilᵊt 'I became long'. Moreover, this phenomenon occurs regardless of the phonetic environment, and the /i/ is inserted also after emphatic and guttural consonants, e.g., ʾxḏ̣āṛ 'he became green', ʾxḏ̣irᵊt 'she became green' (Ritt-Benmimoun 2014, 385).

4.0. Conclusions

The analysis presented above enables us to assess to what extent the verbal system of the Jewish dialect of Gabes is similar to other Maghrebi dialects, on the one hand, and what the points of disagreement are, on the other. Unlike Jewish Tunis, both Jewish Gabes and Jewish Djerba have gender distinction in the 2FS forms, which are marked by the /-i/ suffix. In Jewish Tunis, on the other hand, this distinction does not exist and masculine forms are used also for the feminine. The data analysed in this chapter confirms the sedentary character of Jewish Gabes, since the suffix of verbs with a weak third radical in stem I is /-āw/, and not /u/, as found in the Bedouin dialects. Concerning the vowel distribution of verbal forms of stem I, Jewish Gabes exhibits several commonalities with neighbouring Jewish dialects, particularly in the use of /ə/ as the basic theme vowel, which is lowered to /a/ in the vicinity of gutturals. Muslim dialects and Jewish Wad-Souf, on the contrary, demonstrate a much wider array of vowel qualities. Moreover, as has been argued (§2.2), Jewish Gabes has developed an alternative way of expressing the passive, by means of a bipartite construction involving an active verb with a personal object pronoun.

4. NOMINAL MORPHOLOGY

The present section describes the nominal morphology of Jewish Gabes. Since in many aspects it does not differ from other dialects, this survey aims at a detailed presentation of the collected data. I will first provide some theoretical preliminaries on the characteristics of the nominal morphology of Jewish Gabes, and subsequently, I will present all the attested patterns, first of singular nouns, and then of plural.

1.0. Theoretical Preliminaries

1.1. The Definition of 'Noun' and the Classification of the Nominal Patterns

In the present study, I will not apply a differentiation between nouns, adjectives, and numerals, since Jewish Gabes, like many other modern Arabic dialects, does not make any morphological distinction between them, and adjectives very often function as substantives. In this respect, I will follow the method of Yoda (2005, 197), rather than that of Cohen (1975, 140), who sets a very clear distinction between these parts of speech. The lexical items found in this chapter have been classified according to their morphological structure, and not their properties as parts of speech; hence, along with substantives, adjectives, prepositions, and numerals have been included. This approach is analogous to Wright's (2005, 104) definition of the noun, which includes: substantives, adjectives, numerals, demonstratives, conjunctions, and pronouns.

It has been mentioned that various grammars differ in terms of the definition of the noun. An additional point of divergence is the way the nominal patterns are organised, particularly when it comes to the choice between diachronic and synchronic approaches. Both approaches have their advantages and disadvantages. The diachronic one can be considerably confusing for the reader, as it is not clear whether semi-consonants like /و/, /ي/, or long /ā/ *alif* are to be considered consonants and therefore part of the root, or should rather be perceived as a vocalic element of a pattern. For example, *bāb* 'door' can theoretically be classified both as CV̄C and, if one considers *alif* part of the root, as CvCC. The distinction between triliteral and biliteral nouns seems to be somewhat inconsistent and vague as well. Yoda (2005, 215, 218) classifies *mṛa* 'woman' (< CA *marʔa*) as a biliteral noun, while *ġda* 'medicine' (< CA *ġadāʔ*) is classified as a triliteral noun with third radical y/h, placed in the pattern CvCC, even though both of them have two strong consonants and *hamza*.

On the other hand, the synchronic approach tends to lack information on the historical development that led to the present situation. In light of these observations, I decided to apply a blend of both approaches, namely to focus on synchronic classification of the patterns, but simultaneously to give the corresponding CA forms.[1] This means, therefore, that words like *līl* 'night' and *bīr* 'well' are both classified under the same CV̄C pattern, but have been broken down in two categories, since /ī/ is

---

[1] A similar approach has been applied by Veronika Ritt-Benmimoun (2014) in her description of the Bedouin dialect of Douz.

brought about in the former by contraction of the diphthong /ay/, but in the latter by the elimination of *hamza*. I hope this method will facilitate navigation of the text, while simultaneously providing some crucial historical data.

Finally, in contrast to the method of Cohen (1975, 143), I decided not to break down into separate categories those roots with semivowels where the semivowels do not bring about any morphological change; for example, the word *dənya* 'world', with third radical /y/, does not differ morphologically from *ṣəžṛa* 'tree', which has three regular consonants. I did, however, separate the roots whose second and third radical are alike, in order to avoid any confusion with the patterns that possess geminated consonants.

1.2. Gender

Jewish Gabes possesses two genders, namely masculine and feminine, but only the feminine is morphologically marked, by an /-a/ suffix, e.g., *mṛa* 'woman', *ḍəṛba* 'slap', *fəṛṣa* 'mare', *kbīra* 'big', *ždīda* 'new', *ḥābla* 'pregnant'. This corresponds to several CA endings marking the feminine, i.e., /-t/, /-ah, /at/, /-ā/, /āʔ/ (Wright 2005, 169). When the masculine form finishes with /-i/, the feminine one admits the ending /-ya/, e.g., *tūnši–tūnšīya* 'Tunisian'. Nonetheless, there are exceptions to this rule, and some feminine nouns are unmarked. This group includes some words that are feminine by default, e.g., *umm/omm* 'mother'; parts of the body: *ʕīn* 'eye', *yədd* 'hand', *bṭən* 'belly', *wdən* 'ear'; cities: *tūnəš* 'Tunis'; and others, like, for example, *aṛḍ* 'Earth, soil, land', *bīt* 'room', ḍāṛ 'house, family', šəmš 'sun', ṭrīq 'road'. Yoda (2005, 201) classifies also əxt 'sister' and bənt 'daughter' as exceptions; however, taking into account the historical background of these forms, they should be considered vestiges of the original feminine /t/ marker, rather than exceptions.

On the other hand, there exist also nouns that resemble the feminine because of their /-a/ suffix, but whose gender is masculine, e.g., dwa ṃaṛṛ 'bitter medicine'.

In some dialects, certain feminine nouns that in Jewish Gabes possess the /-a/ marker are listed as unmarked and presumably reflect an earlier stage of linguistic development. Items like ʕᵃzūz 'old woman' and fṛaṣ 'mare' in the Bedouin dialect of Douz correspond to Jewish Gabes ʕažūža and fəṛṣa (Ritt-Benmimoun 2014, 210).[2] In addition to the cross-dialectal differences, Jewish Gabes exhibits some differences in gender in comparison to CA. Below I present several selected nouns:

Table 45: Gender divergence in Jewish Gabes as compared to CA

Jewish Gabes–masculine	CA–feminine
drāʕ 'arm'	ḏirāʕ
ṣbaʕ 'finger'	ʔiṣbaʕ
fxaḍ 'shin'	faxiḏ
qdəm 'heel'	qadam
ktəf 'shoulder'	kataf
bīr 'well'	biʔr

In addition to the alternations of CA feminine–Jewish Gabes masculine, there are also reversed alternations, i.e., words which

---

[2] The form ʕazūz has been attested in Jewish Wad-Souf.

were of masculine gender in CA are feminine in Jewish Gabes, e.g., *bīt* (F) 'room'–CA *bayt* (M), *kās̄* (F) 'cup'–CA *kaʔs* (M).

There exists a group of nouns wherein the feminine form originates from a root that is wholly distinct from its masculine counterpart. Below one can find a list of the most commonly used pairs in Jewish Gabes:

Table 46: Nouns with irregular gender formation

Masculine	Feminine
ḅu 'father'	uṃṃ/oṃṃ 'mother'
ḥsān 'horse'	fərṣa 'mare'
rāžəl / rāẓəl 'man'	mra 'wife'
šəbbāni 'old man'	ʕažūža 'old woman, dowager'
šīd 'master'	ləlla 'madam'
wəld 'boy'	bənt 'girl'
xu 'brother'	uxt 'sister'

1.3. Definite Article

In Jewish Gabes, as in many other North African dialects, /l-/ serves as the definite article. The CA rule of the assimilation of /l-/ before the solar letters operates also in Jewish Gabes. Similarly to other dialects, like Jewish Tripoli for example, the assimilation results in the emergence of a short auxiliary vowel /ə/ before the geminated consonant. Below one can find a list of all the consonants which bring about the assimilation of /l-/, along with examples. The list does not include the emphatic variants of some non-phonemic consonants, like /ḷ/ for example, as the assimilation of the article is not subject to any fluctuations in this respect, and non-phonemic emphasis tends to be irregular and depend on the speaker.

l + d > dd, e.g., əd-drūž 'the stairs';
l + ḍ > ḍḍ, e.g., əḍ-ḍhəṛṛ 'the back';
l + l > ll, e.g., əl-līl 'the night';
l + n > nn, e.g., ən-nhār 'day';
l + t > tt, e.g., ət-tānya 'the second';
l + ṭ > ṭṭ, e.g., əṭ-ṭayba 'the cooked, ripe (F)';
l + r > rr, e.g., ər-rīḥa 'the smell, scent';
l + ṛ > ṛṛ, e.g., əṛ-ṛmān 'the pomegranate';
l + ṣ > ṣṣ, e.g., əṣ-ṣəlṭān 'the sultan';
l + š > šš, e.g., əš-šhūd 'the witnesses';
l + ẓ > ẓẓ, e.g., əẓ-ẓġīr 'the small one';
l + ž > žž, e.g., əž-žnūn 'the ghosts'.

1.4. Construct State

In Jewish Gabes, the distribution of the construct state is rather limited, as this construction, widely used in CA, has been replaced in the majority of cases by the analytic construction involving the genitive marker *(n)tāʕ*. Nonetheless, in some instances, the analytic construction is impossible, and the construct state is used instead. Its specific distribution will be explained in chapter 5, §2.3; here I will limit myself only to the morphological aspects of this construction.

Forming the construct state of masculine nouns does not involve any morphological change, e.g., *ʕžəb ṛəbbi* 'the miracle of God'. In turn, feminine nouns terminating with /-a/ admit /-t/. Monosyllabic nouns, like *ṣla* 'synagogue' or *šma* 'sky', turn their final /-a/ into /-t/ without any change within the syllable structure, e.g., ṣlāt əl-blād 'the synagogue of the city'. The only exception to this rule is the word mṛa 'woman', which in the construct state becomes məṛt, e.g., məṛt bu 'father's wife, step-mother'. Other feminine nouns, i.e., those not belonging to the pattern CCv, admit the ending /-ət/, e.g., maklət əž-žməl 'the camel's food', šxānət əṣ-ṣīf 'the heat of the summer'.

It is worth mentioning that words related to the semantic field of family and affinity usually appear in the construct state and not in the analytic construction. Therefore, most speakers will say: bənt uxti 'the daughter of my sister', rather than *bənt tāʕ uxti. Some of these expressions are fixed, like məṛt būya 'my step-mother', ṛāẓəl bənti 'my daughter's husband, son-in-law',[3] wəld wəldi 'my grandson'.[4] In the case of some words denoting family relations, both the construct state and a specific term are used interchangeably, e.g., məṛt wəldi–kənti 'my daughter-in-law'.

1.5. Number

In Jewish Gabes, there are three types of number, i.e., singular, dual, and plural. The usage of the second one is very limited, and, as pointed out by Cohen (1975, 186), all the Maghrebi dialects either have already lost or are in the process of losing the dual. Jewish Gabes represents in this respect an example of gradual

---

[3] The word nšīb also serves as the equivalent of son-in-law, but the expression ṛāẓəl bənt is much more popular. nšīb / nšība designates all kinds of affinity acquired through marriage.

[4] As far as I could establish, Jewish Gabes does not have one specific word for 'grandson', unlike Jewish Tunis, where ḥfīdi 'my grandson' exists.

substitution of the CA ending /-ayn/ by the analytic construction with žūž 'two'. There are, however, several exceptions.

1.5.1. Dual

The dual in CA is one of three types of number and its distribution is widely attested. It designates a group of two individuals and can be formed from any noun by adding the suffix /-āni/ to the root of the noun (Wright 2005, 189). In case of feminine nouns ending in /-a/, the final ة changes into ت, just like in the construct state. As has been mentioned above, this is not the case in the North African dialects. In his description of Jewish Algiers, Marcel Cohen (1912, 289) reports that there are two types of number in this dialect, namely singular and plural, simultaneously excluding the dual due to a limited number of attested examples. The elimination of the dual seems to exceed the boundaries of the sedentary dialects, as limited distribution of the dual is also attested in the Bedouin dialect of Douz (Ritt-Benmimoun 2014, 220). There, as in other dialects, the classical dual has been replaced by the analytic construction and survives only in words denoting time and measures.

In Jewish Gabes, the distribution of the dual is similar. Due to contraction of diphthongs, the suffix of the dual is /-īn/. Below I present two semantic groups where the dual occurs:

1. Parts of the body

Singular	Dual	Meaning
ʕīn	ʕinīn	eyes
yədd	yəddīn	hands
ržəl	rəžlīn	legs
wdən	wədnīn	ears
drāʕ	darʕīn	arms

Not every paired part of the body can be formed in this way. Some nouns that, in other Semitic languages—for example in Hebrew—form the dual, like *xədd* 'cheek', form only the internal plural, i.e., *xdūd*. Similarly, some nouns that possess dual forms have also parallel plural forms that can function as duals, e.g., *ʕyūn* 'eyes'.

2. Time expressions

Singular	Dual	Meaning
ʕām	ʕāmīn	two years
līl	līltīn	two nights
marra	martīn	twice
nhār	nharīn	two days
šāʕa	šāʕtīn	two hours
ṣhaṛ	ṣahrīn	two months
tqīqa	tqiqtīn	two minutes

In the case of time expressions, the differentiation between dual and plural is very clear and marked morphologically, e.g., *ṣahrīn–ṣhūr* 'two months–months'. Therefore, the dual and the plural forms cannot be used interchangeably, as they can in the case of other nouns, e.g., *ʕinīn–ʕyūn* 'eyes'.

1.5.2. Plural

Two basic ways of forming the plural can be distinguished. The first one involves addition of a suffix at the end of a noun, while the other can be defined as an 'internal plural' and entails rearrangement of the order of the sounds within the word. The dual, as described above, belongs to the former category. Both substantives and adjectives form the dual/plural and very often, when combined, they follow different paths of formation, e.g., *rəžlīn ṭwāl* 'long legs', where the first word represents the dual, which is formed externally, and the other the internal plural. As has been pointed out by Cohen (1975, 188), the internal plural is much more prevalent than the external one, and indeed the majority of nouns form their plural in this way. On the other hand, the external plural is applied in words of foreign origin, hence, as observed by Cohen (1975, 188), it has a propensity to expand.

The internal plural will be analysed, together with its patterns, in §3.0; here I will limit myself to presenting the distribution of the external plural. The following suffixes can be distinguished as markers of the external plural:

1. /-īn/

    This suffix corresponds to the CA termination -ūna / -īna, which characterises the so-called *pluralis sanus* (Wright 2005, 192). It can mark the plural of both masculine and feminine nouns (Cohen 1975, 189). As concerns its distribution, below are listed the major grammatical groups in which it appears:

    - active and passive participles of the first stem: *ʕāyəš–ʕāyšīn* 'alive', *dāxəl–dāxlīn* 'entering', *xārəž–*

xāržīn 'exiting', *məktūb–məktubīn* 'written', *maqlī–maqlīyīn* 'fried', *māši–māšīyīn* 'going';[5]
- nouns of the pattern with geminated second radical (CvC²C²v̄C) that denote names of professions and occupations, e.g., *kəddāb–kəddābīn* 'liars', *ṣarrāq–ṣarrāqīn* 'thieves', *xabbāž–xabbāžīn* 'bakers', *xaddām–xaddāmīn* 'slaves, workers';[6]
- adjectives terminating with /-ān/, e.g., *farḥān–farḥānīn* 'happy', *ġədbān–ġədbānīn* 'angry', *məlyān–məlyānīn* 'full', *ḥafyān–ḥafyānīn* 'barefoot';
- adjectives terminating with /-i/:[7] *axxrāni–axxrānīn* 'last, final', *fuqqāni–fuqqānīn* 'upper', *lūṭāni–lūṭānīn* 'lower';
- some adjectives with second radical semi-vowel, e.g., *ḍəyyəq–ḍəyyqīn* 'narrow', *məyyət–məyytīn* 'dead';
- some adjectives of the pattern CCūC, e.g., *ḥlu–ḥlūwīn* 'sweet', *šxūn–šxūnīn* 'hot';

---

[5] It is worth noting that, in the case of the active participle, the original long /ā/ following the first consonant, e.g., *māši* 'the one who is going', is significantly shortened when the plural marker is added, mostly due to the repositioning of the stress.

[6] It is important to note, however, that these nouns can also form the plural by means of the /-a/ suffix, e.g., *xaddāma* 'slaves'.

[7] In Jewish Tunis, this suffix shifts to /-ən/ when added to an adjective ending with /-i/, e.g., *axxrāni–axxranīyən* 'last, final' (Cohen 1975, 190). Contrary to this, in Jewish Gabes, the suffix maintains its original form and, as a result, the /i/ is geminated.

- some adjectives with second and third radicals alike, e.g., *ḥərr–ḥərrīn* 'hot', *ḥayy–ḥayyīn* 'alive', *mərr–mərrīn* 'bitter'.

2. /-āt/

The /-āt/ ending has /-wāt/ and /-yāt/ variants, which occur when the noun terminates with /-u/ or /-a/ respectively (Cohen 1912, 296). In Jewish Gabes, as in Jewish Tunis, this suffix is much more frequent than /-īn/ (Cohen 1975, 190). The vast majority of nouns that admit this ending are feminine. The following items form their plural with /-āt/:

- nouns ending with /-a/, e.g., *ḥarka–ḥarkāt* 'movements', *qābla–qablāt* 'midwives', *ṣəẓra–ṣəẓrāt* 'trees'. Also included in this category are nouns of unity (singulatives), which usually terminate with /-a/ and are formed from collectives without the /-a/ ending. However, when reference is being made to a real plural, which is usually preceded by a number, rather than to a collective, a plural form is used, e.g., *bəṭṭīx* 'melons (coll.)', *bəṭṭīxa* 'a melon (singulative)', *tlāta bəṭṭīxāt* 'three melons'; similarly: *nəmmāla* 'an ant (singulative)', *nəmmālāt* 'ants (PL)'; *xūxa* 'a peach (singulative)', *xūxāt* 'peaches' (PL);
- some nouns of the pattern CCa, which in the plural admit the suffix /-wāt/, e.g., *bla–blāwāt* 'disasters', *ṣla–ṣlāwāt* 'synagogues', *šma–šmāwāt* 'sky';

- some nouns of the pattern CCa, which in the plural admit the termination /-yāt/, e.g., *dwa–dwāyāt* 'medicaments', *rḍa–rḍāyāt* 'agreements';
- some feminine nouns that do not have the typical feminine marker, e.g., *umm–ummāt* 'mothers';
- some masculine nouns admit the -/āt/ ending, e.g., *ʕamm–ʕammāt* 'paternal uncles', *lbāš–lbāšāt* 'clothing', *qbūr–qbūrāt* 'graves', *xāl–xālāt* 'maternal uncles', *žnāḥ–žnāḥāt* 'wings', *žwāb–žwābāt* 'letters';
- numerous nouns of foreign origin form their plural with /-āt/, e.g., *ḫābūr–ḫābūrāt* 'ships', *balkūn–balkūnāt* 'balconies', *famīlya–fāmiliyāt* 'families', *šbīrītu–šbīrītwāt* 'high-percentage alcohols, poison'.

1.5.3. Collective

The collective as a grammatical notion is on the border between singular and plural. It can be perceived as a separate category of the plural denoting a group of objects without specific individual identities, but at the same time, the plurality it conveys is treated as a unit, hence it is often treated as a type of singular (Ferrando 2011). The Arabic term designating the collective is either *ism al-jins* or *ism al-jamʕ*, indicating that this category covers nouns denoting different species (*jins*) and simultaneously refers to the notion of plurality (*jamʕ*; Dayf 1990, 57). Usually, the use of the collective is determined by the lack of a numerical specification preceding the noun, namely, it never appears when the quantity is clearly specified. In that case, the plural is used instead. Nouns that form the collective often refer to animals, plants, vegetables, and fruits:

Table 47: Formation of the collective in Jewish Gabes

Singular	Collective	Plural	
bəṭṭixa	bəṭṭix	bəṭṭixāt	'melons'
xūxa	xūx	xūxāt	'peaches'
nəmmāla	nəmmāl	nəmmālāt	'ants'

2.0. Singular Nominal Patterns

2.1. Patterns with One Consonant

This small group includes words which in CA contain *hamza*: *ma* 'water' (corresponding to CA *māʔ*), *bu* (corresponding to CA construct state of أبُ i.e., *ʔabū*), *xu* (corresponding to CA construct state of خُ, i.e., *ʔaxū*; Yoda 2005, 215).

2.2. Patterns with Two Consonants

2.2.1. CvC

These forms correspond to the CA patterns CvC, CaʔC, and CawC/CayC and include roots with second radical ʔ/w/y. In Jewish Tunis, the group CawC/CayC has been preserved in an unaltered form, while in Jewish Gabes, the diphthongs have been contracted to a single vowel, namely, /aw/ has contracted either to /ō/ or to /ū/, while /ay/ has contracted to /ī/. This pattern contains, among others, nouns designating collectives which correspond to singulative nouns of the pattern CvCa.

a) corresponding to CA CāC/CaʔC:
ʕām 'year', bāb 'door', ḍāṛ 'house', fāṛ 'mouse', fāš 'pick-axe, hoe', ḥāl 'situation', kāš 'cup', nāṛ 'fire', nāṣ 'people', ṛāṣ 'head', rāy 'opinion',[8] tāž 'crown', xāl 'maternal uncle',[9] ẓāṛ 'neighbour';

b) corresponding to CA CīC/CiʔC:
ʕīd 'festival', bīr 'well', dīb 'wolf', dīl 'tail', dīn 'religion, debt', fīl 'elephant', rīḥ 'wind', rīq 'saliva', xīr 'better';

c) corresponding to CA CayC:
ʕīn 'eye', bīt 'room', dīn 'debt', ǵīr 'without', kīf 'enjoyment, pleasure', līl 'night', ṣīf 'summer', šīf 'sword', ṭīṛ 'bird', xīr 'better', xīṭ 'thread', žīb 'pocket', žīn 'beauty', žīt 'oil';

d) corresponding to CA CūC:
būq 'trumpet', fūl 'beans',[10] rūḥ 'spirit', ṣūq 'market', šūk 'thorn (coll.)', tūm 'garlic (coll.)';

---

[8] This word can be found in the expression: kull ḥadd ʕal rāyu 'everyone acts according to their opinion, judgement'.

[9] This word appears in a proverb related to the relationship between a daughter and her paternal and maternal uncles: žīt l-ʕammi ʕammāni, žīt l-xāli xallāni 'I came to my paternal uncle—he made me blind, I came to my maternal uncle—he secretly talked to me'. Usually, the paternal uncle was perceived as a serious and uncompromising figure, while the maternal one was associated with affection and understanding.

[10] There is an incredibly rich assortment of proverbs and riddles involving this word in Jewish Gabes, e.g., ṛəbbi yaʕṭi əl-fūl li ma ʕandūš əẓ-ẓṛūṣ 'God gives beans to one who does not have chewing teeth' (Tobi 2016, 270).

e) corresponding to CA CawC:

dūd 'worms (coll.)', *fūq* 'above', *ḥūt* 'fish' (coll.),[11] *lūn* 'colour', *mūt* 'death', *ṣūṭ* 'voice, sound', *tūt* 'berries' (coll.), *xūx* 'peaches' (coll.), *žūž* 'two'.

2.2.2. CvCa

This group principally includes feminine nouns of roots with second radical ʔ/w/y. From a semantic point of view, some nouns of this group designate collectivity.

a) corresponding to CA CāCah, CaʔCah:

ġāba 'forest', *ḥāra* 'Jewish quarter', *ḥāža* 'thing, something', *nāga* 'female camel', *šāʕa* 'hour', *ẓāṛa* 'neighbour (F)';

b) corresponding to CA CayCah, CīCah:

bīḍa 'white (F)', *dīma* 'always', *ġība* 'absence', *ḥīla* 'fraud', *mīla* 'circumcision', *mīya* 'hundred', *rīha* 'smell', *rīya* 'lung', *šīra* 'side',[12] *xība* 'disappointment';

c) corresponding to CA CawCa, CūCah:

dūda 'worm', *ḍūra* 'round trip', *ḥūta* 'a fish',[13] *lūḥa* 'board, wood', *šūda* 'black (F)', *šūka* 'thorn', *tūma* 'garlic clove'.

---

[11] Due to social taboo, it is prohibited to pronounce this word, and instead the expression *fi-wažž l-ʕadū* 'on the face of the enemy' is used.

[12] This word occurs in the expression *mən šīra wāḥda… wa mən oxra…* 'on the one hand… on the other…'.

[13] This word also serves a female name. Interestingly, its diminutive *ḥwīṭa* is a male name (e.g., rabbi Hwita Cohen from Djerba).

2.2.3. CCv

Words classified in this group derive from CA roots with third radical *hamza*, i.e., CvCā?, and words with third radical semi-vowel:

ʕṣa 'stick', ʕša 'dinner',[14] *bla* 'problems, worries',[15] *dwa* 'medicine', *ḥlu* 'sweet', *ḥma* 'mother-in-law',[16] *kra* 'rent', *mṛa* 'woman', *ṛḍa* 'God's will', *šma* 'sky', *šta* 'winter', *ṣla* 'synagogue' (< CA ṣalāh), *ṣqa* 'fatigue'.

2.2.4. vCC

Words in this group derive from CA words with first radical *alif*:

āmš 'yesterday', *aṛḍ* 'soil, Earth', *ašm* 'name', *aṣḷ* 'origin', *uṃṃ/oṃṃ* 'mother'.

---

[14] This corresponds to the CA word ʕašā? which was originally masculine. Jewish Gabes has retained the masculine gender of this word and therefore the final /a/ does not turn into /t/ when a personal pronoun is added, e.g., ʕašāna 'our dinner'. Contrary to this, in Jewish Tripoli, this word is feminine (Yoda 2005, 218).

[15] This noun designating troubles and quarrels appears in the following proverb: *yəṭlab l-bla, lqa l-bla qāllu: əža ʕandi* 'the person who is looking for troubles, found troubles and told them: come to me'—meaning that problematic people attract problems by themselves.

[16] In Djerba, the word for mother-in-law is ʕažūža, literally 'old woman'. The figure of the mother-in-law occurs in a plethora of poems, songs, and proverbs used in Jewish Gabes, e.g., *məktūb ʕla bāb əž-žənna / ḥatta ḥma ma tḥabb əl-kənna* 'On the door of the Garden of Eden is written: no mother-in-law likes her bride' (see Tobi 2016, 314).

2.2.5. CāCi

From a diachronic perspective, items belonging to this group should be classified as triliteral words of the pattern *fāʕil*, since in CA, many of them have either *hamza* or /y/ as their third radical. Nonetheless, the final consonants have been reduced without any compensatory vowel lengthening, and therefore, on the synchronic level, roots with third radical *hamza* or /y/ belonging in CA to the pattern *fāʕil* should be classified as CāCi:

a) corresponding to CA third radical *hamza*:
dāfi 'mild, warm', *ḥāfi* 'barefoot',[17] *wāṭi* 'low, flat', *xāṭi* 'not belonging to anyone';

b) corresponding to CA third radical /y/:
bāhi 'good', *ġāli* 'expensive', *lāhi* 'busy, occupied', *ṣāfi* 'clear, pure', *tāli* 'last, previous', *tāni* 'second'.

2.2.6. CvCa

The word *lūṭa* 'ground, floor' is the only item attested in this pattern. It appears in two variants with different stress placement, i.e., *lúṭa* 'down', and *lūṭá* 'floor'. The latter has a shorter variant, *wṭa*.[18]

---

[17] Apart from its basic meaning, this word also denotes a lack of any additions, e.g., *āna ka-nākəl xabž ḥāfi* 'I am eating bread without anything', i.e., there is nothing on the top of the slice.

[18] The equivalent of this word in the northern communities, like Moknin and Tunis, is *qāʕa*.

2.3. Patterns with Three Consonants

The nominal forms with one short vowel before or after the second radical constitute the biggest group among all the patterns in the Maghrebi dialects. This group covers a wide array of nominal patterns known from CA, which, due to various historical changes like reduction of the vowel system or disappearance of *hamza*, have lost their distinctiveness from one another. In addition, in Jewish Gabes, as in many other Maghrebi dialects, there is a general tendency to geminate the last consonant in monosyllabic words, and therefore words that, in CA, had two consonants, like فم 'mouth' or يد 'hand', are, on the synchronic level, triliteral, i.e., *fumm, yədd*.

2.3.1. CvCC

- three strong consonants, $C^1vC^2C^3$:
  ʕarš 'wedding', *ʕaql* 'brain', *baʕd* 'after, afterwards', *bənt* 'girl, daughter', *bard* 'cold', *ḍuww* 'light', *farx* 'little bird, bastard, naughty child', *ġalṭ* 'errors (coll.)', *ḥabš* 'prison', *fərn* 'oven', *kəbš* 'lamb', *kəlb* 'dog',[19] *məlḥ* 'salt', *nəfš* 'spirit', *qəlb* 'heart, centre', *ṣarq* 'east', *ṣarf* 'change (coins)', *šəlf* 'brother-in-law', *šəmš* 'sun', *taʕb* 'tiredness', *taḥt* 'under, beneath', *ṭarf* 'piece', *təlž* 'snow', *waqt* 'time', *xabž* 'bread', *xamš* 'five', *žəld* 'leather', *žənš* 'kind';

---

[19] This word served also as a disdainful synonym for 'Jewish' among Muslim speakers of Gabes Arabic. Interestingly, Jews used to refer to Muslims in the same way, changing the initial /k/ into /x/, i.e., *xlāb* 'Muslims' (disdainful).

- second and third radical alike, C¹vC²C²:
  baṛṛ 'continent, remote place', *bəyy* 'ruler, bey', *dəmm* 'blood', *fəmm* 'mouth', *ḥašš* 'voice', *ḥaqq* 'justice', *ḥažž* 'pilgrimage to Mecca', *maxx* 'brain', *məṛṛ* 'bitter', *qadd* 'size', *ṣaṛṛ* 'secret, mystery', *šənn* 'tooth', *šəyy* 'nothing', *yədd* 'hand', *wəžž* 'face', *xədd* 'cheek', *žədd* 'grandfather, ancestor'.

2.3.2. CCvC

ʕbəd 'man', *ʕdəš* 'lentils', *ʕmər* 'age', *ʕqal* 'intelligence', *ʕraq* 'sweat', *ʕšal* 'honey', *bdən* 'body, corpse',[20] *bḥar* 'sea', *blaḥ* 'dates (coll.), *braq* 'lightning (coll.)', *bṣal* 'onion (coll.)', *bṭan* 'stomach',[21] *ḥbəl* 'rope', *ḥnəš* 'snake', *ḥṭab* 'fire logs (coll.)', *qwəy* 'strong', *mṭaṛ* 'rain', *nšər* 'eagle', *ṣʕar* 'hair', *ṣbaʕ* 'finger', *ṣqaf* 'roof', *šdər* 'chest, breast', *tlət* 'a third', *tmən* 'eighth', *wdən* 'ear', *xšəm* 'nose', *žbəl* 'mountain', *žməl* 'camel', *žnəb* 'side'.

2.3.3. CvCCa

This category includes a wide array of grammatical forms. Many words classified here are feminine counterparts of the patterns CvCC and CCvC, feminine nouns designating abstract objects,

---

[20] A more popular word for 'body' in Jewish Gabes is the Hebrew word *gūf*. The word *bdən* appears, however, in the expression *ṣaḥḥat bdən* 'good physical condition'.

[21] In Jewish Tunis, this word has two variants, namely, it appears also with a short vowel after the first consonant. Contrary to this, in Jewish Gabes, only *bṭan* is used. The communities in the North use *žūf* as the word for 'stomach'.

and feminine names of colours. In addition, singulative forms of collectives of the pattern CCvC have been included here:

- three different consonants, C¹vC²C³a:
ʕaḍma 'egg',[22] ʕafya 'fire', ʕaqrəb 'scorpion',[23] baqra 'cow', bəlḥa 'a date', bəlġa 'slipper', baṣla 'an onion',[24] ḍarba 'blow, bump', dənya 'world', dəxla 'entry', farḥa 'happiness', fərṣa 'mare', ġadwa 'tomorrow', ġaṣra 'worry', ḥamra 'red (F)',[25] ḥalwa 'candies (coll.)', kəlba 'bitch', kəlma 'word', kəlša 'sock', kəmša 'handful', kəšwa 'costume, clothing', laġwa 'language', laḥya 'beard', nədwa 'dew', nəšda 'question', nəxla 'palm tree', qaffa 'basket',

---

[22] In Jewish Tripoli, dəḥya is used instead (Yoda 2005, 321). Interestingly, in Jewish Gabes, the word ʕaḍma has bad connotations linked to the evil eye, similarly to the number five. Euphemistically, speakers use ʕīn l-ʕadu 'the eye of the enemy' as the equivalent of 'egg'.

[23] The figure of the scorpion in folktales and proverbs is a symbol of danger, e.g., rəbbi u l-ʕaqrəb rəḍḍi bālək taqrəb 'it is better to avoid rabbi and scorpion'.

[24] Onion, similarly to beans, appears in multiple folktales, proverbs, and expressions, e.g., bṣəltu tḥarqət, literally: 'his onion got burned', an expression used for a person who is in a hurry without any reason.

[25] All the names of colours have ultimate stress, unlike in Jewish Tunis, where they have penultimate stress. In terms of stress placement in adjectives, Jewish Gabes seems to be somewhere in the middle between Jewish Tunis, where all the female adjectives are paroxytone, and Jewish Tripoli, in which the stress falls on the last syllable (Cohen 1975, 150; Yoda 2005, 200).

qahwa 'coffee', ṣaʕra 'hair',[26] ṣaḥba 'friendship', ṣaḥra 'desert', ṣarba 'drinking', ṣafrá 'yellow (F)', šəmʕa 'candle', ṭawla 'table', xabža 'bread', wərta 'heritage', wəzġa 'lizard', xaḍrá 'green (F)', yəbra 'needle', ẓənqa 'blind alley', ẓarqá 'blue (F)', ẓərwa 'puppy'.

- second and third radical alike, C¹vC²C²a:
  bənna 'taste', barra 'outside', ḥakka 'little box for tobacco', ḥənna 'henna', marra 'time', nəffa 'tobacco', šəbba 'reason', šənna 'custom, habit', ṣaḥḥa 'health', ṣəwwa 'desert', tuwwa 'now'.

2.3.4. CvCvC

The words that belong to this pattern are principally active participles of the CA pattern *fāʕil* that have lost their verbal properties and started functioning as substantives. The phenomenon of the transition of this pattern from a verbal form into a noun is already known from CA (Wright 2005, 130). In fact, as is shown in chapter 6, §2.7.3, *fāʕil* bearing the meaning of an active participle survived in Jewish Gabes only in some isolated forms. Finally, the ordinal numbers have been assigned to this group:

ʕāṣər 'tenth', bārəd 'cold', ġāmaq 'dark', ḥāḍar 'ready, prepared', ḥādəq 'stingy', ḥādəš 'eleventh', ḥāyəf 'barefoot', ḥāžəb

---

[26] The figure of a hair appears in the blessing against the evil eye: *ynaḥḥi mənnək əl-ʕīn kīf ma ynaḥḥiw ṣaʕra mən ʕažīn* 'may the evil eye leave you like a hair is taken out of the dough'. Interestingly, a similar use of the image of a hair appears in the Babylonian Talmud in the context of a painless death: מיתת נשיקה – דמיא כמשחל בניתא מחלבא 'painless death is similar to the removal of the hair from the milk' (b. Berakhot 8a).

'eyebrow',[27] *kātəb* 'scribe', *mālaḥ* 'salty', *ṛābaʕ* 'fourth', *ṛāẓəl* 'man', *ṣāḥəb* 'friend', *ṣārəq* 'thief', *ṣāyəb* 'hard, difficult', *šābaʕ* 'seventh', *šāhəd* 'witness', *šāhəl* 'easy', *šārəb* 'lip', *šātət* 'sixth', *tālət* 'third', *tāmən* 'eighth', *tānəš* 'twelfth', *tāšaʕ* 'ninth', *wāḥəd* 'one, someone', *xādəm* 'slave',[28] *xāməš* 'fifth', *žāyəd* 'additional'.

2.3.5. CV̄CCa

This group comprises the feminine counterparts of items belonging to the pattern CV̄CvC. The addition of the final /-a/ brings about a change in the syllable structure in order to avoid a short vowel in an open syllable:

- three regular consonants, C¹v̄C²C³a:
  ʕālya 'tall' (F), *ʕāṣra* 'tenth (F)', *būnya* 'fist' (< Ital. *pugno*), *fāyda* 'benefit', *ġālya* 'expensive (F)', *ḥādša* 'eleventh (F)', *qābla* 'midwife', *rābʕa* 'fourth (F)', *ṣābʕa* 'seventh (F)', *ṣāḥba* 'female friend', *šāyba* 'old woman', *tālta* 'third', *tāmna* 'eighth (F)', *tānya* 'second (F)', *ṭānša* 'twelfth (F)', *xāmša* 'fifth (F)', *žābya* 'pool';

---

[27] This word appears in the expression: *ḥāžb tāʕ hlāli* 'the moon eyebrow', describing a pretty woman.

[28] Even though, morphologically, this word should be perceived as masculine, it was used to indicate slaves of both genders and mostly female ones. It is accompanied by a female demonstrative pronoun, e.g., *hādi əl-xādəm* 'this female slave', and when a pronominal suffix is added, it acquires the feminine marker, e.g., *xadəmti* 'my female slave'.

- second and third radical alike, C¹v̄C²C²a:

    ḍārra 'second wife', *šābba* 'pretty, beautiful', *šātta* 'sixth (F)'.

2.3.6. CCv̄C

The historical development of the CA vowel system that has led to the reduction of short vowels in open syllables in the Maghrebi dialects has significantly contributed to the productivity of this pattern: the classical patterns *faʕāl*, *fuʕāl*, and *fiʕāl*—and their feminine counterparts with the /-a/ suffix—after losing the short vowel in the first syllable, shifted to the pattern CCv̄C (Cohen 1975, 154).

- three regular consonants, C¹C²v̄C³:

    blād 'city', *ḍlām* 'darkness', *flān* 'anonymous', *ḥmār* 'donkey', *ḥsān* 'horse', *ḥžām* 'belt, loins',[29] *nzās* 'pears (coll.)', *qbūr* 'grave', *rmād* 'ashes', *ṣrāb* 'wine', *šlām* 'peace', *šmāḥ* 'pardon', *šrāḥ* 'permission', *štār* 'curtain', *trāb* 'soil', *wṣīf* 'black person', *ysār* 'left', *žmān* 'time',[30] *žnāḥ* 'wing', *žwāb* 'response, letter';

- second and third consonant alike, C¹C²v̄C²:

    rṣāṣ 'lead', *sqāq* 'exterior, street'.

---

[29] In Jewish Gabes this word serves for both 'belt' and 'loins'. It appears in the blessing: *nṣalla zġārək mən ḥžārək* 'may your offspring come out of your loins'.

[30] This word connotes a higher register, while *wuqt* is used in an ordinary communicative situation.

2.3.7. CCv̄Ca

This group contains only physical objects and abstract nouns:

dbāra 'advice', ḥkāya 'story', mrāya 'mirror',[31] mšāḥa 'towel', nẓāṣa 'pear', qrāya 'lecture, reading', krūma 'neck', rxāma 'marble', šnāša 'custom', šxāna 'heat', zyāra 'visit to a holy site'.

2.3.8. CCīC

The pattern CCīC corresponds to the CA pattern faʕīl and covers many adjectives, as well as some collectives:

- three regular consonants, C¹C²īC³:
  bʕīd 'distant, remote', ḍʕīf 'skinny, slim', mlīḥ 'good', mrīḍ 'sick', nsīb 'a person close to the family', qdīm 'old', qrīb 'close', qṣīr 'short', šʕīr 'barley', šmīn 'fat', ṭwīl 'long', xrīf 'autumn', ẓġīr 'small', zbīb 'raisins',[32] žmīʕ 'together', žrīd 'palms (coll.)';
- second and third consonant alike, C¹C²īC²:
  bnīn 'tasty', ḥdīd 'iron', ḥrīr 'silk', ḥšīš 'herb', ṣḥīḥ 'healthy', xfīf 'light', ždīd 'new'.

2.3.9. CCīCa

- three regular consonants, C¹C²īC³a:
  dbīḥa 'slaughter', ktība 'writing', mžīya 'favour', nbīla 'kind of bracelet', qṭīla 'killing', tnīya 'route, way';

---

[31] The plural form of this noun, mrāyāt, means also 'glasses'.

[32] This occurs in a proverb related to friendship: *məʕand ḥbība ḥatta žbība*, literally: 'from a friend, even a raisin', meaning that even a small gift from a friend brings a lot of joy.

- second and third consonant alike, C¹C²īC²a:
  ḥdīda 'bracelet', tšīša 'a bit' (mostly used in Djerba).

2.3.10. CCūC

- three regular consonants, C¹C²ūC³:
  dxūl 'entering',[33] flūš 'money', ṣxūn/šxūn 'hot', xrūž 'leaving';
- second and third consonant alike, C¹C²ūC²:
  ḥmūm 'soot, bad thing, misery'.

2.3.11. CCūCa

- three regular consonants, C¹C²ūC³a:
  ʕqūba 'punishment', flūka 'ship, boat', ʕrūṣa 'bride';
- second and third consonant alike, C¹C²ūC²a:
  ʕžūža 'old woman', ḍrūra 'harm'.

2.3.12. C¹vC²C²āC³

The aforementioned process of the loss of short vowels in open syllables has brought about a vast unification of various intensive patterns known from CA, which have as a distinctive feature the gemination of the second radical followed by a long vowel. Historically, the CvCCāC pattern comprises principally nouns indicating professions, but the whole CvCCv̄C group includes also some intensive adjectives (Wright 2005, 137). The patterns with

---

[33] dxūl designates the action of entering, as opposed to dəxla, which means the physical entrance of a house. The night of the wedding, the Hebrew ליל החופה, is called in Jewish Gabes līlət əd-dxūl, namely the night when the bride enters the house of the groom.

geminated second radical are often called 'intensive', as they denote agents who repeatedly perform an action (Cohen 1975, 162):

- three different consonants, $C^1vC^2C^2\bar{a}C^3$:
  bənnāy 'builder', *bəyyāʕ* 'vendor', *dəbbāġ* 'tanner',[34] *dəbbāḥ* 'butcher', *dəbbān* 'flies (coll.)', *dəllāʕ* 'watermelon', *dəxxān* 'smoker', *fəllāḥ* 'farmer', *gəddāb* 'liar', *ġannāy* 'singer', *ḥammāl* 'porter', *ḥaššād* 'jealous person',[35] *ḥawwāt* 'fisherman', *ṣayyād* 'hunter', *šəbbāt* 'Sabbath', *təffāḥ* 'apples (coll.)', *ṭabbāx* 'cook', *xabbāž* 'baker', *xannāb* 'thief', *xarrāž* 'outdoors merchant', *xawwān* 'swindler, fraud', *xayyāṭ* 'tailor', *ṣəḅḅāṭ* 'shoe';
- second and third radicals alike, $C^1vC^2C^2\bar{a}C^2$:
  ʕaššāš 'guard, watchman', *ḥaddād* 'blacksmith', *ḥammām* 'bath', *ḥaṭṭāb* 'lumberjack'.

2.3.13. $C^1vC^2C^2\bar{a}C^3a$

Most of the items in this group designate feminine names of occupations, as well as names of instruments and tools:

---

[34] This appears in the proverb: *əbṭən ətžīb sabbāġ o dabbāġ* 'the same belly can give birth to either a tanner or a painter', meaning that the same mother can give birth to two very different children.

[35] The figure of the jealous person is strongly connected to the phenomenon of the evil eye, and the word *ḥaššād* therefore appears in multiple proverbs and prayers against the evil eye, which are called *təlwīda*, e.g., *ʕīn l-aḥšūd fīha ʕūd, məlḥ wəddād fi ʕīn əl-ḥaššād* 'splinter in the eye of jealousy, salt and repelling smoke in the eye of a jealous person' (Tobi 2016, 286).

dəbbāna 'fly', fəllāya 'thin comb', məllāḥa 'salt cellar', nəmmāla 'ant', ṣəkrāna 'drunk (F)', xarrāfa 'story, anecdote', ẓəffāra 'whistle', žəbbāna 'cemetery', žərrāya 'mattress'.

2.3.14. C¹vC²C²ūC³

As has been noted by Cohen (1975, 164), the aspect of intensity is hardly perceivable in this pattern. It includes, nevertheless, some items denoting tools and concrete substantives:

ʕallūš 'lamb', bəkkūš 'mute', fərrūž 'cock', faqqūṣ 'cucumbers (coll.)', kəmmūn 'cumin', qaṭṭūṣ 'cat', səllūm 'ladder', xarrūb 'carobs (coll.)', žəllūž 'almonds (coll.)'.

2.3.15. C¹vC²C²ūC³a

ḥallūṭa 'earring', dabbūža 'bottle', kəmmūna 'Kəmmūna' (female proper name), žəllūža 'almond'.

2.3.16. C¹vC²C²īC³

bəṭṭīx 'melons (coll.)', šəbbīk 'window'.[36]

2.3.17. C¹vC²C²īC³a

rəttīla 'spider' (possibly < Ital. *rangatela* 'spiderweb'), šəkkīna[37] 'knife', šurrīya 'shirt'.

---

[36] There exists also a variant šəbbāk.

[37] This item in Jewish Tunis is masculine and has the form šəkkīn (Cohen 1975, 185).

2.4. Patterns with Four Consonants

It is rather difficult to ascribe one specific semantic value to this pattern. In some respects, it collects items of similar meaning to words of the $C^1vC^2C^2\bar{v}C^3$ pattern, namely, nouns denoting instruments and professions. Additionally, items of a foreign provenance have been included in this paradigm. It is worth noting that many of the items found here in fact repeat the first two consonants of the root in the second syllable of the word, i.e., $C^1vC^2C^1\bar{v}C^2$.

- $C^1vC^2C^3\bar{v}C^4$:
  fənžān 'coffee cup', *məšmāš* 'apricots (coll.)', *qəbqāb* 'wooden shoe', *səlṭān* 'sultan', *səmsār* 'mediator, go-between';
- $C^1vC^2C^3\bar{v}C^4a$:
  məšmāša 'apricot', *ṣaqṣāqa* 'savings box, puppet making noise', *šaqlāla* 'scandal', *šərlīya* 'lock';
- $C^1vC^2C^3\bar{u}C^4$:
  baʕbūṣ 'female reproductive organ',[38] *barkūn* 'balcony',[39] *darbūž* 'balustrade', *gənfūd* 'hedgehog',[40] *karmūṣ* 'figs

---

[38] Surprisingly, this rather low-register and vulgar word denotes, in Jewish Tunis, the tail of an animal (Cohen 1975, 170). Due to the connotation of this word, Jewish speakers from Gabes use *dīl* to denote 'tail'.

[39] This word comes from Italian and appears also as *balkūn* due to the interchanges of the liquids.

[40] The hedgehog is a symbol of something unimportant and insignificant. It appears in the proverb: *ʕīṭa u šhūd ʕal dbīḥāt ganfūd*, literally 'shouting and testimony because of the slaughter of a hedgehog', meaning that there is a lot of fuss for no significant reason.

(coll.)', *šəlšūl* 'spinal column', *šərdūk* 'cock', *ṣəndūq* 'box, case', *ẓaṛbūʕ* 'rat';

- C¹vC²C³ūC⁴a:
  ḥarbūša 'pill', *gəržūma* 'throat',[41] *šakšūka* 'shakshouka', *xənfūša* 'beetle, cockroach';
- C¹vC²C³īC⁴:
  barmīl 'barrel',[42] *yaṣmīn* 'jasmine (coll.)';
- C¹vC²C³vC⁴:
  fəlfəl 'pepper', *kərkəm* 'turmeric', *šaḥləb* 'sweet beverage made of sorghum', *zəʕtər* 'thyme';
- C¹Cv²C³C⁴:
  krəmb 'cabbage', *šfənž* 'doughnut';
- C¹vC²C³C⁴a:
  fədkla 'joke', *žəlžla* 'earthquake'.

2.5. Items with Five Consonants

This small group contains mostly items of foreign origin: *sfaržəl* 'quinces (coll.)', *qranfəl* 'carnation', *zmagārd* 'emerald'.

---

[41] On the metaphorical level, this word serves also as a synonym for 'beautiful voice', e.g., *ʕandu gəržūma* 'he has beautiful voice, he sings very well'.

[42] Metaphorically, this word also designates an obese person.

2.6. Patterns with Prefixes

2.6.1. Prefix /m-/

As has been noticed by Yoda (2005, 233), patterns with the prefix /m-/ represent a wide array of morphological functions, including names of places and names of instruments, as well as verbal nouns, participles of derived stems, and passive participles of the first stem. Many of the passive participles have acquired properties of nouns and function in the dialect as items independent from the verbal form.

- mvCāC:
  məžān 'scale';
- mvCCūC:
  mahbūl 'crazy, insane', *maḥlūl* 'open', *məktūb* 'written', *maqrūḍ* 'sweet pastry made of honey', *mažrūḥ* 'hurt, wounded', *məlbūš* 'dressed';
- mvCCāC:
  məftāḥ 'key', *məṣmār* 'nail';
- mvCCvC:
  mənkəb 'elbow',[43] *məšləm* 'Muslim', *maxžən* 'storeroom, shed', *məžləš* 'council';
- mCvCCa:
  mġərfa 'spoon', *mṭərqa* 'hammer';

---

[43] This item appears in the proverb: *mūt l-mṛa l-ṛāžəl kīf ḍəṛba fi-l-mənkəb tūžaʕ wa fīsʕa təmši* 'when one's wife dies it is like hitting an elbow—it hurts a lot, but it goes away quickly'.

- mvCCāCa:
  mərwāḥa 'fan'.

2.6.2. Prefix /v-/

Historically, this pattern corresponds to CA *ʔafʕal* and includes adjectives in the comparative and superlative. Names of colours and physical features are also classified in this group.

- vCCv

  Nouns classified in this pattern have as the third radical of their root /w/ or /y/:

  aḥla 'sweeter' (< *ḥlūw*), *aġla* 'more expensive' (< *ġāli*);

- vCCvC:

  əbrəd 'colder', *abyəḍ* 'white', *ədyəq* 'narrower', *aḥdəq* 'stingier', *aḥmar* 'red', *akbər* 'bigger', *ašwəd* 'blacker', *aṭraṣ* 'deaf', *awšaʕ* 'wider', *axfəf* 'easier', *azġər* 'smaller'.

2.7. Patterns with Suffixes

2.7.1. Suffix /-ān/

In Jewish Gabes, as in other Maghrebi dialects, this scheme corresponds to the CA forms *faʕlān*, *fuʕlān*, and *fiʕlān* (Wright 2005, 111). As has been pointed out by Cohen (1912, 281), this suffix indicates a state, rather than a quality. From a morphological point of view, many of the items in this group are verbal nouns of the first stem.

- three regular consonants:

  ʕaryān 'naked', *ʕaṭšān* 'thirsty', *bənyān* 'action of constructing', *ġoẓlān* 'gazelles (coll.)', *ḥafyān* 'barefoot', *ṣəkrān* 'drunk', ṣəryān 'buying, action of purchase', žaʕān 'hungry'.

2.7.2. Suffix /-i/

As in CA, the /-i/ suffix is added to nouns to turn them into adjectives, i.e., designating the property denoted by the root. From a morphological point of view, compared to CA, in the Maghrebi dialects, this suffix has been reduced to a single /-i/ vowel, which corresponds to the suffix /-ya/ in the feminine. Among many functions of this suffix, it is worth noting that, when added to the name of a country or city, it designates nationality or provenience, e.g., tūnəš 'Tunis'–tūnši 'Tunisian'.

- CV̄Ci:
  žīri 'Algerian';
- CvCCi:
  baḥri 'marine, western',[44] gabši 'from Gabes', maṣri 'Egyptian', ṣayfi 'summery', šətwi 'wintry', žərbi 'from Djerba';
- CV̄CCi / CCV̄Ci:
  flāni 'anonymous', grīgi 'Greek', šwāki 'brown-red'.[45]

---

[44] The basic meaning of this adjective is 'marine', as it derives from bḥar 'sea'. However, probably due to association with the sunset, it also means 'western'. In Jewish Gabes, this form replaced the original CA word for 'western', i.e., ġarbi.

[45] This word designates also shells of unripe nuts which were used by women to dye their lips. Chewing the peel gave the lips a brown-red tinge, hence the name of the colour. In addition, these nutshells were used to dye clothes. The colour of clothes dyed in this way is called ḥrām šwāki.

2.7.3. Suffix /-īya/

gabšīya 'woman from Gabes',[46] *grigrīya* 'Greek woman', *tūnšīya* 'woman from Tunis', *žīrīya* 'woman from Algeria' (also a female proper name), *žərbīya* 'woman from Djerba'.

2.7.4. Suffix /-āni/

The morpheme /-āni/ is characteristic of adjectives formed from prepositions denoting location or time, hence Cohen (1975, 180) calls them "the adjectives of position:"

axrāni 'last, the one that is at the end', *barrāni* 'external, foreigner, the one that is outside', *dəxlāni* 'interior, the one that is inside', *fuqqāni* 'the one that is below, beneath', *lūṭāni* 'lower, the one that is on the ground', *wuṣṭāni* 'middle, the one that is between'.

2.7.5. Suffix /-ži/

This suffix is of Turkish origin and designates names of professions. As mentioned by Cohen (1975, 180), the morpheme in question is already attested in CA, but its distribution in the Tunisian dialect intensified over time:

ḥammāmži 'owner of the hammam', *qahwāži* 'owner of the coffee shop'.

---

[46] This word appears in the proverb: *ya wāxəd gabšəya, ṭəmṛa ʕala mšīya* 'when a man gets married to a woman from Gabes, she is like a precious date'.

2.7.6. Suffix /-ūt/

Similarly to the morpheme mentioned above, the suffix /-ūt/ is also of foreign origin, namely, it is a loan from Hebrew. In Jewish Gabes, as in Hebrew, it denotes abstract nouns. Some words with this ending have been assimilated into the dialect whole, while others have an Arabic root combined with the Hebrew suffix:

šaḥḥūt 'avarice',[47] tmimūt 'naivety', xẓariūt 'cruelty'.

2.8. Irregular Nouns

This group contains nouns that are formed irregularly and to which no CA pattern can be ascribed. The vast majority of them are loans from other languages, mostly Italian, Turkish, French, and Spanish:

buḷṣu 'wrist' (< Ital. polso), brūdu 'stock' (< Ital. brodo), fāmīlya 'family' (< Ital. famiglia), gərṛa 'war' (< Ital. guerra), gūf 'body' (< Heb. גוף), mistru 'teacher, professor' (< Ital. maestro), mubīlya 'furniture' (< Ital. mobilia), rfūa 'medicine, medication (< Heb. רפואה), rīgālu 'gift' (< Ital. regalo), ḥānūt 'shop' (< Heb. חנות), tīla (< Sp. tela) 'fabric'.

---

[47] While the other two words listed here are of clearly Hebrew provenience, the case of šaḥḥūt is interesting from both a morphological and an etymological point of view. It consists of the Arabic root š.ḥ.ḥ., to which has been agglutinated the Hebrew morpheme /-ūt/. The basic meaning of the root is 'dry', which was subsequently extended to denote also lack of generosity.

3.0. Internal Plural Patterns

As I have already mentioned in §1.5.2, there exist in Jewish Gabes two types of plural, namely the external, which is formed by the addition of fixed suffixes, and the internal, which is characterised by a high degree of unpredictability. The formation of the internal plural is based on the allomorphy developed by the transition of a singular pattern into a different syllabic structure denoting the plural. This change might involve the input of additional consonants or vowels of a new quality (Ratcliffe 2011). As observed by Cohen (1975, 194), the number of possible plural patterns has significantly shrunk compared to CA. In Jewish Tunis, seventeen patterns are attested, as opposed to the twenty-six of the classical language. Wright (2005, 199) gives an even higher number, twenty-nine, of which five are defined as rare. As in the case of singular patterns, the reason behind this reduction is the loss of *hamza* and elision of short vowels in open syllables.

In the vast majority of grammars, both of CA and of Maghrebi dialects, the topic of the broken plural is limited to an analytic presentation of all the attested patterns along with their examples; sporadically, the corresponding singular patterns are given. As argued by Ratcliffe (2011), this approach might suggest that the broken plural is formed in a completely random way and there is no phonological or morphological motivation behind the way the singular is associated with the plural. However, numerous studies have undermined this assumption, showing that the distribution of the plural patterns is conditioned by a few factors. For CA, five principal criteria have been established with reference to the singular form that determine the distribution of its plural counterpart: (1) prosodic structure of the singular stem, moraic, then syllabic; (2) presence of the gender marker; (3) quality of the stem vowel; (4) word class (adjective/noun); (5) rational or non-rational referent (Ratcliffe 2002, 89). These factors differ in terms of their nature, namely, (1) and (3) are phonological, (2) is formal, and (4) and (5) are functional. Therefore, it is virtually impossible to build any taxonomy of the singular based on all the criteria. Ratcliffe chose the first three factors, grouping the singular patterns into six categories and assigning to them attested plural patterns. This scheme involves only items attested in CA and shows that both phonological factors (e.g., presence of a glide or a weak consonant) and morphological ones (e.g., gender marker) condition the choice of a plural pattern.

As has already been mentioned previously, the system of plural patterns in modern dialects of Arabic is considerably different from the one described above. One might posit a question as to whether the incorporation of new nouns in modern dialects leads to the reinforcement of already existing patterns, or, on the contrary, brings about the emergence of new allomorphs. Ratcliffe (2002, 103) studied a corpus of nouns in Moroccan Arabic and reached the conclusion that the natural loss of allomorphs is followed by changes in the distribution of others, and, finally, by the creation of new patterns. This discovery provides evidence that native speakers are indeed capable of developing new grammatical rules regarding the allomorphs, and therefore that they possess deep morphological comprehension.

The present section will therefore have three principal aims: (1) presentation of the collected data, (2) establishment of possible rules conditioning the association of singular patterns with a given plural allomorph, (3) detection of possible new internal plural patterns in Jewish Gabes.

3.1. Patterns with Two Consonants and One Long Vowel

- CūC:
  dūd (< dūda) 'worms', ṣūd (< aṣwad) 'black';
- CīC:
  ḥīl (< ḥāyl) 'not fertilised';
- CCa:
  nša 'women'.[48]

3.2. Patterns with Three Consonants

3.2.1. CCvC

As this allomorph is associated with several singular patterns, I will break down the paradigms according to their singular forms:

a) singular feminine forms of the pattern CvCCa:
ʕḍam (< ʕaḍma) 'eggs', ʕləb (< ʕalba) 'tins', ʕləq (< ʕalqa) 'leeches', ʕṛəm (< ʕaṛma) 'piles', ġləl (< ġalla) 'fruits', ẓnəq (< ẓənqa) 'blind alleys';

b) singular nouns and adjectives with long /ī/:
qdəm (< qdīm) 'old', ṭrəq (< ṭrīq) 'roads', ždəd (< ždīd) 'new';

---

[48] There exists also another variant of the plural of this word, found predominantly in Bedouin dialects, namely, nšāwīn 'women'.

c) singular adjectives designating colours and properties:
ʕwər (< aʕwər) 'one-eyed', kḥəl (< akḥal) 'black', zrəq (< azraq) 'blue'.

3.2.2. CəCCa

ṭəbba (< ṭbīb) 'doctors', wəžra (< wžīr) 'ministers'.

3.2.3. CCāC

The following groups are associated with this pattern:

a) nouns of the singular schemes CvCC(a) and CCvC(a):
ʕbād (<ʕbəd) 'people, men', ʕwām (<ʕām) 'years', ʕrās̆ (<ʕars̆) 'weddings', bgār (<bəgra) 'cows', bnāt (<bənt) 'daughters', ffām (<fəmm) 'mouth', ḥbāl (< ḥbəl) 'ropes', ḥbās̆ (<ḥabs̆) 'prisons', kbās̆ (< kəbs̆) 'muttons', klāb (<kəlb) 'dogs', nfāṣ (< nəfṣ) 'halves', ryāḥ (<rīḥ) 'winds', s̆wād (<əs̆wəd) 'black', ṭfār (<ṭfər) 'nails', wdān (< wudən) 'ears', wqāt (< wuqt) 'times', xs̆ām (< xs̆əm) 'noses', žnās̆ (< žəns̆) 'species, kinds', žbāl (< žbəl) 'mountains', žmāl (< žməl) 'camels';

b) nouns of the patterns CūC, CāC, and CīC, where the second radical semi-vowel reappears in the plural:
ʕyād (<ʕīd) 'festivals', dyāṛ (<dāṛ) 'houses', ḥwās̆ (< ḥūs̆) 'houses, properties', lwāḥ (<lūḥ) 'planks, boards', ṣwāq (<ṣūq) 'souks';

c) adjectives of the pattern CCīC:
bnān (<bnīn) 'tasty', ḥbāb (<ḥbīb) 'beloved, dear', ġlāḍ (< ġlīḍ) 'thick', kbār (<kbīr) 'big', mlāḥ (<mlīḥ) 'good', ṃṛāḍ (<ṃṛīḍ) 'sick', nḍāf (<nḍīf) 'clean', qrāb (<qrīb)

'near, close', šmān (<šmīn) 'fat', ṭwāl (< ṭwīl) 'long', xfāf (<xfīf) 'light, easy', zġār (<zġīr) 'small (PL), children', ždād (<ždīd) 'new';

d) some nouns of the pattern CāCvC:
ṛžāl (< ṛāzəl) 'men', ṣḥāb (<ṣāḥəb) 'friends'.

3.2.4. CCūC

This allomorph is closely related to the CCāC pattern and covers a similar range of singular schemes:

a) nouns of the pattern CvCC(a)/CCvC:
bṭūn (<bṭən) 'bellies', byūr (<bīr) 'water wells', drūʕ (<drāʕ) 'arms', drūž (<dərža) 'stairs', dyūb (<dīb) 'wolves', flūš 'money', frūx (<farx) 'little birds, bastards', mlūk (<məlk) 'kings', ktūf (<ktəf) 'shoulders', kṭūṭ (<kəṭṭ) 'cats', nžūm (<nəžma) 'stars', qlūb (<qəlb) 'hearts', ṛyūṣ (<ṛāṣ) 'heads', ṣyūf (<ṣīf) 'summers', šhūd (<šāhəd) 'witnesses', šhūr (<šhər) 'months', šyūf (<šīf) 'swords', ṭrūf (<ṭarf) 'pieces', ṭyūr (<ṭīr) 'birds', žlūd (<žəld) 'belts', žnūb (<žnəb) 'sides', žnūn (< žənn) 'ghosts', žyūt (<žīt) 'olives';

b) nouns of the pattern CvC²C²:
dmūm (<dəmm) 'blood', ṣṛūṛ (<ṣaṛṛ) 'secrets',[49] šnūn (<šənn) 'teeth', xdūd (<xədd) 'cheeks', ždūd (<žədd) 'ancestors, grandparents';

---

[49] The vowel quality of this form is conditioned by the phonetic environment, namely, in lieu of the expected /ū/, the /ō/ vowel occurs due to vowel rounding between two instances of emphatic /ṛ/.

c) nouns of the pattern CīC:

byūt (<*bīt*) 'rooms', *dyūl* (<*dīl*) 'tails', *dyūn* (<*dīn*) 'debts', *xyūṭ* (<*xīṭ*) 'sewing threads'.

3.2.5. CCīC

This pattern is extremely rare in Jewish Gabes, just as it is in CA. Cohen (1975, 196) points out that, in Jewish Tunis, there is only one noun that forms its plural in this way, namely *maʕža–mʕīž* 'goats'. In Jewish Gabes *ḥmār–ḥmīr* 'donkeys' is also attested. In Jewish Tripoli and Muslim Tunis, apart from the two paradigms mentioned here, one can find also *ʕabd–ʕbīd* 'black servants' (Singer 1985, 583; Yoda 2005, 240).

3.2.6. CvC²C²āC

This corresponds to the CA pattern *fuʕʕāl* and is associated with the singular pattern Cv̄CvC, which usually denotes names of professions (Wright 2005, 206; Cohen 1975, 196):

ḥakkām (<*ḥākəm*) 'judges', *kəffār* (<*kāfər*) 'blasphemers', *šəkkān* (<*šākən*) 'inhabitants', *ṣarrāq* (<*ṣārəq*) 'thieves', *xaddām* (<*xādəm*) 'servants'.

3.2.7. CCāyvC

Most of the plural forms in this class derive from the singular pattern CCv̄C(a). Nonetheless, occasionally some nouns of the CvCC(a) pattern are associated with this allomorph as well:

ḥdāyəd (<*ḥdīda*) 'bracelets', *ḥṣāyən* (<*ḥṣān*) 'horses', *qmāyəž* (<*qməžža*) 'shirts', *šlāyəf* (<*šəlfa*) 'sisters-in-law', *ṭbāyəx*

(<ṭbīxa) 'meals, foods', dqāyəq (<dqīqa) 'minutes', xlāyəq (< xlīqa) 'figures, shapes, creatures', ḥwāyəž (<ḥāža) 'things'.

3.2.8. Suffix /-ān/

Here have been classified both forms possessing three regular radicals (CvCCān) and forms with second radical semi-vowel (C¹vC³ān). The second group is particularly abundant:

a) nouns with three regular consonants:
bəldān (<blād) 'cities', xərfān (<xrūf) 'lambs';

b) nouns of the singular pattern CāC (second radical semi-vowel):
bībān (<bāb) 'doors', bīṭān (<bāṭ) 'armpits', fīrān (<fāṛ) 'mice', ḥīṭān (<ḥīṭ) 'walls', kīšān (<kāš) 'mugs', šīšān (<šāš) 'foundations', žīrān (<žār) 'neighbours';

c) nouns of the singular pattern CCv̄ (third radical semi-vowel):
ʕadwān (<ʕdū) 'enemies', ʕaṣyān (<ʕṣa) 'sticks'.

3.3. Patterns with Four Consonants

This pattern corresponds to two CA patterns, namely CaCāCiC and CaCāCīC (Yoda 2005, 241). A wide array of singular patterns form the plural by means of this allomorph, including both nouns with geminated second radicals and nouns with four radicals.

a) nouns with four radicals:
ʕqārəb (<ʕaqrab) 'scorpions', ʕṣāfər (<ʕaṣfūr) 'birds', fkārən (< fakrūn) 'tortoises', fnāžən (<fənžān) 'coffee cups', kwākəb (<kawkəb) 'planets', mnākəb (<mənkəb) 'elbows', m̥ṣāmər (<m̥əṣmār) 'nails', ṣbābət (<ṣəbbāt)

'shoes', ṣmāṣaṛ (<ṣamṣāṛ) 'brokers', ṣnādaq (<ṣandūq) 'boxes', škākən (<šəkkīna) 'knives', šnāšəl (< šənšla) 'chains', xrārəž (<xərrāža) 'drains';

b) nouns with second radical geminated:
blālət (<bəllūta) 'earrings', bžāžəl (<bažžūla) 'udders', kšākəš (<kəškāš) 'colanders', šbābəl (<šəbbāla) 'fountains';

c) there is one attested noun which originally had *hamza* as its first radical that forms its plural according to this scheme:
arānəb (<arnəb) 'rabbits'.

3.3.1. CwāCəC

In the vast majority of the grammars, this pattern is not treated separately, but rather is classified as an allomorph of the CCv̄CvC pattern (Cohen 1975, 198; Yoda 2005, 242; Ritt-Benmimoun 2014, 254). Nonetheless, I decided to give it the status of a separate pattern, as there is a regular shift from the /ā/ vowel in the singular to /-wa/ in the plural, similar to that of long /ī/ to /ay/ in the CCayvC pattern. The shift is attested in nouns that, in the singular, contain both long and short /a/:

a) nouns with long /ā/ after the first radical:
ḥwāžəb (<ḥāžəb) 'eyebrows', mwākəl (<mākla) 'foods', šwārəb (<šārəb) 'lips', šwāraʕ (<šāraʕ) 'streets', ṭwāwil (<ṭāwla) 'tables', žwāmaʕ (<žāmaʕ) 'mosques';

b) nouns with short /a/ after the first radical:
dwāməš (<damūš) 'caves, tunnels', kwānən (<kanūn) 'ovens', ṣwābən (<ṣabūn) 'soaps, detergents';

c) some monosyllabic words possessing short /ā/ also form their plural in this way:

ḍwāfar (<*ḍfar*) 'nails', *ṣwābaʕ* (<*ṣbaʕ*) 'fingers', *žwānaḥ* (<*žnāḥ*) 'wings'.

3.4. Patterns with Suffixes

3.4.1. Suffix /-i/

As in Jewish Tunis, this pattern in Jewish Gabes is highly productive and covers a variety of singular patterns, the majority of which are feminine. The only masculine noun in this pattern is *krāši* (<*kərši*) 'chairs'.

a) feminine nouns with suffixes /-īya/ and /-ya/:
fwāki (<*fākya*) 'dried fruits', *wẓāġi* (<*wəẓġa*) 'lizards', *ẓṛābi* (<*ẓaṛbīya*) 'carpet';

b) feminine nouns with geminated second radical and third radical /y/:
flāli (<*fəllāya*) 'combs', *ẓrāri* (<*ẓərrāya*) 'mattresses';

c) feminine nouns with third radical /w/:
kšāwi (<*kəšwa*) 'costumes', *lġāwi* (<*ləġwa*) 'languages';

d) some nouns of the pattern CCā:
ʕašāwi (<*ʕaša*) 'dinners', *rdāwi* (<*rda*) 'curtains, blinds';

e) some nouns with first radical /a/ or /y/ due to the loss of *hamza*:
aṛāḍi (<*aṛḍ*) 'grounds', *ašāmi* (<*əšm*) 'names', *ybāri* (<*yəbra*) 'needles'.

3.4.2. Suffix /-a/

There is a relatively small group of plural patterns that, in addition to the internal modulation of syllable structure, also admit the /-a/ suffix. This type of pattern has been termed a 'mixed' plural by Cohen (1975, 201), due to the double marking.

CvCCa

All the examples classified in this category derive from the singular pattern CCīC:

ḥarfa (<ḥrīf) 'clients', šərka (<šrīk) 'companies, firms', ṣəlba (<ṣlīb) 'crosses', ṭəbba (<ṭbīb) 'doctors'.

CCāCa

Some items of the pattern CvCCān form their plural in this way:

ʕrāya (<ʕaryān) 'naked', ḥfāya (<ḥafyān) 'barefoot', xḍāra 'vegetables'.

Additionally, some names of origins and ethnicities are associated with this allomorph:

ġrāba (<ġarbi) 'Moroccans', rwāma (<rūmi) 'Christians', žrāba (<žərbi) 'from Djerba'.

CCūCa

dkūra (<dkar) 'males', ṣyūḍa (<ṣayḍ) 'lions'.

CwāCCa

ṣwālda (<ṣūldi) 'pennies', twānša (<tūnši) 'Tunisians'.

4.0. Diminutive

Both substantives and adjectives can form the diminutive. The CA pattern of the masculine diminutive, *CuCayC*, has been replaced in Jewish Gabes, as well as in Jewish Tripoli and Jewish Tunis, by *CCəyyəC* (Cohen 1975, 204; Yoda 2005, 244). As pointed out by Cohen (1975, 204), the use of the diminutive is limited to women and children, and men use it mostly in an ironic context. Selected examples:

- biliteral nouns, e.g., Cv̄C > CCv̄Ca, *ḍāṛ* > *ḍwīṛa* 'little house';
- triliteral nouns, e.g., CCvC / CvCC > CCvyyvC: *kəlb* > *kləyyəb* 'small dog', *nəfṣ* > *nfəyyəṣ* 'small half',[50] *wəld* > *wləyyəd* 'little boy';
- CaCCa > CCīCCa, e.g., *ṭawla* > *ṭwīwla* 'little table';
- CvCCi > CCv̄Ci, e.g., *kərši* > *krīši* 'little chair';
- quadrilateral nouns, e.g, CvCCūCa, CvCCāC > CCīCīCa: *qaṭṭūṣa* > *qṭīṭīṣa* 'kitten', *ṣəbbāṭ* > *ṣbībīṭ* 'small shoe'.

5.0. Numerals

5.1. One to Ten

Counted nouns appear in the plural only when preceded by numbers 2–10. When accompanied by any higher numbers, the counted noun is in the singular. Below have been listed cardinal numbers with examples of masculine and feminine nouns. As can

---

[50] The etymological form of this item is *nəṣf*, but in Jewish Gabes there exists also a parallel form with metathesis, i.e., *nəfṣ*.

be inferred, only number 1 distinguishes formally between the two genders and causes inversion of the word order:

1. ʕabd wāḥəd, mṛa waḥda 'one man, one woman';
2. žūž ṛəžžāla, žūž amṛá 'two men, two women';
3. tlāt ẓġāṛ, tlāt əbnāt 'three boys, three girls';
4. arbʕa ḥyūt, arbʕa xūxāt 'four fish, four peaches';
5. xamš(a) aṛwāẓəl, xamša amṛá 'five men, five women';
6. šətta wlād, šəta amṛa 'six boys, six women';
7. šəbʕa aṛwāẓəl, šəbʕa amṛá 'seven men, seven women';
8. tmənīya aṛwāẓəl, tmənīya amṛá 'eight men, eight women';
9. təsʕa ḍyāṛ, təsʕa amṛá 'nine houses, nine women';
10. ʕaṣra qbūrāt, ʕaṣra amṛá 'ten graves, ten women'.

5.2. Eleven to Nineteen

11 ḥdāš, 12 taẓẓīna, 13 təlləṭāṣ, 14 aṛbʕaṭāṣ, 15 xaməṣṭāṣ, 16 ṣəṭṭāṣ, 17 ṣəbʕaṭāṣ, 18 təmənṭāṣ, 19 təsʕaṭāṣ.

5.3. Twenty to Ninety

The units always precede the tens.

    20 ʕaṣrīn, wāḥəd wa ʕaṣrīn, 30 tlatīn, wāḥəd wa ʕaṣrīn, 40 aṛbʕīn, wāḥəd wa aṛbʕīn, 50 xamšīn, wāḥəd wa xamšīn, 60 ṣəttīn, wāḥəd wa ṣəttīn, 70 šəbʕīn, wāḥəd wa šəbʕīn, 80 tmanīn, wāḥəd wa tmanīn, 90 təsʕīn, wāḥəd wa təsʕīn.

5.4. Hundreds and Thousands

Unlike with tens, when units appear with hundreds, they are placed after the hundreds.

100 mīya, 101 mīya wa wāḥəd, 102 mīya wa tnīn, 103 mīya wa tlāta, 132 mīya u tnīn u tlatīn, 200 miytīn, 300 tlat mīya, 400 arbʕa mīya, 500 xəmša mīya, 1000 alf, 2000 alfīn, 3000 tlāt alāf.

5.5. Days of the Week

nhār əl-ḥadd 'Sunday', nhār ət-tnīn 'Monday', nhār ət-tlāt 'Tuesday', nhār əl-arbʕa 'Wednesday', nhār əl-xmīš[51] 'Thursday', nhār žəmʕa 'Friday', nhār šəbbāt 'Saturday'.

6.0. Pronouns

6.1. Personal Pronouns

6.1.1. Independent Personal Pronouns

Table 48: Independent personal pronouns

	Singular	Plural
3M	hūwa	humma/hūma
3F	hiya	
2M	ənti / ənta	əntūm
2F	ənti	
1	āná / ána	aḥna

The stress in the first person singular and plural is not fixed and varies between ultimate and penultimate. In other dialects of the region, on the contrary, we observe a form with penultimate stress, i.e., ána (Cohen 1975, 210; Singer 1984, 250; Yoda 2005, 115). The classical form of the first-person plural, i.e., naḥnu, has

---

[51] Due to the social taboo relating to the evil eye, this day has two additional names: nhār əl-fardi 'unpaired day' and nhār ʕīn əl-ʕdu 'day in the eye of the enemy'.

been reduced in the majority of the Maghrebi dialects to ḥna/ ḥnān. The absence of the initial /n/ has been explained by Cohen (1912, 87) as dissimilation, which is supposedly an early development, given its wide distribution among the dialects of Arabic. The /a/ quality of the initial vowel in Jewish Gabes is the same as in Muslim Tunis (Singer 1984, 250) and can be explained by the proximity of the pharyngeal /ḥ/. Contrary to this, Jewish Tunis has in this place a rather unexpected /ə/ vowel (Cohen 1975, 211). In the Bedouin dialect of Maṛāzīg, both singular and plural forms of the first person have long ē at the end, i.e., anē 'I', ᵊḥnē 'we' (Ritt-Benmimoun 2014, 66).

Across many Jewish dialects of the region, the initial /h/ sound in the third person singular and plural is omitted; however, in the case of Jewish Gabes, the original consonantal manifestation is retained, mirroring a similar phenomenon found in Muslim dialects (Singer 1985, 250). Conversely, in various other Jewish dialects, this initial consonant has been excised, consequently giving rise to the emergence of the ūwa form (Cohen 1912, 336; Cohen 1985, 210; Yoda 2005, 115).

The forms of the second person singular are also somewhat exceptional compared to other Maghrebi dialects and especially the Jewish ones. The general tendency across the majority of the dialects is for the the feminine form to be used for both feminine and masculine (Cohen 1975, 211).[52] Jewish Djerba utilises ənti

---

[52] The historical background of this phenomenon has been given by Cohen (1975, 211), who claims that the predominance of the feminine form is related to the agglutination of the particle /-ya/ to the masculine form ənta in some dialects, i.e., əntīya. This hypothesis is supported by

for 2MS and *əntīn* for 2FS (Behnstedt 1998, 72). There is a similar situation in Jewish Algiers, where the latter has the form *əntīna* (Cohen 1912, 336). On the other hand, Muslim Algiers, Jewish Wad-Souf, and Bedouin Douz (Ritt-Benmimoun 2014, 66) have both forms. Jewish Gabes utilises both of these forms, with *ənti* being the dominant variant. Interstingly, the merger of these pronouns has not affected the verbal morphology, where the feminine forms of the second person are marked as such. The second person plural in Jewish Gabes preserves the classical form *ʔantum*, unlike Jewish Tunis and Jewish Algiers, which use a variant *(ə)ntumān*, or Jewish Djerba, where we find *əntūn*. As explained by Cohen (1975, 212), the /-ān/ suffix in this form could be an analogy to the plural marker of the nouns.

6.1.2. Pronominal Suffixes

Table 49: Pronominal suffixes

	Singular	Plural
3M	-u, -ū, -h	-həm
3F	-ha/-a	
2M	-ək, -k	-kəm
1	-i, -ni, -ya	-na

The distribution of the variations of some suffixes depends on the ending of the default form, namely, whether it ends with a consonant or a vowel. In the third person masculine singular, when a verb or a noun has a /u/ vowel at the end, the /u/ of the pro-

---

evidence from the dialect of Djidjelli, where the masculine form has two variants, i.e., *ənta* and *əntīna*.

noun is assimilated and subsequently long ū emerges, which attracts the stress. This phenomenon is attested in many Maghrebi dialects; however, some of them still possess traces of the original /h/. As reported by Cohen (1912, 338), in Muslim Algiers, nouns ending with a vowel regularly admit /-h/, e.g., ʕadūh 'his enemy'. When it comes to the Jewish speakers of Algiers, most of them tend to omit the final /h/, but, as pointed out by Cohen (1912, 339), some individuals do pronounce /h/, especially in 3PL forms of the past tense, e.g. *(h)ašplū^hu* 'they destroyed him'. Interestingly, in the same form, Muslim speakers use an /-ah/ suffix, e.g., *nsāuah* 'they forgot him' (Cohen 1912, 339). In Jewish Gabes, the original /h/ is attested to a limited extent, in past-tense forms of verbs with a weak third radical that have an /a/ vowel in the third person singular. In this case, instead of /u/, /h/ is added, e.g., *nšāh* 'he forgot him'. Alternatively, an extra long /ā/ vowel emerges, e.g., *xda* 'he took', *xdā* 'he took him'. Also, nouns ending with /-a/ admit the /h/ suffix (see *ġda* 'lunch' below).

In the second person singular, the CA suffix /-ka/ contracted in the Maghrebi dialects to /-k/ when a word finishes with a vowel, and to /-ək/ when the ending is consonantal. The same variation is attested in Jewish Tunis (Cohen 1975, 213). In the plural, the suffix corresponds to classical /-kum/, and in Jewish Gabes, as in other dialects, can be realised either as /-kəm/ or, in a labial and pharyngeal context, as /-kom/.

The suffix of the first person singular has three possible variants, namely /-ni/, /-i/, and /-ya/. Their distribution is conditioned grammatically, namely, /-ni/ is added only to verbs, /-i/

and /-ya/ to nouns. The latter is applied only to nouns ending with vowels.

Nouns ending with /-i/, like kərši 'chair', constitute a separate category. As is demonstrated below, the final vowel is elided in the singular and the personal pronouns are added to the root kərš-, but the final vowel is retained in the rest of the persons, where the suffix starts with a consonant. Contrary to this, in Jewish Tripoli, the final vowel of the noun is preserved throughout the whole inflection (Yoda 2005, 121).

Below are presented some examples including both consonantal and vocalic endings.

Table 50: Examples of nouns with pronominal suffixes

3MS	qalbu	his heart	xū(h)[53]	his brother
3FS	qalbha	her heart	xūha	her brother
2MS	qalbək	your heart	xūk	your brother
1SG	qalbi	my heart	xūya	my brother
3PL	qalbhəm	their heart	xūhəm	their brother
2PL	qalbkəm	your (PL) heart	xūkəm	your (PL) brother
1PL	qalbna	our heart	xūna	our brother
3MS	ġdāh	his lunch	kəršu	his chair
3FS	ġdāha	her lunch	kəršha	her chair
2MS	ġdāk	your lunch	kəršək	your chair
1SG	ġdāya	my lunch	kərši	my chair
3PL	ġdāhəm	their lunch	kəršīhəm	their chair
2PL	ġdākəm	your (PL) lunch	kəršīkəm	your (PL) chair
1PL	ġdāna	our lunch	kəršīna	our chair

The aforementioned examples do not demonstrate any fluctuations in terms of syllable structure. Nonetheless, some nominal

---

[53] The final /h/ is usually audible when an informant is asked to pronounce an isolated form; in free speech it tends to be elided.

patterns require replacement or deletion of a vowel once the pronoun is added. This is the case, for example, in disyllabic nouns with a short last vowel, e.g., ṣāḥəb 'friend'–ṣāḥbi 'my friend'. In turn, in nouns of the pattern CCəC, the position of the short vowel /ə/ is changed after adding the pronominal suffix in order to avoid a short vowel in an open syllable. Below the example of ṣḍəṛ 'breast' is given:

Table 51: ṣḍəṛ 'breast' with pronominal suffixes

3MS	ṣəḍṛu	his breast
3FS	ṣḍəṛha	her breast
2MS	ṣəḍṛək	your breast
1SG	ṣəḍṛi	my breast
3PL	ṣḍəṛhəm	their breast
2PL	ṣḍəṛkəm	your (PL) breast
1PL	ṣḍəṛna	our breast

Many words, however, do not admit pronominal suffixes, and instead the possessive particle *(ə)ntāʕ* is used. This applies particularly to words of foreign origin.

Table 52: *livro* (Ital.) 'book' with possessive particle

3MS	livro əntāʕu	his book
3FS	livro əntāha	her book
2MS	livro əntāʕk	your book
1SG	livro əntāʕay	my book
3PL	livro əntāhəm	their book
2PL	livro əntāʕkəm	your (PL) book
1PL	livro əntāʕna	our book

Below are presented examples of the weak verbs *nša* 'he forgot', which has a vocalic ending, and *žāt* 'she came', which has a consonantal ending, with personal pronouns added.

Table 53: *nša* 'he forgot' and *žāt* 'she came' with pronominal suffixes

3MS	nšāh	he forgot him	žātu	she came to him
3FS	nšāha	he forgot her	žātha	she came to her
2MS	nšāk	he forgot you	žātək	she came to you
1SG	nšāni	he forgot me	žātni	she came to me
3PL	nšāhəm	he forgot them	žāthəm	she came to them
2PL	nšākəm	he forgot you (PL)	žātkəm	she came to you (PL)
1PL	nšāna	he forgot us	žātna	she came to us

It is worth noting, however, that in Jewish Gabes the verb *ža* with a personal pronoun in the role of direct object is used to refer to abstract phenomena rather than people. It occurs often in expressions related to health conditions, e.g., *ṣ-ṣhar l-lāxər žātni šxāna* 'last month I got fever', *žātha* 'she got her period'. In turn, when it comes to a meeting of two people, a particle *ʕandi* or /-li/ is used, e.g., *hīya žāt ʕandna* 'she came to us'.

Above I presented short verbs, which do not change their syllable structure when a personal pronoun is added. In the case of verbs with three full radicals, however, the syllabification is modified:

Table 54: Strong verb with pronominal suffixes

3MS	qatlu	he killed him
3FS	qtəlha	he killed her
2MS	qatlək	he killed you
1SG	qtəlni	he killed me
3PL	qtəlhəm	he killed them
2PL	qtəlkəm	he killed you (PL)
1PL	qtəlna	he killed us

6.1.3. Dative Marker /l-/

In addition to regular agglutination of a personal pronoun as a direct object, some verbs admit also what Yoda (2005, 126) calls the 'enclitic dative marker', which corresponds to the classical preposition /-li/. The order is therefore as follows: verb, pronominal suffix, dative marker, pronominal suffix. Below I present examples of the prefix conjugation:

Table 55: Prefix conjugation with enclitic dative marker

3MS	yžībūlu	he brings him to him
3FS	yžībūlha	he brings him to her
2MS	yžībūlək	he brings him to you
1SG	yžībūli	he brings him to me
3PL	yžībūlhəm	he brings him to them
2PL	yžībūlkəm	he brings him to you (PL)
1PL	yžībūlna	he brings him to us

The inflection presented above includes only verbs with a vocalic ending. Below one can find an inflection with a consonantal ending:

Table 56: Suffix conjugation with enclitic dative marker

3MS	žābəthālu	she brought her to him
3FS	žābəthəlha	she brought her to her
2MS	žābəthālək	she brought her to you
1SG	žābəthāli	she brought her to me
3PL	žābəthalhəm	she brought her to them
2PL	žābəthalkəm	she brought her to you (PL)
1PL	žābəthalna	she brought her to us

6.2. Reflexive Pronoun

In Jewish Gabes, as in many other dialects of Arabic, the particle /rūḥ-/ is used to express reflexivity. It is inflected as follows:

Table 57: Inflection of particle /rūḥ-/

3MS	hažž rūḥu	he raised himself
3FS	qaṭlət rūḥḥa	she killed herself
2MS	ḍarriti rūḥək	you (FS) harmed yourself
1SG	ḍarrīt rūḥi	I harmed myself
3PL	ḍərbu rūḥḥəm	they hit themselves
2PL	ḍrəbtu rūḥkəm	you (PL) hit yourselves
1PL	ḍrəbna rūḥna	we hit ourselves

Another reflexive pronoun used in Jewish Gabes is /nəfš-/. This, however, has slightly different connotations. While /rūḥ-/ expresses physical reflexivity, /nəfš-/ is used in a more abstract context, e.g., *aḥšəb nəfšək li qāʕad fi-žnān* 'imagine yourself sitting in the garden'.[54] However, some verbs admit both variants. One of them is the verb 'to become', which in Jewish Gabes is expressed by the verb ʕməl + reflexive pronoun. In this case, both /rūḥ-/ and /nəfš-/ are correct. In Jewish Tunis, the situation is exactly the opposite: /nəfš-/ is predominant, while /rūḥ-/ serves to express reflexivity in more specific contexts (Cohen 1975, 218). Moreover, /rūḥ-/ forms another pronoun, namely /brūḥ-/ meaning 'by oneself', e.g., *žīt brūḥi* 'I came alone'. The most popular expression for 'by oneself, alone' in Jewish Gabes, however, is /waḥd-/, which has the following inflection:

---

[54] Interestingly, when *nəfš* stands alone it means 'evil eye', e.g., *ʕandu nəfš* 'he is sick because of the evil eye'.

Table 58: Inflection of particle /waḥd-/

3MS	ža waḥdu	he came alone
3FS	žāt wḥadha	she came alone
2MS	žīt waḥdək	you came alone
1SG	žīt waḥdi	I came alone
3PL	žāw wḥadhəm	they came alone
2PL	žītu wḥadkəm	you (PL) came alone
1PL	žīna wḥadna	we came alone

This pronoun seems to be very common in Tunisia, although there exist several exceptions; for example, Muslim Tunis uses /bid-/ to express the meaning 'by oneself' (Singer 1985, 257), while Jewish Tripoli prefers /brūḥ-/ (Yoda 2005, 129). Nonetheless, /waḥd-/ has been attested in Jewish Algiers (Cohen 1912, 355).

6.3. Relative Pronoun

The principal pronoun that introduces relative clauses in Jewish Gabes is *li*, which is not affected by gender or number, e.g. *tlāta baṭṭīxāt li bʕaṭəthəm bəntək* 'three melons that your daughter has sent you', *təmma wāḥəd li hūwa ma tḥarrəkš* 'there is a man who does not move', *āna hūwa li žītək āmš* 'I am the one who came to you yesterday', *li nḥabb humma liāvər li šəfthəm* 'what I want is the book that I saw'. There exists also an allomorphic variant *əlli*. The use of the relative pronoun in Jewish Gabes will be analysed more closely in chapter 6, §1.1.

Apart from the aforementioned *li*, which prevails in Jewish Gabes, one can find in Muslim Tunis also a widespread vestigial use of the pronoun *ma* (Singer 1985, 260), e.g., *xūd ma tḥabb* 'take whatever you want'. It has been replaced by *li* in the role of the relative pronoun, probably in order to avoid misunderstanding due to the second function of *ma*, which is as a negation particle, e.g., *āna ma nḥabbūš* 'I do not like him'. In Jewish Gabes, the pronoun *ma* does exist, but it serves as a highlighter of the object, often contradicting the statement or the presumption of the collocutor, e.g., *māk klīt baʕda* 'but you have already eaten', *māni qaltlək* 'I already told you'.

6.4. Reciprocal Pronoun

As in other Maghrebi dialects, *mʕa bʕaḍ* is an equivalent of 'each other', e.g., *āna wa ənti nəmšīw mʕa bʕaḍna* 'I and you will go together', *humma tnīn žāw mʕa bʕaḍhəm* 'they came together', *əẓ-ẓġār yəḍərbu mʕa bʕaḍhəm* 'the children hit each other'.

6.5. Interrogative Pronouns

- *šnūwa, aš* 'what':
  šnūwa nqūllək? 'what will I tell you?', *aš yaʕməl?* 'what will he do?', *šnūwa šāʕa?* 'what time is it?' *waqt wṣəlt l-hūni šnūwa šāʕa li kānət?* 'when you arrived in here, what was the time?', *šnūwa maʕnatha?* 'what is the meaning (of the word)?';
- *(h)āni* 'which':
  (h)āni tnīya nūṣəl bīha fi-l-blād? 'which way will lead us to the city?', *(h)āni ṭawla tḥəbbi?* 'which table do you like?', *(h)āni liāvər tḥəbb?* 'which book would you like?', *(h)āni ašəm ʕṭīti l-wəldək?* 'what name have you given to your child?', *mən (h)āni blād žīt?* 'which country did you come from?';

- *škūn, aškūn* 'who':
  škūn әṛ-ṛāẓәl li ža āmәš? 'who is the man who came yesterday?' *aškūn l-mra li žāt?* 'who is the woman who has come?' *aškūn nāš šәft fi-ṣ-ṣūq?* 'which people did you see in the market?' *škūn әnti?* 'who are you?', *wәld škūn әnta?* 'whose son are you?'.

This interrogative pronoun is usually not inflected. However, in Jewish Gabes, one can occasionally find forms like *škūnәk?* 'who are you?' *škun hūwa?* 'who is he?'.

- *kәddāš* 'how much/how many'
  kәddāš tḥabbi tәffāḥ? 'how many apples would you like?'
- *kīfāš, ša* 'how'
  ša yšәmmīw? 'what is he called?', *ša ḥālәk?* 'how are you?', *kīfāš ʕamәlt hāda?* 'how did you do that?'.

6.6. Exclamative Pronouns

The particle *ma-* serves to form the following exclamative pronouns:

- *madabi-*
  This word is used to express a wish that it is possible may come true. It is inflected regularly, i.e. *madabīya, madabīk*, etc.
- *mā-/ša-* + elative
  This construction expresses amazement, astonishment, or surprise. It brings about some fluctuations within the syllable structure of an adjective as it admits the personal suffixes, e.g.:

Table 59: mā-/ša- + elative with pronominal suffixes

Elative	Masculine	Feminine
akbər 'bigger'	ma-kabru 'how big he is!'	ma-kbarha 'how big she is!'
azġar 'smaller'	ma-zaġru 'how small he is!'	ma-zġarha 'how small she is!'
aṭwəl 'longer'	ša-ṭūlu 'how long he is!'	ša-ṭūlha 'how long she is!'
axəff 'lighter'	ma-xaffu 'how light he is!'	ma-xfəfha 'how light she is!'
aḥla 'sweeter'	ma-ḥla(h) 'how sweet he is!'	ma-ḥlāha 'how sweet she is!'
axyəb 'worse'	ma-xaybu/xību 'how bad he is!'	ma-xayba/xība 'how bad she is!'
ṣaḥḥ 'stronger'	ma-ṣḥāhu 'how strong he is!'	ma-ṣaḥḥa/ṣḥīha 'how strong she is!'[55]

6.7. Demonstrative Pronouns

6.7.1. Near Reference

Table 60: Near demonstrative pronouns

	Singular	Plural
Masculine	hāda	hādu
Feminine	hādi	

The position of the pronoun within the sentence is not fixed, and it can either follow the noun, e.g., əl-ḥṣān hāda 'this horse', or precede it, e.g., hāda ər-ṛāẓəl 'this man'.

---

[55] The primary meaning of this adjective is 'strong'; however, due to the social taboo, it serves also as a euphemistic equivalent of 'fat', especially with reference to a woman, e.g. ʕanda ṣḥīha, literally 'she has a strength'.

6.7.2. Far Reference

Table 61: Far demonstrative pronouns

	Singular	Plural
Masculine	hādāk	hādūk
Feminine	hādīk	

There exists in Jewish Gabes also another pronoun indicating far reference, namely, hāk-əl, e.g., hāk-əṛṛāẓəl 'that man'. It is attested also in Jewish Tunis, where the initial /h/ is elided, i.e., āk-əl (Cohen 1975, 225). As suggested by Cohen, this form probably stems from CA hādāk-əl. Interestingly, in Jewish Gabes, only the masculine form is attested. It seems to be the same situation also in Jewish Tunis, since Cohen (1975, 225) presents only the masculine form, without mentioning its feminine counterpart. In Jewish Algiers, in turn, one can find an abbreviation of hādāk, namely dāk (Cohen 1912, 346).

6.7.3. Vestiges of /-ha/

The particle /-ha/, known from CA as a component of the demonstrative hāḏā, forms in Jewish Tunis a separate demonstrative pronoun inflected for person and number, and indicating the physical presence of someone (Singer 1985, 259). As reported by Cohen (1975, 225), the pronoun in question is represented in Jewish Tunis by a compound form awāda (< *hāhu hāḏā). In Jewish Gabes it seems to have survived only in two isolated forms, i.e., hāni (< *hā + āna) and hawwa (< *hā + huwwa). The second form serves as a demonstrative pronoun not only for the third person singular, but also for all the persons except the first person singular, which has its own form, namely *hāni*, e.g., *hāni žīt* 'here I came', *hāwwa ža* 'here he came', *hāwwa žīna* 'here we came'.

6.8. Indefinite Pronouns

- *wāḥəd, waḥda* 'someone';
- *mnādəm* 'somebody, one' (< Heb. בן אדם);
- *ʕbəd* 'a person, somebody', e.g., *təmma ʕbəd wāḥad f-əd-dāṛ* 'there is someone at home';
- *ḥadd* 'no one'
  This pronoun is used exclusively in negative sentences or in the expression *kəll ḥadd* 'everyone', e.g., *ma təmma ḥadd f-əd-dāṛ* 'there is no one at home', *ḥadd ma ža* 'no one came', *ḥadd ma xnəbhəm* 'no one stole them';
- *bʕaḍ əl-ḥadd* 'unknown person, someone', e.g., *qəlt l-ummi li bʕaḍ əl-ḥadd ža* 'I told my mother that someone came', *bʕaḍ əl-ḥadd hūni* 'someone is here';
- *bʕaḍ* 'some, unspecified place or item, few', e.g., *ʕla bāli šəftu fi-bʕaḍ əl-blād* 'in my opinion, I have seen him in a town', *bʕaḍ ən-nāš žāw* 'few people came', *hūwa ṣalla bʕaḍ ṣlawāt* 'he prayed some prayers';
- *flān* 'someone'
  This pronoun is used only for human beings and cannot be followed by any noun, e.g., *flān wṣəl l-d-dāṛ* 'someone has arrived at home' (i.e., not: *flān ṛāžəl wṣəl*);
- *ḥāža* 'something', e.g., *madabīya ḥāža naṣrabha* 'I would like to drink something', *nḥabb nqūllək ḥāža* 'I would like to tell you something', *təmma ḥāža li thayyərni* 'there is

something that worries me', *aʕṭīni hādīk əl-ḥāža* 'give me that thing';
- *bʕaḍ əl-ḥāža* 'something', e.g., *aʕṭīni bʕaḍ əl-ḥāža* 'give me something';
- *šəyy* 'nothing', used only in negative sentences, e.g., *ma ʕandīš šəyy* 'I have nothing', *ma nḥabb šəyy* 'I do not want anything';
- *šwīya*[56] 'a bit', e.g., *aʕṭīni šwīya mənha* 'give me just a bit of this';
- *āxər/ōxər* 'another', e.g., *žāt mra āxra* 'another woman came', *šəft nāš oxrīn* 'I saw other people', *nḥabb ḥāža āxra* 'I want something else', *aʕṭīni təffāḥa oxra* 'give me one more apple'.

6.9. Pronouns Related to Quantity

- *ṭrəyyəf* 'a slice, a piece', e.g., *ʕṭīthu ṭrəyyəf xabž* 'I gave him a small slice of bread';
- *bərša* 'many, a lot', e.g., *hūwa yḥabb bərša ḥwāyəž* 'he wants many things', *ma təmmāš bərša rmān* 'there are not many pomegranates';
- *yāsər* 'many, a lot', e.g., *təmma nāš yāsər* 'there are a lot of people';
- *kattər* 'the majority' (in Muslim Tunis: *mukter*; see Singer 1985, 286), e.g., *kattər əl-nāš yḥabbu yəmšīw l-ṣla* 'the majority of people want to go to the synagogue';

---

[56] In Jewish Djerba, instead of *šwīya*, *tšīša* is used.

- *bāqəl* 'the rest, the leftovers', e.g., *nāxəd əl-bāqəl* 'I will take the rest';
- *kull* 'all, every, whole', e.g., *xdəmt nhār kullu* 'I worked all day', *əl-nāš əl-kull žāw hūni* 'all the people came here', *kull ʕāyla ʕandha žūžẓġār* 'in every family there are two children'.

PART III
DIACHRONIC AND COMPARATIVE STUDIES IN SYNTAX

Introduction

The study presented below investigates several syntactic phenomena attested in Jewish Gabes. Since no comparative description of North African Arabic syntax exists, the selection of topics studied here has been made based on Kristen Brustad's (2000) work on the syntax of spoken Arabic, but several modifications have been made as well. One of the major differences is the methodology adopted in this chapter, namely, the syntax of Jewish Gabes has been approached from a typological and historical point of view. The data for every topic has been extracted from the text corpus and is presented at the beginning of every section. The comparative analysis is of particular importance in this chapter, since data from the neighbouring dialects can provide valuable information for understanding the development of syntax in Jewish Gabes.

5. SYNTAX OF NOUNS

1.0. Definiteness

1.1. Introduction

The primary aim of this section is to specify the nature of definiteness in Jewish Gabes based on the data presented below. I am going to study the factors determining the level of definiteness and revisit the rules established for CA and other dialects. The primary question posed in this survey is whether definiteness is a fixed grammatical category, or should rather be perceived functionally as a result of interaction between different grammatical features. The second question addressed in this section is of a comparative nature, namely, whether the same factors condition definiteness in all the North African dialects, or some variations occur.

1.2. Data

Definite

1. *l-kbīra xdāha ṛāẓəl, xda wəld wžīr, wa l-tānya xdāha ṛāẓəl* (2:13)
   'He married the eldest to a man, the son of the minister, he married also the second one.'

2. *humma mšāw yāsər, ət-tnīya ṭwīla u ufālhəm əl-ma* (2:56)
   'They walked a lot, the way was long and they ran out of water.'

3. *əl-bāba ṣəlṭān ža: wīn bənti?* (4:12)
   'The father sultan came: where is my daughter?'

Indefinite

4. ḥaṭṭi šəkkīna u nqaṣṣūha (1:22)
   'Bring a knife and we will cut it.'

5. rqāt mṛa ʕamya (4:18)
   'She found a blind woman.'

6. dəxlət, tərqa šūbīrya kbīṛa (4:25)
   'She entered and found a big bowl.'

Indefinite Specific

7. wāḥəd mša yəṭlab ya krīm tāʕ aḷḷa (1:2)
   'A man went to beg for money.'

8. qāmət ʕamlətlu wāḥda oxra (1:31)
   'She got up to make another one.'

9. šūfu wāḥəd l-əktər agžān, l-əktər məxnān, l-əktər ẓāwāli, xūdūla (2:14)
   'Look for the one that is the laziest, the dirtiest and the poorest and marry her to him.'

1.3. The Arabic System of Definiteness and its Challenges

Most grammars of Arabic present the system of definiteness dichotomically, implying that nouns can be either marked by the definite article and therefore definite, or unmarked and therefore indefinite. In the case of Jewish Gabes, as in many other modern dialects, this approach is inaccurate and fails to represent multiple levels of definiteness in natural language. As has been mentioned by Brustad (2000, 18), native speakers of Arabic make flexible use of various shades of definiteness in order to manipulate the discourse. The same observation has been made by Dominique Caubet (1993, 185) in her analysis of the morphosyntax of Moroccan Arabic.

What characterises the North African group in terms of definiteness is the use of the article *wāḥəd*, meaning 'someone, one, somebody'. Its occurrence is attested particularly frequently in Moroccan Arabic, but it occasionally appears also in the Eastern dialects, e.g., in Syrian and in Egyptian dialects, in the latter being used exclusively with nouns that refer to humans. In addition to *wāḥəd*, one can find in Maghrebi Arabic also *šəy*, meaning 'some'.[1] The particle *šəy* is also attested in Syrian; however, it has been pointed out that it functions there more as a partitive noun (Cowell 1964, 467). These two articles, therefore, prove that there is a 'grey space' between the classic extrema of definiteness and indefiniteness, within which native speakers exercise different degrees of determination. Caubet (1993, 185) associates them with the action of extraction, as a result of which an item becomes separated from the anonymous whole and acquires some kind of specificity, yet remains anonymous.

Before establishing the rules that govern the system of definiteness and indefiniteness in Jewish Gabes, I would like to discuss some additional grammatical concepts that might have an impact on the notion of definiteness. I will adopt the view of Brustad (2000, 18), who argues that definiteness constitutes a continuum interacting with concepts like number and animacy.

---

[1] The particle *wāḥəd* finds its parallel in Berber *jirane* 'one, someone'.

1.4. Animacy—Individuation—Discourse

Definiteness is a notion closely related to a speaker's perception and their idea of discourse. The speaker chooses to assign greater definiteness to items that they can see by themselves or are close and akin to them. The egocentric dimension of definiteness has been already noted by many scholars, including Khan (1988, XXXVI), but it is crucial to highlight also in the present study that the choice of a specific level of definiteness is embedded in the perceptual subjectivity of the speaker, and it therefore might not be correlate with commonly established grammatical rules. There are, however, several other factors which might help explain the system of definiteness and indefiniteness in Jewish Gabes.

To begin with, definiteness as a concept of perceptual salience formally reflected in the language has some parallels with animacy (in general linguistics) and virility (in Slavic languages). Animacy can be explained as the ability of a noun to be alive and animate, i.e., to act in a conscious manner. Thus, in order to establish the definition of animacy, Comrie (1981, 185) proposes the following hierarchy: human > animals > inanimate, arguing that it is relevant for numerous morphosyntactic developments cross-linguistically, but at the same time interacts with other parameters rather than functioning independently. Comrie's hierarchy notwithstanding, the most common and most attested distinction within the category of animacy is that of human and non-human. In terms of definiteness, therefore, human referents are more definite than other items, as they are aware of their acts and thus they acquire more prominence.

5. Syntax of Nouns

However, the concept of animacy is not reflected equally in every language, and therefore the phenomena stemming from it can be manifold.[2] Perception of which nouns have the ability to act in an aware way depends to a large extent on socio-cultural factors in each speech community. Some languages make a more specific distinction as to what deserves an additional marking in the language as being more animate/salient, disambiguating nouns related to kinship from the rest by means of clitic doubling. Both in Berber and in Maghrebi Arabic, the possessors of kinship terms are often doubled, resulting in the construction: kinship term + pronominal clitic + genitive particle + possessor, e.g., *yəmmā-ha ntāʕ bāya* 'the mother of Baya' (Souag 2017, 58). Some examples of the impact of animacy can be found also in Northwest Semitic. As argued by scholars of Biblical Hebrew, the direct object marker את *ʔēṯ* occurs often with definite and animate nouns (Khan 1988; Bekins 2014). In terms of subject-verb agreement, it has been argued that, similarly to Ancient Greek, inanimate collectives in Hebrew are accompanied by singular verbs when in the position of subject, e.g., לֹא תָבוֹא דִמְעָתֶךָ 'and nor shall your tears run down' (Ezek. 24.16; Gzella 2013, 110). This kind of morphological marking reflects the way in which speech communities perceive which referents are more animate and alive.

---

[2] As an example, consider Russian and Polish, where in the former, plurality increases the degree of animacy, and causes a noun to admit a special animate accusative morpheme, while in the latter, the situation is exactly the opposite (Comrie 1981, 188).

Another parameter relevant for noun phrases with regard to animacy is gender. This is of special significance in Slavic languages, where the discriminating category has been called 'virility' by Janda (1999, 209). It has multiple morphological implications and as a term is not dichotomous, but, similarly to definiteness in spoken Arabic, demonstrates diversification. Different levels of virility are reflected in the declension of human nouns in Polish, which, when in the nominative, might admit three possible endings: honorific virile, neutral virile and deprecatory non-virile (Janda 1999, 202). As has been suggested by Janda, the most animate and the most prominent category, honorific virile, was shaped by a sociolinguistic concept of the idealised and prototypical self, which is highly specific and unique. The personal and perceptual dimension of virility/animacy therefore corresponds to the egocentric hierarchy of salience. A parallel discriminative distinction was suggested for the Proto-Semitic morpheme /-t/, which originally marked inferiority, being used especially for diminutives and pejoratives, and subsequently acquired the function of the feminine marker (Hasselbach 2014, 324).[3]

Bearing in mind that various aspects of animacy may have an impact on the system of definiteness and indefiniteness, I

---

[3] The /t/ morpheme as a marker of inferiority is a widespread phenomenon not only in Proto-Semitic, but in the entire Afro-Asiatic group; it is attested, among others, in the Bantu languages. The cross-linguistic regularity of this morpheme was observed at an early stage of Semitic scholarship (Brockelmann 1908).

would now like to discuss another satellite concept, namely individuation. This serves as one of the key factors relevant to the Transitivity Hypothesis formulated by Hopper and Thompson (1980) in their cross-linguistic study of transitivity and its discourse implications. In their view, transitivity is a global phenomenon which is central in every natural language and has multiple, predictable grammatical consequences. Rejecting the classical definition of transitivity as the presence or absence of an object, they propose to interpret it as a continuum consisting of various components that determine whether a clause is more or less transitive. Their hypothesis also has other aspects relevant for discourse analysis, but for the time being, I would like to focus on the parameters of transitivity formulated by Hopper and Thompson (1980, 252):

Table 62: Hopper and Thompson's parameters of transitivity

	HIGH	LOW
PARTICIPANTS	two or more participants	one participant
KINESIS	action	non-action
ASPECT	telic	atelic
PUNCTUALITY	punctual	non-punctual
VOLITIONALITY	volitional	non-volitional
AFFIRMATION	affirmative	negative
MODE	realis	irrealis
AGENCY	agent high in potency	agent low in potency
AFFECTEDNESS OF OBJECT	object totally affected	object not affected
INDIVIDUATION OF OBJECT	object highly individuated	object not individuated

This table shows that individuation correlates with other grammatical categories and participates in much wider processes like transitivity, which subsequently has serious discourse implications. Definiteness, animacy, and individuation of an object affect the syntax of most of the natural languages. Hopper and Thompson illustrate the importance of these features in several languages. In Hungarian, the word order of a sentence reflects the level of individuation of the object, while in Chukchee, when the object is non-referential and non-individuated, it is incorporated into a verb, which is in turn marked as intransitive (Comrie 1973, 243–44; Hopper and Thompson 1980, 257). It can be assumed, therefore, that there is a clear correlation between the categories of individuation of an object and transitivity of a verb. This statement can be reformulated in the following way: individuated nouns tend to occur in telic and punctual verbal clauses expressing actions. Contrary to this, atelic, non-punctual verbal forms, which do not significantly affect the object, attract non-individuated and indefinite objects.

The Transitivity Hypothesis has been widely discussed and reanalysed, especially within the framework of a single language. Čech and Pajas (2009) have tested its effectiveness in Czech and, based on their data, rejected some of Hopper and Thompson's predications related to the number of participants. I would like to pay special attention to their findings regarding the language form (spoken vs written), as it is of a special relevance for the study of individuation/definiteness in Jewish Gabes. Hopper and Thompson (1980, 53) have argued that spoken language forms like conversation are low in transitivity, because speakers tend to talk about themselves, describing views and attitudes rather than relating actions, which, as has been pointed out, have high levels of transitivity. This hypothesis was rejected for Czech, as the data analysed by Čech and Pajas (2009, 47) clearly indicate that, statistically, there are no differences in distribution between one- and two- and more-participant clauses in spoken and written language. Hence, a corpus of transcribed spoken language can serve as a basis for analysis of definiteness.

A dichotomic hierarchy parallel to that of Hopper and Thompson has been proposed by Khan (1988) in his study of object marking and agreement pronouns in Semitic in the context of individuation. According to this model, there are eight qualities that determine whether a noun is individuated and salient or non-individuated and non-salient. Brustad (2000, 23), in turn, has expanded Khan's hierarchies by adding, among others, the notion of agency, understood as an ability to act independently. Both Hopper and Thompson and Khan define individuation as distinctness of a nominal form from other forms found in a clause, but also from the background. Out of all the hierarchies proposed by the aforementioned scholars, some are more accurate, while others contain qualities not necessarily applicable in Jewish Gabes. Below I propose a provisional hierarchy of individuation, which matches my findings in the most accurate way:

Table 63: Hierarchy of individuation based on Khan (1988)

INDIVIDUATED	NON-INDIVIDUATED
Definite	Indefinite
Animate	Inanimate
Specific	General
Count	Mass
Textually prominent	Secondary for the discourse
Concrete	Abstract

These features designate tendencies rather than fixed rules.[4] Nonetheless, I would like to pay special attention to the relationship between discourse and individuation, which in my view has a critical impact on the syntactic behaviour of nouns. Nominals that are of relevance to the line of discourse are almost always more individuated and definite. Therefore, the pair singular vs plural that appears in Hopper and Thompson's hierarchy is not always relevant, since plural entities relevant to the discourse will usually be definite and individuated. On the other hand, the category of agency proposed by Brustad would acquire more importance, as entities acting independently are usually more prominent in the discourse.

The correspondence between discourse and definiteness is of special importance in this study, as the vast majority of the collected text corpus consists of folktales, where discourse span and topics are clearly marked. In a situation where a speaker delivers to a hearer a story that is unknown to them, the definiteness of the entities appearing in this story depends to a great extent on the degree to which the hearer is familiar with them (Khan 1988, XXXVII). Therefore, if the storyteller assumes that the hearer is able to retrieve a nominal from their memory or knowledge, this nominal will acquire more individuation and definiteness, namely, a noun will function as an associative anaphora. The new information in a story can therefore be twofold; it can be either discourse-related, or part of assumed famil-

---

[4] The vagueness of this kind of hierarchy has already been highlighted by Brustad (2000, 24).

iarity-related newness/givenness. This distinction was first introduced by Prince (1981) and subsequently extended by other scholars including Rudy Loock (2013). The latter proposed the following hearer-orientated definition of information in the discourse: HEARER NEW vs HEARER OLD INFORMATION—is the information given or new, depending on the speaker's assumption as to the state of knowledge of his/her addressee(s) (Loock 2013, 88)? Hence, the speaker matches the degree of definiteness of the nominals used in the story to the state of knowledge of the hearer.

Theoretically, it could be established, therefore, that there is a straightforward correspondence between individuation/textual prominence and definiteness. This hypothesis, even though it is applicable in many cases, has some impediments. In particular, in Arabic, as in many other languages, abstract and generic nouns attract the definite article. An example of this exceptional behaviour is found in passage (1:3). This sentence appears at the very beginning of the story and the house at which the beggar arrives is unknown to the reader. The house itself will not play any significant role in the further discourse of the story, neither will the door. Nonetheless, they are both marked with the definite article. The first is definite due to its generic character. As argued by Krifka (1987, 19), a kind-referring generic nominal phrase can occur in an object position and can fulfil several roles, one of them being representation. A representative object in this case refers to a "typical representative of this kind." Namely, the speaker did not mean any specific house, as it does not have any significance for the story, but rather refers to an entity representative of the ontological category of houses.[5] The definiteness of the noun 'door' can be explained by the phenomenon of associative anaphora. As every house usually has a door, the speaker uses the definite article in the frame of cognitive psychology. Löbner (1998, 1) argues that "associative anaphora involves a hidden link or anchor which has to be introduced earlier." In the analysed passage, therefore, the definiteness of the door is anchored in the cognitive frame of the house.

1.5. The Indefinite-Specific and New Topic Marking

I already have pointed out that this study takes a particular interest in the space between absolute definiteness and absolute indefiniteness, namely, different degrees of individuation. As observed by Khan (1988, XXXVIII): "It is more accurate to state that some [nominals] are more individuated than others." One instance of such ambiguity is the indefinite-specific, which designates nouns that are syntactically indefinite, but possess a higher level of referentiality than indefinite nouns normally do (Wald 1983; Brustad 2000, 26). In Jewish Gabes, *wāḥəd* functions as the marker of indefinite-specific nouns, while simultaneously playing an important role in the discourse, namely, introducing a new topic. This article seems to be well-established in the dialect and its occurrence is relatively high, as can be inferred from the data

---

[5] Similar interpretation of the term 'generic' appears in the Egyptian joke provided by Brustad (2000, 32). There, parallel to the definiteness of the house in the passage I am analysing, a restaurant occurring at the very beginning of the joke bears the definite article.

presented above. This calls into question the statement made by Marçais (1977, 163), who claims that the distribution of *wāḥəd* in Maghrebi Arabic follows a decreasing tendency from West to East, with extremely high occurrence in Morocco and vestigial distribution in Libya and Tunisia, where it is "impossible." Both my findings and a text from Jewish Tripoli prove this statement to be wrong (Yoda 2005).

Brustad (2000, 36) argues that a new topic can be introduced in many ways in different dialects of Arabic, and can be indefinite, indefinite-specific, or sometimes definite. Based on her data, she established that the last option is particularly well attested in Moroccan. In contradistinction, in Jewish Gabes, the indefinite-specific almost always introduces a character who is new to the hearer but will reoccur and play a significant role in the discourse, like in the following example:

(1) mša **l-wāḥda** ʕažūža u qālla
    go.SFX DEF-one.FS old woman and say.SFX.3MS.her
    aʕməlli mžīya əmši u əxṭbīha
    make.IMP.FS.me favour go.IMP.FS and ask.IMP.FS.her
    'He went to an old woman and said to her: please do me a favour, go and ask her for her hand.' (5:16)

Here the old woman is preceded by *wāḥəd* by virtue of her newness in the story, but simultaneously, soon she will become one of the key figures in this part of the tale, and the speaker therefore needed to highlight her textual prominence.[6] Very often, a nominal that is at first marked by *wāḥəd* is immediately repeated followed by the definite marker and proximal demonstrative pronoun:

(2) *təmma ṣəlṭān **wāḥəd** əṣ-ṣəlṭān hāda*
    there.is sultan INDF DEF-sultan this
    ʕandu bənt ʕžīža ʕalī yāsər
    at.him daughter dear.FS on.him a lot
    'There was a sultan, this sultan had a daughter who was very dear to him.' (4:1–2)

Example (2) illustrates the mechanism by which a figure that was introduced as unknown to the hearer is at the same time one of the key players of the discourse. Apart from the discourse dimension of this example of indefinite-specific marking, a sultan, as an entity of high animacy and agency, always attracts definiteness and individuation. A similar way of introducing a textually prominent yet indefinite figure entails a relative clause. The following example comes from Jewish Tunis, and the boy who appears in this passage is at the same time the main topic of the discourse:

---

[6] Another difference between Moroccan and Jewish Gabes is that, in the former, *wāḥəd* is followed by the definite article and a noun. By contrast, in Jewish Gabes, the noun is usually not preceded by the definite article.

(3) māš   nədūyu   ʕla wāḥəd wləd **əlli**
    go.AP.MS talk.PFX.1PL on   INDF   boy   REL
    ža   l-waqt   tāʕu   bāš yəlbəš   tfəllīmu
    come.SFX.3MS   DEF-time of.him SUB wear.PFX.3MS tefilin.his

'Nous allons parler d'un garçon qui a attaint l'âge auquel on procède à la cérémonie de la majorité religieuse.' (Cohen 1964, 28)

Contrary to this example, in some instances, a nominal which will not play any role in the discourse and is of low animacy is not marked in any way:

(4) **təmma bīr   ġārəq   yāsər**   wa l-bīr   hāda
    there.is well deep   a lot   and DEF-well this
    li   yədxal   fī   ymūt   ma   yəṭlaʕṣ
    REL   enter.PFX.3MS in.it   die.PFX.3MS   NEG leave.PFX.3MS.NEG

'There was a very deep well and whoever goes in dies, does not go out.' (2:57)

As the above example indicates, the adjective that follows the nominal changes its status from indefinite to something that can be described as unmarked indefinite specific. The speaker states the existence of the specific water well, but at the same time, it will not reappear in the discourse and it could therefore not admit *wāḥəd*.

The same rule of a lack of any marking on textually non-prominent nouns applies also to animate entities, as in the following example:

(5) rqāt   mṛa   ʕamya u   tərḥi   fi-l-qamḥ
    find.SFX.3FS woman blind and grind.PFX.3FS in-DEF-wheat

'She found a blind woman, she was grinding wheat.' (4:18–19)

Here again, the indefinite and general character of this woman is cancelled by additional information about her provided by the adjective and the following verbal clause. Nevertheless, the referent does not have discourse prominence and therefore is not flagged by the indefinite specific.

1.6. Definite Marking in Jewish Gabes as opposed to Moroccan

To delineate the fundamental characteristics of the definiteness system in Jewish Gabes, I intend to scrutinise specific examples from Moroccan Arabic and subsequently juxtapose them with analogous usages in Jewish Gabes. According to Brustad's (2000, 36) analysis, among all Arabic dialects, Moroccan Arabic exhibits the highest prevalence of definite nouns, often contravening established definiteness norms. Consequently, this typological comparison has the capacity to unveil substantial disparities in the definiteness framework within the same dialectal cluster, i.e., the Maghrebi varieties. One notable instance of unexpected definite article usage occurs in the initial mention of an entity in a story:

Table 64: Points of divergence between the system of definiteness in Jewish Gabes and Moroccan Arabic

Jewish Gabes	**Moroccan**[7]
(1) l-məštaġni ma ʕandūš wlād u l-ẓāwāli ʕandu yāsər zġār (3:3) 'The rich one does not have children and the poor one has a lot of them.'	hāda wāḥəd ər-rāžəl maʕandūš l-wlād, ʕandu ġi[r] l-mra 'This is a man who has no children. He has only a wife.'
(2) kif ənti māši l-ṛabbi, aṭəlbu ʕalāš āna ma ʕandīš ḥūt fi-l-bḥar (3:19) 'Once you go to God, ask him why I do not have fish in the sea.'	maši tšūf b-ʕink tqūl rāh kāyn l-ḥūt 'You will see with your own eyes and say there are fish.'
(3) hrab mən-l-blād u sfāṛ l-blād oxra (6:66) 'He fled from the town and travelled to another city.'	xəllāwha b-l-kərš w xwāw blād w ʕammərū blād 'They left her pregnant and moved to another city.'

As can be seen in the first two examples, the dialects differ in terms of the use of the definite article. In example (1) in Moroccan, the non-existent noun is marked as definite despite the low level of salience. On the other hand, the same noun in Jewish Gabes is treated as non-individuated and therefore indefinite. In a similar vein, in example (2), a generic and non-specific noun 'fish' is marked as definite, while in this specific passage in Jewish Gabes, it is indefinite.[8] Contrary to this, an indefinite noun

---

[7] The examples have been borrowed from Brustad (2000, 36-37).

[8] In the final part of the story, this noun reappears in the same question and is marked as definite. This discrepancy is presumably owed to the fact that 'fish' were mentioned previously and are therefore textually more specific in this context.

occurs in both dialects in the third example. The syntactic behaviour exhibited by Jewish Gabes is in line with the usual grammatical rules, namely, first mentions of non-individuated nouns are usually unmarked.

The unexpected definite marking in Moroccan, according to Brustad (2000, 38), is best explained by the specificity and animacy factors. All three examples from Moroccan are of low individuation and salience, but the first two are animate and hence the definite marking appears. In Jewish Gabes, the animacy factor is operational, but only in a limited way, namely, inanimate nouns of low individuation are almost always unmarked, but, as the above examples show, some animate entities are not marked either. Passages (1:22), (4:25), (4:63), and (4:92) contain exclusively inanimate nouns with zero marking. Passage (7:85) is an example that could theoretically call this statement into question, since animate entities with low individuation are marked as definite:

(6) *qām   f-əṣ-ṣbāḥ   u   lqa   l-qaṭṭūṣa*
    get up.SFX.3MS in-DEF-morning and find.SFX.3MS DEF-cat

    tmaʕʕwi   u   l-ǧāǧa   tgərgər   u   hāda
    meow.PFX.3FS and DEF-hen   chirp.PFX.3FS and this

    qāllu: šnūwa   hāda?
    say.SFX.3MS.him what   this

'He woke up in the morning and found a cat meowing and a hen crowing and he said: what is that?' (7:85)

Similarly to passage (4:18–19), one would expect here zero marking, signalling the first mention on the one hand, and the hearer's unfamiliarity with the referent on the other. The sultan fell victim to his wife's ambush and woke up in a completely unknown place. The reason why these nouns are definite is their high agency, as they are agents of verbs. Here, in this particular topic span, they play an active role in the dynamic of the situation; it is the end of the story, and this scene leads the sultan to the final confrontation with his wife, hence the agency and definite marking.

Another example of an unusual use of the definite article is related to what has previously been mentioned in this chapter as virility. Brustad (2000, 38) quotes a woman who, when referring to giving birth to a girl, does not use any marking, but the definite article appears when she says that she delivered a son. Below, one can find the example in question with parallel examples from Jewish Gabes containing word *wəld* 'son':

(7) Moroccan:

gā[l]t-lu wlədt bənt. gāl-lha gūli-li šnu wlədti rāh ʔila wlədti l-bənt⁹ ġa-ndəbḥk wndbəḥha. Ta šāft-u zāyd-lha b-l-mūs, gā[l]t-lu hda, wlədt l-wəld

'She told him, "I had a girl." He told her, "Tell me what you had—if you had a girl, I will slay you and slay her." Until she saw him coming at her with the knife. She told him, "Calm down, I had a son."'

---

[9] The definite marking of the 'daughter' in this sentence is presumably due to its mention in the previous sentence.

(8) Jewish Gabes:

mərtu əl-lūwla kānət žərbīya mātətlu, kānu ʕandu bənt u wəld, əl-bənt xdāha rəbbi bīrəṣ, u l-wəld ḥrəq rūḥu, xāṭər šāf ša ʕamlu fi-ruṣalayim, ma tāqəṣ (8:20)

'His first wife was from Djerba, she died, he had a daughter and a son, the daughter got married to rabbi Peretz, while the son killed himself because he had seen what they did in Jerusalem, he did not stand it.'

(9) *əl-mra ḥablət, tžīb wəld, ma təmmaš škūn yaqtlu* (2:55)

'The woman was pregnant, gave birth to a son, there is no one to kill him.'

(10) *baʕd yāmāt, hīya žābət wəld* (4:45)

'After some time, she gave birth to a boy.'

(11) *hīya žābət wəld, ḥaṭṭətlo bəžawonk ʕal fxəddu* (6:12)

'She gave birth to a boy and put the bracelet on his shin.'

The examples from Jewish Gabes clearly indicate that the concept of 'virility' does not attract definite marking as it does in Moroccan. The gender of a child notwithstanding, it is the first mention which brings about the encoding of the item as indefinite.[10] Similarly, in the Bedouin dialect of Douz, the factor of virility does not seem to affect the system of definiteness (e.g.,

---

[10] In Jewish Tripoli, similarly to Jewish Gabes, the gender of a child does not affect the indefinite marking (Yoda 2005, 298).

yžahhim ʕalā wⁱlad b-is-sīr kābis nuṣṣa,[11] Ritt-Benmimoun 2011, 280).

Nonetheless, there are some similarities between Moroccan and Jewish Gabes in terms of definite marking. One of them is inalienable possession, especially in the context of nouns designating familial relations. As has been observed by Brustad (2000, 39), these nouns in Moroccan almost never occur without any marking. This is also the case in Jewish Gabes, where all of them either are preceded by the definite article or have a possessive pronoun.

(12) oṃha   ʕṭātam   flūš   ʕṭātam
     mother.her give.SFX.3FS.them money give.SFX.3FS.them
     əlbāš u   mšāw
     clothes and go.SFX.3PL
     'Her mother gave them money, gave them clothes and they left.' (2:21)

(13) waqt l-oṃṃa   kānət   fi-l-kūžīna   əl-bənt
     when DEF-mother be.SFX.3FS in-DEF-kitchen   DEF-daughter
     ḥaṭṭətla   šəmm   wa l-oṃṃa   ma   ʕarfətš
     put.SFX.3FS.her poison and DEF-mother NEG understand.SFX.3FS.NEG
     'While the mother was in the kitchen, the daughter put poison [in the mother's food], but the mother did not know that.' (4:118)

---

[11] Ritt-Benmimoun gives the following translation: "Es jagt einem Jungen Furcht ein, der mit einem Riemen seine Körperhälfte zusammenschnürt."

Another point of convergence between Moroccan and Jewish Gabes is an asymmetry of noun-adjective phrases. According to the rules of Arabic, when a phrase is definite, both its members should be definite.[12] However, as shown by Brustad (2000, 41), in Moroccan, a definite phrase where only the noun bears the definite article is permitted. A similar example has been found in Jewish Gabes:

(14) Moroccan:

    ka-ytbāʕu   f-l-ḥānūt ʕaṣri
    PVPT-be.sold.PFX.3PL in-DEF-shop modern
    'They are sold in a modern house.'

(15) Jewish Gabes:

    xdāw   rəbṭū   fi-l-ḥbəl   ġliḍ
    take.SFX.3PL tied.up.SFX.3PL.him in-DEF-rope thick

    u   daxxlū   hbaṭ   ḷūṭa
    and enter.SFX.3PL.him descend.SFX.3MS down
    'They took him and tied him up with a thick rope and put him [in the well], he descended.' (2:62)

This inconsistency can potentially be explained by the continuum of individuation. The less individuated the noun, the higher the probability that the adjective will not be definite (Brustad 2000, 42). Such an explanation would be valid for Jewish Gabes, since the 'thick rope' from the above example is inanimate, non-individuated, and textually non-prominent. Nonetheless, the phrase

---

[12] Despite this general tendency, there are in Classical Arabic cases of noun phrases where only the first part of the construct state is marked by the definite article, e.g., *ath-thalāthu rijālin* 'the three men' (Wright 2005, II:264).

is definite by virtue of associative anaphora, i.e., the action of tying someone up presupposes the use of a rope.

Lack of agreement between definiteness of noun and adjective is not only a characteristic feature of the aforementioned North African dialects, but also plays a part in the discussion regarding the very origin of the definite article in Semitic. According to the common explanation, the definite article in West Semitic, reconstructed as *han* for Arabic and Hebrew, derives from an attributive demonstrative (Rubin 2005, 72–76). However, as has been shown by Pat-El (2009, 42), this theory is at odds with numerous examples of the use of the definite article in Semitic languages. Based on her findings, she argues that, originally, the article was attached only to non-predicative adjectival forms, and only later was it expanded also to the head noun. Indeed, there are numerous languages, including Judaeo-Arabic and modern Arabic dialects (especially those of the Gulf and the Levant), where only the adjective bears the definite article (Blau 1952, 33; Pat-El 2009, 33). Both Blau (1961, 161) and Feghali (1928) attempted to explain this inconsistency through 'compositum', namely, according to this theory, speakers treat a noun modified by an adjective as one entity. Pat-El (2009, 37) rejected this assumption, arguing that, if the phrase were supposed to be understood as a whole, the article would be prefixed and not medial. In the case of Jewish Gabes and Moroccan, where the nominal phrase is indeed preceded by the definite article, this assumption would be valid, and thus it may be concluded that speakers would indeed treat a nominal phrase of low animacy and individuation as a single whole.

1.7. The Animacy Factor in Jewish Gabes

It has previously been mentioned that textually non-prominent entities with low animacy usually tend to be unmarked. Nonetheless, in my data from Jewish Gabes, there are a few exceptional instances, where an inanimate noun acquires animacy through a literary device. Text (7) contains several examples of anthropomorphism, which is the principal feature of the metaphoric language of the main character of the story:

Table 65: Anthropomorphism in Text (7)

Inanimate definite article	Anthropomorphic use
əṣ-ṣəlṭān tʕadda, lqā yəẓra fi-l-bṣəl (7:7) 'When the sultan was passing by, he found [him] planting onion.'	qāllu: əl-bṣəl hāda, tāklu wəlla yāklək? (7:8) 'He asked him: this onion, you will eat it, or will it eat you?'
qāllu: tuwwa nḥabbək tqūlli əẓ-ẓrāṛa (7:21) 'He said: now I want you to tell me, a water well.'	kīf ytạllʕu ṣṭall mən bīr, šnūwa yqūl (7:22) 'When people take out a bucket from a well, what does it say?'
nḥabbək tqūlli: šnūwa yqūlu, əš-šəžwa, kīf ḥaṭṭūha ʕal əl-nāṛ (7:16) 'I want you to tell me now: what they would say, a coffee kettle, when they put it on the fire.'	šnūwa tqūl, kīf ytạyybu əl-qahwa bə-šəžwa, šnūwa tqūl? (7:16) 'What does it say? When people prepare a coffee in a kettle, what does it say?'

In all three examples, the highlighted nouns occur in questions and seemingly do not have any textual prominence, yet they are marked as definite. Their definiteness is best explained as being rooted in their level of animacy. Every question presupposes that the entity is able to speak. In the answers given to the sultan, these entities turn out also to be able to act independently, and thus they possess some degree of agency.

1.8. Conclusions

This section has shown that the notion of definiteness does not function independently, but rather coexists with other linguistic concepts in creating various shades of specificity present in a natural language. Of the wide array of different qualities that condition the definiteness of a noun, there are in Jewish Gabes two factors that should be highlighted: animacy and textual prominence. The latter is of special importance, since, as this study has proven, textual prominence as a quality is more important than other features. The comparison with Moroccan indicates that Jewish Gabes is not governed by the same rules of definiteness, and the factors of animacy and virility do not operate in the two dialects in question in the same way. Finally, this study has confirmed that the traditional dichotomic approach to definiteness is inaccurate in the case of Jewish Gabes, and speakers utilise other syntactic devices in order to differentiate levels of definiteness.

2.0. Genitive Constructions

This section aims to explore genitive constructions present in Jewish Gabes. As in virtually every modern Arabic dialect, the genitive can be expressed in two ways, namely synthetically or analytically. Eksell (2009, 35) argues that these two forms of a genitive relationship in fact represent two parallel systems, each possessing its own dynamics. From a historical point of view, the analytic system, which encodes the genitive by means of a special exponent, is a dialectal innovation (Eksell 1980, 10). Indeed, in CA, the default way to express a genitive relationship is through annexation of two terms and inflection of the second one with the genitive case. Nevertheless, throughout the history of Arabic, there also existed alternative, analytic, means of expressing a genitive. Blau (1965, 82) mentions the particles *li* 'for, belonging to' and *min* 'of' as ways of introducing genitive constructions in Medieval Judaeo-Arabic. The emergence of a fully established and functional analytical genitive construction can be accounted for by the fact that almost all modern Arabic dialects have lost their case system.[13] Nowadays, both systems coexist and encode different types of possession. The present study will attempt to determine the factors conditioning the distribution of the two types of genitive construction in Jewish Gabes, as well as identifying some cross-dialectal parallels.

2.1. Data

Construct State

1. *šnūwa **yhūd žbəl** yaʕmlu? ya žbāli, əl-ʕōmər kla bhīm*
   'And what were the Jews of mountains doing? O mountaineer, a donkey has eaten the Omer.'

2. *qāl: āna* ᴴᴱʕaníᴴᴱ *u əl-xabža nḥabb nākəlha, aʕṭīni **nfayyəṣ xabža**, wa aʕṭīni ḥžina šmīʕa, u **qrīṭiṣ wqīḍ** bāš nəšʕlha* (1:19)
   'He said: I am poor and I would like to eat the bread, so give me half of it and give me a (poor, miserable) candle and a box of matches so I can light it.'

---

[13] Vestiges of the case system can be found in some Bedouin dialects of the Gulf, especially in the poetic register and in speech of some less educated speakers, where a suffix /-in/ denotes an indefinite noun (Brustad 2000, 28).

3. *aʕmlīlu ḥžīna oxra u dəxlīlu **kəmša lwiž** fi-l-ʕažīn* (1:38)
   'Make another [pitiful bread] and put a handful of coins inside the dough.'

Genitive Exponent

4. *yāxdu šwəya mən **məlḥ tāʕ ōmer** waqt yəmšīw yṣallīw*
   'They were taking a bit of the Omer salt when they were going to pray.'

5. *təmma wāḥəd, yəqʕad taḥt **šəǧra tāʕ blaḥ*** (2:15)
   'There was a man who was sitting beneath a date palm.'

6. *mšāt **l-naxla tāʕ ṛman**, qaṣṣət l-ʕarūf, nəẓṛəthum u tədṛəblu fi-rəžlīh mən lūṭa* (2:23)
   'She went to the pomegranate tree, collected some branches, bound them, and started hitting his feet from beneath.'

2.2. The Genitive Exponent from a Cross-Dialectal Perspective

The distribution of genitive exponents is uneven, both typologically and geographically, across the Arabic-speaking world. It has been pointed out by many scholars (Marçais 1977; Eksell 1980; Naim 2011) that the synthetic construction is preferred in the Bedouin dialects of the Sahara, while the analytic one prevails in sedentary dialects. One can expect, therefore, that the distribution of *iḍāfa* in Jewish Gabes will be considerably limited. Below, one can find some selected genitive exponents from different geographical regions:[14]

---

[14] The table is based mostly on Naim (2011).

Table 66: Genitive exponents in selected dialects of Arabic

Genitive exponent	Region
dyāl / d-	Morocco
əddi (Djidjelli), əlli (Constantine)	Algeria
ntāʕ, mtāʕ, tāʕ	Libya, Tunisia
ḥagg, ḥaqq	Arabian Peninsula, Galilee Bedouin, Sudan
māl	Iraq, Oman, Yemen
dīl, dēl	Qəltu dialects of upper and lower Iraq, Anatolia, Syria–Lebanon–Palestine
lēl	Qəltu dialects, Daragözü, Sudan
bitāʕ	Egypt

This provisional comparison clearly indicates that the genitive exponent in various dialects has different etymological origins. Eksell (2009, 39) divides them in two main groups: those deriving from a noun denoting possession, e.g., *ḥagg* in Ṣanʕānī Arabic, which, when isolated, means 'property, right' (Watson 1993, 220), and those that originate in a relative/demonstrative pronoun, e.g., CA *allāḏī* > Moroccan *dyāl*. Tunisian *ntāʕ* would therefore fall into the first category, as it originally denoted property or possession.

From a historical point of view, the function of *ntāʕ* as a genitive exponent is already attested in Medieval Judaeo-Arabic (Blau 1961, 159). It is well established in a wide array of the North African dialects and is particularly operative in sedentary dialects. Similarly widespread is Moroccan *dyāl*, which, according to Brustad (2000, 85), is found in the highest frequency of any genitive particle among all Arabic dialects covered by her research. On the other hand, *dēl–lēl* exponents in Mesopotamia and Anatolia are obsolete and not productive. This discrepancy has been explained by Eksell (2009, 48) by means of an Aramaic substratum. According to Eksell, while Moroccan *dyāl* seems to derive from *allāḏi*, Mesopotamian *ḏēl* presumably originates in the Aramaic particle /d-/ and therefore has ultimately been rejected as a foreign element. Nevertheless, as argued by Heath (2015), the Arabic-internal origin of the Moroccan particle *dyal* is dubious. Instead, it has been suggested that *dyal* stems from the Late Latin genitive particle *dē* and reflects the earliest stages of the formation of Moroccan Arabic.

2.3. The Synthetic Genitive in Jewish Gabes

In this section, I shall discuss two types of synthetic genitive present in Jewish Gabes, namely, an annexation phrase consisting of two nominals, and an annexation phrase in which the annexed term is modified by a pronoun.[15] Several restrictions govern the first type of annexation: the annexed term cannot admit the definite article, nor can it be an inherently definite noun, like a proper name or pronoun. When a phrase is definite, only the annex takes the definite article. In an annexation phrase, when the annexed term ends with /-a/, this is replaced by an allomorph -ət/at. Jewish Gabes, like many other modern Arabic dialects, does not usually permit a phrase consisting of more than two nominal annexes.[16] Potential multiple annexation strings are broken by the genitive exponent. An annexation phrase can be

---

[15] These terms have been borrowed from the syntax of Ṣanʕānī dialect (Watson 1993, 173).

[16] The same rule exists, *inter alia,* in Ṣanʕānī Arabic and in other Maghrebi dialects (Marçais 1977, 171; Watson 1993, 176).

modified attributively by an adjective or demonstrative pronoun, in which case the attribute is mandatorily in agreement with the annexed term.

An annexation phrase is applied in a number of genitive constructions associated with certain semantic fields. Below I present the main types of genitive occurring in Jewish Gabes, named after the semantic value of the relationship they denote. Their character can be either identificatory, indicating the relationship of possession, or classificatory, indicating a type or kind of the annexed term.[17] The examples come from both the text corpus and questionnaires.

2.3.1. Synthetic Genitive of Place

The first example is clearly classificatory, as it distinguishes the group of the Jews living in the mountains from other Jews. The next two examples are identificatory and indicate an inalienable possession. While, in the first and second examples, the synthetic genitive could be replaced respectively by the analytic prepositional construction with *ntāʕ* and by the preposition *fi* 'in', i.e., **yhūd ntāʕ žbəl* and **žāra fi-l-ḥamma* (lit. 'pilgrimage in El-Hamma'), in the third one, meaning literally 'the heart of the house', such replacement is rejected as ungrammatical, probably due to the fixed character of the phrase.

---

[17] This distinction has been borrowed from *A Reference Grammar of Syrian Arabic* by Mark W. Cowell (1964, 458).

1. yhūd əž-žbəl   'Jews of mountains'
2. žyārat əl-ḥamma   'pilgrimage to El-Hamma'
3. qəlb əḍ-ḍāṛ   'the house interior'

2.3.2. Synthetic Genitive of Quantity

This type of annexation is exclusively classificatory and, contrary to Moroccan, cannot be replaced analytically by means of *ntāʕ*.[18] As can be inferred from the following examples, the genitive of quantity is very often indefinite:

1. nfayyəṣ xabža   'little half a bread loaf'
2. nəfṣ šāʕa   'half an hour'
3. ṛāṣ əl-bṣəl   'one onion'

2.3.3. Synthetic Genitive of Description

The basic function of the genitive of description is to add an attributive value to the annexed term. Therefore, the type of annexation it represents should be defined as classificatory. It can be replaced periphrastically by the genitive exponent.

1. lḥam ʕallūš   'lamb meat'
2. ṣəṭṭ əl-bḥar   'seashore'
3. žīn əl-gumra   'the beauty of the moon'

---

[18] Brustad (2000, 89) gives an example of *xəmsa d drāhəm* 'five drahms', which in Jewish Gabes was categorically rejected as ungrammatical. Similarly, in Ṣanʕānī Arabic, the use of the genitive exponent is not permitted in this case; nonetheless, a periphrasis with the preposition *min* is acceptable (Watson 1993, 186).

2.3.4. Synthetic Genitive of Possession

This type of genitive covers both alienable (e.g., house) and inalienable (e.g., parts of the body) possession. It is particularly operative in the semantic field of kinship and parts of the body. As the first example demonstrates, the annex can be indefinite. While an alienable possession can be expressed analytically, e.g., ḍāṛ ntāʕ bābāy 'my father's house', some phrases expressing human relationships cannot. An informant categorically rejected the forms *l-umm ntāʕk 'your mother', *l-bū ntāʕk 'your father', and *l-xū ntāʕk 'your brother' as ungrammatical, but accepted the form wəld ntāḥḥa 'her child' as an indicative equivalent of wəldha. On the other hand, body parts are acceptable in a periphrasis, e.g., l-wdən ntāʕk 'your ear'.

1.	məṛt xūya	'the sister of my brother'
2.	wəld əṣ-ṣəlṭān	'the sultan's son'
3.	ḍāṛ bābāy	'my father's house'
4.	wədnək wa yəddək	'your ear and your hand'

2.4. The Analytic Genitive in Jewish Gabes

The genitive exponent *ntāʕ* in Jewish Gabes has several truncated allomorphs: *tāʕ, taʕ,* and *ta*. Eksell (2009, 36) points out that, in Morocco and Algeria, the analytic genitive is the ordinary way to express the genitive. This suggests, therefore, that its occurrence would be high in Tunisia also, especially among sedentary dialects. Indeed, as can be inferred from my data, the use of the analytic genitive in Jewish Gabes is much more frequent than that of the synthetic one. As has been mentioned above, in many cases, the analytic annexation can replace the synthetic one, but there are cases where only the periphrasis is possible.

In Jewish Gabes, the exponent does not exhibit number or gender agreement with the annexed term. Despite the fact that lack of agreement is the prevalent option in the Maghrebi dialects, some Bedouin dialects of Algeria and Morocco possess also feminine *mtāʕət* and plural *mtāwʕ* forms. Similarly, parallel forms have been attested in several Bedouin dialects of Southern Tunisia and Libya, where one finds also distinct plural forms: *mtāʕīn* and *mtāʕāt* (Marçais 1977, 168). However, among all the Arabic dialects, only in Egyptian are gender and number agreement obligatory (Brustad 2000, 72).

Following the taxonomy applied to the synthetic genitive, I shall now itemise the main types of the analytic genitive in Jewish Gabes.

2.4.1. Analytic Genitive of Alienable Possession

This type of genitive can be used interchangeably with the synthetic genitive of possession; however, the analytic genitive highlights the annexed term, often in a contrastive manner:

1. *l-žnəbb ntāʕ l-bənt* 'the daughter's side'
2. *əṣ-ṣūra tāʕ l-ʕarūṣa* 'the bride's dowry'
3. *l-məžān tāʕkəm* 'your scale'
4. *ləbša tāʕ* [HE]saba[HE] *u* [HE]sāvta[HE] 'grandfather and grandmother's clothes'

2.4.2. Analytic Genitive of Attribution

This corresponds to the synthetic genitive of description and can potentially be replaced by it. It seems, however, that the analytic annexation denotes more individuated referents:

1. ṣəžra kbīra tāʕ blaḥ   'the big fruit tree'
2. naxla tāʕ ṛmān   'the pomegranate tree'
3. məlḥ tāʕ ᴴᴱōmerᴴᴱ   'the Omer salt'

2.4.3. Analytic Genitive of Time

While the first two examples can be replaced by synthetic annexation, expression of time can only be achieved analytically, either by means of the genitive exponent, or by the preposition *fi*.

1. ᴴᴱxōdəšᴴᴱ tāʕ ᴴᴱnissanᴴᴱ 'the month of Nissan'
2. līl tāʕ ᴴᴱbišaḥᴴᴱ   'the night of Passover'
3. tlāta tāʕ ṣbāḥ   'three in the morning'

2.4.4. Analytic Genitive of Place

The basic function of this type of genitive is to narrow the focus of the annexed term. It can potentially be replaced by the synthetic construction, but the two types of genitive differ in meaning. While *yhūd tūnəš* bears the meaning of classification, pointing taxonomically to the distinctiveness of the Jews of Tunis from other Jews, *yhūd tāʕ tūnəš* is focusing on the place of their origin. In the sentence: *žāw yhūd tāʕ tūnəš* 'the Jews of Tunis came', the speaker is stressing the fact that the Jews came <u>from</u> Tunis, and therefore the focus is on their place of origin, and not on their ethnic distinctiveness from other Jews.

1. *yhūd tāʕ tūnəš*   'the Jews of Tunis'
2. *əẓ-ẓġār tāʕ škūla*   'the children of the school'
3. *xabž tāʕ ṣūq*   'bread of the market'

2.5. Formal Restrictions

As has been observed by many scholars (Marçais 1977, 171; Eksell 1980, 106; Brustad 2000, 74), the choice between the synthetic and the analytic genitive is very often restricted by some formal factors. In the case of Jewish Gabes, a few motivations can be distinguished. The first of them is related to the high occurrence of Hebrew loans, which never form synthetic annexation. My data includes the following examples: ᴴᴱagadaᴴᴱ *ntāʕna* 'our Aggada', ᴴᴱabīlᴴᴱ *ntāʕu* 'his mourning', ᴴᴱšəbbatᴴᴱ *ntāʕu* 'his shabbat', *məlḥ tāʕ* ᴴᴱōmerᴴᴱ 'the Omer salt'. Secondly, a multi-term noun phrase is usually broken by the genitive exponent, e.g., ᴴᴱrōšᴴᴱ *əl-*ᴴᴱxōdəšᴴᴱ *tāʕa* ᴴᴱnissānᴴᴱ 'the beginning of the month of Nissan'. Finally, the syllable structure of some words does not permit direct annexation, namely, when a noun ends with a vowel other than the feminine marker /-a/, e.g., *əl-kərši ntāʕi* 'my chair', *əḍ-ḍuww ntāʕha* 'her light'.

2.6. The Genitive and Definiteness

It is widely accepted that the genitive exponent in the dialects of Arabic is the domain of specific and individuated phrases, as opposed to the construct phrase, which tends to be correlated with general relations of kinship and possession (Brustad 2000, 80). I also previously mentioned another distinction, namely, that any type of genitive can function either for individuation, or for classification. The former is closely related to the notion of possession, and therefore denotes highly individuated items, which can potentially also be expressed by synthetic annexation with a pronoun. Contrary to this, the classificatory genitive is associated with annexation phrases of low individuation and general identity, which function as generic examples of their kind (Brustad 2000, 80). Nonetheless, this distinction is not always completely clear. For example, Brustad (2000, 80) argues that the example from Egyptian given by Eksell (1980, 87), *il-kitāb bitāʕ is-siḥr* 'the book of magic', demonstrates the use of a classificatory construction, since it refers to a specific type of book. This interpretation rather goes against the rules established by Cowell (1964, 461) for Syrian Arabic. Even though the phrase is definite, the type of genitive indicates a type of book, i.e., a book of magic and not, for example, a book of prayers, and thus does not contain the element of possession required for identification.

Brustad (2000, 81) also noticed that, while Egyptian Arabic uses the exponent only to identify and not to classify, in Moroccan and Kuwaiti it serves both purposes. It could be assumed, therefore, that the individuation and specificity of a noun do not entirely dictate the use of the genitive exponent in Moroccan, as it also fulfils a classificatory function, which is usually associated with low-individuation phrases. The situation in Jewish Gabes seems to resemble that of Moroccan, namely, the individuation and definiteness of the annexed term are only tangentially related to the distribution of the genitive exponent, i.e., the genitive exponent does not occur exclusively in definite phrases. However, depending on the definiteness of the phrase, it can fulfil different functions. When it is found in a definite phrase, it can have contrastive or deictic value, while in an indefinite phrase, its function is mainly classificatory. An example of the latter is seen in the following passage:

(1) *mšāt*   *l-naxla tāʕ ṛmān*   *qaṣṣət*   *l-ʕrūf*
    go.SFX.3FS to-palm GEN pomegranate cut.PFX.3FS DEF-branches
    'She went to the pomegranate tree, cut some sticks.' (2:23)

The reference here is the type of tree, namely, the speaker highlights that it is a pomegranate tree because it has sharp branches, and this in turn will be important in the following part of the story. On the other hand, when the exponent functions as identificatory in a definite phrase, it can have a contrastive aspect:

(2) *ʕamlət*   *kəṣkṣu* *u*   *ḥaṭṭətla*
    make.SFX.3FS couscous and put.SFX.3FS.her
    šəmm *fi-l-žnəbb* *tāʕ l-bənt*
    poison in-DEF-side GEN DEF-daughter
    'She prepared couscous and put poison on the daughter's side.' (4:116)

In this example, the exponent introduces a contrast between the side of the daughter, which has poison, and the side of the mother. This distinction plays a key role in the story, because ultimately the daughter will change the sides and, as a consequence, cause the death of her mother-in-law.

Another role of the analytic genitive particle is to draw special attention to the annex through the function of deixis, e.g.:

(3) əl-wəld **tāʕ** hādi əl-mṛa
    DEF-boy GEN this DEF-woman
    'The child of this woman.'

However, in some cases, the definiteness of an analytic annexation is affected by associative anaphora. In the following example, there is no reference to any specific dowry. The passage comes from the description of a typical wedding in Gabes, and the general and universal dimension of this narrative is reflected by the impersonal verb form. Nonetheless, the dowry, notwithstanding its non-individuated character, is definite, since every wedding presupposes the existence of a dowry:

(4) l-nhār yəxšlu   əṣ-ṣūra   **tāʕ** l-ʕarūṣa yaʕmlu
    DEF-day clean.PFX.3PL DEF-dowry GEN DEF-bride   make.PFX.3PL
    u   mən ġadwa   ṣḥābha   yḥaddədu
    and from tomorrow   friends.her   iron.PFX.3PL
    'One day they would clean the dowry of the bride, make it up, the day after the friends of the bride would iron.'

In sum, it can be established that the genitive exponent in Jewish Gabes plays a classificatory role when in an indefinite phrase, and an identificatory (contrastive, expositive, deictic) role when in a definite one. This assumption confirms Cowell's (1964, 458) argument that "identification is fundamentally a function of definiteness and classification a function of indefiniteness."

3.0. Grammatical Concord[19]

In this section, I will present the main features of the agreement system in Jewish Gabes, simultaneously outlining the historical background of this phenomenon in Semitic. The term 'agreement' denotes a syntactic congruence of words in gender, number, person, and determination (Levi 2013). My investigation will focus primarily on the agreement between adjective and head noun and between subject and predicate. As argued by Hasselbach (2014, 35), agreement depends either on syntax, or on semantics of the phrase. She gives an example of the word 'committee', which can be perceived as a unity and therefore take singular agreement, or the focus can be placed on the plurality of its members, in which case the agreement will be plural.[20] The semantic perception of the head noun by the speaker will be of particular interest in the following part of the discussion.

3.1. Historical Perspective

Semitic languages exhibit several agreement systems, the origins of which are still matter of discussion among scholars. In North-West Semitic, and especially in Biblical Hebrew and in Aramaic, strict agreement in gender and in number is a general rule gov-

---

[19] An extended version of this section can be found in a paper 'Between Analogy and Language Contact: A Case Study of Grammatical Change in Maghrebi Judaeo-Arabic Dialects' (Gębski, forthcoming b).

[20] Following Corbett (2006, 4), in my study, I will apply the following terminology: 'controller', i.e., the element determining agreement, and 'target', i.e., a form determined by agreement (Hasselbach 2014, 35).

erning syntactic relationships between both head nouns and attributive adjectives, and subjects and predicates.[21] In Classical Ethiopic, on the other hand, only nouns denoting human beings form agreement, while all other animate and inanimate entities lack any agreement. Somewhere between these two extrema is CA, where agreement depends both on animacy, i.e., inanimate nouns take feminine singular agreement, and on position in the sentence, i.e., the subject agrees with the predicate only when it precedes it, not when it follows.

From a historical point of view, nominal agreement arose in different circumstances from verbal agreement. The latter, as argued by Givón (1976) and Hasselbach (2014, 41), is closely related to the grammaticalisation of pronouns, which began with appositional constructions, and subsequently became incorporated into the verb. This theory is supported by evidence from Akkadian and Neo-Aramaic dialects. However, the origin of nominal agreement is less straightforward. One of the theories is related to grammaticalisation, namely, that nominal agreement could have arisen from weak deictic pronouns (Lehmann 1988, 59–60). An alternative explanation, based on parallels found in the Bantu languages, suggests that agreement stems from noun classifiers such as 'human', 'abstract/mass', etc., which originally had their own markers.

The emergence of agreement is closely related to the rise of gender marking. In Semitic, masculine is the default gender and

---

[21] There are numerous examples of incongruence in Biblical Hebrew, stemming from re-writing and editing of the biblical text in different periods of time (Levi 2013).

is unmarked, while feminine is marked by the /-(a)t/ suffix. There are, however, numerous exceptions to this rule, and every Semitic language has a set of unmarked feminine nouns denoting basic vocabulary, like, for example, *ummum* 'mother', as well as nouns of variable gender (Hasselbach 2014, 44). Moreover, Semitic has many examples of heteroclisis, i.e., some nouns exhibit mismatch between plural form and gender marker. How exactly the feminine marking arose is still matter of debate among scholars. It is widely accepted that, at an early stage of Semitic, the gender was not marked by an affix, but rather through vowel ablaut and suppletion, and only highly animate nouns were marked for gender. Subsequently, gender marking by means of suffixes started appearing on some targets, while controllers remained unchanged. This suggests that nominal agreement is a secondary development, stemming from gender marking on adjectives, which later spread onto controllers. Beyond this point, each language applied its own rules governing agreement. In the case of CA, two restrictions were imposed, i.e., animacy and position.

3.2. Data Analysis

The data presented below has been obtained by means of a questionnaire:

1. Human feminine plural head nouns:
    1. *ən-nša žāw yəṭlbu l-ma*
       'The women came to ask for water.'
    2. *ən-nša l-oxrīn kānu yxāfu mənhu*
       'Other women were scared of him.'

3. *bnāt məžyānīn yžīw l-ʕarš*
   'Beautiful women will come for the wedding.'

4. *šāʕāt l-bnāt yəmšīw yəṣthu*
   'Sometimes girls go to dance.'

5. *qbəl kānu nša yūldu fi-l-gīṭūn*
   'Earlier women would give birth in tents.'

2. Human masculine plural head nouns:

   1. *fi-bdu l-ʕarš əržāla yəṣrbu qahwa*
      'At the beginning of the wedding men drink coffee.'

   2. *zġīrāt dīma yəlʕabu f-əṣ-ṣətwān*
      'Boys would always play in the court.'

   3. *l-nās l-əkbār žāw*
      'The elders have arrived.'

   4. *nāš l-kull/kulla žāw yšūfu l-ʕarūṣa*
      'Everyone came to see the bride.'

   5. *l-ʕbād l-kbār ma yəṭlaʕūṣ mən ḍārhəm*
      'The elderly people do not leave their homes.'

3. Singular nouns denoting groups of people:

   1. *ḍāṛ l-ʕarīš bdāw yġannīw*
      'The family of the groom started singing.'

   2. *l-būlīṣīya žāw u ḥabbšūhum l-kull*
      'The police came and arrested everyone.'

4. Animal head nouns:

   1. *l-ʕalālīš mšāw əl-l-wād yəṣrbu l-ma*
      'Lambs went to the river to have some water.'

   2. *l-ʕṣāfīr əlli šəfthəm āməš žāw mən əṣ-ṣaḥra*
      'The birds that you saw yesterday had come from the desert.'

3. *l-ṭyūr žāw*
   'Birds have come.'
4. *tlāta aḥṣānāt, xamṣa bgār*
   'Three horses, five cows.'
5. *əl-bgār ndəbḥu qbəl l-ʕīd*
   'The cows are slaughtered before the festival.'

5. Inanimate head nouns:

   1. *ṣrīna bībān əždəd*
      'We bought new doors.'
   2. *əl-nhārāt yətʕaddu bə-šwīya*
      'The days pass by slowly.'
   3. *tmənya nəxlāt hādu*
      'These eight palm trees.'
   4. *tlāta xabžāt hādu*
      'These three loaves of bread.'
   5. *šəbʕa ḥažrāt mdəwwrīn u nfatḥīn*
      'Seven round and flat rocks.'

The data presented above clearly demonstrate that there is strict agreement in Jewish Gabes in both the nominal and verbal phrase. The examples have been classified according to the categories of animacy and gender. As can be inferred, regardless of the gender or level of animacy of the controller, almost all the targets are in complete agreement. In what follows, I shall discuss this phenomenon in the wider context of the Jewish and Muslim dialects of North Africa.

Patterns of grammatical agreement have recently gained a lot of attention in scholarship on both literary and dialectal forms of Arabic. The general interest in grammatical concord resulted in several pioneering studies that cast new light on its diachronic development. In dialectology, agreement patterns in Tunisian Arabic are well described thanks to studies on the Southern Bedouin dialects of Tunisian Arabic (Ritt-Benmimoun 2017), as well as those of the urban north (Procházka and Gabsi 2017). There exist numerous studies on this phenomenon in Cairene Arabic (Belnap 1991; 1993; 1994; 1999), the Libyan dialect of Fezzan (D'Anna 2017), and Omani Arabic (Bettega 2018). Similarly, in the realm of Quranic and Classical Arabic, the topic has received a lot of scholarly attention (Ferguson 1989; Belnap and Shabaneh 1992; 1994; Dror 2013; 2016; D'Anna 2020). Finally, the problem of grammatical concord in both written and spoken forms of Arabic has been extensively treated in Bettega and D'Anna (2022). Against this background, grammatical concord in Jewish varieties of North African Arabic remains *terra incognita*. The exception to this tendency is the grammar of Jewish Tripoli, where Yoda (2005, 285) mentions that plural nouns always agree with their arguments.

A study of grammatical concord in Judaeo-Arabic has the potential to make a significant contribution to our knowledge of this grammatical phenomenon for two reasons. Firstly, there exists a wealth of textual Judaeo-Arabic sources, which reflect both the literary and the colloquial language alike, and therefore might reveal invaluable information about the diachronic development of agreement. Secondly, since Judaeo-Arabic dialects were, in the second half of the twentieth century, transplanted from their natural environment into Hebrew-speaking Israel, one can assume that the Israeli Hebrew system of strict agreement has affected the Judaeo-Arabic system. The study of this phenomenon could be crucial for establishing the sensitivity of grammatical concord in a language contact situation. To this end, in the following paragraphs, I will analyse several examples of grammatical concord in a few dialects of North African Arabic, simultaneously providing historical data where possible. I argue that, as in the case of the /t-/ prefix marking the passive (see chapter 3, §2.2), the generalisation of strict agreement in modern dialects of Maghrebi Judaeo-Arabic took place at the intersection of analogy and language contact.

One of the most striking features of the syntax of the surviving varieties of Maghrebi Judaeo-Arabic is their strict grammatical agreement. This tendency stands in striking contrast to the Muslim and Bedouin dialects, where plural controllers low in animacy and individuation trigger agreement with the third person singular feminine. This latter type of agreement will, in the present study, be called 'deflected'.[22] The situation prevalent in these Muslim and Bedouin dialects has in fact a long historical tradition. Some modern dialects, like Cairene and Damascus Arabic, feature a variation between strict and deflected agreement similar to that found in Old Arabic sources (e.g., pre-Islamic poetry) and Christian Middle Arabic, where it reflects colloquial language (Belnap and Gee 1994, 131). In contradistinction to this tendency, in Classical Arabic, a rapid generalisation of the rule

---

[22] This term has been chosen following Belnap and Gee (1994) and Ritt-Benmimoun (2017).

of deflected agreement with nonhuman controllers took place.[23] Against this historical background, two questions arise regarding the evolution of agreement in Judaeo-Arabic. Firstly, do Judaeo-Arabic sources reflecting the spoken language point to a similar level of variation, or rather, has the distribution of deflected agreement in this variety always been rather limited? And secondly, has the prevalence of strict agreement in modern varieties been caused by language contact with Israeli Hebrew, or is it rather rooted in the internal development of Judaeo-Arabic?

In order to better understand the nature of agreement in Judaeo-Arabic, let us first discuss this phenomenon in non-Jewish Arabic from a diachronic perspective. As pointed out below, we can assume with a high degree of certainty that, in contradistinction to Classical Arabic, the system of agreement in non-Jewish Arabic has remained relatively stable, exhibiting variation between the strict and the deflected options. Belnap and Gee (1994), in their quantitative study of the occurrence of different variants of agreement in textual sources from between the sixth and fourteenth centuries, demonstrate that agreement with nonhuman plural heads was at first almost equally distributed between feminine singular, feminine plural, and broken plural. For instance, in works of Imru' al-Qays, from the sixth century, these categories account respectively for 38, 31, and 31 percent of the occurrences, while in Al-Xansaa', from the seventh century, they

---

[23] As argued by Belnap and Gee (1994, 141), the generalisation of the pre-existing deflected agreement in CA might have taken place due to the scribal practices of non-native speakers of Arabic, who were unsure of the rules of variation between the two types of agreement.

account for 48, 27, and 25 percent. These proportions are disrupted from the seventh century onwards, when deflected agreement becomes the only option for non-human heads. The explanation for this development is rather complex, but we can assume that, with the introduction of the Quran and the activities of grammarians and intellectuals who were not native speakers of Arabic, written Arabic became more prescriptive and more detached from the spoken language.

As stated above, many modern dialects of Arabic still reflect the OA system, which exhibits the two types of agreement. This is also the case in North African dialects when the head is low in individuation and generic. Some examples from Muslim Tunis can be found below (elicited from an informant):

(1) l-klēb   bdēt   tēkəl
     DEF-dogs start.SFX.3FS eat.PFX.3FS
     'The dogs started eating.'

(2) kif   l-ʕbēd   bdēt   təžri   l-qtaṭes harbət
     when DEF-people   start.SFX.3FS run.PFX.3FS   DEF-cats flee.SFX.3FS
     'When people started running, the cats fled.'

However, controllers with a higher degree of individuation are in strict agreement with their targets:[24]

(3) ər-ržēl   qāʕdīn   yošrbu   fi-qahwa
     DEF.men   sit.AP.PL   drink.PFX.3PL in-coffee
     'The men are drinking coffee.'

---

[24] As pointed out by Brustad (2000, 38), the gender of the controller can also affect the choice of agreement, with masculine nouns being more individuated and animate.

As confirmed by Procházka and Gabsi (2017, 245), deflected agreement with human controllers is rather rare and limited to *nās* and *ʕabēd* as collectives denoting people, but other groups of nouns demonstrate a wide array of variation. A similar tendency is attested in the Bedouin dialect of Nifzāwa (Tunisia) and in Benghazi (Libya; Benkato 2014, 88; Ritt-Benmimoun 2017).[25]

Against this background, in several Jewish dialects of North African Arabic, strict agreement is the only available variant. This has already been pointed out by Yoda (2005) with regard to Jewish Tripoli. Jewish Gabes (Southern Tunisia) and Wad-Souf (Eastern Algeria) are an additional two dialects where, at least synchronically, we observe this tendency. Let us have a look at several examples from Jewish Wad-Souf:

(4) kān ṣəkkāt kānu yuḍrubu nṣāwinhəm maʕrūfīn
be.SFX.3MS families be.SFX.3PL hit.PFX.3PL women know.PP
'There were families, which were known for hitting their women.'

(5) kānu nās ygūlu hāḏi əṣ-ṣəkka ṣəkkət əẓ-ẓəbda
be.SFX.3PL people say.PFX.3PL this DEF-family family DEF-butter
'People would say: this family is very mild (literally: this family is a family of butter).'

---

[25] This tendency is attested to a lesser extent in the south-Libyan dialect of Fezzan, where deflected agreement accounts for only 10% of occurrences of plural heads. Nevertheless, the data for this dialect do not contain abstract and less individuated nouns and are therefore not representative of the overall distribution of deflected agreement (D'Anna 2017, 119).

(6) *l-mʕāz mātu bi-l-mrāḍ*
DEF-sheep die.SFX.3PL in-DEF-disease
'The sheep perished because of the disease.'

(7) *l-wlād l-kull xaržu mən madrāsa*
DEF-children DEF-all exist.SFX.3PL from school
'All the children went out of school.'

(8) *kānu ʕanda tlāṯa arbaʕ xarrāfāt tʕāwəd*
be.SFX.3PL at.her three four tales repeat.PFX.3FS
ʕalīm kull marra hāḏākum xarrāfāt
on.them.3PL every time those.3PL tales
'She had three or four tales, she would repeat them every time, those tales.'

These examples clearly indicate that strict agreement is the general rule in the dialects in question, regardless of the level of individuation, human/non-human distinction, or abstract/concrete distinction. Since neither the dialect of Gabes nor that of Wad-Souf preserved the feminine forms of the plural, all the plural controllers are followed by targets in the masculine form of the plural. This tendency is particularly surprising in the case of Wad-Souf. Inasmuch as Gabes is a first-wave, sedentary dialect, Wad-Souf exhibits numerous Bedouin features, e.g., the realisation of /q/ as /g/ as in *ygūlu* 'they say'; preservation of interdentals, as in *hāḏi* 'this (FS)'; and the plural form *nsāwīn* 'women', instead of the sedentary form *nsa*. One would expect, therefore, that this explicitly conservative dialect would also reflect the Bedouin-type pattern of agreement, characterised by widespread variation between the strict and deflected options. Since no case of deflected agreement has been attested in this conservative variety, it seems that either its distribution in the past was only marginal, or that it has never been an option. This assumption is further confirmed by a statistical survey of agreement in Jewish Tunis. Below one can find a table summarising my survey of Cohen's text corpus from 1964:[26]

Table 67: Agreement patterns in Jewish Tunis (Cohen 1964)

	Verbs	%	Adjectives	%	Pronouns	%	Total %
Masculine plural	104	**90**	17	100	31	100	**93**
Feminine singular	11	**10**	0	0	0	0	**7**
Total	115		17		31		

The corpus in question contains mainly transcriptions of free-speech narratives related to the Jewish community in Tunis, but several poems have been included too. The survey has revealed several striking tendencies. Firstly, deflected agreement occurs only in verbs. No occurrences of deflected agreement have been found in adjectives or pronouns. Secondly, out of 163 occurrences of plural heads with targets, only 11 of the targets are in 3FS, which amounts to only seven percent of all the examples. It is important to notice, however, that out of the 11 examples of deflected agreement, three appear in poetry, where they were apparently conditioned by rhyme, as in the following example (Cohen 1964, 123):

---

[26] If a plural head is followed by more than one target in the same person, they have been counted as one. Generic sentences without a subject always contain the verb in the 3PL form and have therefore not been considered in the survey. The system of transcription used for the examples from Jewish Tunis has been adopted from the source.

(9) yūm žəmʕa ʕal-bəkrīya
    Friday   early
    rūḥi   xaržət   **wəntfāt**
    spirit.mine leave.SFX.3FS and.extinguish.SFX.3FS
    'Early on Friday, my soul left and extinguished.'

    ḥīn   šəmʕat   ənnās bīya
    immediately   hear.SFX.3FS people in-her
    zġāṛ   u-kbāṛ   ʕalīya **bkāt**
    small.PL   and-big.PL   on-her cry.SFX.3FS
    'Immediately people learn about it, young and old cry over me.'

Another unexpected tendency is that all 11 occurrences of deflected targets accompany human controllers; these are usually *nās* 'people', *nša* 'women', or *ʕawwadīya* 'musicians'. Surprisingly, non-human controllers that are low in individuation trigger strict agreement: *daxlu lə-qṭāṭoṣ* 'the cats entered', *wel-fonctions ntaḥḥa yəlzəmməm yəbdāw doubles* 'her functions must start being double' (Cohen 1964, 136, 49). This significantly differs from the situation found in Muslim Tunis, where groups of animals treated as a whole and abstract nouns trigger deflected agreement (Procházka and Gabsi 2017).

The data from Jewish Tunis is of paramount importance, as it has been recorded in its natural environment, without any interference from Israeli Hebrew. The question arises as to whether this type of marginal deflected agreement with non-individuated plural human controllers reflects a situation common to all the varieties of spoken Judaeo-Arabic of the region, or different dialects utilise different types of agreement. Unfortunately, a diachronic survey, which could potentially elucidate this issue, is hindered by a lack of available textual Judaeo-Arabic sources from the Maghreb that reflect the spoken language. Nevertheless, various studies on pre-modern Judaeo-Arabic suggest that deflected agreement has never reached the same level of distribution there as in the Muslim varieties, but has rather remained marginal throughout history.

Blau (1961, 131) points out that, in Medieval Judaeo-Arabic, strict agreement is almost the rule in verb-subject alignment. Both animal and non-animate heads trigger strict agreement in this type of sentence. Interestingly, the only exception to this rule is human controllers, in which case the verb is occasionally in the 3FS form. Similarly, non-human controllers are in strict grammatical agreement with their targets as far as subject-verb alignment is concerned. On the other hand, human controllers sporadically trigger deflected agreement. This situation reveals a striking resemblance to Jewish Tunis, where no cases of non-human heads with deflected agreement have been attested. The rule of strict grammatical agreement has also been attested in sources containing the Egyptian *šarḥ*, i.e., translations of the Bible into Judaeo-Arabic. Although one might argue that this tendency could stem from verbatim translation of the Hebrew text, where strict agreement prevails, Hary (2009, 275) argues that strict grammatical concord is a feature of both Classical Judaeo-Arabic and colloquial Jewish Egyptian. This evidence could potentially point to a difference between the Judaeo-Arabic system of agreement, and the Muslim one, where, as argued before, deflected agreement remained an option with non-individuated plural heads.[27]

After discussing patterns of agreement from a comparative perspective, let us now return to the question posited in the first paragraphs: has the strict agreement of some Jewish dialects of the Maghreb (Tripoli, Gabes, Wad-Souf) been triggered by Israeli Hebrew, or is it rather a result of the internal evolution of Judaeo-Arabic? The textual evidence from Judaeo-Arabic, in conjunction with Cohen's transcriptions from 1964, suggests that the system of agreement in Judaeo-Arabic differs from that in the continuum of pre-Classical poetry and modern Muslim dialects. Specifically, in the latter group, deflected agreement exists as an option with both human and non-human plural controllers, while in the former it is primarily applied with human ones, and only

---

[27] I am aware of two types of Judaeo-Arabic sources where deflected agreement appears with non-human plural heads. I have spotted a couple such cases in Egyptian folktales and letters of merchants also from Egypt and the Maghreb (Connolly 2018; Wagner 2010). Nevertheless, since no transcription corpus is available, nor does a systematic description of agreement in these sources exist, it is difficult to draw any conclusions. Naturally, Judaeo-Arabic did not evolve in complete isolation and one should therefore assume that there were cases of interference of the Muslim variety, or imitation of it. Wagner (2010, 14) points out that the Egyptian varieties of Judaeo-Arabic, which were more central within the Muslim empire, were generally more progressive than the peripheral Maghrebi ones, which retained more conservative features. Thus, examples of deflected agreement with non-human controllers from Egyptian sources should be taken with a pinch of salt, as they might have been affected by the non-Jewish varieties.

to a very limited extent. It is rather difficult to offer a historical explanation of how this discrepancy emerged, as the past of the spoken language is poorly documented. Nevertheless, one can assume that the correlation between deflected agreement and non-individuated controllers has never been fully adopted in spoken Maghrebi Judaeo-Arabic. This state of affairs might tentatively be accounted for by languages that Jews had been speaking before the first wave of Arabisation of the Maghreb, i.e., Late Latin, Berber, and presumably Punic, as in none of these languages does deflected agreement exist. The liturgical usage of Hebrew and Aramaic could also potentially have contributed to the emergence of the Judaeo-Arabic system of agreement. Nevertheless, if we accept the assumption that there existed a limited usage of deflected agreement in different Jewish dialects of Arabic, how do we explain its complete absence in Jewish Tripoli, Gabes, and Wad-Souf? *Prima facie* the easiest explanation is the influence of Israeli Hebrew, which does not utilise agreement with 3FS. However, as the above study demonstrates, deflected agreement has never been used to the same extent in Judaeo-Arabic as in Muslim Arabic. I would thus like to raise the possibility that, as in the case of the /t-/ prefix, the rejection of deflected agreement came about at the intersection of language contact and analogy. Since there existed within Judaeo-Arabic itself potential for the analogical extension of strict agreement, i.e., deflected agreement has never been fully adopted as a viable option, language contact with Israeli Hebrew triggered the definitive extension of this pattern. It is plausible that analogical extension of the strict pattern had been operating at different stages of the historical development of Judaeo-Arabic, preventing the spread of deflected agreement, whose presence is attested in historical sources. In this way, in the second half of the twentieth century, deflected agreement, additionally weakened by Israeli Hebrew, has been entirely replaced through analogical extension of strict agreement, which, historically, had been by far the most common variant.[28]

3.3. Conclusions

As has been demonstrated, Jewish Gabes exhibits a pattern of strict agreement. In this respect, it aligns with several other Jewish dialects of the region. It is reasonable to presuppose that, at an earlier stage, it had a mixed type, similar to that of Jewish Tunis, in which both animacy and position played a role. I have argued that the uniformity of the agreement system in Jewish Gabes could potentially be explained by a conjunction of two factors: analogy and language contact with Modern Hebrew. The historical sources suggest that deflected agreement has never been fully adopted in the Jewish dialects. A North-West Semitic substrate, in which strict agreement prevails, could be a plausible

---

[28] Using Optimality Theory, the divergence between the Jewish and Muslim dialects in terms of their choice of agreement pattern can be accounted for by distinct ranking of the output constraints (Prince and Smolensky 2004; Archangeli 1999). The Evaluation mechanism in the Jewish dialects ranks the rule of grammatical agreement between the subject and its modifiers higher than the level of its individuation and animacy. On the other hand, the evaluation of the input in the Muslim dialects is conditioned by the requirement to adjust the grammatical form of the modifier to the identity of the subject.

explanation of the peculiarity of the Jewish varieties in this sense.[29] A historical investigation involving a text corpus reflecting spoken language in Gabes in the nineteenth and twentieth centuries, as well as a comparative study of Jewish Gabes with its Muslim counterpart, would certainly shed more light on the development of agreement patterns.

---

[29] A hypothesis related to a North-West Semitic substrate in Judaeo-Arabic is discussed in greater detail in chapter 6, §2.0.

6. SYNTAX OF VERBS AND CLAUSES

1.0. Clausal Subordination

According to the definition of subordination, it "refers to a syntactic dependency between clauses in a multiclausal sentence, in which the subordinate clause must be annexed to an independent clause but not conversely" (LeTourneau 2011). On the other hand, Pat-El (2012, 21), following Otto Jespersen, applied, in her study on the historical development of Aramaic syntax, a definition of subordination based on the 'nexal hierarchy', where the main nexus contains the lower one, which is syntactically dependent on it. The term 'subordination', therefore, is perceived as the opposite of 'coordination', which describes the relationship between two independent clauses that are not embedded.[1] From both definitions quoted here, one can gather that subordination is a relatively wide category, which covers numerous types of syntactic dependency. In my study of subordination in Jewish Gabes, I will consider three types of subordinate clauses: relative clauses, adverbial clauses, and complements. I shall analyse these syntactic structures from two perspectives, namely, the historical one, aimed at demonstrating the place of Jewish Gabes in a wider Semitic framework, and the cross-linguistic one, which will enable a typological approach.

---

[1] As will be shown in the course of this chapter, this is not always the case, and the two categories can interconnect.

1.1. Relative Clauses

The relative clause is a syntactic construction that permits description and specification of the noun it modifies in a form of a clause. In this sense, the relative clause functions as an adjective, since it provides additional information about the item. Any relative clause has the following components: (1) head noun, often referred to in this study as 'head', (2) relative pronoun, which, as will be demonstrated, is omitted in asyndetic constructions, and (3) clause. In terms of the spectrum that relative clauses cover, we can distinguish two types, namely, restrictive and non-restrictive. The former limits the reference of the head noun in order to assist the hearer in identifying its referent. The function of a non-restrictive relative clause, on the other hand, is to add information about the head noun, whose referent is already identifiable by the hearer. Another distinction, which will be of special interest in my investigation, is that between attributive and non-attributive relative clauses. The attributive type assigns a feature or property to the noun. Therefore, both restrictive and non-restrictive clauses are included in this category. On the other hand, non-attributive clauses do not specify the item, but rather have an 'open' reference, which in English is introduced by pronouns like 'whoever', 'whatever', 'everyone', etc.

In this section, I will discuss several types of relative clauses present in Jewish Gabes. I will analyse both attributive and non-attributive relative clauses, paying special attention to the syntactical behaviour of definite and indefinite heads. Before demonstrating the structure of relative clauses in Jewish Gabes, I shall present some typological aspects of relative clauses, followed by a brief outline of the development of relative clauses in Semitic. This approach may help explain the syntactic behaviour of some types of relative clauses in Jewish Gabes.

1.1.1. Data

Below, I present examples of relativisation occurring in Jewish Gabes. The passages that are followed by a number placed in brackets have been taken from the text corpus and thus represent free speech, while those that are not followed by a number have been obtained by means of a questionnaire. It should be marked, therefore, that the latter, notwithstanding their correctness, do not reflect the most acceptable and natural relative clauses.

The examples presented below have been divided into groups with definite and indefinite heads, and subsequently further classified according to the position of the head noun.[2]

1. Attributive clause with definite head noun
    a. Head that has the grammatical role of object
        1. hāk əl-xabža li ʕṭīthālək ša ʕməlt bīha? (1:27)
           'The bread that I gave to you, what have you done with it?'
        2. hāk əṛ-ṛāẓəl li ʕaḍḍātu l-kəlba hūwa ṣāḥbi
           'That man whom the bitch bit is my friend.'

---

[2] This taxonomy has been borrowed from the grammar of ṢanʕānĪ Arabic (Watson 1993, 230), and the reason I find it useful is its relevance for examination of the Accessibility Hierarchy proposed by Keenan and Comrie (1977).

3. *l-ʕṣāfīr əlli šəfthəm āməš žāw mən əṣ-ṣaḥra*
   'The birds that you saw yesterday had come from the desert.'

b. Head that has the grammatical role of subject

4. *əršəm əl-yədd li ʕṭātni (ə)l-kəff tətqaṣṣ* (6:85)
   'Write: the hand that hit me will be cut.'

5. *l-ḥāža əlli ʕažiža ʕalīk xūdīha* (7:89)
   'The thing that is valuable for you, take it.'

6. *nhār wāḥəd žāt əxt l-mṛa hādīk li təṣri mənhu əl-kmāž*
   'One day the sister of that woman who buys from him fabric came.'

7. *əxti rāxəl əlli təškən fi-tūnəš žāt tẓūrna*
   'My sister Rachel, who lives in Tunis, came to visit us.'

c. Head that has a noun as an annex

8. *əl-mṛa ḍāṛha kbīra bəṛša*
   'The woman whose house is big.'

d. Head that is the complement of a preposition

9. *əl-bīr əlli nša yāxdu mənnu l-ma*
   'The well from which women take water.'

2. Attributive clause with indefinite/indefinite-specific head noun

a. Head that has the grammatical role of object

1. *ma ʕandūš mākla yaʕṭi l-ẓġāru* (3:4)
   '[he] does not have food to feed his children.'

6. Syntax of Verbs and Clauses

b. Head that has the grammatical role of subject

2. *təmma wāḥəd li hūwa ma tḥarrəkš, hūwa yəstənna ḥatt ytīḥlu mākla fi-fəmmu* (2:16)
   'There is a man who does not move, he waits for the food to fall down in his mouth.'

3. *qāllu: škūn li qāʕəd mxabbi* (4:37)
   'They said: who is the person who is hiding?'

4. *kānu žūž famīlyāt yətʕārqu mʕa bināthəm*
   'There were two families, which were arguing with each other.'

5. *tʕadda ḥda ṛāẓəl u kān rāqəd*
   'He passed next to a man who was sleeping.'

6. *rqāt mra ʕamya u tərḥi fi-l-qamḥ* (4:18–19)
   'She found a blind woman who was grinding wheat.'

c. Head that is the complement of a preposition

7. *ər-ṛāẓəl ṭlaʕ u rqa žməl ʕali ṣəndūq kbīr* (4:85)
   'The man came out and found the camel with a big box on it.'

8. *ṛqa hādīk əl-məṛt wāḥda li ʕandha ḍaṛba* (2:47)
   'He found that woman who has a mark.'

9. *ḥānūt kbīra wa fīha wāḥəd ybīʕ kmāž*
   'A big shop, in which a man was selling fabric.'

The relative particle in Jewish Gabes is either *əlli* or *li*. As in virtually all modern Arabic dialects, the relative particle in Jewish Gabes is not inflected for gender, number, or person. As argued by some scholars, it stems from the CA relative pronoun *allaḏī*, which was inflected for gender, person, and number (Wright

2005, I:270).³ Three components of this pronoun can be identified, namely the demonstrative element /al/, the demonstrative morpheme /l/, and the demonstrative pronoun *ḏā* or *ḏū*. The relationship between the relative pronoun and demonstratives is attested also in Biblical Hebrew, which, according to historical-comparative reconstruction, used at an early stage to utilise the near demonstratives as relative pronouns (Holmstedt 2011).⁴

1.1.2. Cross-Linguistic Typology

Relative clauses, due to their complex character, can be divided into multiple categories based on various criteria. In terms of the position of the head noun, a relative clause can be either postnominal (as in English and Jewish Gabes, for example), prenominal (as in Alambak, a variety of languages spoken in Papua New Guinea), or internal, where the head occurs within the restricting

---

³ As observed by Pat-El (2017, 257), there is no phonological motivation behind this etymology. It is more plausible that the CA relative pronoun is an innovation combining the two elements /l/ and /d/, which already existed in the dialects. The vast majority of modern varieties of Arabic use the /lli/ variant, whose relationship to the CA one is disputable. It is worth noting, however, that there are dialects which use the /d/ variant, presumably reflecting the Proto-Semitic relative morpheme /d/, e.g., Cypriot Arabic, and some varieties of Moroccan and Yemeni Arabic. The closest dialect to Jewish Gabes which uses this pronoun is Djidjelli, where one finds /əddi/ (Marçais 1956).

⁴ Apart from a presumed early relative strategy involving near demonstratives, Biblical Hebrew also possesses another relative complementiser of a dual nature, namely, the definite article /ha-/ (Holmstedt 2011). This in turn indicates a similarity between relative clauses and attributive adjectives (Goldenberg 1995).

clause (as in languages spoken in Southern California and North-West Mexico). Moreover, within the category of internally headed relative clauses, scholars distinguish also correlative clauses, in which the relative clause is outside the main clause, but linked anaphorically to the noun phrase (Dryer 2005).[5] Thus, a more general division can be drawn based on the position of the head noun, namely, relative clauses can be either externally-headed or internally-headed (Holmstedt 2011). As will be shown in §1.1.4, Jewish Gabes uses external, postnominal relative clauses.

In an extensive study of the formation of relative clauses in about fifty languages, Keenan and Comrie (1977, 66) attempted to produce a set of universal properties shared by relative clauses appearing in all those languages. They pointed out a further division of relative clauses, based on the strategy of their formation: case+/case -. In the case strategy, the nominal element in the restricting phrase unequivocally codes the grammatical role of the head noun that is being relativised. This strategy is particularly common in languages which possess a case-marking system (e.g., Slavic languages). Nonetheless, languages without cases can also utilise the case strategy by means of prepositional phrases, e.g., 'the house in which the family lived'. Here the preposition 'in' is included in the restrictive clause and clearly indicates which grammatical role of the head noun is relativised. This

---

[5] Some more detailed divisions include also adjoined relative clauses, present in some Australian languages (e.g., Diyari), and double-headed relative clauses, represented by a single language, Kombai (Trans-New Guinea; Austin 1981, 188; Dryer 2005).

strategy will also be relevant to the formation of relative clauses in Jewish Gabes.

The investigation conducted by Keenan and Comrie resulted in the establishment of the Accessibility Hierarchy, which aims to indicate the positions in a sentence from which a noun phrase can be relativised. Keenan and Comrie claim that the relativisability of these positions is uneven and can be presented in the form of a gradually decreasing sequence, where the left extreme designates the most relativisable position, while the right one marks a position that is unlikely to be relativised:

> Subject > Direct Object > Indirect Object > Oblique > Genitive > Object of Comparison (Keenan and Comrie 1977, 66)

This means that, from a cross-linguistic perspective, the subject is the position of the head noun that is most frequently relativised by a restrictive phrase, while an object of comparison would usually not be.[6] The hierarchy has some constraints, however, and languages usually allow only certain positions to be relativised

---

[6] This is the case in some Romance languages, where the comparative preposition and the relative pronoun are homonymous or closely related, and therefore objects of comparison are not relativisable. For example, in Spanish, any preposition in a restrictive clause precedes the relative particle, e.g., *el cajon del que saqué el arma* 'the drawer from which I took the gun'. The relative pronoun used for inanimate nouns has the same form as the comparative particle, i.e., /que/, thus a sentence where the homonyms stand next to each other is ungrammatical, e.g., * *la casa que que mi casa es mas alta* 'the house than which my house is higher'. The same situation is found in French (Keenan and Comrie 1977, 74).

by means of the primary strategy (i.e., without promoting the noun phrase to the position of subject by, for example, changing the voice). Thus, one finds languages where only a subject can be relativised (Western Malayo-Polynesian languages), only subjects and direct objects (Welsh), only subjects and indirect objects (Basque), etc. According to the results of the investigation, virtually all the languages permit only the subject to be relativised by means of the primary strategy. The explanation of the constraints of the Accessibility Hierarchy proposed in the study involves a psychological dimension of comprehensibility (Keenan and Comrie 1977, 88). It has been demonstrated by various additional studies that speakers deal with the unacceptability of certain positions being relativised by reformulating the idea expressed by the unacceptable sentence. My informant of Spanish categorically rejected as ungrammatical the following phrase involving relativisation of an object of comparison: *el hombre que que Maria es mas alta 'the man whom Maria is taller than', and immediately proposed: el hombre, que es mas bajo de Maria 'the man who is shorter than Maria', where 'the man' has been promoted from object of comparison to subject. In Modern Hebrew, in turn, an object of comparison seems to be more acceptable when followed by a verb. My informant accepted the following sentence as natural and correct: הגבר שרחל גבוהה יותר ממנו, דחף אותה 'the man, whom Rachel is taller than, pushed her' but found the sentence without the predicate somewhat unnatural.

Hence, it can be assumed that an accessibility hierarchy established for a certain language based on free speech will represent the most acceptable instances of relativisation, which were judged by a speaker as most comprehensible and natural. Keenan and Comrie (1977, 90) point out that their hierarchy should not be treated as a fixed grammatical order but rather as a continuum of acceptability. It is plausible, therefore, that some positions will not be relativised in free speech but will be accepted by the speaker to some degree in a questionnaire.

1.1.3. Relative Clauses from a Semitic Perspective

The nature of relative clauses has been discussed extensively in scholarship on Semitic languages. Undoubtedly, relativisation constitutes a sort of 'promotion' of the head noun, which, by means of extraposition, acquires a higher level of prominence. Holmstedt (2011), in his description of relative clauses in Biblical Hebrew, points out that every relative clause can be characterised by two factors, namely, subordination, since the relativised clause is syntactically dependent on the head noun; and the pivot constituent, which relates to the polyfunctionality of the head noun in a relative clause.

From a historical point of view, relative clauses are linked to the construct state. As pointed out by Pat-El (2012), all Semitic languages have two strategies for marking nominal attribution, namely, nominal dependents and adnominal complements. Relativisation in Proto-Semitic was expressed by means of a relative-determinative pronoun *dV/tV, which was fully inflected for gender, number, and case (Huehnergard 2006). Moreover, it was in the construct state and the clause following it depended on it. At a later stage, the pronoun lost its inflection and became a particle. It has been assumed, therefore, that the original construction used to express adnominal attribution was the construct state. As has been demonstrated by Goldenberg (1995), adjectives and relative clauses in Semitic also originally reflected dependence on a head noun. Numerous examples from Akkadian indicate that both the head noun and the attributive verb bear marks of attribution (lack of case marking in the former, and a 'subjunctive' -u suffix in the latter). Biblical Hebrew too reflects vestiges of an attributive structure of relative clauses: קריית חנה דוד 'the city where David settled' (Isa 29.1).

This type of syntax is reflected in some modern dialects of Arabic. In the dialect of the mountain Arabs in northern Morocco who are known as Žbāla, variants of the particle /d/ are used both in relatives and in genitives.[7] A similar function is performed by the Aleppan particle /il/, which nominalises the relative clause and stands in the construct state as *nomen regens* of the head noun (Brustad 2000, 101, 109). As will be demonstrated in §1.3.5, some temporal clauses reflect a parallel construction.

---

[7] The fact that the /d/ element marking genitives is attested almost exclusively in the western Maghreb (Morocco and Algeria) means that it could have emerged due to contact with Romance languages. In opposition to this claim, it could be argued that the /d/ genitive exponent is attested, albeit scarcely, in the Quran, and therefore reflects the original morpheme. As an alternative solution, it could be proposed that the /d/ element existed as an obsolete form in some varieties of Arabic, but the presence of a Romance-speaking population in north-western Africa, and the fact that these languages utilise a homonymic morpheme to mark a genitive relationship, might have brought the /d/ element into wider use (Heath 2015).

One of the central questions in investigation of the syntax of relative clauses is whether the relative pronoun syntactically operates within the relative clause. This question has already been addressed by Pat-El and Treiger (2008), and their study of CA is of particular interest for understanding the modern dialects as well. Unlike most other Semitic languages, Arabic does demonstrate case inflection of relative pronouns in the dual, and the syntactic function of the relative pronoun can therefore be precisely determined (Wright 2005, I:271). Contrary to what has been argued by some Semitists (Reckendorf 1921, 428), the relative pronoun is conditioned by the syntagm of the noun phrase, and not by the relative clause. This is the major difference between Semitic and Indo-European languages.[8] The two following examples should illustrate this difference:

(1) Arabic:

arinā š-šayṭānayni lladayni ʔaḍallānā[9]

show.IMP.us devil.DU.ACC REL.ACC lead.astray.SFX.DU.us

(2) Polish:

wskaż nam dwóch diabłow którzy nas zwiedli

show.IMP us two.ACC devils.ACC REL.NOM us lead.astray.PERF

'Show us two devils who led us astray.'

In Polish, which is an Indo-European language with an abundantly developed case system, the case of the relative pronoun (*który*) is conditioned by the syntax of the relative clause, while

---

[8] This discrepancy has already been observed by Wright (2005, II:320).

[9] This example originally occurs in Wright (2005 II:320); the transcription is quoted according to Pat-El and Treiger (2008). The translation in Polish has been done by the author.

in Arabic, it agrees with the head noun. Nonetheless, the gender and number inflection of the relative pronouns in Indo-European languages is derived from the head (pro)noun. It can therefore be assumed that, in Indo-European languages, the relative pronoun constitutes a syntactic link between the head (pro)noun and the relative clause. In Semitic languages, on the other hand, the (pro)nominal phrase is connected to the relative clause by means of the resumptive pronoun.

In sum, previous studies undertaken in the historical syntax of Semitic clearly indicate that adjectives, genitives, relative clauses, and prepositional clauses are manifestations of the same attributive relation. The relative pronoun is best explained as a substantival modifier standing in apposition to the head (pro)noun. As a result of this assumption, the relative clause in Semitic is treated syntactically as a substantive (Pat-El and Treiger 2008).

1.1.4. Data Analysis

I shall start the discussion of the syntactic behaviour of relative clauses in Jewish Gabes by arguing against the claim made by Harell (1962, 164) regarding Moroccan Arabic that the subordinate clause is a restrictive adjectival modifier. Not only is this statement not true for Moroccan Arabic, as has been proven by Brustad (2000, 89), but it does not hold water in other Arabic dialects either. In Jewish Gabes, relative clauses can modify restricted and non-restricted nouns alike. Example (1.7) above (§1.1.1) confirms this assumption, i.e., the head noun 'my sister

Rachel' is already restricted and there is no doubt which sister the speaker is referring to.

The data clearly demonstrates that relative clauses in Jewish Gabes display different behaviour depending on the definiteness of the head noun. First, the relative pronoun tends to occur primarily in sentences with highly individuated antecedents. Therefore, the *li/əlli* pronoun often, as in examples (1.1) and (1.2), accompanies nouns preceded by demonstrative pronouns, whose referent is very clearly specified. Similarly, in example (1.6), the elder woman had appeared in the story before, and thus her individuation and textual prominence are well established.

Apart from the instances of conspicuous specificity of the head noun, the relative pronoun occurs also in clauses whose antecedent is indefinite-specific. In this kind of sentence, the referent, notwithstanding its formally indefinite character, is in fact narrow and textually prominent. In example (2.3), the identity of the man is not specified, but the speaker is referring to a specific person possessing a defined quality. Example (2.8) represents a usage of the indefinite-specific article that is even more explicit, since it is preceded by a demonstrative, and there is hence no doubt that the referent is individuated.

On the other hand, clauses modifying entities of low individuation that are textually non-prominent lack the relative pronoun. This is the case, for example, in statements of non-existence, as in (2.1). In addition to the omission of the relative pronoun, in some indefinite clauses, a conjunctive particle occurs, as demonstrated by examples (2.3) and (2.6). The question arises as to the type of circumstances in which an indefinite head noun is relativised asyndetically, and when, on the other hand, the relativisation is realised by means of coordination. It seems that, in asyndetic clauses, the verb functions as an adjectival modifier, as in example (2.4), i.e., 'there were two arguing families'. On the other hand, /wa/ or /u/ introduces a verbal modifier, and the focus is on the actual action, as in example (2.6), rather than on the quality of the modified term.

Relativisation coded by means of coordination is of particular typological interest. It can be analysed in terms of the so-called Mismatch Problem discussed by Cristofaro (2005, 21) in her study on subordination. In a number of languages, the relationship between coordination and subordination is vague, and the meaning must be inferred from two non-embedded juxtaposed clauses. This is the case in Gumbaynggir (Australia), which does not utilise any grammaticalised construction to convey relativisation. Jewish Gabes, on the other hand, does possess a specific construction for clearly coding relativisation, but examples (2.5) and (2.9) suggest that, in sentences with an indefinite head noun followed by a relative clause containing a verb, the coordinative structure, with or without *waw*, is preferred. Such syntactic behaviour is best explained by a continuum approach, according to which clause linkage is not seen as a fixed grammatical category, but rather in terms of coordinate-like or subordinate-like types (Foley and Van Valin 1984). Consequently, based on the criteria of dependency and embedding, a third category has been proposed, namely co-subordination (Van Valin and LaPolla 1997, chapter 8). It combines the lack of embedding typical of coordination on the one hand, and the dependency that characterises subordination on the other. Therefore, the instances of ambiguous relativisation in examples (2.5) and (2.9) could be explained as co-subordinative, since they do not involve embedding, but they do involve the dependency of one action upon another, i.e., in (2.5), the action of seeing semantically engages the action of sleeping.

The correlation between the indefinite-specific category and the occurrence of the *li/əlli* pronoun is attested in many modern Arabic dialects. Even though Brustad (2000, 95) does not present any examples of indefinite noun phrases with conjunctive relative clauses, she reaches the same conclusion regarding indefinite nouns followed by *əlli*, namely, the primary function of this construction is to narrow the reference of the head noun. Nonetheless, in her data, only unmarked indefinite-specific nouns are treated in this way, while those accompanied by *wāḥəd* behave like indefinites (Brustad 2000, 96). This is a rather paradoxical conclusion, since *wāḥəd* usually marks indefinite-specific nouns with a higher degree of individuation and textual prominence (new topic marker). In Jewish Gabes, by contrast, *wāḥəd* does attract the relativiser. Brustad mentions, however, that in Moroccan Arabic, nouns marked with another indefinite-specific article *ši* can be relativised with *li*. It might be possible, therefore, that North African dialects permit the relativisation of indefinite-specific nouns with the relativiser, but to different degrees.

The lack of a straightforward correlation between definiteness and use of relative pronouns does not seem to be an innovation of modern Arabic dialects. As has been observed by Blau

(1961, 232), in Mediaeval Judaeo-Arabic, there are numerous cases of interchanges between asyndetic and syndetic relative clauses.[10] Usually, when an indefinite head noun is followed by the syndetic construction, either it has a distributive meaning, it is an ordinal number, or the head noun is generic (Blau 1979, 232). In other words, the head noun displays some features of definiteness, as ordinal numbers tend to narrow the reference, while generic nouns fall under the category of generic definiteness (see chapter 5, §1.4). This is the case with the use of *wāḥəd* followed by the relative pronoun in Jewish Gabes. As has been shown in chapter 5, §1.5, the indefinite-specific article often refers to an individuated entity. At the other extreme lie definite head nouns followed by an asyndetic construction. These are well attested in CA, especially in sentences where the head noun bears the definite article due to its genericity (Wright 2005, II:318). In Jewish Gabes, however, this usage seems to be limited only to heads followed by a nominal phrase with a possessive pronoun.

Another aspect of the syntactic behaviour of relative clauses related to the definiteness of the head noun is the resumptive pronoun. Here, again, the presence of the resumptive pronoun seems to be conditioned by the individuation of the head noun, namely, it is mandatory when the head noun is definite. The examples from Jewish Gabes confirm this assumption. All five passages where the relativised position is the object pronoun

---

[10] Another type of interchange found in Mediaeval Judaeo-Arabic involves mismatch between the gender/number of the head noun and the form of the relative pronoun (Blau 1961, 235–37).

possess a resumptive pronoun. On the other hand, no instances of indefinite head nouns with resumption have been attested.

This relatively uniform system, which prevails in many modern dialects, diverges significantly from Medieval Judaeo-Arabic, where one finds numerous cases of omission of the resumptive pronoun in both syndetic and asyndetic constructions (Blau 1961, 240). Similarly, in Moroccan Arabic, resumption does not take place in all positions. As reported by Brustad (2000, 109), a resumptive pronoun in the position of direct object is rare. However, when the syntactic position of the referent of the head noun is that of a genitive or the object of a preposition, it is obligatory. Contrary to this, in Jewish Gabes, resumption occurs with both direct objects and objects of prepositions.

Finally, based on the examples of relativisation in Jewish Gabes, one can affirm the applicability of the Accessibility Hierarchy. Indeed, the subject (four examples) and the direct object (five examples) are the two single positions that are most commonly relativised in Jewish Gabes. The third most frequent type is relative clauses with a prepositional annex, which occur mostly with indefinite nouns. While it is possible that one may also find other positions relativised in free speech, these constructions are the ones speakers find the most understandable and natural.

To sum up, relative clauses in Jewish Gabes display a strong dependence on the definiteness of the head noun: the more individuated it is, the higher the probability that the *li/əlli* pronoun will occur. Indefinite-specific nouns are very often followed by the relative pronoun, which indicates that they fall within the definite range of the definiteness hierarchy, in contrast to the situation in the dialects studied by Brustad, including Moroccan. In addition, it has been shown that some indefinite head nouns form relative-like clauses by means of coordination coded by *waw* or asydetically. This can be explained by the category of co-subordination, which combines features of both subordination and co-ordination. Finally, as has been demonstrated, the relative pronoun *li/əlli* can introduce both restrictive and non-restrictive clauses.

The present study has been based mostly on spoken, colloquial language, which is characterised by a relative lack of syntactic complexity. In these forms of speech, asydetic constructions are much more widespread than in literary, written language. This assumption is confirmed by Wagner, who finds numerous cases of mismatch between the definiteness of the antecedent and the occurrence of the relative pronoun. Based on letters from the Cairo Genizah, which often reflect a spoken and informal register, Wagner (2010, 217) has demonstrated that, very often, a definite head is followed by an asydetic relative clause. As will be shown in §1.3, adverbial constructions also very often tend to be constructed asydetically. This phenomenon, attested also in Late Judaeo-Arabic, seems to be one of the traits of the spoken register, which, in contradistinction to the written language, demonstrates less syntactic complexity and morphological marking (Wagner 2014).

1.2. Non-Attributive Relative Clauses

Head which has the grammatical role of object

1. *wa ʕāwəḍ li ʕməl mbāraḥ* (1:34)
   'And he repeated the same as he did yesterday.'

2. *qāllu: ngədd, li tḥabb naʕməllək* (2:28)
   'He told him: I will guard, I will do whatever you want.'

Head which has the grammatical role of subject

3. *ža li wāqəf ʕaləyəm, qālla: žībi* (2:26)
   'The person in charge came and told her: bring him!'

4. *əl-mṛa ḥablət, džīb wəld, ma təmmaš škūn yaqtlu* (2:55)
   'The woman was pregnant, gave birth to a son, there is no one to kill him.'

5. *təmma bīr ġārəq yāsər wa l-bīr hāda li yədxal fi ymūt, ma yəṭlaʕṣ* (2:57)
   'There was a very deep well and whoever goes in dies, does not go out.'

6. *āna qahwa wa li yəṣṛəbni šahwa wa li yətʕalləm bīha təmknu daʕwa* (7:19)
   'I am coffee, and those who drink me enjoy, and those who get used to me, I become their curse.'

In addition to the relative clauses analysed in the previous section (§1.1), Jewish Gabes also possesses two types of non-attributive clauses. The first one involves the relative pronoun *li/əlli* without a head noun. As can be seen, this type is the most prevalent in the above examples, and its reference can be either human (e.g., 5) or non-human (e.g., 2). The second type, which occurs across the dialects of Arabic, utilises non-specific, non-attributive pronouns. In Jewish Gabes, however, this is attested only scarcely.[11] The majority of dialects employ *ma* for 'what' and *mīn* for 'who(m)' (Brustad 2000, 99). As demonstrated by example (4), the interrogative particle *škūn* functions in Jewish Gabes as a non-specific relativiser for human referents, while non-human referents are relativised by *li*, as exemplified by example (2). Finally, applying the Accessibility Hierarchy, one can infer that the subject position by far outranks the object.

1.3. Adverbial Clauses

In this section, I shall consider adverbial clauses occurring in Jewish Gabes. To this end, I will first present some preliminary notes on the definition of an adverbial clause and its various types. The theoretical underpinnings of this section are mainly based on a study by Cristofaro (2005, chapter VI).[12] Subsequently, I shall discuss some aspects of the historical development of adverbial clauses in Semitic and some Arabic dialects.

---

[11] The occurrence of the two particles seems to be uneven and conditioned geographically. According to Brustad (2000, 100), while *ma* is well attested in Moroccan, it has not been found in Kuwaiti, and in Egyptian and Syrian Arabic it is used irregularly. On the other hand, *mīn* is often employed by speakers of Syrian Arabic, but has not been attested in Moroccan.

[12] In my study, I will utilise terminology applied by Cristofaro in her study on subordination. The events coded by the main and the dependent clause shall therefore be referred to as 'states of affairs'. This term has been borrowed from Functional Grammar (Siewierska 1991) and is

1.3.1. Definition and Cross-Linguistic Typology

An adverbial construction combines two clauses in such a way that the clause conveying a dependent state of affairs describes the circumstances under which the main state of affairs (henceforth: SoA) takes place. Following Cristofaro (2005, 155), I shall reject the traditional definition, which stipulates that the dependent clause is embedded in the main one. As will be shown in the following analysis, adverbial relations in Jewish Gabes are not always expressed by means of embedding, and, similarly to relative clauses, can be coded by coordination.

The following types of state of affairs will be examined in my investigation:

- i) purpose
- ii) temporal
- iii) conditional
- iv) reason
- v) manner
- vi) contradiction

This taxonomy aims to capture the types of adverbial clause as precisely as possible. Therefore, building on Cristofaro's model, which was based on the studies of other typologists (Givón, Kortmann, Thompson, and Longacre), I decided to expand it and add the two last categories.

Apart from the different semantic values ascribed to each type of dependent SoA, adverbial clauses differ also in terms of

---

more precise than 'event', as the latter implies dynamicity and punctuality (Cristofaro 2005, 25).

predetermination of some grammatical features represented by the SoAs. Thus, temporal and purpose clauses predetermine the time reference of the SoAs, by indicating their sequential time order (e.g., a purpose clause presumes that the independent SoA is anterior to the dependent one), or simultaneous co-realisation, as in temporal overlap. On the other hand, conditional or reason clauses do not have any inherent time reference, and their time coding depends on the context. Adverbial clauses vary also in terms of semantic integration of the linked SoAs. Purpose clauses consist of two semantically interconnected entities, which imply that the realisation of the main SoA is motivated by the dependent one. Temporal clauses, by contrast, do not convey any semantic relation between SoAs, as they occur independently of each other (Cristofaro 2005, 167).

From a cross-linguistic point of view, it is worth noting that languages code adverbial relations in various different ways. In terms of the form of the verb, a verb occurring in a dependent SoA can be either unaltered (balanced) or modified (deranked). Deranking often involves reduction of time, aspect, mood, or person agreement distinctions, resulting in a form that cannot be used independently. One of the languages that codes adverbial relations in this way is Tamil, which utilises a nominalised form with a special case marker (Cristofaro 2005, 56). The CA subjunctive can also be interpreted as a sort of deranked form, since it is marked by *fatḥa* at the end of the imperfective form, as opposed to *ḍamma* in the indicative (Wright 2005, II:60). Contrary to this, Jewish Gabes demonstrates a balanced strategy, coding subordination by means of structurally equal forms.

1.3.2. Semitic Perspective

The development of adverbial subordination in Semitic is parallel to that of relative clauses. Presumably, adverbial clauses have their origin in the same model as relative clauses, where the relative pronoun was in the construct state as the *nomen regens* of the following adnominal complement.[13] When the pronoun lost its inflection, it became a frozen particle treated as the marker of adnominal attribution, and not as part of the matrix sentence (Pat-El 2012, 24). Similarly, some nouns denoting time or place underwent a process of grammaticalisation and started functioning as adverbial particles. Arabic, following the path of North-West Semitic, Ugaritic, Akkadian, and Ethiopic, developed a system of nominal markers introducing adverbial subordination.[14]

In CA, the accusative serves as a default marker of adverbial relations. There are numerous cases of nouns which acquire adverbial function when inflected in the accusative case, e.g., *marrat-an* 'once'. Alongside these forms exist also adverbs marked by the archaic suffix /-u/, e.g., *qabl-u* 'previously', and entities that function purely as adverbs, e.g., *ġad-an* 'tomorrow', though

---

[13] This proves the claim made in §1.1.3, that the construct state was the default way of expressing attribution in Semitic (Goldenberg 1995; Pat-El 2008).

[14] As has been shown by Pat-El (2012, 28), Aramaic diverged significantly from other Semitic languages in terms of subordination strategies. It did not utilise nominal dependence and the only way of coding subordination was by means of the determinative-relative pronoun.

their distribution is limited (Watson 2011). The adverbial function of the accusative is conspicuous also in locative adverbs and adverbs of direction, e.g., *qarīb-an* 'near', *dāxil-an* 'inside'.

It can therefore be established that, in CA, the vast majority of adverbials are derived from nouns which function also outside adverbial contexts. This is not the case in modern dialects of Arabic, where one finds predominantly pure adverbs (Watson 2011).

1.3.3. Purpose Clauses

1. *wāḥəd mša yəṭlab ya krīm tāʕ aḷḷa* (1:2)
   'A man went to beg for money.'

2. *ma yaʕrfūṣ škūn yāxdu yəqṭlu* (2:37)
   'They did not know who took it to kill it.'

3. *aʕṭīni ḥžina šmīʕa, u qrīṭīṣ wqiḍ bāš nəššalha* (1:19)
   'Give me a (poor, miserable) candle and a box of matches so I can light it.'

4. *baʕtu bāš ymūt* (2:60)
   'They sent him to death.'

5. *hāk əẓ-ẓāwāḷi kull nhār xmīš, yəmši l-xu yaʕṭī flūš* (3:2)
   'That poor one goes every Thursday to his brother so he gives him money.'

6. *xūya kīf yži aʕṭī flūš bāš yaʕməl šəbbāt* (3:9)
   'If my brother comes, give him money so he can have shabbat.'

7. *qāllu: āna māši l-ṛabbi yaʕṭīni bāš nwəkkəl ẓġāri* (3:18)
   'He said to him: I am going to God so he gives me something and I feed my children.'

8. *qāl: mšīt l-ṛabbi nžībəlkəm bāš tāklu* (3:42)
   'He said: I went to God to bring you (food) so you can eat.'

9. *lāžma ṭṭabḫaṣ bāš tədxəl* (4:16)
 'She had to lean down to go in.'

10. *ža wāḥəd əl-*^HE*mélex*^HE *yəškīlu* (7:66)
 'A man came to the king to complain to him.'

Judging from the data above, two types of purpose clauses can be distinguished in Jewish Gabes: (1) an asyndetic type, where the subordinated verb has a prefix form and is not preceded by any particle; (2) a syndetic type, where the purpose clause is introduced by means of the particle *bāš*. The rule governing the distribution of the variant with the particle seems to combine two factors:

1. It is utilised in the case of what can be defined as switch-reference. This term is traditionally used to describe a phenomenon in some languages of Australia, New Guinea, Northern Asia, and both Americas, which entails "verbal affixing systems indicating whether or not the subject of the affixed verb is coreferential with the subject of some other verb" (Cristofaro 2012, 70). This definition cannot be directly applied to Jewish Gabes, but without doubt, *bāš* can function as a switch-reference device.[15] In other words, it appears when the subject of the predicate in the main clause is not co-referential with the subject of the dependent clause. For instance, in example (4), the subject of the verb *bʕaṭu* is different from that of *ymūt*, hence the particle. On the other hand, in example (1), the

---

[15] Switch-reference morphology and personal agreement might interact in many ways. As pointed out by Cristofaro (2012, 70), modifications of personal agreement can be used to code switch-reference.

subject of both verbs is co-referential—*wāḥəd mša yəṭlab*—and therefore *bāš* does not occur.

2. *bāš* is applied in multi-verbal clauses in order to break a chain of predicates referring to the same subject. Example (9) demonstrates this usage of *bāš*.

1.3.4. Temporal Clauses

1. *aʕṭyī əl-xabža yəštaġna bīha wa waqt ywəlli* ᴴᴱ*aʕšīr*ᴴᴱ, *nāxdu* (1:13)
   'Give him this bread so that he becomes rich from it and when he is already rich, we will marry him [to you].'

2. *waqt l-omma kānət fi-l-kūžīna əl-bənt kānət taxšəl əl-fxār*
   'While the mother was in the kitchen, the daughter was washing the dishes.'

3. *nhār li nāxdək ma tədwəyyəš mʕa əl-nās* (7:64)
   'From the day I marry you, you will not talk to people.'

4. *taʕddāw šəbʕa ayyām mən ən-nhār əlli mša*
   'Seven days have passed since the day he left.'

5. *līlətha li ʕarrəš, yaḥləm wāḥəd ḍərbu kəff* (6:64)
   'On the night of the wedding he had a dream that someone hit him with the palm of a hand.'

6. *kull mṛa li tūləd, tlāt arbʕa ayyām u yāxdu l-wəld yləwwḥu* (2:36)
   'Every woman who gives birth, after three or four days someone would take the child and throw it away.'

7. *yḥall fəmmu wa yəštənna ḥatt əl-blaḥ ytīḥlu fi-fəmmu* (2:15)
   'He would open his mouth and he would wait until the date fell into it.'

8. waqt hūwa ka-yʕašš fi-nəfṣ əl-līl, žāt waḥda mṛa, žāt u ləwwḥat ḥāža, hūwa yḥabb yaʕṛəf šnūwa ləwwḥat (2:32)
   'While he was guarding at midnight, a woman came, she came and threw something, he wanted to know what she had thrown.'

9. hūwa ka-yəmši fə-ṣəṭṭ əl-bḥar mḥayrān, wa hīya qaʕdət fi-l-balkūn šāfəthu yəmši (7:70)
   'While he was walking worried on the beach, she sat down on the balcony and saw him walking.'

10. yāxdu šwəyy mən məlḥ tāʕ ^{HE}ōmer^{HE} waqt yəmšīw yṣallīw
    'They would take a bit of the Omer salt when going to pray.'

11. baʕd təsʕ u arbʕīn ykəmməlu l-^{HE}ōmər^{HE} u yaʕlqu l-məlḥ
    'After forty-nine days they would complete the Omer by hanging the salt.'

12. kīf ža ʕammi āna ma kənts fə-ḍ-ḍāṛ
    'When my uncle came, I was not at home.'

13. hūwa, kānt mīta hūwa bāš ymūt ʕaləya, kān yži yərqa ʕāyša, mšāt ʕaləya (4:102)
    'He, when she was dead, was ready to die for her, so now if he comes and finds her alive, she will be in real trouble.'

14. aṣ-ṣəlṭān tʕadda, lqā yəẓṛaʕ fi-l-bṣəl (7:7)
    'When the sultan was passing by, he found him planting onions.'

15. baʕd ma mātət ʕarrəš mʕa mṛa oxra
    'After [his wife] died, he got married to another woman.'

16. aqbəl ma bdīt naxdəm kənt lāhi b-ommi
    'Before I started working, I had been taking care of my mother.'

The data presented above includes different types of temporal clauses in Jewish Gabes. The vast majority of the passages consist of two adjacent verbal clauses, one of which represents a dependent SoA, and the other the major one. However, there have been included in the data pool also a few examples of adverbial clauses which do not possess a dependent SoA, like example (11).

Typologically, three principal types of temporal clauses can be distinguished with respect to the temporal position of the dependent clause in relation to the main one (Cristofaro 2012, 159):[16]

i) temporal posteriority ('before' relations), where the dependent clause occurs after the main clause, as exemplified by example (16);
ii) temporal overlap ('when' relations), where both the dependent SoA and the main one occur at the same time, as in example (8), in which the main clause, i.e., the coming of the woman, falls within the temporal span of the dependent clause, i.e., the guarding of the livestock;
iii) temporal anteriority ('after' relations), where the dependent SoA takes place before the main clause, as exemplified in example (1), i.e., first the man will become rich (dependent SoA) and then the wedding will take place (main SoA).

This somewhat general and simplified taxonomy fails to cover some aspects of temporal relations expressed by adverbial

---

[16] Other scholars, for example Givón (1990, 330), propose a taxonomy based on the temporal position of the main clause in relation to the dependent one; according to his classification, therefore, Cristofaro's temporal posteriority is classified as 'precedence'.

clauses. I shall therefore propose a more detailed classification, aimed at a more accurate description of the temporal clauses present in Jewish Gabes. The division below is based on the studies of Givón (1990, II:330) and Kortmann (1997, 80), and supplements the three main types proposed by Cristofaro:

Simultaneity Overlap 'when': one of the SoAs is punctual, while the other one is continuous:

12. *kīf ža ʕammi āna ma kənts fə-ḍ-ḍāṛ*
    when come.SFX.3MS uncle.my I NEG be.SFX.1SG in-DEF-house
    'When my uncle came, I was not at home.'

Simultaneity Duration 'while': indicates two continuous SoAs overlapping in the time:

2. *waqt l-omma kānət fi-l-kūžīna*
    while DEF-mother be.SFX.3FS in-DEF-kitchen
    əl-bənt kānət taxšəl əl-fxār
    DEF-daughter be.SFX.3FS wash.PFX.3FS DEF-dishes
    'While the mother was in the kitchen, the daughter was washing the dishes.'

Point of coincidence: the dependent SoA is continuous and is interrupted by a punctual independent SoA:

14. *aṣ-ṣəlṭān tʕadda lqā yəẓraʕ fi-l-bṣəl*
    DEF-sultan pass.SFX.3MS find.SFX.3MS.him sow.PFX.3MS in-DEF-onion
    'When the sultan was passing by, he found him planting onion.' (7:7)

Terminal boundary: the dependent SoA indicates the final point of the independent SoA:

7. yḥall fəmmu wa yəštənna
   open.PFX.3MS mouth.his and wait. PFX.3MS
   ḥatt əl-blaḥ yṭīḥlu fi-fəmmu
   until DEF-date fall.PFX.3MS.to.him in-mouth.his
   'He would open his mouth and he would wait until the date fell into it.' (2:15)

Initial boundary: the dependent SoA indicates the initial point of a continuous SoA expressed by the main clause:

3. n-nhār li nāxdək ma tədwīyəš mʕa ən-nāš
   DEF-day REL take.PFX.1SG.you NEG talk.PFX.2FS.NEG with DEF-people
   'From the day I marry you, you will not talk to people.' (7:64)

As can be seen in the above examples, Jewish Gabes utilises several ways of expressing temporal relations in adverbial clauses. The most common particle is the grammaticalised CA noun *waqt* 'time'. It is principally used to introduce a dependent SoA of a continuous or repetitive character, as in (2) and (8). On the other hand, *kīf* marks punctual and singular SoAs, as in (12). Terminal boundary relations are marked by *ḥatta*.

In addition to the syndetic constructions, Jewish Gabes also employs the asyndetic option in temporal clauses. Among other scenarios, this occurs when the dependent SoA contains the verb 'to be', as in (13), where the particle is omitted. The coordinative type of adverbial clause is also employed in the passage exemplifying a point of coincidence, (14). Here, the continuous character of the dependent SoA is expressed by the verb itself, which implies an extended duration of time. Similarly, in example (9), the imperfective aspect of the verb is marked by the preverbal particle /ka-/. Hence, it can be tentatively established that the coordinative construction is preferred when the dependent clause contains a continuous verb.

Adverbial clauses involving temporal nouns can be formed by means of either parataxis or hypotaxis. In the former, there is no formal relativisation, while in the latter, the temporal noun is followed by the relative particle *əlli/li*. The status of this particle is somewhat problematic, as, in this construction, it relativises indefinite nouns. Brustad (2000, 102) has observed that, in some modern dialects of Arabic, the *illi* particle can function as a nominaliser of an adverbial phrase when the head noun refers to time and is of low individuation. This resembles the original Semitic structure of nominal dependence employed with adjectives and relative clauses (Goldenberg 1995). Moreover, these constructions very often occur at the beginning of the sentence and therefore function as topic markers. This use of 'quasi-relativisation', or co-subordination, is exemplified by passage (3) and can be contrasted with passage (4), which contains the same temporal noun, but in a fully-fledged relative clause.

In sum, temporal clauses in Jewish Gabes can be expressed either through subordination by means of a temporal particle, or through co-subordination, where two SoAs are juxtaposed without any lexical link.[17] Regarding the temporal particles, it has been pointed out that *waqt* tends to mark continuous or repetitive actions, while *kīf* is generally used for punctual and singular ones. The classification proposed by Cristofaro has been expanded by several more specific categories borrowed from Givón and Kortmann.

1.3.5. Conditional Clauses

1. *ma naqtlūkš kān tžībna agžān mən Baġdād* (2:65)
   'We will not kill you if you bring us the idle man from Baghdad.'

2. *twəlli žīn kān yži hadāk əl-ʕagžān mən Baġdād* (2:67)
   'You will turn back into a ghost if the idle man from Baghdad comes here.'

3. *kān ənti təṭlab mənni bāš(i) nži, nžīk*
   'If you ask me to come, I will come to you.'

4. *kān ʕraft li ənti qāʕad fi-l-blād, kənt nži nẓūrək*
   'If I had known that you were in the town, I would have come to visit you.'

5. *hūwa, kānt mīta hūwa bāš ymūt ʕaləya, kān yži yərqa ʕāyša, mšāt ʕaləyha* (4:102)
   'He, when she was dead, was ready to die for her, so now if he comes back and finds her alive, she will be in real trouble.'

---

[17] The pitfalls of the traditional distinction between subordination and coordination, and the fact that subordination does not necessarily involve clauses, have also been pointed out in relation to European languages (Kortmann 1997, 57).

6. *kān štənnītni tqīqa wa āna dawwītək* (5:40)
   'If you had waited for me a minute, I would have cured you.'

The particle *kān* introduces conditional clauses in Jewish Gabes. Following the distinction proposed by Givón, the above passages can be classified in two groups (Givón 1990, II:331):

1) irrealis: (1), (2), (3), (5);
2) counterfactual: (4), (6).

The structure of the first group involves two clauses, a protasis and an apodosis, and the truth value of the SoA in the apodosis is contingent on the truth value of the SoA in the protasis. The apodosis has a future time reference relative to the protasis. The irrealis is encoded by use of the p-stem in both parts of the sentence:[18]

kān + p-stem	p-stem
protasis	*apodosis*

On the other hand, the counterfactual conditional clause does not have any factual truth value. Since the condition expressed by the SoA in the protasis has not been met, the main apodosis clause is false. In Jewish Gabes, counterfactual clauses have the following structure:

kān + s-stem	s-stem form of the verb 'to be' + p-stem verb form
protasis	*apodosis*

---

[18] Although the Bedouin dialect of Nifzāwa, spoken in the south of Tunisia, often features the s-stem in the protasis (Ritt-Benmimoun 2020), I have not found any examples of this construction in my corpus. This could potentially point to language contact with Israeli Hebrew, where the p-stem in the protasis of the irrealis is the norm.

However, they can also occasionally have the structure exemplified by passage (6):

kān + s-stem	s-stem verb form
protasis	apodosis

It seems that, in the latter type, the main clause bears some degree of probability, albeit very low. The perfective form in example (6) apparently signals that the woman still has some hope of saving the man, although she is aware of his terminal condition. This use of the perfect to express low-likelihood SoAs is attested also in Biblical Hebrew (Givón 1990, II:334; 1997).

1.3.6. Clauses of Reason

1. ənti ʕala xāṭər ṣāḥbi āna nʕāwnək
   'Because you are my friend, I will help you.'

2. ma mšāš l-xadma ʕala xāṭər mṛīḍ
   'He did not go to work because he was sick.'

3. hīya habṭat lūṭa, u l-bīt krātha xāṭər xāyba mātu fīha bərša zġār
   'She went down and rented the room because it was bad, too many children had died in it.'

4. l-wəld ḥrəq rūḥu, xāṭər šāf ša ʕamlu fi-rusalaym
   'The son burnt himself because of what they had done in Jerusalem.'

5. āna ma žəlt ma ʕarrəšts mʕāha li ma ʕṭītīks l-mahar (2:88)
   'I have not married her yet because I did not give you the mahr.'

This type of adverbial clause combines two SoAs connected through the logical relation of cause and effect. The dependent SoA expresses the reason for the occurrence of the main one. In Jewish Gabes, the reason relationship is expressed through *xāṭər* or *aʕla xāṭər*, or through the explanatory particle *li*. The former is widely used across the North African dialects and is attested, among others, in Jewish Tripoli (Yoda 2005, 263). As the above examples demonstrate, no co-subordination occurs in this type of adverbial clause.

Typologically and semantically, reason subordination is related to 'when' and 'after' temporal clauses, in the sense that both of them are causally related. Moreover, the dependent SoA of a reason clause, just like that of a temporal clause, is factual. For this reason, many languages code both types of subordination with the same morphology. Cristofaro (2012, 162) presents the example of the Greek particle *hōs*, which in the Homeric language coded purpose and 'when' clauses, whereas in Classical Greek it was extended to express relations of reason too. In Jewish Gabes, the factual value of the dependent SoA is signalled by elision of the verb 'to be' before predicative adjectives. While example (1) is referring to the present, and the dependent clause in example (2) could refer to both past and present, example (3) has clear past reference.

1.3.7. Clauses of Manner

1. *rākəb ʕal əl-bhīm u rəžlīn fi-lūṭa* (7:34)
   'He rides the donkey with his legs on the floor.'

2. *baʕd təšʕ u arbʕīn ykəmmlu l-*^HE^*ōmər*^HE^ *u yaʕlqu l-məlḥ*
   'After forty-nine days they would complete the Omer by hanging the salt.'

3. *yḍūru fi-l-blād wa yšūfu kifāš əl-ʕbād yʕīšu*
   'They would patrol the city, looking at how people live.'

4. *hūwa yxayyəṭ wa yqīm ṛāṣu fūq*
   'He sews raising up his head.'

Manner constructions consist of two SoAs, the dependent SoA indicating how the main one is executed. In Jewish Gabes, this construction is expressed by means of coordination. Unlike in the majority of other adverbial clauses, in manner constructions, the main SoA comes first, before the dependent one.

1.3.8. Concessive Clauses

1. *ma xašləts̆ əl-fxār u āna ṭḷəbt mənha bāš taxšəl*
   'She did not wash the dishes even though I asked her to do so.'
2. *ḥatta kān l̩-mṭar əqwīya, məlžūm ʕalīna nəṭlʕu mən əḍ-ḍāṛ*
   'Although there was heavy rain, we had to leave the house.'
3. *kānət m̩rīḍa bərša u qāmət (qadrət) təlləf bi ẓġārha*
   'Despite her severe illness, she made an effort to take care of her children.'

Concessive adverbial constructions consist of two SoAs which are linked by a relationship of opposition. The dependent clause expresses circumstances that theoretically should have prevented the occurrence of the main clause, but the event nevertheless takes place, as in examples (2) and (3); or the dependent clause theoretically should have brought about the occurrence of the event in the main clause, but it did not take place, as in (1). Therefore, the dependent SoA is always factual. In Jewish Gabes, the concessive relation can be expressed either coordinatively, as in examples (1) and (3), or through the concessive particle *ḥatta*.

1.3.9. Summary

To sum up the syntactic behaviour of adverbial constructions in Jewish Gabes, several points should be made. The primary strategy used in the dialect is balancing, although some degree of deranking can be identified as well, since the verb in some dependent clauses (e.g., purpose clauses) cannot admit verbal particles (e.g., the /ka-/ particle indicating a continuous action). The semantic classification based on Cristofaro's model has been expanded by several additional categories. Special attention was paid to the distinction between subordination and coordination. As I have shown, some adverbial constructions—like, for example, clauses of manner and concessive clauses—show a strong tendency towards coordination.

1.4. Complementation

In my investigation of complementation in Jewish Gabes, I shall apply the following definition of complementation, proposed by M. Noonan (2007, 52): "the syntactic situation that arises when a notional sentence or predication is an argument of a predicate." In other words, complementation provides information which is necessary for conveying the full meaning of a sentence. In this respect, complement clauses differ from those types of subordinate clauses that provide additional information without which the sentence would remain grammatically correct. Modern studies try to avoid defining complementation in terms of embedding, since, in many languages, complementation can take place without formal embedding (Cristofaro 2012, 96).

1.4.1. Typological Preliminaries

Numerous historical studies of various languages indicate that complementation derives from non-embedded, apposition-like structures involving nouns and pronouns (Noonan 2007, 57). In this kind of construction, which was particularly common in the early stages of development of Indo-European languages, the main clause contained a pronominal element, while the dependent clause presented further specification about it and was connected to the main one through a resumptive pronoun.

The morphology of complements varies from one language to another and can be coded by means of different grammatical categories; nevertheless, several types can be distinguished cross-linguistically. The most common type is a sentence-like complement, which can have two kinds of form. The first one behaves like an independent sentence, and the predicate is in the indicative mood. The second type involves subjunctive forms, which are morphologically distinct from the indicative ones and, in virtually all languages, can stand in an independent sentence in several grammatical contexts (imperative, cohortative, irrealis, etc.). The subjunctive often conveys a sense of doubt and therefore accompanies negated main clauses. This is exemplified by the usage of the particle *by* in Russian, or the distribution of subjunctive forms in negated sentences in Spanish. Complements may be preceded by a complementiser, but some languages convey complementation by means of parataxis and verb serialisation, a method that is particularly common in sub-Saharan languages. Moreover, a single grammatical form can serve as a complement, e.g., an infinitive or a participle. The former, depending on the language, can code a variety of SoAs. In Ancient Greek, infinitives express a full range of tenses, while in Slavic languages, they are coded for aspect and voice (Noonan 2007, 68).

Syntactically, complements can function as subjects or objects of the matrix clause. There is a number of phenomena related to the syntactic behaviour of complements. Some of the most common of them will be mentioned here. Firstly, many of the world's languages make use of what Noonan (2007, 75) calls 'equi-deletion' (henceforth: equi). As a result of this process, a predicate argument of the complement clause is deleted when it is co-referential with the matrix, and the complement becomes of non-sentence-like type. Equi is found mostly in languages where the use of an overt subject is necessary, and therefore will not take place in those that code the subject by means of verb morphology. On the other hand, the phenomenon by which, despite the deletion of an independent subject constituent, the complement remains a sentence, is called anaphoric ellipsis. Applying this rule to Jewish Gabes, one should expect to find the phenomenon of anaphoric ellipsis rather than equi, since deletion of an overt subject from the complement does not bring about a non-sentence-like constituent.

Another phenomenon that is related to the syntagm of complements and involves deletion of an argument is raising. It entails removing an argument of the predication from the dependent SoA and promoting it to the matrix; as a result, the argument acquires a new grammatical function. This process usually takes place when the raised argument is syntactically part of the complement, but semantically constitutes part of the matrix (Noonan 2007, 79). The most common type of this process is subject-to-object raising, which occurs in desiderative and volitive clauses.

It involves promotion of the subject argument from the dependent SoA in an embedded structure to the direct object of the predicate in the matrix. According to Noonan, raising, similarly to equi, brings about a non-sentence-like complement.[19]

Complement clauses are prone to undergoing various kinds of reduction, of which two deserve special attention. Simple clause reduction takes place in three-place manipulative predicates, where, notwithstanding equi-deletion of the subject of the complement predicate, the complement maintains a grammatical structure independent from the syntagm of the matrix. On the other hand, a process called clause union causes both matrix and dependent clause to share the same grammatical features (Noonan 2007, 83). This process usually involves the merging of both predicates in such a way that all the arguments of the sentence are subordinated to the same syntagm. An example from French can provide further explanation of this phenomenon: *Roger laissera manger les pommes à Marie* 'Roger will let Marie eat the apples' (Noonan 2007, 84). In this sentence, 'let' and 'eat' from a ditransitive predicate, both of them having the same arguments, namely, 'Roger', 'apples', and 'Marie'.

So far, I have discussed morphological and syntactical relations between the matrix and complement clauses. I have pointed out the distinction between indicative and subjunctive forms and briefly described the processes of deletion and raising of comple-

---

[19] Another type of raising common across world's languages is negative raising, which entails removing the negative particle from the complement and promoting it to the matrix clause (Noonan 2007, 100).

ments. At this point, it should be argued that both the morphology and the syntax of the complements are, to a large extent, governed by the semantics of the matrix predicate, which can in turn produce a number of interconnections between the two clauses. The semantic integration between the matrix and the complement SoAs has been the subject of extensive studies. Givón (1990, 526) has observed that the semantic interconnection between the clauses is stronger when the agent of the matrix controls the realisation of the complement. According to this statement, manipulative predicates will generate stronger semantic correlation with the complement, than, for example, utterance or proposition. Moreover, Givón (1990, 526) has suggested that, due to semantic integration, events from both clauses merge into one spatio-temporal dimension.[20] This view has been called into question by Cristofaro (2012, 119), who adduces a number of cases where, despite spatio-temporal integration, there is no semantic correlation between the clauses.

The semantics of the matrix predicate are the decisive factor also when it comes to the mood and tense reference of the complement. In this respect, the complement predicate is dependent on the matrix when part of the information it conveys is coded by the main predicate (Noonan 2007, 102). The dependency of the complement on the matrix predicate can be threefold.

---

[20] As pointed out by Noonan (2007, 101), the syntax of the complement can also signal the degree to which the clauses are semantically integrated. Sentence-like complements tend to be more independent than reduced ones, which, due to their incorporation into the matrix, represent a higher degree of semantic integration.

The first type of dependency is time reference, which is sometimes also referred to as time predetermination (Cristofaro 2012, 116). With this dependency, the tense coding of the complement predicate is dictated by the meaning of the matrix predicate. Otherwise, the complement can have a tense constituency of its own, in which case it is described as having indetermined tense reference (Noonan 2007, 103). The former situation is exemplified by predicates expressing a wish, order, command, or desire, since the predicate of the following component will always have future reference. On the other hand, knowledge and utterance predicates do not imply any particular time reference for the complement.

Another dimension of clause dependency is truth-value, or epistemic dependency. This means that the epistemic status of the complement clause depends on the level of truthfulness and probability expressed by the matrix predicate. This type of dependency has indetermined tense reference. As has already been mentioned, some languages code the irrealis mood of the complement by means of the subjunctive (e.g., Spanish) or a distinct form of complementiser (e.g., Russian).

In sum, the world's languages utilise various types of morphological and syntactical reduction in complements that exhibit dependency on the matrix clause. This behaviour can be explained through pragmatic concepts, such as syntagmatic economy and information recoverability (Cristofaro 2012, 248). Usually, when mood and tense are not coded by the complement predicate, this information is recoverable from the matrix predicate, and therefore the reduction reflects the tendency to reduce the complexity of the message. This is also the case when the participant of the dependent SoA is coreferential with the participant of the matrix. Moreover, some of the processes involving merging of the clauses discussed above can be seen as manifestations of aspects of iconicity, namely iconicity of independence and iconicity of distance (Givón 1980; Cristofaro 2012, 251). According to the former, linguistically independent forms represent independence of the concepts that the forms code. Similarly, iconicity of distance points to the correlation between formal distance between forms and their conceptual distance. In light of these statements, it becomes clear why desiderative and modal predicates tend to bring about merging of the clauses by means of raising, namely, the will of the agent and the target of his/her will are conceptually interconnected.[21] On the other hand, utterance predicates almost always involve use of a complementiser, because the act of speaking and its content are not related conceptually.

1.4.2. Complementation in CA

In the previous section (§1.4.1), it was pointed out that the world's languages code complement dependency by means of different syntactical and morphological devices. In what follows, I

---

[21] In CA, this correlation is exemplified by, among others, interchangeability between the complementiser *ʔan al-maṣdariyya* and the actual *maṣdar* in desiderative clauses whose matrix and complement have coreferential subjects. In this case, the conceptual closeness between the wish and its content is expressed by a reduced, nominalised form of the complement (LeTourneau 2011).

shall briefly discuss forms of complementation present in CA. The grammarians distinguish three types of complementiser in CA, each of them being associated with different semantic values of the complement.[22] The first one, ʔanna, follows propositional predicates denoting factual assertions, and therefore the tense reference is often past (Wright 2005, II:26). The predicate in the complement is in the indicative, while its subject is in the accusative case. The second kind of complementiser is ʔinna, which occurs exclusively after the utterance predicate qāla. Finally, the third type, namely ʔan, has a twofold usage. It can follow predicates expressing order, necessity, duty, permission, etc., and in this case, the predicate in the complement clause is in the subjunctive. The tense reference of the complement is therefore future. On the other hand, ʔan can also accompany emotive or knowledge predicates, in which case the reference can be present or past, and the complement predicate is in the indicative. Traditionally, the former is called ʔan an-nāṣibatu 'the ʔan that governs the subjunctive' and the latter is called ʔan muxaffafa 'the lightened ʔan' (LeTourneau 2011).

It can be inferred, therefore, that the semantics of the matrix predicate in CA are the factor that conditions the syntactic behaviour of the complement. On this basis, one would expect to find in CA the syntactic processes described in §1.4.1. Indeed, Persson (1999), in a study of complement-taking predicates in Arabic, observes that raising occurs when the agent of the matrix

---

[22] Some linguists add to the list of the CA complementisers also allaði since it appears in the expression: al-ḥamdu li-llāhi lladī 'God be praised that...' (Spitaler 1962).

is able to control the way the agent of the complement acts. This proves that there is a strong relationship between the type of predicate in the matrix and the form of the whole complement sentence.

1.4.3. Semantic Taxonomy of Complement-Taking Predicates[23] in Jewish Gabes

In the previous sections (§§1.4.1–1.4.2), it has been repeatedly highlighted that there is a strong correlation between the semantics of a complement and its syntax. As has been observed by Givón (1990, II:40), the isomorphism of these two dimensions gives rise to clause union and event integration, which in turn significantly affects the syntax of the entire sentence. Bearing in mind the importance of the semantics of the matrix predicate, in what follows, I shall categorise the passages containing complements according to the meaning of the complement-taking predicate (henceforth: CTP). They have been taken from the text corpus and from questionnaires.

Noonan (2007, 121), in his cross-linguistic study on complementation, proposed a very detailed taxonomy of CTPs appearing in various languages. Some of them are only sporadically attested and do not demonstrate any syntactic peculiarities. Hence, I will follow rather the model proposed by Cristofaro

---

[23] Following Noonan (2007, 121), henceforth, the abbreviation CTP will be used.

(2012, 99), which outlines the most common categories, with some minor modifications.[24]

1.4.4. Modal

1. lāžəm nšūfu šnūwa ʕandu fi-l-bīt (4:91)
   'We must see what he keeps in his room.'
2. ġadwa əl-mélex fi-šətta tāʕ ṣbāḥ lāžəm yətmašša ʕal ṣəṭṭ l-bḥar (7:75)
   'Tomorrow at six in the morning the king is supposed to take a stroll on the beach.'
3. muš lāžəm nədfnūha (4:79)
   'We cannot bury her.'
4. tnəžžəm tədxəl tuwwa
   'You can enter now.'
5. ma ynəžžmūš yədxlu ʕla xāṭər ma ʕandhumš əl-məftāḥ
   'They cannot enter because they do not have the key.'
6. məlžūm ʕalīya bāš nəmši əl-yūm l-ṭbīb
   'I must go to the doctor today.'
7. baʕd ma tkaṣṣrət rəžlu tuwwa ma ynəžžəmš yəmši ʕalīha
   'After he broke his leg, he cannot walk yet.'
8. ḥatta kān l-mṭar əqwīya, məlžūm ʕalīna nəṭlʕu mən əḍ-ḍāṛ
   'Although there was a heavy rain, we had to leave the house.'
9. yəlžəmha ṭṭabbaṣ bāš tədxəl (4:16)
   'She had to lean down to enter.'

---

[24] Givón (1990, II:41) proposes an even more general classification of CTPs, outlining three main categories: modality verbs, manipulation verbs, and perception-cognition-utterance (PCU) verbs.

It is widely recognised by linguists that there are two main distinct types of modality (Comrie 1985; Givón 1990 II, 52; Cristofaro 2012, 60). The first is epistemic modality, which refers to the speaker's degree of commitment to the truth of the proposition. The other is deontic modality, which conveys obligation or permission regarding an event as yet unrealised. A third type relates to ability and is sometimes termed dynamic modality.

As the above passages demonstrate, Jewish Gabes utilises three different ways of conveying modality. The distinction between ability and obligation is clearly marked lexically and syntactically. Thus, the former is expressed by means of conjugated verbal forms of the root /nžm/.

Obligation, on the other hand, can be conveyed in several ways, depending on the nature of the obligation. The first one involves an uninflected particle *lāžəm* and is used when the subject feels an internal need or moral obligation to perform the action expressed by the complement.[25] However, as example (2) demonstrates, the particle in question also has another usage, namely, it can introduce an event that is highly likely to occur. In example (2), *lāžəm* does not denote a personal need or obligation of the king to walk, but rather indicates that this is what he usually does, or what he has planned, and it is therefore reasonable to assume that tomorrow he will walk on the seashore. This, therefore, expresses epistemic necessity.

---

[25] This uninflected particle is widespread in modern varieties of Arabic. It has been attested, among others, in Gulf Arabic (Holes 1990, 201) and in Ṣanʕānī Arabic, where it can occur in a hypotactic construction with the complementiser /innih/ (Watson 1993, 160).

Apart from the particle *lāžəm*, obligation is expressed also by means of a construction involving the passive participle *məlžūm* and the inflected preposition *ʕal*.[26] However, unlike *lāžəm*, which denotes the personal obligation of the subject, this construction is used when the subject is forced by a third person to perform the action conveyed by the complement, or when the obligation is conditioned by external factors. Thus, in example (6), the subject is forced to go to the doctor by their health condition. Similarly, in example (8), the subject does not feel an independent and personal need to leave, but rather is forced by external conditions.

Example (9) presents yet another way of expressing obligation. It involves the 3MS form of the root /lžm/ followed by a direct object pronoun. In this construction, the verb form is impersonal and the subject who is obliged to perform the action expressed by the complement is coded by the direct object. Jewish Tunis supplies numerous examples demonstrating the syntactic behaviour of this form:[27]

(1) *mṛa **yəlzəmha** taʕməl fonctions tāʕ ṛāžəl*
'une femme (…) doit remplir les fonctions d'un homme'

(2) *əlli umān «ḥəšbūn iš» u **yəlzəmma** taʕməl əl-fonctions ntāʕ ṛāžəl*
'qui est le compte de ʔiš et doit exercer les fonctions d'un homme'

(3) *wəl-fonctions ntaḥḥa **yəlazmmam** yəbdāw doubles*
'et dont les fonctions vont être doubles'

---

[26] In Jewish Tunis, there exists also the variant *lāžəm ʕal* (Cohen 1964, 48). However, this has not been attested in Jewish Gabes.

[27] All the examples have been borrowed from Cohen (1964, 48-60).

(4) ma **yəlzəmnāši** bāš baṛmənnām baṛmənnām nqūlu lli isṛail zāda ġalṭin
'nous ne devons pas dire que Israël est dans l'erreur'

(5) flān **yəlzəməlna** nuqfūlu, ulā flān «baṛmənnām baṛmənnām nəftāṛ» **yəlzəmna** bāš nūqfu fi rīgla-lli-īya **təlzəm**
'nous assurer la défence d'un tel, ou bien, helas, un tel est décédé, nous devons nous mobiliser pour telle chose qui est nécessaire'

The semantic value of this construction is by no means homogenous. The first three examples illustrate an obligation being the result of external circumstances. Thus, the subject is involuntarily forced to perform the action expressed by the complement. On the other hand, in examples (4) and (5), *yəlzəm* denotes an obligation that is dictated by morality. The subject is not forced to undertake an action, but is required on a personal level to act in a certain way. Nonetheless, as can be inferred from the above passages, *yəlzəm* never represents an internal, personal need of a subject. Its primary function is hence to denote external obligation.

1.4.5. Phasal

1. **bdāt təmši** təmši təmši (4:16)
   'She started walking, she walked, and walked.'

2. təḍṛəblu fi-ṛəžlīh mən lūṭa ḥatta əl-ṛāẓəl **bda yətḥarrək** wa dəmmu **bda yəẓri** (2:23)
   '[She] started hitting his feet from beneath until the man started moving and the blood started running in his body, he stood up on his feet and started walking.'

3. humma **wəqfu yəbniw** əl-ḍāṛ
   'They stopped building the house.'

4. *əržaʕt naxdəm kif ma kənt aqbəl*
   'I continued working as I worked before.'

5. **kəmmalt nṭəyyəb əl-marqa**
   'I finished cooking the soup.'

The function of phasal predicates is to mark the point in time when the complement SoA is happening. Thus, it can express either the onset of an action, its continuation, its cessation, or its termination. Unlike aspectual operators, phasal predicates do not modify the temporal constituency of the complement predicate (Siewierska 1991, 118; Cristofaro 2012, 102). This assumption is confirmed by example (3), where the reference being made is only the suspension of the construction and not its temporal aspect. In other words, we learn about the development of the construction with reference to its own time-frame, but there is no information about when this SoA takes place.[28]

Jewish Gabes utilises several verbs to express the phase in which the dependent SoA is:

onset	continuation	cessation	completion
bda	ržaʕ	wqəf	kəmmal

It is worth noting that the verb *ržaʕ* 'to come back, to return', in other dialects of Arabic, codes different temporal categories. While, in Jewish Gabes, it means to come back to the point where

---

[28] The distinction between internal and external temporal constituency is coded by different grammatical categories. As has been observed by Siewierska (1991, 118), external time reference is rendered by adverbs or other aspectual operators, which place certain SoAs on a timeline. Contrary to this, phasal predicates code only internal progress of the SoA, and therefore cannot be regarded as aspectual operators.

the action was suspended, and therefore 'to continue', in Moroccan Arabic, it designates a start of the action (Brustad 2000, 215). On the other hand, in some varieties of Syrian Arabic, it denotes a repetitive action.[29] Interestingly, due to language contact, the iterative meaning of *ržaʕ* has also been adopted in the Western Neo-Aramaic dialect of Maʕlūla, where it occurs in the asyndetic construction *rkʕ* + verb (Correll 1978, 83).[30]

The time reference of the complements is predetermined by the matrix predicate (Noonan 2007, 139). Since phasal predicates indicate a stage of an action, and not a punctual event, complement predicates always have a prefix form.

1.4.6. Manipulative

1. *hūwa ṭləb mənni bāš nəmši bə-šwīya*
   'He asked me to walk slowly.'

2. *hūwa li **xallāha** bāš təqṭəl rāẓəlha*
   'It is he who made her kill her husband.'

3. ***dabbərt** ʕali bāš yšəlləfha flūs*
   'I convinced him to lend her money.'

4. *hūwa **ġaṣṣabha** bāš tākəl*
   'He forced her to eat.'

Manipulative CTPs can be divided into two principal groups: (1) expressions of causation (force, make, persuade) and (2) expressions of request (ask, order, request, command). Within both

---

[29] Other varieties of Syrian Arabic, like, for example, the dialect of Damascus, utilise the verb *radd* (Grotzfeld 1965, 90).

[30] I am indebted to Dr Ivri Bunis for providing me with the comparative data from the dialect of Maʕlūla.

those groups, the agent causes an affectee to perform the action expressed by the complement. Similarly to phasal predicates, manipulative CTPs also have predetermined time reference, since the complement SoA always takes place after the matrix predicate.

In Jewish Gabes, manipulative predicates are followed by the particle *bāš*, due to the lack of coreference between the matrix and the complement subjects. Example (1) represents a request predicate, while the other examples fall within the category of causation.

1.4.7. Desiderative

1. *tuwwa bnīwli qṣaṟṟ qbal ḍāṟ bābāy, xīr mən tāʕu, u **nḥabba** ṣahrīn takməl* (2:82)
   'Now build me a castle in front of my father's house, even better than his, and I want it to be finished within two weeks.'

2. *hūwa **yḥabb** yaʕṟəf šnūwa ləwwḥat* (2:32)
   'He wanted to know what she had thrown.'

3. *t**ḥabb** tədxal ənti?* (2:58)
   'Would you like to go in?'

4. *tuwwa **nḥabbək** tqūlli škūn hādi li qāʕda tfaššərlək fi-ḥwāyəž hādi kulla*
   'Now I want you to tell me who this person is, who explains all those things.'

5. *āməš **ḥabbītək** tži tʕāwənni*
   'Yesterday I wanted you to come and help me.'

6. *qāl: āna ᴴᴱʕanī ᴴᴱ u əl-xabža **nḥabb** nākəlha* (1:19)
   'I am poor and I would like to eat the bread.'

7. *ma **ḥabbūš** yqūlūla qatlū l-ʕaṟāb*
   'They did not want to tell her that the Arabs had killed him.'

Desiderative CTPs express a wish for the realisation of an action conveyed by the complement predicate. Either the subject of the matrix predicate may be coreferential with the experiencer of the complement, or the dependent clause may be brought about by a third person (Cristofaro 2012, 103). The time reference of desiderative predicates is predetermined, and the complement predicate always has future meaning.

In Jewish Gabes, the verb associated with this class is invariably *ḥabb*. As examples (1), (4), and (5) demonstrate, *ḥabb* very often brings about raising of the subject from the complement clause to the position of the direct object in the matrix. According to Noonan's (2007, 79) definition, one of the outcomes of raising is a non-sentence-like complement type. However, in light of the data from Jewish Gabes, this assumption turns out to be inadequate. Without doubt, raising takes place, since the argument of the lower clause is promoted to the higher one, but the complement remains a sentence-like type. Example (5) is equal to: *āməš ḥabbīt tži tʕāwənni*, where the subject of the complement predicate, coded by verbal inflection, is in the nominative case. Once raising is applied, it is coded by a pronominal object suffix. Nonetheless, the promotion of the argument does not affect the grammatical independence of the complement.

1.4.8. Perception

1. *āna wəld ṣəlṭān, šmaʕt li taʕməl ʕarš tāʕ bəntək* (6:91)
   'I am a son of the sultan and I have heard that you held a wedding for your daughter.'

2. *šmaʕt tədwi wāḥda u baʕd dənya šəktət wa rqītha mīta* (4:77)
   'I heard a woman talking and then everything became silent and I found her dead.'

3. *f-əl-līl šmaʕtu yətkəlləm mʕa əẓ-ẓāṛ*
   'At night I heard him talking to the neighbour.'

4. *əl-būlīṣi šāf əl-xannāb kīf ṭlaʕ mən əl-*[HE]*xanūt*[HE]
   'The policeman saw the thief escaping from the shop.'

Perception predicates are applied in sentences where the subject witnesses, by hearing or seeing, an event coded by the complement. Their tense reference is predetermined, since the act of perception takes place at the same time as the event itself (Noonan 2007, 142). In Jewish Gabes, as in many other languages, the subject of the complement predicate is coded as the direct object of the CTP. The complement predicate is, in the majority of the examples, in the prefix conjugation, indicating the durative character of the verb.[31] Example (4) is an exception to this rule, as the dependent predicate is punctual and thus the perceived SoA is coded by the suffix inflection. Somewhat problematic is example (1). Lexically, it belongs to the perception category, since it includes the verb 'to hear', but the form of the complement suggests that it could also be classified in the next group, namely, CTPs of knowledge.

---

[31] Due to the immediate and durative character of the act of perception, it is common across the world's languages to code the complement predicate with a participle (Noonan 2007, 142).

1.4.9. Knowledge

1. *l-kbīra taʕrəf li ma ʕandhāš šəmm wa əẓ-ẓġīra taʕrəf li ḥaṭṭətla* (4:121)
   'The old one knew she did not have any poison and the young one knew she did give her poison.'

2. *l-bnāt ʕarfu li ma ʕandīš ġləmm*
   'The girls learnt that I did not have livestock.'

3. *yəšhədu ʕalīya ənžūm u šma li āna žītək* (5:40)
   'My witnesses the moon, the stars and the sky that I have come.'

Knowledge CTPs indicate either a state of knowledge, or the process in the course of which the subject acquires certain knowledge. In Jewish Gabes, the same verb *ʕrəf* expresses both possibilities. Example (3), which contains the verb *šədd* 'to witness', has been classified in this group, since the act of witnessing represents a level of knowledge. Both *ʕrəf* and *šədd* are followed by the complementiser *li*, which nominalises the complement.

1.4.10. Propositional Attitude

1. *ʕandək əl-ḥaqq li šahrīn ma mšītš, nəmšīlo* (5:10)
   'You are right that I have not gone to him for two months, I will go to him now.'

2. *āna fi-bāli əlli hūwa mūš ḥabb yərbaḥ*
   'I think he is not going to win.'

Through propositional CTPs, the subject expresses an evaluation of the content conveyed by the complement. Since this evaluation usually pertains to the truth of the dependent clause, the matrix predicate will involve verbs relating to thinking, believing, expressing opinion, etc. In Jewish Gabes, this class is scarcely attested, and comprises two expressions, both of them followed by the complementiser. Their time reference is undetermined, since the complement of example (1) refers to the past, and that of example (2) to the future.

1.4.11. Utterance

1. *hūwa qālli ʕamru ma yəržaʕ əl-hūni*
   'He told me that he would never come back to this place.'

2. *āna qatlu ma ʕātəš təmma məlžūm bāš tbəddəl šəlha*
   'I told him that it was not possible to change the stock.'

Utterance predicates describe a process of transferal of the information which is coded by the complement. As pointed out by Cristofaro (2012, 121), the transferred information can be expressed in the form of either direct or indirect quotation. The vast majority of utterance predicates in Jewish Gabes function within direct discourse, and therefore cannot be analysed in terms of complementation. Both of the examples presented above have been obtained by means of a questionnaire. It is worth noting that no complementiser occurs in them, and as a matter of fact the dependent clause has a form similar to that of direct speech.

1.4.12. Emotion

1. *farḥat mərt būha li žāt* (4:66)
   'The step-mother was happy that she came.'

2. *āna nādəm əlli ma ʕāwəntūš waqt əlli kān m̱rīḍ*
   'I regret that I did not help him when he was sick.'

3. *āna ġlat li ma qbəltš əl-xadma hādi*
   'I am sorry that you have not got this job.'

This category is not included either in Cristofaro's model or in Noonan's.[32] Predicates of emotion express an emotional attitude of the subject towards the SoA expressed by the complement. Their time reference is not predetermined. In Jewish Gabes, they attract the occurrence of the *li-əlli* complementiser.

1.5. Summary

After analysing the three types of subordination, some conclusions can be drawn regarding the coding of dependency in Jewish Gabes. Throughout the course of my investigation, two dimensions were considered—a cross-linguistic and a Semitic one. The latter was aimed at demonstrating the origins of relative and adverbial clauses. The former approach, on the other hand, was applied in order to place Jewish Gabes within a wider typological framework.

I have argued that relative clauses in Jewish Gabes are of an external, post-nominal type and can be either restrictive or non-restrictive. Historically, they derive from the pattern of nominal dependency, similarly to adjectives and adverbial clauses. As in many other modern Arabic dialects, the syntactic behaviour of relative clauses in Jewish Gabes is, to a large extent, dependent on the definiteness of the head noun. It has been demonstrated that definite nouns attract the relative pronoun and bring about resumption in the relative clause. On the other hand, when the relativised item is indefinite, relativisation tends to be realised by means of coordination or asyndetically. Finally, my data have

---

[32] Noonan's model includes, however, predicates of fearing: see Noonan (2012, 130).

confirmed the accurateness of the Accessibility Hierarchy, demonstrating that subject and direct object are the two most relativised positions in Jewish Gabes.

The investigation of adverbial clauses provided a thorough presentation and taxonomy of data. It was argued that, historically, Semitic languages used nominal dependency to express adverbial relations, and at a later stage, some grammaticalised nouns started serving as adverb markers. The data analysis involved six semantic groups of adverbial clauses in Jewish Gabes. Special attention was paid to temporal clauses. I utilised the model proposed by Givón (1990, II:330) and Kortmann (1997, 80), which allowed me to demonstrate different aspects of temporal dependency. In addition, I argued that some clauses use coordination in order to render adverbial relations. This was the case in some temporal clauses, as well as clauses of manner and concessive clauses.

The analysis of the third type of subordination, complementation, was primarily concerned with syntactic phenomena caused by the semantics of the matrix predicate. I argued that the meaning of the main predicate to a large extent conditions the syntagm of the complement. From a historical point of view, it was demonstrated that CA utilises three types of complements depending on the semantics of the main predicate. Subsequently, a semantic taxonomy of complement-taking predicates was presented. Each class of complements has been classified with respect to tense predetermination. I have argued that Jewish Gabes makes a clear distinction between deontic and epistemic modality. Moreover, I have shown different ways of expressing obligation in the dialect, involving the particle *lāžəm*, *məlžūm ʕal*, and *yəlžəm* + personal pronoun. Finally, it has been demonstrated that some types of predicate, like for example desiderative predicates, bring about raising of the complement subject to the position of the direct object of the matrix predicate.

2.0. Expressions of Tense and Aspect

2.1. Introduction[33]

There is a general scholarly consensus that the verbal system of modern Arabic dialects incorporates both aspect- and tense-coding devices (Eisele 1991, 193; Brustad 2000, 203).[34] Indeed, these two categories are inextricably linked, and both play a part in expressing events. However, Brustad (2000, 202), after comparing data from several dialects, reaches the conclusion that it is aspect that prevails in the verbal system of spoken Arabic, and indicates that separate mechanisms are used to convey time. This might give the impression that all Arabic dialects code aspect and tense in the same way. Unsurprisingly, this is far from correct. The dialects in fact display immense differences in their verbal

---

[33] This section is a modified version of my paper: 'Expressions of Tense and Aspect in the Tunisian Varieties of Arabic: A Comparative Study of Jewish and Muslim Dialects' (Gębski 2022).

[34] It is worth noting that the debate on the nature of the verbal system is not limited only to Arabic. The puzzling relationship between tense and aspect seems to be one of the most frequently discussed issues in scholarship on Semitic languages, the best example being Biblical Hebrew.

syntax (use of participles, preverbal particles, auxiliary verbs), which, in turn, have a significant impact on the coding of the two categories in question. The aim of the present study, therefore, is to present a thorough investigation of the relationship between tense and aspect in Jewish Gabes, and of its wider context in relation to other Arabic dialects. Comparative material has been excerpted from Jewish Tunis (Cohen 1964, 1975), Muslim Tunis (interview with an informant), ʕAulād Msalləm (Simeone-Senelle 1985), the Bedouin dialect of Douz in Southern Tunisia (Ritt-Benmimoun 2011; 2014), and Jewish Tripoli (Yoda 2005). The introductory remarks include a short presentation of the verbal system of Jewish Gabes, as well as discussion of the origin of the /ka-/ preverbal particle. In §2.7, I demonstrate that the p-stem and the s-stem in Jewish Gabes are mostly aspectual, and their temporal value is conveyed by external elements. Subsequently, I discuss the expressions of the perfect in modern Tunisian dialects, where, as will be shown, there are salient functional divergences between the Jewish and Muslim varieties. I provide an explanation of this phenomenon involving a North-West Semitic substrate underlying the Jewish dialects. The final part of the section (§2.8) deals with the compound forms of the p-stem (/qāʕd/, /qāʕ/, /ḵa/, /kān/, and /ḥabb/).

2.2. Syntax of Verbs in Jewish Gabes

The structure of the verb phrase in Jewish Gabes comprises the following primary elements: the verb itself, negation particles, and preverbal particles or auxiliary verbs. The inventory of the last two elements differs from dialect to dialect. This issue will be analysed more closely in the following section (§2.3).

The two basic forms of the verb in Jewish Gabes are called in the present study the s-stem (ffʕəl) and the p-stem (yəffʕəl). Scholars of spoken Arabic have also been known to use the terms perfective and imperfective (e.g., Brustad 2000), the former occasionally being replaced by the term 'perfect' (Eisele 1990, 174). This terminology in Jewish Gabes is not always accurate, especially in light of the distinction between lexical and formal (viewpoint) aspect, and the possible tense-related implications it might bear. Thus, in order to avoid any imprecisions, in what follows, I will be using terminology based on morphology. Moreover, the term 'perfect', in some studies, designates a specific aspectual value coded formally by the active participle (Eisele 1990, 173; Brustad 2000, 142). As will be shown in §§2.7.3–2.7.4, the active participle in Jewish Gabes has limited usage, and fulfils a different function. As regards negation, the dialect in question has two basic patterns: (1) verbal negation, expressed by *mā* verb + /š/ clitic, and (2) predicate negation, expressed by the particle *muš*.

2.3. Distinction between Preverbal Particles and Auxiliaries

The emergence of preverbal particles in any language is closely related to its internal, diachronic processes of grammaticalisation and morphological reduction (Owens 1998, 105). The category of preverbal particles is, in Jewish Gabes, interconnected with that of auxiliary verbs, and it is therefore sometimes difficult to unequivocally draw a distinction between them. Certain verbs are in the process of a functional ramification, serving on the one hand as fully-fledged, inflected verbal forms, and on the other as frozen particles. Their double nature seems to present some difficulties for the analysis of Arabic dialects. Harrell (1962, 178) classifies under the category of 'auxiliaries' in Moroccan both those items lacking a full conjugation and those with regular verbal forms. Contrary to this, Eisele (1992, 160), when investigating auxiliaries in Egyptian Arabic, sets out four features they display, one of which is obligatory subject coreferentiality among members of the verb phrase. In the present section, following Eisele, a clear distinction between these two categories is made. Thus, lexical items lacking a full conjugation will be classified as preverbal particles, while verbs coreferential with the subject will be grouped under the category of auxiliaries.

2.4. The Origin of Preverbal Particles in Jewish Gabes

Four preverbal particles can be distinguished in Jewish Gabes. They stem from two separate verbal forms, namely, *qāʕəd* and *kān*. The first particle is an uninflected form of the active participle *qāʕəd*. As I shall argue, this form gave rise to a number of clitics, the most obvious being *qāʕ*, which presumably emerged due to the loss of the final consonant. This might have taken place after it underwent devoicing to [t] and subsequent assimilation to the [t] prefix of the 2SG, 3FS, and 2PL.[35] The two other particles

---

[35] The tendency of the preverbal particles to assimilate to the personal prefixes of the main verb has already been pointed out by Stewart (1998, 117), who gives the example of the Egyptian /bi-/ clitic turning into /mi-/ in the 1PL, i.e., *minākul* 'we are eating', instead of *binākul*.

are /ka-/[36] and *kān*. While the latter is no doubt a grammaticalised form of the 3MS s-stem form of the verb 'to be', the origin of the former is less certain. Two possible paths of development can be proposed. The particle could have emerged due to the loss of the final [n] sound of the form *kān*. Again, this could have been caused by assimilation to the /n-/ prefix of the 1SG/PL. As will be shown later, however, this explanation does not hold water in light of the data. On the contrary, as I shall argue, /ḵā-/ developed from the participle *qāʕəd*, being the next stage in the development of the particle *qāʕ*.[37]

As reflected in emphasis spread, the sound [q] in Jewish Gabes is the weakest of the emphatic consonants. The sound [q] could therefore have undergone de-emphaticisation, turning into the unaspirated stop [k]. It is also worth noting that, cross-dialectally, the fronting of [q] to the post-velar position, which also reflects its weakness as an emphatic, is one of the characteristic traits of sedentary dialects (Aguadé 2018, 45). Similarly, the realisation of [ʕ] in the dialect is much weaker than in other varieties of Arabic, especially the eastern ones. Instances of the elision of [ʕ] are also attested in neighbouring Jewish Tripoli,

---

[36] In the transcription, an unaspirated stop is represented as [k̠], its aspirated counterpart as /k/. /k/ in the preverbal particle /ka-/ is always unaspirated, but it is marked as such only when this is relevant for the diachronic reconstruction.

[37] A similar phenomenon of phonetic reduction of a preverbal element is attested in Neo-Aramaic dialects, where the /bət/ particle in the construction *bət-qaṭəl* sometimes turns into /t-/. The parallelism is even more explicit considering that this particle likely originates in the MS form of the active participle of the verb 'to want'.

where one occasionally finds the form *ča*, being a truncated version of the genitive exponent *čāʕ*.[38]

When it comes to the vowel, since the particle always precedes a verbal form and does not constitute an independent entity with its own stress, one can expect length reduction from [ā] to short [a] in the stream of natural speech.[39] Another explanation for the reduction of this vowel could be a de-grammaticalisation of the original verb form. As pointed out by Stewart (1998, 118), some clitics emerge due to the loss of a personal prefix, by which they become grammatically dependent items. In the form *qāʕəd*, the long [ā] vowel is vital for coding the grammatical function of the active participle, and its reduction to a short [a] might therefore be an expression of its syntactic dependence.

In the following paragraphs, I shall present arguments in favour of reconstructing the origin of the particle /ka-/, used to denote progressive events, in the active participle *qāʕəd*. The reconstruction is based on the following phonological processes leading to the emergence of the particle /ka-/ in Jewish Gabes: qāʕəd > *qāʕət > qāʕ > *qaʕ > *qa > ka. It is worth noting

---

[38] This is an observation made on the basis of my own transcriptions of the recordings from Jewish Tripoli available on the website of the Mother Tongue Project: https://www.lashon.org/en/taxonomy/term/58, accessed 30 Nov 2023.

[39] M. Cohen (1924, 57–58) distinguishes three stages in the formation of a clitic: 1) full word, 2) slightly reduced word, 3) considerably reduced word (e.g., the Levantine preverbal particle *ʕammāl* > *ʕa*).

that the same coexistence of *qāʕəd*, *qāʕ*, and *ka* is attested in Jewish Djerba, as opposed to the Ibadite and Malekite varieties, where only *qāʕəd* is used (Behnstedt 1998, 67).

The process described above involves a number of cross-linguistic phenomena related to language change, broadly understood, which have been under investigation over the past few decades (DeLancey 1997; Bybee 2003; Aarts 2004). Namely, as demonstrated above, the evolution of the active participle *qāʕəd* into a progressivity marker was brought about by the subsective gradience of this form, which, in turn, has led to its reanalysis and subsequent grammaticalisation.[40] Moreover, the sequence of synchronically attested forms, *qāʕəd* > *qāʕ* > *ka*, demonstrates that the process underlying this change consists of a number of micro-changes, which represent a gradual development. In other words, the case of the /ka-/ particle and its derivation constitutes a point of intersection between synchronic gradience, and gradualness, which by its nature is diachronic (Traugott and Trousdale 2010, 22). The coexistence in Jewish Gabes of the full verb form alongside the auxiliary and clitics deriving from it therefore offers a unique insight into the dynamics of language change.

---

[40] As explained by Aarts (2004, 361), subsective gradience denotes different levels of membership within the same category (e.g., the adjective and its ability to occur in both attributive and predicative positions). On the other hand, intersective gradience refers to one element having membership of different categories (e.g., some adverbs can mimic the adjective).

2.4.1. The Particle /ka-/ in Other Dialects

The occurrence of the progressive marker /ka-/ is in fact not limited to Jewish Gabes. In a comparative study of a vast variety of Arabic dialects (stretching from Morocco to Iraq) conducted by Agius and Harrak (1987, 164–80), it is argued that numerous dialects from different sub-groups utilise morphological variants of this particle. Agius and Harrak argue that the source of all such particles is the modal participle *qāʕid*. Regarding Moroccan, however, Stewart (1998, 104) calls their claim into question, arguing that the Moroccan particle /ka-/ derives from the perfective form of the verb *kān* used in conditional clauses. Its development from marking conceptual dependency within conditional apodoses to denoting every type of the indicative mood seems to parallel the expansion of the particle /b-/ in other dialects. Owens (2018, 243) argues that the marking of evidentiality with /b-/ was facilitated by its usage in sequences of verbs occurring in narratives. This stage of development is exemplified by Nigerian Arabic. This argument has also been made by other scholars who agree that it was the modal use of the verb 'to be' in conditional clauses that gave rise to the particle /ka-/ (Corriente 1977, 140–41; Hanitsch 2019, 256–58). As argued by Khan (2021), a similar development is evidenced in some NENA dialects, where the construction *bət-qaṭəl*—originally used in the apodosis of conditional clauses—acquired new functions and started denoting discursively dependent events. Khan explains this by means of construction grammar, whereby syntactic spread takes place due to a cognitive schematisation of grammatical constructions.

The model proposed by Stewart and others, which derives /ka-/ in other dialects from the verb *kān* 'to be', does not seem to be plausible in the case of the Jewish Gabes particle /ka-/ denoting the progressive. Rather, Jewish Gabes /ka-/ is more likely to have originated in *qāʕəd*. In support of this, I present two arguments, one phonetic, and the other syntactic. Firstly, within Jewish Gabes, the [k̬] of the particle differs from the [k] in *kān* in terms of aspiration. While the [k̬] of the particle is unaspirated, the [k] in *kān* is conspicuously aspirated [kʰ]. The aspiration of [k] is a widespread phenomenon across Arabic dialects, resulting, in some of them (especially Bedouin dialects of the Gulf and northern Arabia), in further development to [č], e.g., in Baghdadi Arabic (Holes 1991, 655).[41] In Jewish Gabes /k̬a-/, the unaspirated allophone therefore indicates the uvular origin of this consonant.

The second argument is the clear syntactic distinction between the use of *kān* and that of the /ka-/ particle and other forms deriving from *qāʕəd*. Whereas *kān* marks past habitual events and occasionally fulfils a contrastive function (see §2.4.2 below), the latter particles are functionally interchangeable and denote progressivity, albeit with different time references.[42]

---

[41] In some dialects, for example in the Arabic spoken on the south coast of Iran, the affrication of the fronted [k] takes place only in the environment of front vowels, e.g., *samač* 'fish' (Leitner 2021, 230). It is worth noting, however, that the affrication of both [k] and [g] is a feature of Bedouin-type dialects and does not take place in the sedentary ones.

[42] This issue will be further discussed in the analysis.

2.4.2. Origin and Distribution of the /kān/+p-stem Construction

The function of *kān* in Jewish Gabes is relatively similar to its function in CA. According to Marmorstein (2016, 68), the auxiliary *kāna* in CA functions as a temporal adapter, which expresses anteriority of the predominantly aspectual predicate. In addition, as pointed out by Nebes (1982), it denotes the past tense in instances where the time reference cannot be retrieved from the context. Jewish Gabes utilises both *kān* as a frozen form of the verb 'to be', i.e., a preverbal particle, and a fully conjugated form, i.e., an auxiliary, from which the frozen form originates. Both mark past habitual events. This development could be interpreted as the first stage of the cliticisation of the verb 'to be'.

It therefore appears that, in Jewish Gabes, two separate developments led to the emergence of two distinct particles, i.e., /ka-/, from *qāʕəd*, which marks progressive events; and *kān*, which denotes past, predominantly habitual events. The distribution of these particles will be analysed in greater detail below.

2.5. Aspect and Tense: Theoretical Remarks

The relationship between tense and aspect in some languages can be confusing, leading to imprecise conclusions.[43] It is crucial, therefore, to draw clear distinctions between the two categories

---

[43] As pointed out by Comrie (1976, 94), there is a conceptual and terminological confusion of these terms in scholarship on Romance languages. The weakness of the terminology has also been observed by Eisele (1991, 76) and in Woidich's (1975) study on active participle forms in Cairene Arabic.

and precisely define their domains. In what follows, I shall briefly present the terminology used in this section; I shall first define aspect and subsequently contrast it with tense.

2.5.1. Aspect

Aspect can be generally defined as the shape of the event expressed by a verb.[44] It indicates the character of the state of affairs and its internal temporal constituency, i.e., whether an event was punctual or durative (Comrie 1976, 3). Various types of aspect are expressed by binary oppositions used to characterise events.[45] A situation can therefore be viewed as perfective, i.e., temporally bounded, or as imperfective, i.e., expressing duration in time without indicating whether it ended or not (Forsyth 1970, 347). The distinction between these two categories also entails consideration of the way in which they are presented. The perfective presents the situation as a whole, while the imperfective focuses on its phasal nature and sees it from within (Comrie 1976, 16). Although no unequivocal definition of aspect exists, it may be tentatively assumed that, cross-linguistically, the imperfective is associated with continual, habitual, and generic meaning, while the perfective has punctual, iterative, and resultative

---

[44] For the history of scholarship on aspect and the questions it poses, see Binnick (1991, 135–58).

[45] As argued by Sasse (2002, 201), there is presently a scholarly consensus that the common denominator of various aspectual distinctions is the notion of 'boundaries', i.e., the same event can be perceived as having endpoints, or as being temporally unbounded.

connotations (Binnick 1991, 156). In addition, aspect can be divided into two subgroups, namely, formal aspect and lexical aspect (Sasse 2002, 203).

Formal aspect is expressed by the morphology of the verb. In other words, it is the strategy by which the conjugation codes a situation as perfective or imperfective. As pointed out by Eisele (2011), Arabic verb morphology, in contrast to, for example, Slavic languages, is rather poorly equipped for aspect marking. Most of the information about the temporal specification of the situation is provided by external elements—preverbal particles, auxiliaries, and the context of the sentence. Formal aspect is sometimes also called 'viewpoint aspect', as it expresses the way in which a speaker views the situation. Two main types of this formal aspect can be distinguished, i.e., perfective, which views an event from the outside, and imperfective, which depicts it from within.

In contrast to formal aspect, lexical aspect is not grammaticalised, but is expressed by the meaning of the verb itself. A synonymous term used in the literature is Aktionsart, i.e., type of action (Comrie 1976, 6; Eisele 1990, 190; Forsyth 1991, 20; Brustad 2000, 165). Lexical aspect is therefore an inherent semantic feature of a verb. As one might expect, verbs can be divided into multiple semantic categories, which in turn interact in various ways with the formal aspect (Eisele 1990; Brustad 2000, 168). A mere semantic classification of verbs is of little significance and does not provide any crucial information about a language. It is rather the interaction between these classes and the verb morphology that tells us how a language expresses aspect.

In general terms, it can be assumed that the perfective expresses actions with temporal boundaries, i.e., completion, entry into a state, or onset of action, while the imperfective expresses meanings related to habituality, progressivity, or state. Vendler (1957) distinguishes between four classes of lexical aspect: states (like, desire, want, etc.), activity (run, walk, swim, etc.), achievement (lose, find, recognise, etc.), which expresses a punctual event with an endpoint, and accomplishment (build a house, write a novel, etc.), which indicates a process leading to an endpoint. A more detailed classification based on lexical aspect and its relationship with the verbal system in Jewish Gabes will be proposed below.

2.5.2. Tense

In contradistinction to aspect, tense situates an event on a timeline and in reference to some other time, usually the time of speaking (Comrie 1976, 66; Bybee et al. 1994). It can be expressed in various ways, both lexically and by means of verbal morphology. Cross-linguistically, the most common distinction coded morphologically is that of past and non-past. As has already been mentioned, there is some disagreement about how verbal morphology in Semitic languages relates to both aspect and tense. Within the field of Arabic linguistics, scholars generally agree that the Arabic verb expresses aspect rather than tense (Eisele 1990; Brustad 2000, 203; Horesh 2011). If this is indeed the case, a question arises as to the extent to which Arabic verbal morphology provides information about tense. On this topic, in contrast to other topics in the syntax of spoken Arabic, several insightful studies exist (Cowell 1964, 340; Eisele 1990; Horesh 2002). The results of these studies seem to converge and confirm that the only tense feature stable across various dialects is the past encoded by the s-stem.[46] The p-stem, on the other hand, is much more complex, allows for a variety of preverbal elements, and has a tense value which is much more diverse.[47] Very little is actually yet known, however, about the tense and aspect systems specific to North African dialects.

Another important term related to the notion of tense is time reference, one of the three elements in Reichenbach's (1947) system for the temporal structure of verbs. Reichenbach distinguished between three points on the timeline encoding tense: point of speech, point of event, and point of reference. The last of the three orientates an event in relation to another point in time, which is usually another event. As has been established above, tense is usually coded by verb morphology. Time reference, in turn, refers to how tense locates a state of affairs in time and can be produced by both the sentence and the context. As one might expect, in light of the weakness of the Arabic tense system, time reference will be determined primarily by lexical strategies and discourse context (Brustad 2000, 203). Two types of time reference can be distinguished: (1) absolute time reference, which presents the temporal dimension of a verb in relation

---

[46] Even to this rule there are some exceptions. As demonstrated by Horesh (2011), in Palestinian Arabic, some stative verbs in the s-stem might have non-past reference.

[47] The complexity of the p-stem and its dependence on the discourse has also been observed for CA (Marmorstein 2016, 239).

to the time of speaking, and (2) relative time reference, which defines the time of an event in relation to another event (Reichenbach 1947; Comrie 1976, ii). As pointed out by Brustad (2000, 204), and as the following analysis will prove, the Arabic tense system in the main clause is closely related to the time of speaking. On the other hand, the time reference of the dependent clause is determined by the main clause.

2.6. Introduction to Analysis

In the following sections (§§2.7–2.8), I shall analyse the aspectual and temporal functions of the verbal system in Jewish Gabes. I will argue that the verb without any overt time expression is in this dialect mainly aspectual and its temporal dimension is either absent, or secondary. I will apply a modified version of the model used by Simeone-Senelle (1985) in her study on systems of aspect and tense in Tunisian Arabic, which was based on data provided by a female informant from Aʕulād Msalləm (26km north of Sfax).[48] Unfortunately, the communal identity of the informant is unknown. However, certain phonological features (such as the realisation of [q] as [g]) point to a Muslim background. To the best of my knowledge, this is the only available study on aspect and tense in Tunisian Arabic, and it therefore deserves special attention. Simeone-Senelle claims that plain verb forms (i.e., those without temporal adverbial contours) are purely aspectual and do not encode any time reference. She distinguishes two

---

[48] I would like to express my gratitude to Professor Marie-Claude Simeone-Senelle for sharing her article with me and providing me with some insightful comments on Tunisian Arabic.

principal forms, namely imperfective (Fr. *inaccompli*), associated with unfinished, ongoing events, and perfective (*accompli*), which expresses completed, temporally-bounded actions. This binary opposition, in turn, has evolved in order to enable the rendering of concomitance, which is understood as the co-occurrence of an event with another state of affairs—the time of speaking or another point of reference invoked in the utterance (Simeone-Senelle 1985, 58). Thus, the concomitant form of the imperfective is the actual or relative present, while the concomitance of the perfective is expressed by the perfect, which signifies a past event concomitant with the present (as opposed, in some languages, to a non-concomitant aorist that does not have any additional time dimension).

The conclusions of the study in question and the verbal forms provided by the informant differ substantially from the state of affairs in Jewish Gabes. As I shall argue, this dialect does not express the perfect in the same way as ʕAulād Msalləm, and the functional distribution of the active participle is different. Moreover, the two dialects diverge in the way they express the future tense. Not included in Simeone-Senelle's study are compound forms with auxiliary verbs (*kān* + p-stem) or forms with preverbal particles. Since their occurrence in Jewish Gabes is significant and they play an important role in the relationship between tense and aspect, I shall include them in my model. The following analysis is organised according to the morphology of the verb forms attested in Jewish Gabes. The aspectual and temporal values of each of them will be explained.

2.7. Analysis: Plain Forms

2.7.1. P-stem

The temporal value of the p-stem is undefined and strongly dependent on the context. It is compatible with the following types of lexical and viewpoint aspect. For lexical aspect, I adopt Vendler's lexical aspect classes (§2.5.1 above).

Lexical Aspect Class

    (I) State

(1)   *l-kbīra taʕrəf   li   ma ʕandhaš šəmm*
DEF-old know.PFX.3FS that NEG at.her.NEG poison
'The old one knew she did not have any poison.' (4:121)

(2)   *qāllu   la   naʕrfək   u*
say.SFX.3MS.HIM no know.PFX.1SG.you and
la   žītni   u   la   šəftək
no come.SFX.2SG.me and no see.SFX.1SG.you
'He told him: I do not know you, and you did not come to me and I have never seen you.' (6:23)

In both (1) and (2), the time reference is past.

    (II) Activity

(3)   *yəmšīw   l-əl-bḥar   kull   nhār   šəbbāt*
go.PFX.3PL to- DEF-sea every day Saturday
'They go to the sea every Saturday.'

The above example expresses a habitual present. However, an activity with future time reference can also be encoded by the p-stem. This includes both plain verbs, as in (4), and, according to

Simeone-Senelle's terminology, concomitant forms, accompanied by a lexical 'actualiser', i.e., an adverb indicating future reference, as in (5):

(4) āna nʕāwnək
    I   help.PFX.1PL.you
    'I will help you.'

(5) ġadwa nžiblək əl-flūš
    tomorrow bring.PFX.1SG-to.you DEF-money
    'Tomorrow I will bring you money.'

Viewpoint Aspect Class

(I) Habitual

Both past and present habits can be expressed by this form:

(6) yəqʕdu kull līla u yṣallīw
    sit.PFX.3PL every night and pray.PFX.3PL
    'They would sit down every night and pray.'

The above passage comes from a dialogue about the way the Jews of Gabes celebrated the Omer; the reference is therefore past. However, as the next passage demonstrates, the p-stem can also encode the present.

(II) Progressive

(7) qaʕdu u yāklu u yəšrbu
    sit.SFX.3PL and eat.PFX.3PL and drink.PFX.3PL
    u hbəṭ ʕaləhyəm əl-līl
    and fall.SFX.3MS on.them DEF-night
    'They sat down, ate, drank, and the night fell upon them.'
    (2:30)

As the above example demonstrates, the p-stem denotes progressive events stretched over an interval, which are characterised by their homogenous character at every point within the interval.

In sum, it can be established that the p-stem does not have any fixed temporal value and its time reference is entirely dependent on the context. In terms of lexical aspect, the only category from Vendler's model that has not been demonstrated in this stem is accomplishment.

2.7.2. S-stem

The principal role of this form is encoding complete events seen as a bounded whole. In the vast majority of cases, its time reference is past. The following temporal and aspectual features can be distinguished:

Lexical Aspect Class

(I) Activity

(8) hūwa žra   wa xda   ʕaṣa
    he   run.SFX.3MS and take.SFX.3MS stick
    u   ḍrəbha   fi-ḍharha
    and hit.SFX.3MS.her in-back.her
    'He ran and took a stick and hit her on the back.' (2:33)

(II) Accomplishment

(9) šəddi   səlṭān bəntek   əẓ-ẓġīra bnāt   əl-qṣaṛ
    master.my sultan daughter.your DEF-young build.SFX.3FS   DEF-castle
    'Your majesty, it is your youngest daughter who has built this castle.' (2:87)

(III) Achievement

(10) *fahmu tǝmma wāḥǝd hūni*
　　 understand.SFX.3PL there.is one　　here
　　 'They realised that someone was there.' (4:36)

As demonstrated in all the above examples, the s-stem has a past time reference.

Viewpoint Aspect Class

The s-stem is compatible with lexemes implying iterative and perfect meaning:

(I) Iterative

(11) *šallǝf　　 mǝnni　flūš　tlāta marrāt*
　　 borrow.SFX.3MS from.me money three times
　　 'He borrowed money from me three times.'

(II) Perfect

A major difference between Jewish Gabes and other Arabic dialects has to do with encoding the perfect. Whereas in many other dialects the perfect is encoded by the active participle, in Jewish Gabes it is encoded by the s-stem.[49] Thus, an immediate past that bears a relation to the present is expressed by the s-stem:

(12) *tuwwa xrǝž*
　　 now　 go.SFX.3MS
　　 'He has just gone out.'

Similarly, the s-stem also expresses a resultative meaning:

---

[49] In Arabic dialects outside North Africa, the perfect meaning of the active participle is a widespread phenomenon (Brustad 2000, 182).

(13) ʕalāš ənti ʕyīti?
   why you tire.SFX.2FS
   'Why are you tired?'

(14) tuwwa kəmməlt   tanḍīf tāʕ ḍāṛ
   now finish.SFX.1SG cleaning GEN DEF-house
   'I have just finished cleaning the house.'

Such usages of the s-stem with perfect meaning, as in Jewish Gabes (12–14), are in fact found in ʕAulād Msalləm as well, especially with certain verbs of movement and perception (Simeone-Senelle 1985, 71). However, in addition to these, there is a significant group of verbs in that dialect which express the perfect through the *fāʕil* pattern, i.e., the historical active participle. This includes verbs of perception, such as 'to understand', 'to hear', and 'to see', but also various telic and atelic verbs, such as 'to buy', 'to run', and 'to give birth'. The following examples are taken from Simeone-Senelle (1985). Below, they will be contrasted with analogous examples from Jewish Gabes:

(15) fāhma   əd-dərs?
   understand.AC.PTCP.FS DEF-lesson
   'Have you understood the lesson?'

(16) bāni   filla kebīra lāken baʕīda ʕal-blēd
   build.AC.PTCP.MS villa big   but   far.away on-city
   'He has built a big house, but it is far away from the city.'

(17) he-r-rāžel šāri   əž-žmel
   this-the-man buy.AC.PTCP.MS DEF-camel
   'This man has just bought a camel.'

(18) *əl-mrā   wēlda*
    DEF-woman give.birth.AC.PTCP.FS
    'The woman has given birth.'

As can be seen from the above examples, the *fāʕil* pattern in ʕAulād Msalləm covers several types of perfect, such as resultative (17), and recent past (18).[50] According to Simeone-Senelle (1985, 72), the distribution of the s-stem and *fāʕil* pattern is somewhat inconsistent, and certain verbs appear in both forms with perfect meaning. However, the informant notes that *fāʕil* expresses a longer duration from the speaker's point of view in the present.

By contrast, Jewish Gabes never utilises the active participle to encode the perfect. Instead, to render the recent past, it employs the s-stem with an adverbial 'actualiser'. A resultative meaning is inferred from the context. My informant rejected the forms from ʕAulād Msalləm, and interpreted them as bearing a different meaning (the function of these forms will be discussed in detail in §2.7.3) and instead proposed the following:

(19) *fhəmt   əd-dərš?*
    understand.SFX.2MS DEF-lesson
    'Have you understood the lesson?'

(20) *bna   filla kbīra āma baʕīda mən əl-blād*
    build.SFX.3MS villa big   but far.away from DEF-city
    'He has built a big house, but it is far away from the city.'

---

[50] For different types of perfect, see Comrie (1976, 56).

(21) hāk ər-ṛāžel tuwwa sra   əž-žməl
    that DEF-man now buy.SFX.3MS DEF-camel
    'This man has just bought a camel.'

(22) əl-mṛa   wəldət
    DEF-woman give.birth.AC.PTCP.FS
    'The woman just gave birth.'

Due to the lack of sufficient comparative data, it is currently not possible to draw any reliable conclusions regarding the cross-dialectal coding of the perfect in North African Arabic. The use of the active participle to express a past event bearing relevance to time of speech is attested in Muslim Moroccan Arabic, as well as in Muslim Tunis and Douz (Brustad 2000, 183). By contrast, in Jewish Tripoli (Yoda 2005, 308), I have found only one occurrence of the active participle that Yoda (2005, 309) translates using the English present perfect:

(23) ṣ-ṣəlṭan   qaʕəd məzzalu ṭayəḥ
    DEF-sultan PVPT luck.his fall.AC.PTCP.MS
    'The Sultan's luck has run out.'

On the other hand, there are numerous instances of the resultative state being expressed by the s-stem:

(24) ana xalčək u   žič   mən bʕid
    me aunt and come.SFX.1SG from far.away
    u   nḥəm naṛak
    and want see.PFX.1SG.you
    '(…) I am your aunt, I have come from afar, wanting to see you (…)' (Yoda 2005, 302)

Likewise, in the textual corpus of Jewish Tunis (Cohen 1964), I have not found any example of the active participle expressing the perfect.[51] However, there are numerous cases of the s-stem clearly being used in a perfect context. The following passage comes from a story about an alleged appearance of a comet in the sky. One of the characters, who has not seen the comet, asks a random person about the reason for the panic in the city. The person answers:

(25) mnīḥ mā qās tšūf?   əd-dənya
     good NEG PVPT see.PFX.2MS DEF-world
     māš   tūfa   baʕbūṣ   ən-nəžma   xrəž
     FUT   finish.PFX.3FS tail   DEF-star   go.out.SFX.MS

'mais tu ne vois donc pas? C'est la fin du monde, la queue de la comète est sortie' (Cohen 1964, 140)

The appearance of the comet bears clear relevance to the dialogue in the present. Nonetheless, instead of the active participle /xārəž/, the s-stem is used. It seems, therefore, that Jewish Tunis expresses the perfect in the same way as Jewish Gabes. On the other hand, similarly to what Brustad has found in Muslim Moroccan Arabic, the resultative function of the active participle is well documented in the Bedouin dialect of Douz:[52]

(26) hīya ġāsla   šaʕrha
     she wash.AC.PTCP.FS hair.her

'She has washed her hair (and it is still wet).'

These data appear to indicate that, within the Tunisian dialect group, and perhaps within the dialects of North Africa, there is a

---

[51] Other usages of this form in Jewish Tunis will be mentioned in §2.7.3.

[52] The example was provided by Professor Veronika Ritt-Benmimoun in private correspondence with the author.

split between Jewish and Muslim dialects in the encoding of the perfect, with a strong preference among Jewish dialects for expressing this aspect by means of the s-stem.[53]

In what follows, I present a proposed explanation for the lack of use of the active participle with perfect meaning and the strong preference for using the s-stem to express the perfect in Jewish Gabes.

---

[53] From a typological point of view, a parallel to the split between Muslim and Jewish dialects in the encoding of the perfect can be found within Argentinian Spanish, which, of the modern varieties of South American Spanish, is considered to be highly idiosyncratic. Compared to other dialectal variants of Spanish, the use of the *pretérito perfecto compuesto* is extremely limited in the vast majority of regional varieties of Argentinian Spanish, and the simple past tense is used instead. However, in the variety known as *Norteño*, spoken in the province of Tucuman, in the north-western part of the country, speakers use the *pretérito perfecto compuesto* regularly. In contrast to the Argentinian situation, in *Castellano,* i.e., Spanish spoken in Spain, the *pretérito perfecto compuesto* is a widely used tense, with a higher rate of occurrence than the English perfect (for example, it is possible to combine it with time specification, which is ungrammatical in English). Therefore, the sentence: *Carlos ha llegado* in *Castellano* and *Norteño* would be rendered in Argentinian Spanish: *Carlos llego* 'Carlos has arrived'. There is likely no unequivocal explanation of the discrepancy in the expression of the perfect between most varieties of Argentinian Spanish and the dialect of *Norteño,* and between Argentinian Spanish and *Castellano,* but social and cultural separation is one of the possible factors.

2.7.3. Active Participle *fāʕil*

As presented above, in many Arabic dialects, the *fāʕil* pattern, historically the active participle, bears the meaning of the perfect. Scholars of Arabic highlight the resultative (Brustad 2000, 183) and stative (Eisele 1990) nature of this form.[54] In other words, it denotes a state with relevance to the time of speaking. In addition to this principal meaning, Brustad (2000, 185) also notes that the active participle of verbs of motion indicates a progressive.[55]

In Jewish Gabes, the active participle does not have the meaning of the perfect. It denotes events ongoing at speech time. Its distribution is limited to a semantically heterogenous group of verbs including verbs of motion, perception, and state. It is worth noting that the use of the active participle is often optional, and the same meaning can be rendered by the construction *qāʕəd* + p-stem. Listed below are some active participles occurring in the textual corpus and in conversations with the informants:

- *wāqəf* 'standing'
- *ʕārəf* 'understanding'

---

[54] The term 'stative' is rather misleading considering the class of lexical aspect also designated 'stative'.

[55] The double meaning of the active participle has been explained by Brustad (2000, 186). She argues that the distinction between resultative and progressive meaning stems from the opposition between telic and atelic aspect of the verbs of motion, i.e., *māši* can mean both 'to go' and 'to set out'. The progressive meaning, therefore, is a result of semantic expansion of the atelic perfect 'having set out' to 'being in a state of going'.

- *māši* 'going/walking'
- *rāqəd* 'sleeping'
- *šārəb* 'drinking'
- *wākəl* 'eating'
- *šāyəf* 'looking'
- *qāʕəd* 'sitting'
- *šāri* 'buying'
- *rākəb* 'riding'
- *ʕāyəš* 'living'
- *lābəš* 'wearing'

It is worth noting that not every verb can form an active participle. Moreover, the informant indicated regarding some of the forms on the list above that, while they are acceptable, a p-stem form preceded by *qāʕəd* would sound more natural. Specifically, the active participles *māši*, *rāqəd*, *wāqəf*, *lābəš*, and *qāʕəd* were considered the most acceptable, whereas the active participles *šārəb* and *wākəl* were deemed to sound more natural in the *qāʕəd* + p-stem construction. The informant also rejected some forms that occur in Simeone-Senelle's study—namely, *žāri* 'running', *qābəl* 'accepting', *wālda* 'giving birth', and *fāhəm* 'understanding'—indicating that they sounded unnatural.

It should be noted that the distribution of the active participle expressing the perfect also seems to be restricted in Muslim Tunis. It is not possible in Muslim Tunis to express the perfect of the recent past by means of the *fāʕil* pattern. Instead, *ma-zəlt-ki*[56] + s-stem is used.[57]

(27) *ma-zəl-ki xrəž*
    just go.out.SFX.3MS
    'He has just gone out.'

(28) *ma-zəl-ki naḍḍaft əḍ-ḍāṛ*
    just clean.SFX.1SG DEF-house
    'I have just cleaned the house.'

An alternative construction for expressing a very recent event is /tawawīn/ + s-stem:

(29) *əl-film tawwawīn bda*
    DEF-film now start.SFX.3MS
    'The film has just started.'

In this usage, Muslim Tunis converges with Jewish Gabes, which utilises *tuwwa* + s-stem to express the perfect of the recent past, but differs from ʕAulād Msalləm, which uses the *fāʕil* scheme in this context (see example (17) above).

Nonetheless, Muslim Tunis does utilise the active participle to express a resultative aspect, describing a state at the time of speaking that results from a past event:

(30) *šəftu   hādāka? bāni   ḍāṛ kbīra*
    see.SFX.2MS.him that   build.AC.PTCP.MS house big
    'Did you see that man? He has built a big house.'

---

[56] This construction is apparently a variant of the *ma-zal-kif* construction that appears in Singer's (1984, 651) grammar of Muslim Tunis.

[57] I am deeply indebted to Mr Anis Mokni for providing the above examples and for sharing his insightful comments on Muslim Tunis.

(31) šbīha   ma žētš?
    what.in.her   NEG come.SFX.3FS.NEG
    'Why didn't she come?'

(32) māhi   wēlda   ždīda
    but.her give.birth.AC.PTCP.FS   new.FS
    'She has given birth.'

As noted, the use of the active participle to express the perfect occurs across the Muslim varieties of Arabic, as shown by the following examples from three different dialects:

(33) hād-əl-ktāb āna qāṛəh
    this-DEF-book   I   read.AC.PTCP.MS.him
    'Je l'ai lu, ce livre!' (Moroccan; Caubet 1993, 231)

(34) ḥaliyyan   muxtārtu
    as.of.now   chose.AC.PTCP.FS.him
    'As of now, I have chosen him.' (Syrian; Brustad 2000, 189)

(35) il-kahraba   wāṣla?
    DEF-electricity arrive.AC.PTCP.FS
    'Has the electricity arrived?' (Kuwaiti; Brustad 2000, 189)

2.7.4. The Active Participle in Muslim and Jewish Varieties: A Historical Account

As the previous section (§2.7.3) has demonstrated, Jewish and Muslim dialects utilise the active participle in different ways; in the former, it conveys present, ongoing events and is employed with a limited number of verbal lexemes, whereas in the latter, it is used with telic verbs to denote the perfect aspect when the result of an action is still felt. I have shown that this differing usage is not limited geographically, but rather appears to be an isogloss that distinguishes Judaeo-Arabic from its Muslim counterparts in general. This phenomenon is therefore very likely rooted more deeply in the cultural and historical development of the two communities, suggesting the presence of a different substrate underlying Judaeo-Arabic. I would like to offer here a few possible explanations regarding such a possibility, within the context of a multifactorial conditioning of language change.

'Substrate' is a term denoting the result of a language contact situation, in which speakers of one language shift collectively to use of another language, usually due to geopolitical changes (Saarikivi 2006, 11). The receding language, however, leaves some traces in the adopted one, e.g., loanwords, or grammatical constructions, thus forming a stratum, or 'layer'. In the case of North African Arabic, it is generally agreed that two main substrata exist, namely Late Latin and Berber—the former spoken in the coastal cities, the latter used in the hinterland (Aguadé 2018, 34).

A fundamental question in our case is what the language of everyday communication was for the first Jewish communities in North Africa, and in particular, what it was before they began speaking Arabic.[58] There is, however, little to no documentation

---

[58] Although the sources on the first Jewish settlements in North Africa are very scant, it can be assumed that a North-West Semitic language was imported to North Africa as a result of the resettlement of the Jewish population from Palestine. According to Josephus Flavius' treatise *Against Apion* II, the beginning of the Jewish presence in the area west of Egypt was related to the decision of King Ptolemy Lagi (328–285) to settle Jews from Palestine in the Libyan city of Cyrene, which he had

of their languages. Before the advent of Islam and the subsequent spread of Arabic as the language of everyday communication, Aramaic was widely used by Jewish communities throughout the Middle East, such as the Jews of Palestine and Mesopotamia (Gzella 2015, 292, 381). Could it be tentatively assumed that the first communities in North Africa, as in other regions of the present-day Arab world, were also using varieties of Aramaic, a North-West Semitic language, before they adopted Arabic? The distinct use of the active participle in the Jewish varieties of Arabic vis-à-vis their Muslim counterparts appears to suggest this. Alternatively, the first Jewish settlements might have adopted Punic, another North-West Semitic language spoken in North Africa in the first centuries of the first millennium, mainly in the cities (Hirschberg 1974, 40). Both in the Aramaic that predates the spread of Islam (as exemplified by Jewish Palestinian Aramaic; Bunis 2018, 209–10) and in Punic (Krakhmalkov 2001, 199–200), the syntax of the active participle generally parallels that of modern Judaeo-Arabic. Already in pre-Islamic Jewish Palestinian Aramaic and closely related dialects, the active participle is integrated into the verbal system and, replacing the p-stem, encodes the present and immediate future (Stevenson 1924, 56; Gzella 2015, 302; Bunis 2018, 209–10). Moreover, this usage was

---

conquered around the year 300 BC. Another wave of exiles from Palestine came to North Africa after the destruction of the Second Temple (Hirschberg 1974, 24). As far as the linguistic environment of the North African Jewish communities is concerned, P. Sebag (1991, 22) suggests that, before the Roman conquest, the Jews living in the area corresponding to today's Tunisia were using Punic.

retained in certain Aramaic dialects after the spread of Islam and Arabic. This retention is documented in a group of three dialects of modern Aramaic termed Western Neo-Aramaic, which are spoken in present day Syria, in the Qalamun region, 50 kilometres north-east of Damascus. In these dialects, the historic active participle has retained the function of expressing the present and immediate future despite very extensive influence from surrounding Arabic dialects in which the active participle, as in the Muslim dialects I reviewed above, encodes the perfect (Bunis 2021).

I have noted that, in the modern Judaeo-Arabic of Gabes, the active participle is employed with a limited group of semantically heterogenous verbs. However, the common denominator of these verbs is their prevalence in day-to-day usage. It could be argued that, due to their frequent occurrence, they preserved the Aramaic syntax, while less common verbs were more susceptible to assimilation into the Arabic verbal system. With these common verbs, the active participle remained cognitively associated with its earlier morphosyntactic function as in Aramaic, and it is for this reason that the active participle never came to encode the perfect in this dialect.

An additional argument which could point to an Aramaic substrate is perhaps provided by the vowel system of both languages. In North African Arabic, similarly to Aramaic, one observes the phenomenon of pretonic reduction, i.e., the reduction of a short vowel before the stress. This is one of the features that distinguishes Aramaic from Hebrew, where the reverse process took place, namely, pretonic lengthening (Blau 2010, 123). All

Arabic dialects, in comparison to the classical language, demonstrate some degree of reduction of the vowel inventory. Nonetheless, as pointed out by Marçais (1977, 24), the more one moves from east to west, the more conspicuous the vowel reduction becomes. Indeed, in comparison to any eastern dialect, the Maghrebi Arabic vocalic material is much poorer. Below one can find a short comparison between selected eastern and western dialects:

Table 68: Vowel distribution in Eastern and Western dialects of Arabic

Eastern	Western	
kammalat	kəmməlt	'she finished'
Ṣanʕānī	Jewish Gabes	
(Watson 1993, 138)		
xashim	xšəm	'nose'
Gulf	Jewish Tripoli	
(Holes 1990, 286)	(Yoda 2005, 345)	
katab	ktəb	'he wrote'
Cairene	Jewish Tunis	
(Eisele 1990, 174)	(Cohen 1975, 95)	
thalātha	tlāta	'three'
Gulf	Jewish Algiers	
(Holes 1990, 293)	(Cohen 1912, 365)	

It is worth noting that vowel elision is much more prevalent in sedentary North-African dialects than in their Bedouin counterparts, where short vowels are retained under certain circumstances (see Ritt-Benmimoun 2014, 25; Aguadé 2018, 47). Some scholars explain the tendency to drop short vowels in open syllables as a Berber substrate (Diem 1979, 55). This view, however, was called into question by Kossmann (2013, 173), who proposed two separate and independent developments in the two language groups. If we accept this assumption, the question remains as to what triggered the reductive tendency in sedentary Arabic in the first place. The striking similarity in this respect between Aramaic and Arabic might suggest language contact between them, and that the pretonic reduction in the latter was conditioned by the Aramaic substrate. Nonetheless, language contact with Berber cannot be excluded, and the loss of short vowels in open syllables could have been brought about by multiple factors.

The above paragraphs aimed to present similarities between Jewish North African Arabic and Aramaic, especially Palestinian Aramaic, and thereby to propose the existence of an Aramaic substrate in Maghrebi Arabic, especially the Jewish varieties. This proposal is by no means definite and would require a thorough historical investigation of the beginnings of the Jewish presence in North Africa to further support the linguistic findings. Moreover, language change is often multifactorial, and thus Punic influence in the case of the distribution of the active participle, and vowel loss due to contact with Berber, are additional, no less likely, factors.

2.8. Analysis: Compound Forms

2.8.1. /qāʕd/, /qāʕ/, /ka/ + p-stem

The origin of these preverbal particles has been proposed in §2.4. Essentially, I argue that both /qāʕ/ and /ka/ derive from /qāʕd/, and that they reflect different stages within a process of cliticisation. The *qāʕd* particle is attested in both inflected (37) and uninflected (36) forms:

(36) wən mšīt   wən hrabt   qāʕd yəbkīw
     where go.SFX.2MS where flee.SFX.2MS PVPT cry.PFX.3PL
     'Where have you gone, where have you disappeared, they were weeping.' (3:41)

(37) hīya qāʕda tʕayyəṭ
     she   AUX   scream.PFX.3FS
     'She is screaming.'

Example (36) demonstrates how the MS form of the active participle has become frozen. This form, in turn, undergoes further truncation, as outlined below:

(38) āna tuwwa qāʕ nḥaḍḍar   fi mākla
     I   now   PVPT prepare.PFX.1SG in food
     'I am now preparing food.'

(39) ʕašīya əl-wlād ka   yāklu   wa
     evening DEF-boys PVPT eat.PFX.3PL and
     šāfu   əl-žməl ža
     see.SFX.3PL DEF-camel come.SFX.3MS
     'In the evening the boys were eating and saw the camel coming.' (4:109)

The principal function of this preverbal particle is to denote ongoing events stretched over an interval, and its time reference is strongly dependent on the context. Occasionally, it is also used with ingressive verbs to indicate the start of an event, or entry into a state. When the time reference is the present, and the speaker wants to highlight the continuous character of the event, it seems that the conjugated form is preferred. This assumption is confirmed by example (37) above and further examples from

Jewish Tunis, which also include prefixed forms of the root /qʕd/:[59]

(40) ḥīna bāb əḍ-ḍāṛ yoqʕəd maḥlūl u
now door DEF-house AUX open and
qāʕdīn yədəxlu əž-žīrān w-əl-fāmīlya kola
AUX enter.PFX.3PL DEF-guests and-DEF-family all
'Maintenant, la porte de la maison reste ouverte, et les voisins et toute la famille ne cessent d'entrer.'

(41) ən-nās lə-kbāṛ yoqʕədu yəddūyu
DEF-people DEF-big.PL AUX chat.PFX.3PL
'Les grandes personnes bavardent.' (Cohen 1964, 28)

On the other hand, /qāʕ/ and /ka-/ tend to denote durative events without a predetermined time reference. In Jewish Tripoli, /qa-/ denotes both past and present events, as well as protases in conditional clauses. This is indicated by the following examples:

(42) əl-bənt lə-kbira qalč qa
DEF-girl DEF-elder say.SFX.3FS PVPT
čədwi l-əxča qaltla
talk.PFX.3FS to-sister.her say.SFX.3FS-to.her
'The elder sister said, while speaking to her sister, she said to her (…)' (Yoda 2005, 298)

(43) m̥ṣugra duwčək li qa čədwi fīa?
certain.FS story.your that PVPT tell.PFX.2FS in.her
'Is your story that you are telling certain?' (Yoda 2005, 300)

---

[59] I have not found any truncated forms of /qāʕəd/ in Jewish Tunis.

(44) u   kif   čaṛaw   lə-qməžža   qa   čgənni
    and when   see.PFX.2PL DEF-shirt   PVPT   sing.PFX.3FS

'And when you see the shirt singing (...)' (Yoda 2005, 306)

It can therefore be tentatively established that the inflected forms of the active participle *qāʕəd* serve to denote strictly present events, while its truncated variations mark both past and present. However, the common denominator of all of them is the expression of ongoing, durative events.

2.8.2. /kān/ + p-stem

I argue that *kān* undergoes a similar process of cliticisation to that seen in the case of *qāʕəd*. As has already been pointed out, both frozen and conjugated forms are present in Jewish Gabes. The function of both the auxiliary verb and the preverbal particle is to mark past habitual events, whose occurrence is dependent on the circumstances:

(45) qbəl   kānu   nša   yūldu   fi-l-gīṭūn
    before AUX   women   birth.PFX.3PL in-DEF-tent

'Once women used to give birth in tents.'

The auxiliary verb in the above example expresses a characteristic but not completely regular event. As regards the further development of this item, it would be tempting at first glance to think that *kān* gave rise to the preverbal particle /ka-/. As pointed out in §2.4.1, this does indeed seem be the case in Moroccan, where the use of /ka-/ was expanded from conditional clauses to marking the indicative mood in general (Stewart 1998, 104; Brustad 2000, 234). The data explicitly indicates, though, that this is not a plausible explanation in the case of Jewish

Gabes. Firstly, the distribution of *kān* is noticeably different from that of /ka-/. In contrast to *kān*, there is no instance of /ka-/ marking a habitual event or any other dependent state. On the other hand, the function of *qāʕəd* and /ka-/ as markers of durative, ongoing events is identical. In addition, in §2.4, I presented the process of phonological change that explains the origin of /ka-/ in *qāʕəd*. Therefore, although the /ka-/ particles which occur in Moroccan and Jewish Gabes Arabic are homonyms, they have notably different functions and origins.

2.8.3. *ḥabb* + p-stem

This construction is one of the ways of expressing the predictive future in Jewish Gabes. This word derives from the active participle of the volitive verb *ḥābb* 'to want'. In natural, fast speech, one can also find the variant *ḥabb*. It seems, however, that the original meaning of this form has been lost, and, in a similar fashion to *qāʕəd* and *kān*, *ḥābb* is in the process of cliticisation and a semantic shift from volitive to future marker. On the other hand, in Jewish Djerba, the /ḥa-/ prefix is the main device for expressing the future, e.g., *ḥayəmši* 'he will go' (Behnstedt 1998, 67). In light of the data from Jewish Gabes, one can assume, therefore, that this prefix might have emerged from *ḥabb*.[60] Let us consider the following two examples:

---

[60] Behnstedt (1998, 68) argues that this particle originated in *ḥatta* 'until'.

(46) *hūwa ḥābb yʕarrəš*
    he   want.AC.PTCP.MS get.married.PFX.3MS
    mʕa bənt əṣ-ṣəlṭān
    with daughter DEF-sultan
    'He is going to get married to the sultan's daughter.'

(47) *āna fi-bāli əlli hūwa mūš ḥabb yərbaḥ*
    I in-mind.my that he   NEG FUT win.PFX.3MS
    'I think he is not going to win.'

While *ḥabb* in the former example can still be interpreted as a volitive verb producing the meaning 'he wants to get married', this is not the case in the latter. The expansion from volitive verb to predictive future marker is also a feature of other Arabic dialects. To begin with, in the Ibadite dialect of Djerba, one finds a /b-/ prefix marking the future, which, according to Behnstedt (1998, 68), stems from verb *yibġi* 'to want'. The Kuwaiti future marker /b-/ developed from the imperfective stem of the verb *yabi* 'to want' (Brustad 2000, 242; Owens 2018, 206). Outside the Semitic context, there are numerous other examples of this process, e.g., the Greek future marker θα presumably derives from θέλω meaning 'I want' (Pappas and Joseph 2001). Some Arabic dialects, on the other hand, utilise variants of the verb 'to go' to render future reference, e.g., Syrian *raḥ* and Egytpain /ḥa-/ (Brustad 2000, 242).[61] The same strategy is employed in Jewish Tunis:

---

[61] In the Kuwaiti and Syrian dialects, there are two future particles, i.e., /b-/ and /raḥ/, which mark the epistemic and the deontic future respectively (Brustad 2000, 241).

(48) *māš nədūyu ʕla wāḥəd uləd*
    FUT talk.PFX.1PL about one boy
    'Nous allons parler d'un garçon (...)' (Cohen 1964, 28)

Nonetheless, in Jewish Gabes, this construction is not the only way of expressing the future, as the plain p-stem can also do so. The question that arises, therefore, is whether they are in fact free variants, or they encode different types of future. Based on the data and conversations with the informants, I argue that they convey different estimations regarding the probability of future events. Thus, while the p-stem expresses an event whose occurrence is highly probable, *ḥābb* seems to convey the speaker's uncertainty. Let us compare the above examples, (46) and (47), with the following passages:

(49) *qālətlu: əlli taḥkəm yṣīr*
    tell.SFX.3FS.him what rule.PFX.2MS happen.PFX.3MS
    'She told him: whatever you decide will happen.' (7:83)

(50) *āna yžīwni fi-nhār u fi-llīl*
    I come.PFX.3PL.me in-day and in-DEF-night
    nətṣāwər mʕāk u l-maḥkma
    consult.PFX.1SG with.you and DEF-court
    tṣār bərk mən ġadwa
    happen.PFX.3FS only from tomorrow
    'They will come to me in the daytime and at night I will consult with you and the court will only happen the day after, after I consult with you.' (7:91)

Example (49) is an excerpt from a dialogue between the sultan and his wife. In the dialogue, after he instructed her to leave the palace, she obediently promised him that she would do whatever he wishes. Since she is sure about the fulfilment of her promise, she uses the p-stem. Similarly, example (50) is a statement by the sultan regarding his future relationship with his wife. Hence, both the forms he uses are in the p-stem, as the occurrence of the future events is certain.

In sum, the two ways of expressing the future in Jewish Gabes represent different types of future, namely, the epistemic and the deontic. The *ḥābb* particle, which also functions as a volitive verb, indicates an intentive, low-probability mood, while events expressed by the p-stem are characteristically high-probability, factual events. This distinction thus mirrors the two particles marking the epistemic and deontic future in the Syrian and Kuwaiti dialects. It is also worth noting that the functional expansion of *ḥābb* from volitive towards modal epistemic usage is another manifestation of the subsective gradience exemplified by the active participle *qāʕəd*. Aarts (2007, 98) proposes the following scheme of the verbal gradient evolving towards modality: main verb > catenative > semi-auxiliary > modal idiom > marginal idiom > central modal. Nonetheless, as argued by Traugott and Truesdale (2010, 30), a gradual acquisition of modality by a single verb form is more widespread cross-linguistically. The reanalysis of the Jewish Gabes active participle *ḥābb* as a modality marker corroborates this assumption.

2.9. Aspect in Narrative

As has been observed by Brustad (2000, 186), narratives are a particularly important source of knowledge about both aspect and tense in any language, due to the abundance of forms and constructions they represent. In every type of narrative, there are some events which constitute the main story line and move the narrative forward by succeeding one after another, and others which function as a skeleton or background of the main line by cooccurring with it. Hopper (1979, 213) called them respectively foreground and background. As one can expect, the two types of narrative strategies will interact in different ways with aspect.

The findings of Brustad's (2000, 188) analysis seem to confirm Hopper's (1979, 213) statement that perfective forms serve to foreground the narrative, while imperfective ones create the background to the main events. This strategy is also prominent in Jewish Gabes, as exemplified by the following excerpt:

(51)   təmma wāḥad **yəqʕad**   taḥt   ṣəẓra tāʕ
        there.is INDF   sit.PFX.3MS   under tree   GEN

        blaḥ **yḥall**   fəmmu   wa   **yəstənna**   ḥatt
        date   open.PFX.3MS   mouth.his   and   wait.PFX.3MS   until

        əl-blāḥ   yṭīḥlu   fi-fəmmu   fə-l-lāxər
        DEF-fruit   fall.PFX.3MS.to.him in-mouth.his   in-DEF-last

        hūwa **yəqʕad**   əkāk   **žāw**   l-wəžra
        he   sit.PFX.3MS like.this come.SFX.3PL DEF-ministers

'There was a man who was sitting beneath a date palm, he would open his mouth and he would wait until the date fell into it; finally, when he was sitting like this, the ministers came.' (2:15–16)

The story about the lazy man is only tangentially related to the main plot, and therefore this additional package of information is introduced by the p-stem. On the other hand, the visit of the ministers belongs to the main plotline, hence the s-stem is used.

Similarly, background information can be marked by the preverbal particle /ka/:

(52) *waqt hūwa* **ka-yʕašš** *fi-nəfṣ əl-līl žāt*
when he PVPT-guard.PFX.3MS in-night DEF-night come.SFX.3FS
waḥda mṛa žāt u ləwwḥat ḥāža
INDF woman come.SFX.3FS and throw.SFX.3FS thing
'While he was guarding at midnight, a woman came, she came and threw something' (2:32)

The p-stem has another, seemingly contradictory function, namely, it represents the so-called 'historical present'. In a sequence of perfective verbs, the occurrence of a single imperfective verb at the end constitutes a narrative strategy used by the speaker to highlight the present character of the story and give the audience the impression that the events are happening in front of their own eyes. This technique is exemplified by the following excerpts:

(53) *wāḥəd* **mša** *yəṭlab ya-krīm tāʕ alla*
INDF go.SFX.3MS ask.PFX.3MS VOC-merciful GEN God
wṣal *lə-d-dāṛ* **ḍṛəbb** *əb-bāb yəṭlab*
arrive.SFX.3MS to-DEF-house knock.SFX.3MS DEF-door ask.PFX.3MS
'A man went to beg for money, he arrived at a house, knocked on the door and begged.' (1:2-3)

(54) *məṛtu* **ḥallət** *ẓaṛbīya u* **təṛqa**
wife.his open.SFX.3FS carpet and find.PFX.3FS
taḥta žwābāt u **qrātham**
under.her letters and read.SFX.3FS.them
'The wife lifted the carpet and found beneath the letters and read them.' (5:7)

In example (54), the prefix form is found in a sequence of events, between two suffix forms. Since it is rather a punctual verb, one would expect it to be in the s-stem. However, this is not the case. The function of the p-stem in this context is presumably to mark dependency on what precedes. A habitual form, coerced by the narrative context, therefore expresses a single event (Carruthers 2012).

As observed by Hopper (1979, 213), there is a correlation between foregrounding and backgrounding and the lexical aspect of a verb. In other words, the discourse aspect conditions certain types of the lexical one. Thus, foregrounding is associated with kinetic, punctual, and dynamic verbs, while backgrounding usually involves stative and durative aspects. The former is particularly apparent in sequences of verbs:

(55) *hūwa žra   wa xda   ʕaṣa*
     he   run.SFX.3MS and take.SFX.3MS stick
     u   ḍṛəbha   fi-ḍharha   u   harbətlo
     and hit.SFX.3MS.her in-back.her   and run.away.SFX.3FS.him
     'He ran and took a stick and hit her on the back, but she escaped from him.' (2:33)

(56) *žāw   mən xadma əl-wlād*
     come.SFX.3MS from work   DEF-boys
     dəxlu   u   rqāw   šūbīrya
     enter.SFX.3PL and find.SFX.3PL bowl
     'Boys came back from work, entered, and found the bowl.' (4:28)

The above sequences involve kinetic verbs like 'run', 'take', 'hit', and 'enter'. On the other hand, as examples (51) and (52) demonstrate, in backgrounding, stative and atelic verbs are used, like 'sit', 'wait', 'guard', etc.

2.10. Conclusions

This section was concerned with the ways in which the verbal system of Jewish Gabes expresses tense and aspect. The central question was whether an isolated verb form has any temporal value or is mostly aspectual. As I have demonstrated in the course of my analysis, the verb in Jewish Gabes primarily encodes aspect and its tense reference is external, expressed by different lexical means. The aspectual features of the s-stem encompass completeness and punctuality, and therefore its temporal value is past. On the other hand, I have argued that the p-stem is timeless and strongly dependent on the context. In this respect, my findings converge with the observations made by Michal Marmorstein (2016, 239) regarding the function of the *yafʕalu* pattern in CA.

Part of this chapter was devoted to the description of preverbal particles and auxiliaries. I have attempted to establish the origin of the particle /-ka/ by contrasting its functions in Jewish Gabes with its functions in Moroccan Arabic. It is worth noting that the distribution of preverbal particles across the dialects of Arabic is uneven. Some dialects, like Egyptian and Moroccan, have developed particles that mark the indicative mood in general, while others, like Eastern Libyan Arabic or some Algerian dialects, lack any indicative prefixes (Owens 2018, 210). The Tunisian /qāʕəd-/, /qāʕ-/, and /ka-/ particles are in fact aspectual devices indicating durativity and progressivity, which fulfil an important role within the narrative framework. They were analysed as representing different stages of cliticisation. Similarly, it has been argued that *kān* expressing past habituality and *ḥābb* used as a future marker are undergoing the same process.

My investigation was concerned also with different treatment of the *fāʕil* pattern across several Tunisian dialects. I have argued that, in contrast to the Muslim dialects, the Jewish ones do not utilise this form to express the perfect aspect. Presumably under the influence of Aramaic, this form is associated rather with present states, and perfect meaning is achieved by means of the s-stem with adverbs. However, a diachronic comparative study of more Muslim and Jewish varieties of Arabic is needed in order to corroborate the findings of this study.

3.0. Word Order

3.1. Theoretical Preliminaries

The order of the sentence constituents (verb, subject, object) has been an object of interest for typologists in the past century (e.g., Greenberg 1966; Comrie 1981). Different arrangements of these elements are associated with different discourse functions and appear in distinct types of utterance (Brustad 2000, 320). In the field of Arabic, some scholars have repeatedly expressed the view that the predominant word order in the dialects is SVO, as opposed to the VSO order of CA. This was observed, for example, in Egyptian Arabic by Gamaleldin (1967, 58). On the other hand, El Yasin (1985, 107–8) seems to be less radical and points out that both orders are equally well represented, although SVO has become more natural and acceptable in the dialects in contradistinction to CA, where its usage was more limited. From a typological point of view, Arabic shares some syntactic features with other VSO languages, e.g., post-nominal position of adjectives, and prepositions instead of postpositions (Ingham 1994, 37; Brustad 2000, 319).

The two basic types of sentence distinguished by the classical grammarians are called *jumla ismiyya* and *jumla fiʕiliyya*, i.e., nominal and verbal sentence (Wright 2005, II:251). The former is associated with a number of discourse techniques, namely, extraposition, marking of the onset of a topic span, shift in level of description, and shift from foreground to background (Khan 1988, 37). Moreover, in terms of the type of utterance, Dahlgren (2011) observes that SV is much more frequently found in dialogues than in narratives. On the other hand, the VS order prevails in narratives. Dahlgren's analysis of an Early Arabic text clearly indicates that this order occurs much more frequently than SV. This is a natural consequence of the literary form of the text and its descriptive nature. Finally, in the absence of an independent subject, the classical language permits also OV order with fronted, focused object.

A number of pragmatic factors can affect word order. The aforementioned distinction between narratives and dialogues parallels two types of language distinguished by Brown and Yule (1983). In their discourse analysis, they pointed out that language can either express content, or convey personal attitudes and social relations. According to the terminology proposed by these two scholars, the former function is called 'transactional', the latter 'interactional'. As pointed out by Brustad (2000, 320), narratives, which are an example of transactional language, tend to have stable topics, and the expected order is therefore VS. On the other hand, in dialogues, which represent the interactional type, speakers, by expressing their views and attitudes, dynamically change the topic of their conversation, hence the SV order prevails.

3.2. Typological Perspective

An important contribution to the investigation of word order patterns in the world's languages was a study by Li and Thompson (1976), which challenged the view that the basic structure of every language entails subject–predicate (henceforth: S–P) alignment. Based mainly on data from South-East Asia, they argued that, in some languages, the topic–comment structure is much more prominent. Subsequently, they proposed a typological classification, according to which a language can be: only subject prominent, only topic prominent, both subject and topic prominent, or neither category prominent. Although the study in question involves only a limited number of languages, and, as the authors point out, it is rather difficult to establish which type of word order prevails in a language based only on its reference grammar, the methodology used in this article can provide a valuable insight into the discourse strategies present in Jewish Gabes. In what follows, therefore, I shall examine selected passages from the text corpus by applying the classification outlined in the aforementioned study. The result of this investigation will hopefully shed some light on the typological status of Jewish Gabes.

3.3. Subject–Predicate Alignment

3.3.1. Subgroups of Subject-Prominent Type

Subject-prominent types of sentences correspond to what Ingham calls 'uninodal' sentences (1994, 35). A uninodal sentence conveys a completely new piece of information which is delivered to the collocutor as one whole. This kind of sentence usually fronts the verb, which is the main focus of the message. Nevertheless, as will be shown below, uninodal sentences do not necessarily assume VSO form. Binodal sentences, on the other hand, consist of two elements, the first of which is a given piece of information, while the second is a new one. Thus, applying the terminology of Li and Thompson, it can be established that subject-prominent sentences are uninodal, while topic-prominent ones comprise two nodes of information.

Sentences with prevailing subject–predicate alignment can have different permutations of the three basic elements: subject, verb, and object. As demonstrated by the below tables, Jewish Gabes has two main word orders: VSO and SVO, and two peripheral ones: VOS and OSV. No examples of OVS or SOV were detected.

3.3.2. Data

VSO

1. *kānət hāk əl-xabža kbīra ʕalīya* (1:37)
   'The bread was too big for me.'

2. *ṭalʕat ktība fi-l-ḥīṭ* (1:42)
   'An inscription appeared on the wall.'

3. *žāw əž-žnūn qāllu* (2:63)
   'The ghosts came and told him.'

4. *ṭallʕat əl-fəḷḷāya wa l-fəḷḷāya fīha šəmm* (4:70)
   'She took out the comb and the comb had a poison on it.'

5. *ṭalʕat əl-xādma, kān təšbaḥ fī* (1:4)
   'A handmaid went out and kept looking at him.'

6. *fi-l-līl ḥaṭṭəṭlu bənṣ, raqdathu raqda brīma, xdāt əl-frāš ntāʕu, žābət əl-xaddāma ntāʕha u ḥawwlathu l-ḥūš bābāha* (7:84)
   'At night she gave him sleeping drugs, she put him to sleep, took his bed, brought his servants, and moved him to her father's premises.'

SVO

7. *l-žbālīyya yāxdu ḥbəll u kull yūm yaʕqdu ʕaqda*
   'The mountaineers would take a rope and every day they would tie a knot.'

8. *wāḥəd mša yəṭlab ya krīm tāʕ aḷḷa* (1:2)
   'A man went to beg for money.'

9. *bəntek əẓ-ẓġīra bnāt əl-qṣaṛ* (2:87)
   'It is your youngest daughter who has built this castle.'

10. *əl-ʕbəd hāda kān mḥayyər* (7:69)
    'This man was worried.'

11. *hūwa ka-yəmši fə-ṣəṭṭ əl-bḥar mḥayrān, wa hīya qaʕdət fi-l-balkūn šāfəthu yəmši* (7:70)
    'While he was walking worried on the beach, she sat down on the balcony and saw him walking.'

12. *āna ḥkəmt ʕalīk u ənti ma wqəftīs fi-kəlmtək* (7:82)
    'I gave you a condition and you did not keep your promise.'

VOS

13. *xalṭətna moxxna l-mṛa hādi* (7:53)
    'This woman has messed with our heads!'

OSV

14. *hādi l-mṛa ənta tāxəd?* (7:48)
    'Are you going to marry this woman?'

3.3.3. Grammatical Features of S–P Sentences

Li and Thompson (1976) have outlined in their study the main grammatical features of subject-prominent languages, simultaneously indicating points of divergence from the topic-prominent type. The first difference is the definiteness of the noun phrase: in contradistinction to the T–C type, where the topic is definite by default, in the S–P type, the noun can also be indefinite. This can be proven by the indefinite-specific noun *wāḥəd* in example (8), and by the indefinite noun *ktība* in (2). The noun, however, has to be in agreement with the verb, which conveys the main action of the information. As will be shown in §3.5, this is not the case in the T–C structure, where the fronted noun phrase is syntactically independent from the verb in the comment (Li and Thompson 1976, 462). As a result of this assumption, one can infer that, in the T–C type, the verb does not determine the topic.

On the other hand, in the S–P structure, the verb is obligatorily correlated with the subject. From a functional point of view, the subject orientates the hearer in the event and provides insight into the action (Li and Thompson 1976, 464). This is particularly conspicuous in verbs expressing experience, state, etc. As far as position in the sentence is concerned, the above passages indicate that the subject can be located either before or after the verb. In addition, as has been observed by Li and Thompson (1976, 465), the subject is involved in a number of grammatical processes that are not possible in the case of a topic. Thus, for example, equi-deletion or verb serialisation is possible only with a subject.[62] This is exemplified by example (6), where the same subject that occurred in the previous sentence is correlated with every verb in the sequence.

3.3.4. Discourse Features of S–P Sentences

Sentences of S–P structure are event-orientated (Brustad 2000, 329). Since they contain only one node of information, they tend to occur in dynamic narratives, where the plot is moved forward by series of verbs. There is, however, significant variation in their distribution. Using categories of foregrounding and backgrounding, it can be tentatively established that SV dominates in backgrounding, which provides commentary and support to the main storyline, while VS usually occurs in foregrounding, which builds the plot of events. Hopper (1979, 220) notices that foregrounding tends to be pragmatically unmarked. Since foregrounding moves

---

[62] The process of equi-deletion in Jewish Gabes was treated in §1.4.1.

the plot forward and is characterised by high dynamicity, the new information is expressed mostly by predicates and the subject is very often presupposed, hence the VS order. This strategy is exemplified by examples (3) and (4), which contain kinetic verbs like 'to come', 'to take out', etc. On the other hand, close analysis of the backgrounding strategies in different languages, which are associated with stativity and description, indicates that the new information is here introduced by the subject or the object. One should therefore expect to find the SVO/SOV order in commentary and description (Hopper 1979, 220). This strategy is often realised grammatically by means of the preverbal particle /ka-/ (example 11) and the existential verb *kān* (example 10). Moreover, in terms of discourse function, the SVO order is very often applied in order to express contrast between two entities, as in example (12). Another form of contrastive focus is exemplified by passage (9), where the SVO order serves to single out one entity, i.e., a daughter, from a group of the king's daughters.

3.4. Topic–Comment Alignment

3.4.1. Data

Topic is referred to in the comment as a complement of a preposition

15. *hāk əl-xabža yžəyyəd fīha ṛaḅḅi* (1:15)
    'God will add to this bread.'
16. *əl-ḥwāyəž hādu, škūn qāʕd yfəššərlək fīhəm?* (7:26)
    'All these things, who explains them to you?'

17. *(ə)tlāta baṭṭīxāt li baʕṭəthəm bəntək, fīhəm ramz* (2:10)
    'There is a hint in these three melons that your daughter has sent you.'

18. *əl-mélex ṣārlu ʕžəb hādi ḥāža əl-ʕbəd* (7:20)
    'The king was amazed by this man.'

Topic is referred to in the comment by a personal pronoun

19. *əl-ʕamla mšūma ʕaməltha* (7:11)
    'What a mistake I made.'

20. *hādīk əl-maqṣūfāt šəbʕa šnīn, nhār bābāha tʕadda u lqā əṣ-ṣəlṭān* (7:3)
    'This seven-year-old rascal, one day her father was passing and the sultan met him.'

21. *əl-bṣəl hāda, tāklu walla yāklək?* (7:8)
    'This onion, you will eat it or it will eat you?'

22. *əl-məlḥ, yḥaṭṭu fi-ṣrīra u la fi-qrīṭīṣ*
    'The salt, they put it in the pocket, and not in the box.'

23. *hād əl-xabža ʕamri ma rātha ʕīni* (1:21)
    'This bread, my eye has never seen one like this.'

24. *āna, yžīwni fi-n-nhār u fi-l-līl nətṣāwər mʕāk* (7:91)
    'They will come to me in the daytime and at night I will consult with you.'

3.4.2. Grammatical Features of T–C Structures

Topic–comment sentences significantly differ from S–P ones in terms of structure and function. To begin with, applying Ingham's terminology once more, this type of sentence is binodal, i.e., it consists of two pieces of information. The topic constitutes a known piece of information, while in the comment, the speaker delivers a new one. Since the identity of the topic is known to the collocutor, or is easily retrievable from their memory, the topic by default is definite. In the above examples, one can see numerous cases of definite topics preceded by proximal (16) and distal pronouns (15) or followed by a subordinate clause (17). As regards position in the sentence, the topic is always fronted, in contradistinction to the subject, which, as indicated above, can admit different positions. In addition, T–C languages are characterised by low occurrence of passive constructions. Li and Thompson (1976, 467) point out that some languages do not have any form of passivisation (Lahu, Lisu), while others—like Mandarin, for example—make very sporadic use of the passive voice in speech. In Jewish Gabes, as has been indicated in chapter 3, §2.2, CA passive verb stems are obsolete and rarely appear in spoken language. T–C languages are also characterised by a lack of so-called 'dummy' subject constructions, which are common in languages with S–P alignment, e.g., 'it is raining' in English. Jewish Gabes, like other Arabic dialects, does not have this kind of construction (Brustad 2000, 333). On the other hand, dummy subjects often occur in impersonal expressions replacing the passive, e.g., *nəqtəl* 'he was killed' > *yəqtlū* 'they (dummy subject) killed him'. From a functional point of view, the topic sets a thematical domain in whose framework the main predication of the comment takes place. In purely T–C languages, there is no syntactic relation between the two nodes of information. This is not the case in Jewish Gabes, where, despite the lack of agreement between topic and comment predication, the topic is referred to in the comment either as a personal pronoun (19) or with a preposition (17). Nonetheless, Brustad (2000, 336) remarks that most of Li and Thompson's study is based on Mandarin, which does not utilise anaphoric reference. In Arabic, on the other hand, anaphora occupies a significant place in the syntax. Thus, the syntactic relation between topic and comment should not be regarded as an argument against Jewish Gabes being a T–C language, as the absence of such a relation would violate basic rules of the language.

3.5. SVO Versus T–C

The question arises as to whether SVO and topic-prominent sentences are congruent and fulfil the same functions. Khan (1988), in his study of word order in CA, has argued that the discourse functions of the SV order converge with those of the T–C construction. Similarly, Brustad (2000, 336) argues that the SV order can be analysed as topic-prominent. Nonetheless, both the intonation of the sentence and the grammatical features indicate that T–C and SV are two distinct types of information packaging with different discourse functions.

To begin with, in terms of intonation groups, SV contains only one unit, while T–C has a clear prosodic pause separating the topic from the comment. Moreover, the syllable of the topic that contains the nuclear stress is lengthened, and a conspicuous rise in pitch occurs. This phenomenon is also attested in the Neo-Aramaic dialect of Telkepe (Coghill 2018, 309); the prosodic similarities between the two dialects will be discussed further in §3.6. The binodal structure can be represented in the transcription in the following way:

(1) l-ḥwāyəž hādu / škūn qāʕd
    DEF-things these   who   AUX
    yfəššərlək   fīhəm?
    interpret.PFX.3MS.to.you in.them

'All these things, who explains them to you?' (7:40)

In addition, the fact that the topic is almost never in agreement with the subject of the comment proffers another argument against the functional convergence of SVO and T–C. The syntactic independence of the topic furnishes the establishment of a wide, thematical framework, in which both SVO and VSO occur. In other words, within the span of a topic, various types of focus and contrast are conveyed by the SVO order. The following excerpt from text (7) demonstrates how the T–C structure sets the thematical domain of the dialogues:

(2) qālət: təmma wāḥda bnīya yšəmmyūha maqṣūfāt šəbʕa šnīn (3) **hādīk əl-maqṣūfāt šəbʕa šnīn | nhār bābāha |** t*ʕadda u lqā aṣ-ṣəlṭān* (4) qāllu: šnūwa ḥālək wa šnūwa hāda (5) qāllu: naḥəmdu rabbi, la bāš ʕalīna (6) qāllu: nḥabb nəšdək nəšda (7) aaa! aṣ-ṣəlṭān tʕadda lqā yəzraʕ fi-l-bṣəl (8) huwa qāllu: **əl-bṣəl hāda | tāklu wəlla yāklək?** (9) qāllu: əšmaʕ, tlāta ayyām fi-yəddək tžībli əl-xbār.

(2) There was a girl, whom people used to call a 'seven-year-old rascal' (3) This seven-year-old rascal, one day her father was passing and the sultan met him (4) He asked him how are you and so on (5) He said: thank God everything is all right (6) He said to him: I would like to ask you a question (7) Oh! when the sultan was passing by, he found him planting onion (8) He asked him: this onion,

you will eat it or it will eat you? (9) He said: listen, you have three days to bring me the answer

Section (3) of the passage above has a unique T–C structure, containing three nodes of information, with two conspicuous pauses. This structure usually appears at the beginning of a story and introduces the listener to its thematic spectrum. The first topic, i.e., 'the daughter', is the dominant topic of the entire story, thus it is set at its very beginning. The second topic, 'the father', is the main character of the following series of dialogues with the sultan. Finally, the topic of the first dialogue is introduced, i.e., 'the onion'. The distribution of topics in the first part of the story can be represented in the following way:

Figure 6: An example of a thematical span

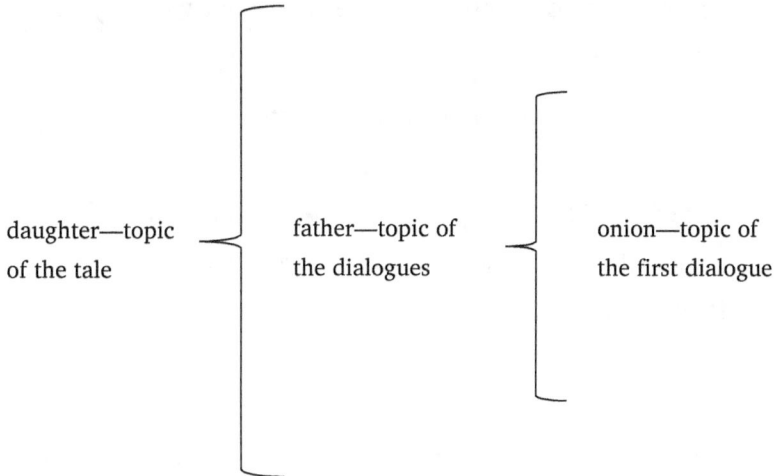

The folktale contains a series of three lexical riddles revolving around three topics: onion, coffee kettle, and water well. Every riddle occurs in a separate dialogue between the sultan and the father and is introduced by the sultan. Subsequently, the same

topic continues in the solution of the riddle delivered by the daughter. The topic of every riddle is introduced by the T–C structure:

(2) **hūwa qāllu əl-bṣəl hāda**
he tell.SFX.3MS.him DEF-onion this
tāklu wəlla yāklək?
eat.PFX.2MS.him or eat.PFX.3MS.you
'This onion, you will eat it, or it will eat you?' (7:8)

(3) **āma nḥabbək tqūlli šnūwa yqūlu**
but like.PFX.1SG.you say.PFX.2MS.me what tell.PFX.3MS
əš-šəžwa kīf ḥaṭṭūha ʕal əl-nāṛ šnūwa tqūl?
DEF-kettle when put.SFX.3PL.her on DEF-fire what say.PFX.3FS
'But I want you to tell me now: what would it say, a coffee kettle, when they put it on the fire, what would you say?' (7:16)

(4) **qāllu tuwwa nḥabbək tqūlli**
say.SFX.3MS.him now like.PFX.1SG.you say.PFX.2MS.me
əẓ-ẓṛāṛa kīf yṭallʕu sṭall mən bīr
water.well when take.out.PFX.3PL bucket from well
šnūwa tqūl?
what say.PFX.3FS
'He said: now I want you to tell me, a water well, when people take out a bucket from a well, what does it say?' (7:21–22)

As stated above, once the main topics are introduced, foregrounding (VSO/VOS) and backgrounding (SVO) take place. The event-orientated and description-orientated types of narrative are exemplified in the above quoted excerpt. Thus, in section (3) of the passage above, the VOS order—*tʕadda u lqā aṣ-ṣəlṭān*—encodes an event, moving the plot forward. On the other hand, in section (7), which is an explanatory comment with the focus on the sultan, one can see SVO: *aṣ-ṣəlṭān tʕadda lqā*.

Nevertheless, there are some rare instances of SVO with the subject functioning as the topic of the sentence. Their occurrence is limited to the presentational verses at the beginning of a tale, in a particular structure consisting of two sentences. Namely, the first sentence introduces the existence of a certain character, while the second one, which contains the topicalised SVO order, provides an additional focus and new information. Despite the clear intonational separation of the topic from the rest of the sentence, it does function as the subject. The following passage illustrates this strategy:

(5)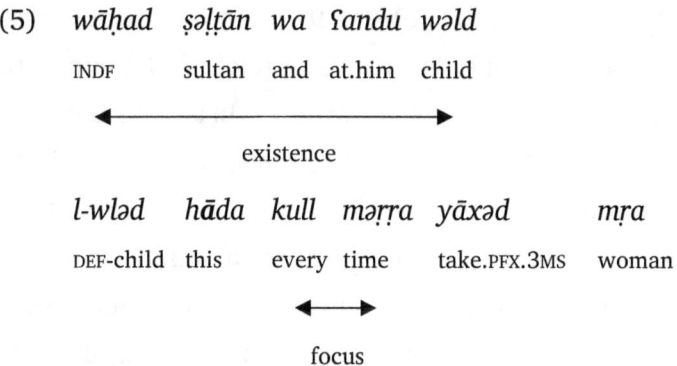

'There is a sultan and he has a son (2) this son, each time he takes a woman (…)' (6:1–2)

In sum, as the above analysis demonstrates, SVO and T–C should generally be regarded as two distinct types of sentence with different discourse functions. In support of this view, I have presented two arguments, related to the intonation and syntax of these sentences. Whereas the topic is conspicuously separated from the comment by a pause, the SVO order constitutes one intonation group. This, in turn, is reflected by the syntactic independence of the topic, which, unlike in an SVO sentence, is not followed by the predicate. The only exception to this rule is SVO with topicalised subject occurring after an introductory statement of existence.

3.6. Points of Convergence and Divergence with NENA

A comparative look at information packaging in the North-East Neo-Aramaic dialect of Telkepe and in Jewish Gabes can yield an interesting picture of the development of sentence structure and narrative strategies in modern Semitic.

Several points of convergence can be identified. To begin with, as observed by Coghill (2018, 309), an intonational phrase which includes only a topic has a rise in pitch at the end with simultaneous lengthening of the last syllable. In Jewish Gabes, it is the penultimate syllable that is lengthened, but, similarly to Telkepe, there is a noticeable rise in the pitch. In addition, both Jewish Gabes and Telkepe share the presence of indefinite topics. Usually, the topic is introduced by a presentational sentence stating the existence of an entity or is flagged by the indefinite-specific marker *wāḥəd* (/xa-/ in Telkepe). In Jewish Gabes, there are also rare instances of a first-mentioned topic, which are not activated in any way:

(6)   ^{HE}zūg^{HE}   yḥabbu   baʕdhəm   yāsər   ʕarršu
        couple   like.PFX.3PL   each.other   a.lot   get.married.SFX.3PL

        u   ma   ṭalʕūš   mən   əḍ-ḍāṛ   mən
        and   NEG   leave.SFX.3PL.NEG   from   DEF-house   from

        əl-ʕarš   ṣahrīn
        DEF-wedding   two.months

'A couple loved each other a lot, they got married and for two months since the wedding have not leave their home.' (5:1–2)

This is the opening sentence of the tale, yet the couple is not definite or introduced by an existential sentence. According to Gundel (1988, 215), indefinite topics are usually anchored in another, definite entity (Coghill 2018, 308). However, as example (6) demonstrates, the topic can appear for the first time as indefinite and unanchored.

Another point of convergence of Jewish Gabes with Telkepe is topicalisation of adverbs or adverbial clauses. In numerous Arabic dialects, it is a common tendency to topicalise temporal verbs, like ṣār 'to become' or kān 'to be', which do not bear any direct syntactic relationship with the main clause (Brustad 2000, 337). Jewish Gabes does not appear to utilise this strategy. However, there are numerous cases of topicalised adverbial clauses, which have the same intonational structure as the T–C sentences:

(7) līla fi-l-līl xūdi li ʕažīž ʕalīk
night in-DEF-night take.IMP.FS REL dear on.you
wa trūḥi l-bābāk
and go.PFX.FS to-father.yours
'Late in the night take whatever is valuable to you and go back to your father.' (7:81)

(8) nhār əl-mélex tʕadda māši ʕal
day DEF-king pass.SFX.3MS go.AP.MS on
əl-bḥar yərqa
DEF-sea find.PFX.3SM
'One day the king was passing by, found (…)' (7:65)

Coghill (2018, 310) reports the same tendency in Telkepe, where topicalised adverbs set the temporal frame of the event.

Despite certain similarities between the two languages, from a wider perspective, the development of word order in Arabic and NENA has followed different paths. Maghrebi Arabic has not been affected by neighbouring, non-Semitic languages to the same extent as NENA. The language contact-induced changes are particularly conspicuous in the region of Western Asia, where sentence typology of both NENA and, to a lesser extent, Arabic has undergone modifications under the influence of Turkic and Iranian languages. In the Jewish dialect of Sanandaj and other NENA dialects of northern Iraq and north-western Iran, the original Semitic VO order switched to OV due to contact with Turkic (Khan 2018, 21). Moreover, in those NENA dialects which adopted OV, syntactic elements expressing goals of verbs of movement are placed after the verb, whereas it is usually the case in OV languages that all the arguments precede the verb (Khan

2018, 23). This development was presumably induced by neighbouring Turkic and Iranian languages. Finally, all the languages in the region, including NENA and Arabic, have an obligatory, clause-final copula, which has diffused from Iranian (Khan 2018, 20).

The situation in North Africa differs considerably from that of Western Asia, mostly because of the relative linguistic uniformity of the region. The only language that has been in contact with Arabic long enough to induce some changes is Berber, where the basic word order is VSO. It has also been argued recently that some varieties of Berber are in the process of shifting to a topic-prominent system (El-Hankari 2015). As this chapter has indicated, however, both VSO and T–C constructions are equally basic in Arabic, hence no contact-induced change could occur with regard to word order.

7. SYNTAX OF PRONOUNS

1.0. Demonstrative Pronouns

1.1. Historical Background

Semitic languages utilise a diverse array of demonstrative pronouns, which can be broadly divided into two categories: near and far deixis. According to Hasselbach's (2007) historical reconstruction, the most common morpheme of the former is /ḏV/, which is widespread across almost all branches of Semitic, including Ethiopic, North-West Semitic, and varieties of Arabic.[1] This base has in some languages the variant /zV/, as for example /zə-/ in Gəʕez, or /ze/ in Hebrew. Apart from the aforementioned basic morpheme, Semitic features a variety of additional demonstrative elements, which either function as near deictics independently, or are attached to other elements to form a cluster of morphemes. The list of demonstrative elements utilised in Semitic includes, among others: /hā/, /la/, /n/, /t/.[2] The extension

---

[1] The /ḏV/ base is not attested in East Semitic, which utilises the /an/ base for near deixis instead.

[2] The /t/ element being a demonstrative element has been a matter of dispute among scholars. It occurs in pronouns like Gəʕez *zəntu* (MS), Hebrew *zōt* (FS), and Arabic *tilka* (FS). Although, according to Bath (1907, 31), the /t/ element represents a Proto-Semitic demonstrative and originally had three gender-sensitive variants—/tu/ (MS), /ti/ (FS), and /ta/ (neuter)—it is more plausible that, in the case of Gəʕez, it derives from the independent pronoun *waʔətu*, while in the rest of the languages where it occurs, it marks the feminine.

of the original /ḏV/ element by these other elements is exemplified by Hebrew *hallāze*, Arabic *ʔallāḏi*, Geʕez *zəntu* (Hasselbach 2007, 2). The plural base /ʔVllV/, which also has a shorter version /ʔVl/, can be extended in the same way. One of the most commonly agglutinated morphemes is the /n/ element, which is present, among others, in Geʕez and Aramaic.

The distribution of the far deixis markers is much less diverse and can be broadly divided into three groups. The first utilises the /k/ element, which is attached to the near deixis marker. This strategy is applied, among others, by virtually all Arabic dialects and by Geʕez. On the other hand, languages like Hebrew and Phoenician do not have a separate morpheme for expressing remote deixis and employ anaphoric pronouns instead. Finally, a small number of languages use demonstrative elements that play a part in the formation of near deixis, like /la/ in the Tigre /lohV-/ base, for example (Hasselbach 2007, 7).

It can therefore be assumed that Proto-Semitic had two demonstrative bases, namely /ḏV/ for the singular, and /ʔVl/ for the plural. The optionality of the demonstrative elements other than /ḏV/, alongside the fact that they are usually attached to other elements, points to their later development. Similarly, the /ʔVllV/ form of the plural seems to consist of the original /ʔVl/ base with an attached /lV/ element. The question remains as to what the relationship is between the singular and plural bases, and if their morphological heterogeneity reflects the original state of affairs. Hasselbach (2007, 1–27) has posed this question in her study on the demonstratives in Semitic. Judging from the oldest textual attestations of demonstratives in Semitic, it is reasonable to assume that the Old Babylonian singular far deictic pronoun *ullûm* contains the Proto-Semitic element /ʔVl/ (Hasselbach 2007, 23). One can therefore not exclude the possibility that this element served to express far deixis at an early stage of Semitic.

1.2. Typological Perspective

Demonstratives, from a cross-linguistic perspective, exhibit an immense diversity and heterogeneity. A few in-depth studies of demonstratives in world's languages are available (Diessel 1999; Bhat 2007). The authors highlight that demonstratives fulfil crucial communicative functions and have multiple pragmatic usages. In addition, Brustad (2000, 113) points to the vital role they play in narratives, where they tend to occur abundantly, and especially in the management of discourse topics. Since my text corpus consists mostly of narratives, analysis thereof should yield a clear and reliable picture of deixis mechanisms in North African Arabic. This section will attempt to outline the main pragmatic functions of demonstratives from a typological perspective and provide solid theoretical underpinnings for further analysis of my data.

To begin with, languages utilise different categories in order to express deixis. The most common deictic criterion is a spatial distinction between near and remote. Bhat (2007, 177) demonstrates that the majority of the world's languages have two-fold spatial categories, although there are some languages in which distinction is based on three or more points. The spatial reference point of the deixis also exhibits enormous diversity across languages. In most of them, the speaker is the centre of the deictic system; nonetheless, there are languages in which the location of the addressee is reflected by demonstratives as well. Apart from the location of the participants in the speech situation, some languages make deictic distinction between visible–invisible, above–below, inside–outside, etc. (Bhat 2007, 177).

Depending on their syntax, demonstratives can be divided into the following four categories: pronominal, adnominal, adverbial, and identificational (Dissel 1999, 4). While pronominal demonstratives function as independent pronouns substituting for a noun or a noun phrase, adnominal usage cooccurs with a noun. Adverbial demonstratives in Jewish Gabes do not exhibit any variation in terms of inflection or syntax, and will therefore not be covered in this chapter. Similarly, identificational demonstratives, which are applied in order to identify an entity appearing in a speech situation, are of no direct significance for the present analysis.

Apart from the above syntactic classification, demonstratives can also be divided according to their pragmatic functions. In scholarship on demonstratives, the most commonly applied division in this respect is that proposed by Halliday and Hasan (1976, 57–76), according to which demonstratives can have either exophoric or endophoric use. The former type of demonstrative is sometimes described as 'pointer', namely, it directs the hearer's attention to entities found in the interlocutors' surroundings. As argued by Diessel (1999, 114), the exophoric use is apparently the basic and the unmarked one, and the other types derive from it. All other three types are classified collectively under the term 'endophoric', since, in contradistinction to the exophoric use, they refer to the internal deixis of the discourse, and not to the entities from the external world. The first type, anaphoric, is utilised in order to track participants previously occurring in the discourse. Anaphoric demonstratives are obligatorily coreferential with the noun they accompany. They are crucial in the narrative, as they navigate the hearer through different layers of the discourse. Similarly, discourse deictic demonstratives, which constitute the second type of endophoric usage, fulfil a language-internal function (Diessel 1999, 101), namely, they refer to propositions expressed in the discourse by indicating a specific aspect of an utterance, like, for example, its truthfulness or falsehood. The last type of endophoric demonstrative is called 'recognitional' and is utilised adnominally to activate a specific item of knowledge shared by both participants in the speech situation. In other words, it introduces a piece of information that is discourse new and hearer old.

Another classification of pronouns, particularly useful in the study of discourse, is that of anaphoric and cataphoric. The former type refers to entities already mentioned in the discourse, while the latter points to elements which will occur later in the discourse.

It is important to point out that demonstratives across all the world's languages present the same tendency towards grammaticalisation. Diessel (2007, 112) argues that the endophoric use of demonstratives can in fact be considered grammaticalised, since it has evolved from a purely deictic exophoric application towards a functional organisation of the discourse information.

1.3. Pragmatic Analysis of the Data

The data pertaining to demonstrative pronouns in Jewish Gabes have been organised according to the criterion of spatial deixis. This includes near deixis, remote deixis, and the unstressed demonstrative pronoun. The morphology of the demonstratives has been treated in detail in chapter 4, §6.7, so, in what follows, I will limit myself to a description of the main pragmatic functions of the demonstratives in Jewish Gabes and in two neighbouring dialects, Jewish Wad-Souf (Algeria) and Jewish Tripoli, in order to obtain a more comprehensive picture of the functionality of pronouns in the region.

1.3.1. Syntactic Distribution

Demonstrative pronouns are usually used adnominally; nonetheless, there are some cases of pronominal usage in the text corpus as well. It appears that demonstratives substituting for nominals are applied to a lesser extent in North Africa than in, for example, the Neo-Aramaic dialect of the Christians of Urmi, where they occur in a variety of syntactic positions (Khan 2016, 238).

In various Arabic dialects, a demonstrative can either precede or follow the noun. Brustad (2000, 129) points out that, in Egyptian, demonstratives mandatorily follow the noun they modify, while in Moroccan, Syrian, and Kuwaiti, the post-nominal placement is obligatory only when the noun is in a genitive construction. Apart from these restrictions, the dialects demonstrate a certain level of variation in terms of the placement of demonstratives, usually motivated by pragmatics. As my data indicates, demonstratives in Jewish Gabes are subject to strict grammatical rules. The proximal demonstrative obligatorily follows the noun, while the distal and the unstressed ones are placed before the noun. This diverges significantly from Moroccan Arabic, where Harrell (1962) does not mention a post-nominal demonstrative construction at all, while Brustad (2000, 129) mentions only a small number of examples occurring in her data. Brustad (2000, 130) proposed a pragmatic explanation of the post-nominal position of the pronoun, pointing out that the pre-nominal position is usually identificatory and deictic, while the post-nominal placement signals an adjectival function. Although my data contains several cases of identificatory pre-nominal demonstratives, there are numerous examples of non-identificatory occurrence as well. This is the case with distal demonstratives, which follow the first mention of a protagonist.

1.3.2. Proximal Demonstratives

Proximal demonstratives fulfil a variety of narrative functions. They modify an item which constitutes the subject of the ongoing discussion:

(1) u bərša nāš kān yaʕmlu l-ḥāža **hādi?**
and a.lot people be.SFX.3MS make.PFX.3PL DEF -thing this
'And many people would do this thing?'

Pronominally, they designate a protagonist of the narrative:

(2) **hāda** dīma yži yʕāwnu
this always come.PFX.3MS help.PFX.3MS.him
u ybīʕu əš-šəlha
and sell.PFX.3PL DEF-stock

'This man always comes to help him sell the stock.' (5:3)

Moreover, they fulfil an identificatory function by narrowing the reference:

(3) žāt bəntu **hādi** mšəmmya
come.SFX.3FS daughter.his this name.her
maqṣūfāt šəbʕa šnīn
rascal seven years

'His daughter came, the one that is called a "seven-year-old rascal".' (7:12)

Similarly, as the following passage demonstrates, proximal demonstratives are utilised as a means of recognition:

(4) qāllu ya šəddi ᴴᴱmélexᴴᴱ **hādi** bənti
say.SFX.3MS.him VOC master.my king this daughter.my
qāllu bəntek **hādi** nḥabb nāxədha
say.SFX.3MS.him daughter.your this like.PFX.1SG take.PFX.1SG

'He said: your majesty, it is my daughter; he told him: this daughter, I would like to marry her.' (7:41–42)

In terms of the management of discourse topics, proximal demonstratives serve to retrieve an entity that recently appeared in the discourse, and therefore they function anaphorically:

(5) əl-ʕbəd **hāda** kān mḥayyər
DEF-man this be.SFX.3MS worried

'This man was worried.' (7:69)

Occasionally, proximal demonstratives can signal a pejorative connotation, expressing a personal disapproval of the speaker. The following passage is at the same time the only example of prenominal occurrence of a proximal demonstrative in my text corpus:

(6) qāllu **hādi** l-mṛa ənta tāxədha?
say.SFX.3MS.him this DEF-woman you take.PFX.2MS. her
hīya mahbūla qālət ʕaqla fi-ḥẓarha
she crazy say.SFX.3FS mind.her in-knees.her
'Are you going to marry this woman? She is insane, she said that her mind is on her knees.' (7:48)

Finally, near deixis is used by speakers to flag an item as particularly prominent in a certain part of the discourse. The water well appearing in the following example is the scene of a significant portion of the story, and is therefore followed by *hāda*:

(7) təmma bīr ġārəq yāsər wa l-bīr
there.is well deep a.lot and DEF -well
hāda li yədxal fī ymūt
this REL enter.PFX.3MS in.it die.PFX.3MS
'There was a very deep well and whoever goes in that well dies, does not go out.' (2:57)

1.3.3. Distal Demonstratives

One of the most important functions of far deixis is marking the crucial figures in the discourse. Usually, this technique occurs at the beginning of the story and involves the first mention of the protagonist flagged by the indefinite-specific article *wāḥəd*, which is subsequently repeated with the accompanying distal demonstrative. In this context, the indefinite-specific has a cataphoric reference:

(8)   təmma   **wāḥda**   bnəyya   yšəmmyūha   maqṣūfāt   šəbʕa
        there.is   INDF   girl   call.PFX.3PL.her   rascal   seven

       šnīn   **hādīk**   əl-maqṣūfāt   šəbʕa   šnīn   nhār
       years   that   DEF-rascal   seven   years   day

       ḅāḅāha   tʕadda   u   lqā   əṣ-ṣəlṭān
       father.her   pass.SFX.3MS   and   find.SFX.3MS.him   DEF-sultan

'There was a girl, whom people used to call a "seven-year-old rascal", this seven-year-old rascal, one day her father was passing and the sultan met him.' (7:2–3)

(9)   kān   ya   ma   kān   ʕala   **wāḥəd**
       be.SFX.3MS   or   NEG   be.SFX.3MS   on   INDF

       ṣəlṭān   **hādāk**   ṣ-ṣəlṭān   qāʕad   yxəmməm   kīfāš
       sultan   that   DEF-sultan   AUX   think.PFX.3MS   how

       yaʕməl   bāš   yāṛa   wlād   l-blād
       make.PFX.3MS   SUB   see.PFX.3MS   people   DEF-city

'Once upon a time there was a Sultan, that Sultan was thinking what to do in order to see the people of the city.' (Jewish Tripoli)

The far deixis forms are also utilised in order to indicate temporal distance, as demonstrated by example (10). In the first passage, *hadāk* marks temporal precedence of the first action, i.e., the man riding the donkey, followed by the more recent action of rubbing an onion:

(10) ət-tīla   fīha   nqāb   wa **hādāk** ʕaryān
　　 DEF-fabric in.her holes and that   naked

　　 u   lābəš   wa hādi xdāt   ṛāṣ
　　 and dressed and this take.SFX.3FS head

　　 əl-bṣəl   u   ḥakkətlo   ʕal žbīnu
　　 DEF-onion and rub.SFX.3FS on forehead.his

'In a fabric there were holes, so he was both naked and dressed, and she took an onion and rubbed it on his forehead.' (7:36–37)

In addition, far deixis can express a spatial distance, as in example (11):

(11) qāl   əntūm mahbūlīn ʕaqla
　　 say.SFX.3MS you.PL crazy   mind.her

　　 fi-ḥẓarha   **hādīk** txallaṣ   fi-ṣaʕrha
　　 in-knees.her that   finish.PFX.3FS in-hair.her

　　 u   ṣaʕrha   wāṣəl   ḥatta rəžlīn
　　 and hair.her arrive.AP.MS until legs

　　 kān   tqūmi   txabbər   əržʕu   l-ġādi
　　 be.SFX.3MS get.up.PFX.3FS inform.PFX.3FS return.IMP.2PL to-there

'He told them: you are insane, her mind was on her knees because she was finishing [combing] her hair and her hair reaches her legs, when she stands up, she will let you know, go back there!' (7:49)

In certain contexts, a remote demonstrative can denote an unspecified entity, which did not occur previously in the discourse. When this is the case, the most accurate translation in English would include the indefinite article 'a':

(12) *humma   žābu   zġār   wa*
     they   bring.SFX.3PL   children   and
     ʕṭāw   l-hādāk   l-ʕaššāš
     give.SFX.3PL   to-that   DEF-guard
     'They would give birth to children and give them to a guard.' (2:52)

Anaphorically, far deixis is utilised to express a referent that has been mentioned previously in the discourse, but the speaker assumes that it is hardly retrievable from the memory of the listener:

(13) *ərra   mən   kull   rqa   hādīk*
     see.SFX.3MS   from   all   find.SFX.3MS   that
     əl-mərt   wāḥda   li   ʕanda   ḍarba
     DEF-woman   INDF   REL   at.her   blast
     'He had a look and found among all of them the woman who has a scar on her back.' (2:47)

(14) *u   l-mra   u   l-rāžəl   li   sāknīn   fi-hādīk*
     and DEF-woman   and   DEF-man   REL   live.AP   in-that
     əl-ḥūš   daxxlu   u   ʕamlūlu   kaḅūḍu
     DEF-house   enter.SFX.3PL.him   and   make.SFX.3PL.him   respect
     'And the woman and man who lived in that house took him inside, and showed him respect.' (Jewish Tripoli)³

Moreover, in terms of managing discourse topics, distal demonstratives occur in a construction that marks the first mention of a

---

[3] This fragment has been excerpted from the following folktale: https://www.lashon.org/1/node/523, accessed 5 March 2024.

secondary story figure. It comprises the unstressed distal demonstrative *hāk* (see §1.3.4) and the distal demonstrative pronoun:

(15) ʕarrəṣt   mʕa **hāk** əṛ-ṛāžəl **hādāk** əṛ-ṛāžəl
marry.SFX.3FS with that DEF-man that DEF-man

yaxdəm   ʕaləyəm   yžīb   u   yəšri
work.PFX.3MS on.them bring.PFX.3MS and buy.PFX.3MS

'She got married to that man, that man would work for them, bring food, buy things.' (Jewish Wad-Souf)

1.3.4. Unstressed Distal Demonstratives

1. ***hāk** əl-qaḍḍ l-ʕažīž, əbṭāt* (1:6)
   'What a precious figure! She was late [going back inside].'
2. *Ṣṭātlu, xūd hād əl-xabža u kūlha, rfaʕha ʕažbathu **hāk** əl-xabža* (1:16)
   'She gave to him saying: take this bread and eat it. He took it and found a favour in the bread.'
3. *fraḥ əṣ-ṣəlṭān, ža l-**hāk** əl-wəld, Ṣṭālo flūš, lwīž* (2:53)
   'The sultan was happy, he came to this man, gave him money, coins.'
4. *žūž axwāt, wāḥəd ẓāwāli wa wāḥəd məštaġni, **hāk** əl-ẓāwāli kull nhār xmīš, yəmši l-xu yaʕṭi flūš* (3:1–2)
   'Two brothers, one poor and the other one rich. That poor one goes every Thursday to his brother, so he gives him money.'
5. *az hīya žābət **hāk** əl-məžān l-oṃha* (3:49)
   'So she brought that scale to the mother.'

In addition to proximal and distal demonstratives, Jewish Gabes utilises also an ungendered, unstressed demonstrative article. Unlike the unstressed demonstrative article /had-/ in Moroccan Arabic, which, as argued by Harrell (1962, 147), does not distinguish between near and far deixis, *hāk* in Jewish Gabes is related to remote deixis and, in some cases, substitutes for the full distal demonstrative.

As shown by the above examples, the functional interchangeability of the two types of demonstratives is significant. To begin with, the use of *hāk* in example (4) suggests that it can replace *hādāk* in the construction that introduces a protagonist. Moreover, as demonstrated by example (3), it functions anaphorically to mark an entity that has already been introduced in the discourse, but is not immediately retrievable from the memory of the listener. Similarly, in examples (1), (2), and (5), *hāk* denotes objects remote from both the speaker and the listener. It is reasonable, therefore, to suppose that *hāk* is not an independent article, like /ha-/ or /had-/ in other dialects, but rather a truncated version of *hādāk*.

1.4. Demonstratives in North African Arabic: A Comparative Perspective

As has already been mentioned, Moroccan Arabic utilises some demonstrative strategies that do not occur in Jewish Gabes. This discrepancy potentially suggests that the western varieties of North African Arabic diverge from their eastern counterparts in terms of expressions of deixis. In the present section, I will investigate the distribution of demonstratives in selected dialects of the region.

A preliminary examination of the data from Jewish Tunis already reveals some differences. Although the forms of near and far deixis converge in both dialects, Jewish Tunis utilises a shortened form of the proximal demonstrative, which Cohen (1975,

224) calls the 'construct state form'. In contradistinction to the full form, which as a rule follows the noun, its short counterpart precedes the noun. Its presence is also attested in Moroccan Arabic, as well as in Syrian and Kuwaiti varieties (Brustad 2000, 115). However, it appears that this form is not utilised in Jewish Gabes. Although *hād* occurs in passage (1:16), I argue that this is *hādi* with elided final vowel, rather than a separate form. The elision of vowels in word-final position, conditioned by the following word starting with a vowel, is a common phenomenon in Jewish Gabes. In addition, Jewish Tunis applies the form *āl* in order to express far deixis, which parallels the Syrian and Kuwaiti unstressed demonstrative article /ha/ (Cohen 1975, 225). This form has not been attested in Jewish Gabes either.

The Bedouin dialect of Douz presents some similarities to Jewish Gabes, namely, it has a set of two full far and near demonstratives and an ungendered *hāk*, but it utilises also the so-called 'double' demonstrative construction, attested, among others, in Syrian and Kuwaiti dialects (Ritt-Benmimoun 2014, 83; Brustad 2000, 131). This construction combines the /ha-/ demonstrative article preceding the noun, and the full near demonstrative in the postnominal position. Similarly to the previous two demonstratives, it has not been attested in Jewish Gabes.

Certain dialects, like Jewish Algiers and some Moroccan varieties, apply, in addition to the basic set of full demonstratives, a shortened form of the remote demonstrative *dāk*. Cohen (1912, 346) merely points out that, in Jewish Algiers, *dāk* is a shorter variant of *hādāk*, without giving any description of its syntactic behaviour. On the other hand, Brustad (2000, 126) notes that, in the region of Fes, *dāk*, which can modify both singular and plural nouns of both genders, functions in a similar manner to the proximal anaphoric *hād*. In the region of Tangiers, this demonstrative has the form *dīk* and, like *dāk*, is anaphoric and ungendered (Brustad 2000, 127).

8. CONCLUSION

This study was concerned with systematic description of the grammar of Jewish Gabes and, by providing comparative data, it attempted to situate it within the dialectological landscape of North African Arabic. It has striven to address several challenges that modern Maghrebi dialectology faces. As was pointed out in the introduction, this field suffers from a lack of a diachronic approach to syntax, particularly from a comparative perspective. The linguistic analysis presented in this volume has hopefully, on the one hand, contributed to a better understanding of Jewish North African dialects, and on the other, cast more light on the differences between Jewish and Muslim dialects. It has been established that Jewish Gabes belongs to the first-layer (pre-Hilāli) dialects of Maghrebi Arabic, which, with the exception of several cities like Mahdia and Tunis, are no longer spoken in Tunisia. The linguistic features of this variety, due to its ancient character, point to a number of substrate and language contact scenarios.

In Part I, on phonology, I demonstrated that the interdental consonants have merged with their plosive counterparts. As is the case with other sedentary dialects, /q/ is generally preserved, although /g/ is found in certain lexemes and there exist minimal pairs proving its phonemic status. When it comes to the distribution of /h/, I have demonstrated that, in contradistinction to Jewish Tunis, this sound has in Jewish Gabes rather stable and audible realisation, except in word-final position. I paid special attention to the development of sibilants in North Africa and argued that plain /s/ and /z/ are not phonemic in Jewish Gabes, although, as demonstrated, the range of emphaticity of /ṣ/ and /ẓ/ is fairly wide. The following part of the chapter dealt with emphasis spread in Jewish Gabes. The preliminary results of this analysis prove, firstly, that the pharyngealised character of /q/ is weak, and secondly, that the emphatic consonants in the dialect in question have different degrees of spreadability. In terms of the vowel inventory, I have demonstrated that Jewish Gabes has three long phonemic vowels: /ī/, /ā/, and /ū/, and three short phonemic vowels: /a/, /ə/, and /o/, although the phonemic status of /o/ is uncertain, as only one minimal pair has been found where the opposition between short /o/ and /a/ differentiates the meaning. I have pointed out a few possible qualities of /ə/, depending on the consonantal environment. My findings prove that, although the vowel inventory of Jewish Gabes is similar to that of Jewish Tunis, the distribution of /o/ in the former is much more limited. On the other hand, short /a/ does seem to be phonemic in Jewish Gabes, in contrast to Jewish Djerba, where only /ə/ is phonemic. Finally, I have demonstrated that David Cohen's (1975, 64) claim about the tendency towards the preservation of diphthongs among Jewish dialects of Tunisian Arabic is not valid for southern Tunisian dialects, where they tend to be contracted.

Part II, on morphology, has demonstrated that the dialect of Gabes differs in some aspects from one of its typologically closest neighbours, namely the Jewish dialect of Tunis. This is the case, for example, with the gender distinction in 2FS forms of both the suffix and prefix conjugations, which does not exist in

Jewish Tunis. Jewish Gabes, similarly to Jewish Djerba, has preserved this distinction. I have paid special attention to the diachronic evolution of the verbal system, which demonstrates a significant departure from the CA stem system. Moreover, as has been argued, Jewish Gabes has developed an alternative way of expressing the passive, by means of a bipartite construction involving an active verb together with a personal object pronoun. I have explained this development by means of analogy. Chapter 4, on nominal morphology, was primarily focused on thorough presentation of the data. Where possible, I have made remarks on semantic differences between selected nouns in Jewish Gabes and in Jewish Tunis. As has been demonstrated, there exist salient lexical differences between Jewish Gabes and the dialects spoken in the North of Tunisia.

Part III was devoted to the investigation of syntax. It included discussion of a number of syntactic phenomena, which were analysed from cross-linguistic and Semitic perspectives. In the section on definiteness, I pointed to salient differences in the way Moroccan Arabic and Jewish Gabes encode definiteness. Subsequently, I presented a classification of genitive exponents, followed by a description of nominal concord. As I have shown, Jewish Gabes, similarly to other Jewish dialects of the region, demonstrates strict syntactic agreement between constituents of the sentence. This phenomenon, which constitutes another isogloss shared by several Jewish dialects of the region, could potentially be explained by language contact with Israeli Hebrew. Nevertheless, in-depth diachronic research into the development of agreement is needed in order to ascertain whether deflected agreement has ever been generalised in Judaeo-Arabic. In contradistinction to this, the second-wave dialects (and some first-wave dialects like Muslim Tunis), have deflected agreement when the subject is of low individuation. In my study of subordination, I have considered three types of subordinate clauses: relative clauses, adverbial clauses, and complements. I have argued that relative clauses in Jewish Gabes are of an external, postnominal type and can be either restrictive or non-restrictive. As in many other modern Arabic dialects, the syntactic behaviour of relative clauses in Jewish Gabes is to a large extent dependent on the definiteness of the head noun. It has been demonstrated that definite nouns attract the relative pronoun and bring about resumption in the relative clause. On the other hand, when the relativised item is indefinite, relativisation tends to be realised by means of coordination or asyndetically. The study of adverbial clauses provided a thorough presentation and taxonomy of data. The data analysis involved six semantic groups of adverbial clauses in Jewish Gabes. Special attention was paid to temporal clauses. The analysis of the third type of subordination, i.e., complementation, was primarily concerned with syntactic phenomena caused by the semantics of the matrix predicate. I argued that the meaning of the main predicate conditions, to a large extent, the syntagm of the complement. In addition, a semantic taxonomy of complement-taking predicates was presented. Each class of complements was classified according to tense predetermination. I have argued that Jewish Gabes makes a clear distinction between deontic and epistemic modality. Moreover, I have shown different ways of expressing obligation in the dialect, involving the particles *lāžəm*, *məlžūm ʕal*, and *yəlžəm* + personal pronoun. §2.0, on expressions of tense and aspect, has demonstrated that the p-stem and s-stem are primarily aspectual, and the temporal dimension is expressed by other constituents of the sentence. I have shown that the active participle in the Jewish dialects encodes the present progressive, while in their Muslim counterparts it functions as a perfect. It has been tentatively suggested that this divergence could point to a North-West Semitic substrate in the Jewish varieties. In the section on word order, I demonstrated that the SVO order differs from T–C, and that these should generally be regarded as two distinct types of sentence with different discourse functions. I have presented two arguments in support of this view, related to the intonation and syntax of these sentences. Finally, in chapter 7, I made a distinction between proximal, distal, and unstressed distal pronouns, simultaneously analysing their discourse functions.

To sum up, as the present volume has demonstrated, Jewish Gabes belongs typologically to the group of first-layer, sedentary dialects, which constitute a minority in the North African dialectal landscape. This is mostly due to an influx of rural and Bedouin populations to Maghrebi cities, which has brought about a merger of the first- and second-layer dialects, resulting in turn in the redefinition of the traditional isoglosses. Part of this volume was devoted to investigation of confessional differences as reflected in the Jewish and Muslim varieties of Arabic. One of the promising pathways of future research would be to extend this line of investigation to other communities, in order to better understand the nature and the development of Judaeo-Arabic. As I have demonstrated, not only do Jewish dialects differ from their Muslim counterparts on the lexical level, but there exist certain salient grammatical divergences as well. Research combining linguistic inquiry with social history could therefore yield some intriguing results.

APPENDIX
A CORPUS OF SELECTED NARRATIVES
QUOTED IN THE VOLUME

1.0. The Tale of the Beggar and the Loaf of Bread

Speaker: Tzivia Tobi, age: 76
Place and time of recording: Israel, December 2016

(1) mūši qāllu: āna fqərtu qūm aġnī, āna qtəltu qūm aḥyī (2) wāḥəd mša yəṭləb ya krīm tāʕ aḷḷa (3) wṣəl l-əḍ-ḍāṛ, ḍrəb əb-bāb, yəṭləb ya krīm tāʕ aḷḷa (4) ṭalʕat əl-xādma, kān təšbaḥ fī (5) fəmm tāqaʕ wa əl-ʕīn baṛṛāqa (6) hāk əl-qaḍḍ l-ʕažīž, əbṭāt (7) nādātha ləllātha (8) qāltəlha: ya xlīqa ka-yəkšəbha ḥadd (9) u qāllək ža yəṭləb (10) ṭalʕat tšūf fī (11) qālətlu: ədxəl! (12) qāltəlha: əšmʕi, xūdi ʕažīn, aʕžnī, u ṭəyyəbi xabža u fi-qalb ʕabbyīha b-əlwīž məndāxəl (13) aʕṭyī əl-xabža yəštaġna bīha wa waqt ywəlli ᴴᴱʕašīrᴴᴱ, nāxdu (14) ṭalʕat əl-xabža wa ʕṭātālhu (15) qātlu: əštənna šwīya, hāk əl-xabža yžəyyəd fīha ṛabbi (16) ʕṭātlu, xūd hād əl-xabža u kūlha (17) rfāḥa ʕažbathu hāk əl-xabža (18) ṭlaʕ, lqa ḥānūt aḥda (19) qāl: āna ᴴᴱʕaníᴴᴱ u əl-xəbža ḥabb nākəlha, aʕṭīni nfayyəṣ xabža, wa aʕṭīni ḥžīna šmīʕa, u qrīṭīṣ wqīḍ bāš nəšʕalha (20) xdāha, ʕṭā nfəyyəṣ xabža oxra (21) rəwwaḥ bīha lə-ḍ-ḍāṛ, qāl əl-mərtu: hād əl-xabža ʕamri ma ṛātha ʕīnī əl-kbāṛ (22) ḥatti šəkkīna u nqaṣṣūha (23) hūwa qaṣṣ, ṭalʕu hāk əl-ḥəžīn əl-lwīž əl-kəll (24) qāʕ l-aḥžīn əmbāṛəq fi-ʕažəb ṛabbi (25) mən ġadwa wəllālha, qāləlha: ya krīm tāʕ aḷḷa (26) qāʕ tšūfi škūn ža?

(1) Moses said to him: I have made him poor, try to make him rich; I have killed him, try to revive him. (2) A man went to beg for money (3) He arrived at a house, knocked on the door and begged. (4) A handmaid went out and kept looking at him. (5) Her mouth was wide open while she was gazing on him (6) What a precious figure! She was late [going back inside] (7) Her mistress called her (8) She said to her: oh, such a figure as no one has ever seen! (9) And he said to you that he came to beg (10) She came out to see him (11) She said to him: come in! (12) She (the mistress) said to her: listen, take dough, knead it and bake bread, filling it inside with coins (13) Give him this bread so that he becomes rich from it and when he is already rich, we will marry him [to you] (14) The bread came out and she gave it to him (15) She said to him: wait a little bit, God will add to this bread (16) She gave to him saying: take this bread and eat it (17) He took it and he liked the bread (18) He went out and found a shop nearby (19) He said: I am poor and I would like to eat the bread, so give me half of it and give me a (poor, miserable)[1] candle and a box of matches so I can light it (20) He took it and gave him half of another bread (21) He (the owner of the shop) came back home with the bread and said to his wife: this bread, my eye has never seen this grandness (22) Bring a knife and we will cut it! (23) He cut it and all the (poor, miserable) coins came out (24) he (the poor, the miserable) was gazing on this miracle of God (25) the next day he (the beggar) came back to her saying: may God have mercy! (26) Can you see who is coming?!

---

[1] The word *ḥažīn/ḥžīna* is introduced in folktales to notify the listener that something bad is going to happen to the main character.

(27) qālətlu: hāk əl-xabža li ʕṭīthālək ša ʕməlt bīha? (28) ya ləlla, nḥabb nākəlha yāsər ʕlīya u kbīra ʕalīya (29) xdīt nfayyəṣ ḥžīna šmīʕa u qrīṭīṣ wqīḍ bāš nətʕašša bīha (30) qāltəlha: aʕmlīlu ḥžīna oxra (31) qāmət ʕamlətlu wāḥda oxra, xīr mən-əl-lūwla (32) qālətlu aqbəl ma ʕṭātālhu: ṛəḍḍ bālək ʕlīha, ṛəḍḍ bālək tbīḥḥa (33) qālha: mlīḥ, u mša l-ḍāṛu (34) fi-tnīya dxəl əl^HE ḥanūt^HE, wa ʕāwəd li ʕməl mbāraḥ (35) ža f-əṣ-ṣbaḥ ya krīm tāʕ alḷa (36) šbīk ržaʕt? (37) ya ləlla, kānət hāk əl-xabža kbīra ʕlīya, ʕṭītha əl ^HE ḥanūt^HE u xdīt nfayyəṣ xabža, u šmīʕa u qrīṭīṣ wqīḍ (38) ʕamlīlu ḥžīna oxra u dəxəllīlu kəmša lwīž fi-l-ʕžīn (39) ṛəḍḍ bālək taʕṭīha l-ḥānūt, kūlha ənti (40) qālha: mlīḥ (41) hūwa hbaṭ mən əd-drūž, l-aḥžīn, ʕtər, ṭāḥ u māt (42) ṭalʕat ktība fi-l-ḥīṭ: āna qtəltu qūm aḥyī, āna fqərtu, qūm aġnī.

(27) The bread that I gave to you, what have you done with it? (28) O my lady, I wanted to eat it but it was too much for me and it was too big (29) I took half of the bread, (the poor, the miserable) candle, and a small box of matches in order to light it (30) She said to her: make him another bread (literally: make him another misery) (31) She got up to make another, better than the first one (32) She said to him before giving it to him: be careful with it, make sure not to sell it (33) He said to her: fine, and went home (34) On his way he walked in the shop and repeated the same as he did yesterday (35) In the morning he came back to beg (36) What is the matter with you? Why did you come back? (37) O my lady, the bread was too big for me, I gave it to the shop and took half of the bread, a candle, and a small box of matches (38) Make another bread and put a handful of coins inside the dough (39) Make sure not to give it to the shop, eat it by yourself (40) He said to her: fine (41) When he was going down on the stairs, poor man, he stumbled, fell down and died (42) An inscription appeared on the wall saying: I have made him poor, try to make him rich; I have killed him, try to revive him.

2.0. The Sultan and Three Daughters

Speaker: Haya Mazouz, age: 76
Place and time of recording: Israel, March 2019

(1) əṣ-ṣəlṭān, ʕandu tlāt bnāt (2) l-kbīra ṣaʕrha bda abyaḍ, u t-tānya bāhya u t-tālta zġīra (3) əẓ-ẓġīra kānət fāyqa (4) mšāt l-əṣ-ṣūq, f-əṣ-ṣūq srāt tlāta bəṭṭīxa (5) hīya mšāt žābət tlāta bəṭṭīxa (6) wāḥda ṭayba, ḥamra, wāḥda xaḍra u wāḥda bāhya (7) wa baʕṭəthəm l-əṣ-ṣəlṭān, lə-bābāha (8) əl-bāba ṭəllaʕ tlāta baṭṭīxa, mabṣūṭ, bəntu baʕṭətlo² baṭṭīxa (9) qaṣṣhəm, əl-lūla ḥamra, u t-tānya ṭāyba u t-tālta xaḍra, nəyya (10) (əž)ža l-wužīr qāllu: əšmaʕ, (ə)tlāta baṭṭīxāt li bʕaṭəthəm bəntək, fīhəm ramz (11) qāllu: l-ḥamra, bəntək l-kbīra kabrat, l-oxra f-ət-tnīya wa ət-tālta zġīra (12) əl-bāba tġaṣṣaṣ, ša ʕməl? (13) l-kbīra xdāha ṛāẓəl, xda wəld wžīr, wa ət-tānya xdāha ṛāẓəl (14) wa hadīk əz-zġīra, qāl, ya kəlba bənt kəlba, qāllhəm: šūfu wāḥəd l-əktər agžān, l-əktər məxnān, l-əktər ẓāwāli, xūdūla (15) təmma wāḥəd, yəqʕad taḥt šəẓra tāʕ blāḥ, yḥall fəmmu wa yštənna ḥatt əl-blāḥ ytīḥlu fi-fəmmu (16) f-əl-lāxər hūwa yəqʕad əkāk, žāw l-wəžra qāllu: təmma wāḥad li hūwa ma tharrəkš, hūwa yštənna ḥatt ytīḥlu mākla fi-fəmmu (17) qāllu: hādāk žību yāxəd əl-bənt (18) žābūla, qərqrū, qāllu: xūdha (19) qāllu: ya šəddi ṣəlṭān, āna ma ʕandəš šnūwa nākəl, wa ənti taʕṭīni bəntək? šnūwa naʕməl bīha? fi-šnu nwəkkəlha?

---

² Occasionally, the preposition *lu* 'to him' interchanges with *lo*, presumably due to the parallel form in Modern Hebrew.

(1) The sultan had three daughters (2) The eldest one started having grey hair, the second one was fine and the third one was still small (3) The young one was smart (4) She went to the souk and bought there three melons (5) She went there and brought three melons (6) One ripe, red, one green, and one fine (7) And she sent them to the sultan, her father (8) The father took out the three melons, happy that his daughter had sent him melons (9) He cut them, the first one was red, the second one was ripe and the third one was still green, unripe (10) The minister came and said to him: listen, there is a hint in these three melons that your daughter has sent you (11) He said to him: the red one – your eldest daughter got old, the other one is on her way (to get old) and the third one is still small (12) The father got angry, what did he do? (13) He married the eldest to a man, the son of the minister, he married also the second one (14) And that small one, he said, the daughter of a bitch, he said to them: look for the one that is the laziest, the dirtiest and the poorest and marry her to him (15) There was a man who was sitting beneath a date palm, he would open his mouth and he would wait until the date fell into it (16) Finally, when he was sitting like this, the ministers came and said to him (the sultan): there is a man who does not move, he waits for the food to fall down into his mouth (17) He said to him: bring that man to marry the daughter (18) They brought him to her, they said to him: marry (her) (19) He said to him: O your majesty, I have nothing to eat and you will give me your daughter? What will I do with her? How will I feed her?

(20) qāllu: āna ma naʕrəfš šəyy, aʕməlli mžīya wa xūd əl-bənt, ma nḥabbš nšūf xlīqatkəm (21) ommha ʕṭātham flūš, ʕṭātham əlbāš u mšāw (22) baʕd nhār žāw taḥt əl-naxla, wa əl-bənt ʕamlət ᴴᴱsukaᴴᴱ (23) mšāt l-naxla tāʕ ṛman, qaṣṣət l-ʕrūf, nəẓṛəthum u təḍṛəblu fi-rəžlīh mən lūṭa ḥatt əṛ-ṛāẓəl bda yətḥarrək wa dəmmu bda yəẓṛi fi ᴴᴱgūfuᴴᴱ, yūqəf ʕal rəžlīh u bda yəmši (24) əl-ḍəṛb qəymu (25) hīya qaʕdət u taʕddāt ᴴᴱšayaraᴴᴱ, qāmət žāt l-əl-kbīr tāḥḥam, qātlo: aʕməlli mžīya, ṛāzli ma ʕandūš xadma, xūdhu maʕkəm, yəxdəm wa yʕāwnək (26) ža li wāqəf ʕaləyhəm, qālla: žībi (27) ža, qāllo: tgədd tʕašš fi-l-līl? (28) qāllu: ngədd, li tḥabb naʕməllək (29) mšāw mšāw mšāw fə-t-tnīya ʕaṭṣu (30) u qaʕdu u yāklu u yəṣṛbu u hbəṭ ʕaləyhəm əl-līl (31) wa qāllu: ənti tʕašš ʕal aḥsānāt (32) waqt hūwa ka-yʕašš fi-nəfṣ əl-līl, žāt wāḥda mra, žāt u ləwwḥat ḥāža, hūwa yḥabb yaʕṛəf šnūwa ləwwḥat (33) hūwa žra wa xda ʕṣa u ḍṛəbha fi-ḍharha u ḥaṛbatlo (34) ṣəbbāḥa ṣbāḥ rqāw wəld məyyət, wəld əṣ-ṣəlṭān (35) l-ṣ-ṣəlṭān ʕandu šəbʕa nša (36) kull mra li tūləd, tlāt arbʕa ayyām u yāxdu l-wəld yləwwḥu (37) ma yaʕṛfuṣ škūn yāxdu yəqtlu (38) wāḥda tžīb u šətta ma yžībuš (39) wāḥda fīhəm tanġa

(20) He said to him: I do not care, do me a favour and take her, I do not want to see either of you (literally: I do not want to see your figure) (21) Her mother gave them money, gave them clothes and they left (22) One day later they came under a palm tree and the girl constructed a tent (23) She went to the pomegranate tree, cut some branches, bound them and started hitting his feet from beneath until the man started moving and the blood started running in his body, he stood up on his feet and started walking (24) The flogging woke him (25) While she was sitting, a caravan was passing by, she stood up and went to talk to the person in charge (literally: to the one who is standing upon them), she said to him: do me a favour, my husband does not have a job, take him with you, he will work and will help you (26) The person in charge came and said to her: bring him! (27) He came and said to him: will you guard the cattle in the night? (28) He said to him: I will guard, I will do whatever you want (29) They walked, walked, walked and on the way they became thirsty (30) They sat down, ate, drank and the night fell upon them (31) And they said to him: will you guard the horses? (32) While he was guarding at midnight, a woman came, she came and threw something, he wanted to know what she had thrown (33) He ran and took a stick and hit her on the back but she escaped from him (34) Early in the morning they found a dead child, the child of a sultan (35) The sultan has seven women (36) Every woman who gives birth, after three or four days someone would take the child and throw it away (37) They did not know who took it to kill it (38) One gives birth and six others do not (39) One of them was jealous

(40) ža l-ṣ-ṣəlṭān, qāllu: ya šəddi ṣəlṭān, āna fi-l-līl nʕašš u žāt xyāl, xbaṭ ḥaža u mšāt (41) kīf xbaṭ āna zrīt wṛā u ḍṛəbta (42) aṣ-ṣəlṭān bda yxəmməm (43) qāllu: taʕṛəf šnu taʕməl? xūd šəbʕa nša ntāʕk, āna ḍṛəbtha fi-ḍ-ḍhar ntāḥḥa (44) šūf škun ʕandu ḍṛabb fi-ḍharha (45) škūn yži yāxdu u yləwwḥu? (46) qāllu: ʕandək ḥaqq ya wəldi (47) əṛṛa mən kull ṛqa hādīk əl-məṛt wāḥda li ʕanda ḍaṛba (48) qālla: ya bənt aḥrām, qaṣṣūla ṛāṣa! (49) šnūwa ᴴᴱmitbarerᴴᴱ? (50) hīya ma tžībš zġār, l-oxrīn yžību, az hīya kānət tanġa (51) humma yūldu wa hīya təqtlu (52) humma žābu zġār, wa ʕṭāw l-hādāk l-ʕššāš (53) fraḥ əṣ-ṣəlṭān, ža l-hāk əl-wəld, ʕṭālo flūš, lwīž (54) qātlo: ənti mənnaʕtni! (55) əl-mra ḥablət, tžīb wəld, ma təmmāš škūn yaqtlu (56) humma mšāw yāsər, ət-tnītya ṭwīla u ufāləm əl-ma (57) ša ʕamlu? təmma bīr ġārəq yāsər wa l-bīr hāda li yədxal fī ymūt, ma yəṭlaʕṣ (58) ža wāḥad mənhum qāllu: tḥabb tədxəl ənti? (59) qāllu: bāhi, nədxəl (60) bʕaṭu bāš ymūt (61) ya yžīb ya ma yžībīš (62) xdāw ṛəbtū fi-l-ḥbəl ġlīḍ u daxxlū, hbaṭ lūṭa (63) žāw əž-žnūn qāllu: šnūwa tḥabb hūni? ʕalāš tqallaqna? (64) qāllu: ʕandna ġləmm, ma ʕandnāš ma

(40) He went to the sultan and said to him: your majesty, at night when I was guarding the livestock, a figure came, it threw something and left (41) When she threw it, I ran behind her and hit her (42) The sultan started thinking (43) He said to him: do you know what you should do? Take your seven women, I have hit the back of a woman (44) Look which of them has the mark of a hit on her back (45) Who was coming to take the child and throw it away? (46) He said to him: you are right, my boy (47) He had a look and found among all of them the woman who has a mark on her back (48) He said to her: O accursed woman! Cut off her head! (49) What happened? (50) She did not give birth, and the others did so she was jealous (51) They would give birth and she would kill (52) They would give birth children and give it to her to look after (53) The sultan was happy, he came to this man, gave him money, coins (54) He said to him: you saved me! (55) The woman was pregnant, gave birth to a son, there is no one to kill him (56) They walked a lot, the way was long, and they ran out of water (57) What did they do? There was a very deep well and whoever goes in dies, does not go out (58) One of them came and asked him: would you like to go in? (59) He said to him: fine, I will go (60) They sent him to death (literally: they sent him so he dies) (61) Either he brings (the water) or he does not (62) They took him and tied him up with a thick rope and put him in the well, he descended (63) The ghosts came and said to him: what do you want here? Why are you disturbing us? (64) He said to him: we have cattle, but we do not have water

(65) qāllu: tuwwa naqtlūk, ma naqtlūkš kān tžībna agžān mən Baġdād, ža hādāk əžžīn wa mərtu ʕaməltlu ᴴᴱbeayotᴴᴱ ma kānətš bāhia mərtu (66) tġaṣṣaṣ ʕaləya, ḍərba ḍərba rəḍḍha aḥṣān (67) qālla: ma twəlli aḥṣān, twəlli žīn, kān yži hādāk əl-agžān mən Baġdād (68) qāllu: kān tžībli agžān mən Baġdād naʕṭīk əl-ma, naʕṭīk li thabb ənti wa mərti təržʕa əžžīna (69) qāllu: āna agžān mən Baġdād! (70) qāllu: ənti?! (71) qāllu: əy (72) qāllu: kīfāš žīt? (73) qāllu: žīb əl-fərṣa! (74) hūwa ḥaṭṭ yəddu ʕal əl-fərṣa wa hīya wəllāt žīn (75) qāllu: ʕandək ḥaqq (76) ʕṭālo dhəbb wa ma (77) ṭlaʕ fīšʕa, əlᴴᴱšayaraᴴᴱ farḥu wa ʕṭāw l-ma l-ġləmm ntāḥəm u rəwwḥu l-əḍ-ḍāṛ (78) žāt əl-mərtu qālətlo: aššnūwa ʕməlt ġādi, šnūwa qbəlt (79) hūwa ʕṭāla dhəbb qālla: ʕamli li thabbi (80) qālətlo: žībtli dənnya kulla! (81) hīya žābət xaddāma qwīyy (82) qāltəlləm: tuwwa bnīyuli qṣaṛ qbal ḍāṛ ḅāḅāy, xīr mən tāʕu, u nḥabba sahrīn takməl (83) fīšʕa bnāw srāw mūḅīlya (84) waqt kull əl-ḅāḅa lāhi bi-l-xadma ntāʕu (85) u nhāṛ wāḥəd žāt əš-šəmš, hūwa qʕad fi-l-balkōn u šāf əq-qṣaṛ (86) qāl: əšškūn kəlb bna ḍāṛ qbəl u xīr mən ḍāṛi? (87) ža wžīr qāllu: ya šəddi ṣəlṭān, bəntek əẓ-ẓġīra bnāt əq-qṣaṛ, li ləwwaḥt mʕa hāda l-agžān

(65) He said to him: We will kill you now, but we will not kill you if you bring us the idle man from Baghdad, a ghost came and his wife was causing him problems, his wife was not good (66) He got angry with her, he hit her, hit her and turned her into a horse (67) He said to her: you will not be a horse and you will turn back into a ghost if the idle man from Baghdad comes here (68) He said to him: if you bring here the idle man from Baghdad, I will give water, I will give you whatever you want and my wife will turn back into a ghost (69) He said to him: I am the idle man from Baghdad! (70) He said to him: you?! (71) He said to him: yes! (72) He said to him: how did you walk? (73) He said to him: bring the mare (74) He put his hand on the mare and she turned into a ghost (75) He said to him: you are right (76) He gave him water and gold (77) He came out quickly, the members of the caravan were happy and gave the cattle water and set off home (78) His wife came and said to him: what did you do down there? What did you receive? (79) He gave her the gold and said to her: do whatever you want (80) She said to him: you have brought me an entire world! (81) She brought strong workers (82) She said to them: now build me a castle in front of my father's house, even better than his, and I want it to be finished within two weeks (83) They built it quickly and bought furniture (84) All this time the father was busy at his work (85) And one day the sun rose, he sat down on the balcony and saw the castle (86) He said: who is this bastard who has built the castle in front of me and even better than mine? (87) A minister came and said to him: your majesty, it is your youngest daughter who has built this castle, the one that you had expelled with the idle man from Baghdad

(88) nādāham, žāt əl-bəntu ža əṛ-ṛāẓəl, qāllu: ya šəddi ṣəlṭān, āna ma žəlt ma ʕarrəšṭṣ mʕāha li ma ʕṭītīkṣ l-māhar, tuwwa naʕṭīk əl-māhar wa tuwwa naʕməl əl-ʕarš (89) ʕamlu ʕarš kbīr u žābu ẓġāru wa qaʕdu fi-qṣaṛ

(88) The father summoned them, the daughter came together with the man, he said to him: I have not married her because I did not give you the mahr, now I will give you the mahr and now we will hold the wedding (89) They held a big wedding and had children and stayed in the castle.

3.0. Two Brothers

Speaker: Haya Mazouz, age: 76
Place and time of recording: Israel, March 2019

(1) žūž axwāt, wāḥad ẓāwāḷi u wāḥad məštaġni (2) hāk əl-ẓāwāḷi kull nhār xmīš yəmši l-xu yaʕṭī flūs (3) l-məštaġni ma ʕandūš wlād u l-ẓāwāli ʕandu yāsər ẓġār (4) l-ẓāwāli ma ʕandūš mākla yaʕṭi l-ẓġāru (5) ma ʕandūš xadma, ma ʕandūš ma yākəl (6) yəmši l-xu, xu məštaġni, ʕandu yāsər flūs, ma ʕandūš ẓġār (7) yaʕṭi nqūl ᴴᴱméa šékelᴴᴱ yaʕməl šəbbāt ntāʕu (8) baʕd yāmāt l-xu l-məštaġni mša l-blād, ṣfāṛ (9) u ža l-məṛtu u qālla: xūya kīf yži aʕṭī flūs bāš yaʕməl šəbbāt (10) qātlu: mlīḥ (11) hūwa ža, qālla: aʕṭīni flūs lə-šəbbāt (12) maṛṛa lūla ʕṭāthu, maṛṛa tānya ʕṭāthu, maṛṛa təlta qātlu: yaḷḷa, əmši l-ṛabbi yəṭləb yaʕṭīk, āna mūš ṛabbi tāʕk (13) aḥšəm u mša l-ḍāṛu yəbki, qām yəmši, yəmši l-ṛabbi (14) bda yəmši yəmši yəmši (15) šəyyəb ḍāṛu u mša (16) wṣəl əl-bḥar (17) qāllu əl-bḥar: wən māši ənti? (18) qāllu: āna māši l-ṛabbi yaʕṭīni bāš nwəkkəl ẓġāri (19) qāllu: yaʕyšək, kīf ənti māši l-ṛabbi, aṭlbu ʕalāš āna ma ʕandīš ḥūt fi-l-bḥar (20) qāllo: bāhi u mša (21) qābəl ṣəẓra kbīra tāʕ blāḥ (22) qʕad taḥta (23) žāt əl-nəxla qāltlu: wən māši? (24) qālla: māši l-ṛabbi nəṭlbu yaʕṭīni bāš nwəkkəl wlādi, ma ʕandīš nwəkkəlhəm qāʕdīn məžžʕānīn u məṛt xūya ḥašmətni

(1) (There were) two brothers, one poor and the other one rich (2) That poor one goes every Thursday to his brother so he gives him money (3) The rich one does not have children and the poor one has a lot of them (4) The poor one does not have food to feed his children (5) He does not have a job, he does not have anything to eat (6) He goes to his brother, he is rich but he does not have children (7) He gives him, let's say, one hundred shekel so he can have shabbat (8) After some days the rich brother went to another city, he travelled (9) And he came to his wife (before he left) and said to her: if my brother comes, give him money so he can have shabbat (10) She said to him: fine (11) He came and said to her: give me money for shabbat (12) The first time she gave him, the second time she gave him, the third time she said to him: go to God and ask him to give you (money), I am not your God (13) He got embarrassed and came back home crying, then he got up and went, he went to God (14) He set off and walked and walked (15) He left his house and walked away (16) He arrived at the sea (17) The sea said to him: where are you going? (18) He said to him: I am going to God so he gives me something and I feed my children (19) He said to him: please, once you go to God, ask him why I do not have fish in the sea (20) He said to him: fine, and left (21) He encountered a big fruit tree (22) He sat down beneath (23) A palm came and asked him: where are you going? (24) He said to her: I am going to God to ask him to give me (money) so I can feed my children, I have nothing to feed them, they are hungry (literally: they are sitting hungry) and my brother's wife embarrassed me

(25) qatlu: ʕayšək, kīf ənti māši l-ṛabbi, qūllu ʕalāš āna ma ʕandīš blāḫ (26) qālla: bāhi u mša (27) žālu ṛāẓəl ṭwīl, məžyān (28) qāllu: wən māši ənti? (29) qāllu: māši l-ṛabbi (30) ʕalāš? (31) qāllu: ma ʕandīš flūš, ma ʕandīš xadma u ma ʕandīš bāš nʕīš (32) qāllu: baṛṛa əmši, əržaʕ ʕal ətnītək (33) qāllu: ʕalāš? (34) qāllu: nšīt nqūllək (35) šnūwa, qāllu? (36) qāllu: əl-nəxla qāl ʕalāš ma ṭəḷḷaʕṣ ġəlla (37) qāllu: baṛṛa əmši aḥfər taḥta u tərqa bəṛma mʕabbya bi-lwīž, baṛṛa əmši l-ḍāṛək (38) hūwa mša wa ḥfər ḥfər ḥfər, u rqa bəṛma kbīra mʕabbya bi-lwīž, xdāha wa mša l-ḍāṛu (39) mša mən tāli əl-bḥar (40) wṣəl əl-ḍāṛ, farḥu bī zġāru, məṛtu l-kull (41) wən mšīt, wən hrabt, qāʕd yəbkīw (42) qāl: mšīt l-ṛabbi nžībəlkəm bāš tāklu (43) hūwa žāb lwīž wa dhəbb wa yḥabbu yūžnhu (44) mšāw lə ᴴᴱgisāᴴᴱ yžību məžān (45) mšāt əl-bənt, qātla: əl-bāḅa yḥabb, aʕṭīni l-məžān tāʕkəm (46) qātla: šnūwa žāblkəm ḅāḅākəm (47) qatla: ma naʕṛafš šnūwa žāb bənna āma ḥabb yūžən, hīya zġīra, ma təfhəmš (48) ʕṭātha əl-məžān u ḥaṭṭət ʕšəl (49) ᴴᴱazᴴᴱ hīya žābət hāk əl-məžān l-omha (50) u qaʕdu yūžnu šnūwa wa kəddāš žāb (51) wəžnu wa tṛəḍḍu əl-məžān (52) əl-məžān kīf yži, žāt tšūf əl-ᴴᴱgisāᴴᴱ, tərqa ᴴᴱyahalomᴴᴱ ləṣqat fi-l-hāk əl-ʕšəl (53) žāt l-ṛāẓəlha qātlo: xūk, mnīn žāb əl ᴴᴱyahalomímᴴᴱ, əl-flūš?

(25) She said to him: please, once you go to God, ask him why I do not have fruits (26) He said to her: fine, and left (27) A tall and handsome man came to him (28) He said to him: where are you going? (29) He said to him: I am going to God (30) Why? (31) He said to him: I do not have money, I do not have work, I do not have anything for a living (32) He said to him: go back on your way (33) He said to him: why? (34) He said to him: I forgot to ask you (35) What? he said (36) He said: why does the palm not have fruits? (37) He said to him: off you go, dig beneath it and you will find a coffer full of coins, then go home (38) He went and dug and dug and dug and found a huge coffer full of coins, he took it and went home (39) He went behind the sea (40) He arrived at home, his wife and children and everyone rejoiced (41) Where have you gone, where have you disappeared, they were weeping (42) He said: I went to God to bring you (food) so you can eat (43) He has brought coins and gold and they wanted to weigh it (44) They went to the sister-in-law to bring a scale (45) The daughter went and said: the father wants (a scale), give me your scale (46) She said to her: what did you father bring you? (47) She said to her: I do not know what he brought but he wants to weigh it; she is small, she does not understand (48) She gave her the scale and put some honey (49) So she brought the scale to the mother (50) So they started weighing what and how much he had brought (51) They weighed and returned the scale (52) When the scale was back (literally: when the scale came), the sister-in-law went to have a look and she found a diamond stuck on that honey (53) She went to her husband and said to him: where did your brother get diamonds, money?

(54) qālla: xallī, xallī, yʕīšu zġāru šnūwa tḥabbīhəm (55) qātlu: la! tuwwa nəmšī l-ḍāṛu u nšūf šnūwa ʕandu (56) mšāt l-ʕandum wa rqāt ṣaʕbu ḍāṛhum, labšu bāhi wa klāw bṛīma (57) qāllu: mnīn ža hāda? (58) qāllu: məṛtək qātli baṛṛa əmši l-ṛabbi, mšīt l-ṛabbi, ṛabbi ʕṭāni (59) qāllu: ᴴᴱlabriut šelxaᴴᴱ wa mšāw l-dāṛhəm (60) žāt l-məṛt əṛ-ṛāžəl qātlo: baṛṛa əmši l-ṛabbi žīb hāda (61) baṛṛa əmši əl-xūk wa žīb bənna (62) hūwa yxāf mənha, ža əl-xu qāllu: hažžni wən mšīt ənti (63) əl-xu nyāl mšāw əl-bḥar (64) ža əl-bḥar qāllu: šbīk ma qətləš ʕalāš ma tətlaʕlīš əl-ḥūt? (65) qāllu: əblaʕ wāḥəd wa ywəllələk əl-ḥūt (66) əl-bḥar blaʕ l-xu (67) qāl əl-məṛt xu: ʕal xāṭṛək hūwa mša, əl-bḥar bəlʕu (68) qaʕdət təbki.

(54) He said to her: leave him in peace, his children will live on it, what do you want from them? (55) She said to him: no! Now we will go to his house and we will see what he has (56) She went there and found out they had fixed the house, they are wearing fine clothes and ate their fill (57) He said to him: where has all this come from? (58) He said to him: your wife told me to go to God, so I went to God and God gave me (59) He said to him: to your health, and they went back home (60) The wife came to the man and said to him: go to God and bring this! (61) Go to your brother and bring us (the same as him) (62) He was afraid of her, he went to his brother and said to him: take me to the place where you have been to (63) The brother was naïve, so they went to the sea (64) He went to the sea and the sea asked him: why didn't you tell me why I do not have fish? (65) He said: swallow a man and you will birth fish (66) The sea swallowed his brother (67) He said to his sister-in-law: because of you he has gone, the sea swallowed him (68) And she wept.

4.0. Beauty of the Moon

Speaker: Haya Mazouz, age: 76
Place and time of recording: Israel, March 2019

(1) təmmaṣəlṭān wāḥəd (2) aṣ-ṣəlṭān hāda ʕandu bənt ʕžīža ʕalī yāsər (3) mәrtu mātət, xda mṛa oxra (4) əl-bənt təṭlaʕ baṛṛa u šəmš təzṛaq (5) mərt būha nəġrat mənna (6) žāt l-ṣānʕa, qatlo: aʕməlli mžīya, xūd əl-bənt u əmši qtəlha (7) əl-ṣānʕa xdāha l-ġāba āma kādu bāš yəqtəlha, qʕad mʕāha wa xəllha, raqdat (8) raqdat, xəllha u mša (9) mša l-ḍ-ḍāṛ, qālətlu: wīnhi? (10) qālla: qtəlta u ləwwaḥta (11) qātlu: ma tqūlš l-bābāha (12) əl-bāba ṣəlṭān ža: wīn bənti? (13) qatlu: ma naʕrafṣ, ṭalʕat ma žātš (14) ʕməl būlīṣīya, ʕbād fərkšu fi-l-blād əl-kulla, ma rqāwaṣ, əl-bənt rāḥət (15) hīya məškīna fāqət, ka-trūḥ fi-l-ġāba (16) bdāt təmši təmši təmši, rqāt ḍāṛ, əl-bāb ᴴᴱagolᴴᴱ zġīr, lāžma ṭṭabbaṣ bāš tədxəl (17) dəxlət (18) rqāt mṛa ʕamya (19) u tərḥa fi-l-qamḥ (20) hīya daxlət bi-škət, bi-škət bi-škət (21) rqāt bīt, əl-bīt fīha tbən (22) qaʕdət tərtāḥ (23) baʕd mərtāḥa hīya žʕāna, ʕaṭṣāna, ṭalʕat bi-škət (24) ṭəlʕat, dəxlət l-məṭbāx (25) dəxlət, tərqa šūbīrya kbīra (26) fīha šəbaʕ laḥmāt, šəbaʕ kaftāt wa kəṣkṣu (27) xdāt žnayyəb u klātu (28) žāw mən xadma əl-wlād, dəxlu u ṛqāw šūbīrya (29) l-oṃṃ ġalṭat əl-yūm, ma tšūfəš (30) ʕamlət bərq šətta

(1) There was a sultan (2) This sultan had a daughter who was very dear to him (3) His wife had died and he married another woman (4) The daughter would go out and the sun would shine (5) The step-mother was jealous about her (6) She went to the servant and said to her: do me a favour, take the girl, go and kill her (7) The servant took her to the forest but it was too painful to kill her (literally: it hurt him to kill her), he sat down with her and left her, she fell asleep (8) As she fell asleep, he left her and went away (9) He went back home and she asked him: where is she? (10) He answered: I killed her and threw away (the corpse) (11) She said to him: do not say anything to her father (12) The father sultan came: where is my daughter? (13) She said to him: I do not know, she left and has not come back (14) They called the police, people were looking for her all over the entire city but did not find her, the daughter is gone (15) The poor girl woke up and started walking in the forest (16) She started walking, she walked, and walked, and found a cottage with small and round door, she had to lean down to enter (17) She went in (18) She found a blind woman (19) She was grinding wheat (20) She went in silently (21) She found a room and in the room, there was a straw (22) She sat down to have some rest (23) Afterwards she was hungry and thirsty, she went out silently (24) She went out and went to the kitchen (25) She entered and found a big bowl (26) In the bowl there were seven pieces of meat, seven meatballs and cuscus (27) She took one portion and ate it (28) Boys came back from work, entered and found the bowl (29) The mother made a mistake today, she did not see (30) She made only six (portions)

(31) qəṣmu mʕa baʕdhəm, klāw u šətku (32) mən ġadwa r̥qāw ᴴᴱotaᴴᴱ ḥkāya, kīf kīf (33) mən baʕd ġadwa kīf kīf (34) qālla: əmma šbīk, ʕalāš taʕmli bərq šətta mūš šəbʕa? wāḥda nāqṣa (35) qātlu: wlīdāti, āna kān naʕməlkəm kīf kīf, kīf dīma (36) fahmu təmma wāḥəd hūni (37) qāllu: škūn li qāʕəd mxabbi? kān wəld ywəlli xūna u kān bənt twəlli axtna wa kān ʕayša twəlli mʕāna (38) hīya ṭəlʕat, əd-dār̥ kulla wəllāt ḍuww (39) qālūla: žīn əl-kulla wa ənti mətxabbya? ənti mən əl-yūm twəlli əxtna (40) farḥu bīha farḥa kbīra (41) u bdāt tnəḍḍəf əd-dār̥, tnaḥḥi l-ʕankbūt u ṭṭayyəb mʕa ḥmāta wa kull brīma (42) əd-dār̥ kulla tabrəq, wa hīya kulla tabrəq, wa yḥabbūha yāsər, wa əl-ḥāma tḥabbha yāsər, wa hīya ʕāyša fi-l-xīr (43) tʕaddu yāmāt, əl-wəld lə-kbīr ᴴᴱhexlítᴴᴱ yʕarrəš ʕaləya (44) ʕamlu ʕarš (45) baʕd yāmāt, hīya žābət wəld (46) yḥalləwha yāsər (47) ža xarrāž, əl-ḥāma qāltla: barr̥i barr̥i əmši šwīya, əṣr̥īlīk ḥwāyəž (48) ḥənna, xrəž, qərfa, šwāk, u qammūn, u bxūr (49) hīya žābətlu ġarbān, ʕabbəthu bi-l-qamḥ (50) hūwa xda əl-qamḥ wa hīya xdāt ḥwāyəž ntāha u dəxlət l-əd-dār̥ (51) dəxlət l-əd-dār̥, taʕməl l-ḥənna, taʕžən fīha, u əl-bxūr tbaxxar (52) wa hūwa mša mən ẓənqa l-ẓənqa (53) wṣəl l-əd-dār̥ mər̥t būha (54) hūwa qālla: āna xarrāž, ṭaḷʕat mər̥t būha

(31) They divided the food between them, ate and did not say anything (32) The next day the same story (33) Also in two days the same (34) He said to her: mother, what is the matter with you? Why are you cooking only six portions and not seven? One is missing (35) She said to him: O my children, I have been cooking for you exactly the same portions, as always (36) They realised that someone was there (37) They said: who is the person who is hiding? If it is a boy, he will be our brother, if it is a girl, she will be our sister, and if it is an animal, it will stay with us (38) She went out and the entire house turned into light (39) They said to her: all this beauty and you are hiding? from now on you will be our sister (40) They rejoiced over her (41) She started cleaning the house, removing spiders, cooking with the mother and everything was fine (42) The entire house was full of shine, she by herself was shining and they loved her a lot and the mother loved her a lot and she was living happily (43) After some days the eldest son decided to marry her (44) A few days later they held the wedding (45) After some time she gave birth to a boy (46) They were spoiling her a lot (47) A merchant came and the mother said to her: go for a bit and buy something for yourself (48) Henna, corals, spices, tooth medicine, cinnamon, and hair conditioner (49) She brought him (in return) a strainer and filled it with wheat (50) He took the wheat, she took her things and went home (51) She entered the house, she made henna, she greased it, and she put the incense on the charcoal (52) And the merchant went from alley to alley (53) He arrived at her stepmother's house (54) He said to her: I am a merchant, and she went out of her home

(55) hīya xdāt ḥwāyəž li ḥabbət (56) u žābətlo kəmša qṣūr ṛmān (57) qālla: ma žībtīli? žībha wəlla žībət žīn əl-gumra! (58) qātlu: qūl šna qəlt maṛṛa tānya (59) qālla: žīn əl-gumra! (60) qātlu: žīn əl-gumra ʕāyša? (61) qālla: ʕāyša, u ʕaršət u ʕanda wlād, u ʕāyša fi-xyāṛ əl-xīr (62) qātlu: kīfāš?! həžžni! (63) dəxlət l-əḍ-ḍāṛ, žābət fəḷḷāya u qumbra (64) qəṛṣathəm fi ᴴᴱnyarᴴᴱ u ṭalʕat mʕam u mšāt l-əḍ-ḍāṛ žīn əl-gumra (65) qātla: žīn əl-gumra? (66) tbawšu, u farḥu u yədwīw, farḥat məṛt būha li žāt (67) qātla: šna³ xdīt mən əl-xarrāž? (68) qātla: xdīt ḥənna l-ṣaʕri (69) qatla: əži, naʕməl ṣaʕrək, naʕməl bxūr (70) ṭaḷḷʕat əl-fəḷḷāya wa l-fəḷḷāya fīha šəmm, ḥaṭṭətəlha fi-ṣaʕrha wa hīya mātət, āma hīya ma mātətš (71) xdīt əl-wəld, ləbšətlo əl-qumbra wa ᴴᴱgamᴴᴱ hūwa məyyət (72) nādāta xmāta: žīn əl-gumra, žīn əl-gumra, ma wāžbətš, la əl-wəld yəbki, la l-mṛa tətkəlləm (73) ma ʕarfətš škūn ža ʕanda (74) nādāt, nādāt, mšāt l-ʕanda, rqātha məyyta (75) qaʕdət təbki (76) ḥatt žāw l-wlād mən xadma fi-ʕašīya (77) qālət: šnūwa nqūlkəm, gumra mātət, šmaʕt tədwi wāḥda u baʕd dənya šəktət wa rqītha məyyta (78) rqāwha mləwwḥa wa bdāw yəbkīw (79) mūš lāžəm nəḍfnūha

---

³ This is a truncated version of *šnūwa*.

(55) She took the things that she liked (56) She brought him a handful of pomegranate peels (57) He said to her: what did you bring me? It does not compare to what žīn əlgumra brought me! (58) She said to him: say again what you just said (59) He said to her: žīn əlgumra! (60) She said to him: žīn əlgumra is alive? (61) He said to her: she is alive and she got married and she has children and she lives the happiest life (62) She said to him: how come?! (63) She went home and took a comb and a small shirt (64) She wrapped them in paper and went to the house of žīn əlgumra (65) She said to her: žīn əlgumra? (66) They kissed, rejoiced and chatted, the stepmother was happy that she came (67) She asked her: what did you take from the merchant? (68) She answered: I have taken henna for my hair (69) She said to her: bring it, we will take care of your hair and we will light the incense (70) She took out the comb and the comb had poison on it, she put it on her hair and she died, but she did not die in fact (71) She took the child and put the shirt on him and he died as well (72) The mother would call her, she called her: žīn əlgumra, žīn əlgumra, but she did not answer, nor did the child cry, nor did the woman talk (73) She did not understand who had come to her (74) She called her and called her, she went to her and found her dead (75) She sat down and wept (76) Until her sons came back from work in the evening (77) What can I say, žīn əlgumra is dead, I heard a woman talking and then everything became silent and I found her dead (78) They found her laid on the floor and started crying (79) We cannot bury her

(80) ʕandəm žməll, ṛəbṭūha bi-l-ṣəndūq, hīya u wəldha, ḥaṭṭūha ʕal žməll u qāllu: ašmaʕ, ma tūqaf kān yqūlūlək əžžaḥ žālək (81) mša əž-žməl u ṛa təmma wāḥəd, ʕandu šəbʕa nša (82) qʕad mʕam u yədwi mʕam (83) ṭalʕatlo kəlma əžžaḥ žālək (84) əž-žməl brəqq u qʕad (85) əṛ-ṛāzəl ṭlaʕ u rqa žməl ʕalī ṣəndūq kbīr (86) škūn bʕaṭ žməl bi-l-ṣəndūq? (87) xda əṣ-ṣəndūq, ḥallu, u dəxxəlu fi-l-bīt (88) yəqʕad mʕāha, yəbki, yəbki, yəbki (89) ṣəkkər əl-bīt bi-l-məftāḥ u ṭlaʕ (90) əl-nās qāllu: šnu ʕandu fi-l-bīt, bda yəbki, ṭlaʕ ʕaynīn dəmʕīn ḥamrīn (91) hūwa mša əl-xadma wa humma qālu: lāžəm nšūfu šnūwa ʕandu fi-l-bīt (92) ḥallu əl-bīt ʕandum məftāḥ u rqāw əṣ-ṣəndūq (93) ḥallu əṣ-ṣəndūq u šāfu əl-mṛa, ᴴᴱbūbaᴴᴱ u dənya kull twəlli ḍuww (94) kīfāš ma yəbkīš hāda, humma qaʕdu u yəbkīw (95) wāḥda qālət: nḥabb mākla mən yəddəyha (96) oxra məššət fi-ṣaʕra u žāt yədda fi-fəḷḷāya, ḥaṭṭət yəddha fi-fəḷḷāya u hīya fāqət (97) qātla: mən aḥyāni ṛāḍət fia əṛ-rūḥ (98) əl-mṛa ʕarfat šnūwa ʕamlət (99) žāt əl-wəld, naḥḥātlo qumbra (100) əl-wəld bda yəbki (101) žābūla mākla tākəl (102) qāllu: əšmʕu tuwwa, hūwa, kānət mīta hūwa bāš ymūt ʕaləya, kān yži yərqa ʕāyša, mšāt ʕaləyha (103) daxxəlūha fə-ṣ-ṣəndūq fīšʕa (104) u ḥaṭṭūha ʕal žməll (105) ʕamlu hāk, xdāwha, ṛəbṭūha fi-l-žməl, ṛəbṭūha bi-l-ḥbəl u ḥaṭṭūha fi-l-qāʕda (106) əl-wəld fi-yəddha

(80) They had a camel, they put her in a box, her and her child, they put them on the camel and said to him: listen, you will not stop until someone tells you 'raise your tail' (81) The camel walked and saw a man who had seven women (82) He sat down and chatted with them (83) Someone said by accident 'raise your tail' (84) The camel kneeled and sat down (85) The man came out and found the camel with a big box on it (86) Who has sent a camel with a box? (87) He took the box, opened it and found inside the girl (88) He sat down with her and wept (89) He locked the room and left (90) The women said: what does he have in the house? He had been crying, then left with red eyes full of tears (91) He left to work and they said: we must see what he keeps in his room (92) As they had the key, they opened the room and found the box (93) They opened the box and found the woman, a doll, filling the entire world with her light (94) How would he not cry? They sat down and wept (95) One of them said: I would like to eat from her hands (96) The other one petted her hair and her hand got to the comb, she put her hand on the comb and the woman woke up (97) She said: the one who animates me brought me back my spirit (98) The woman already knew what had been done (99) She went to the child and took off the shirt (100) The child started crying (101) They brought her food (102) They said: listen now, he, when she was dead, was ready to die for her, so now if he comes back and finds her alive, she will be in real trouble (103) They put her back in the box at once (104) And they put her on the camel (105) This is what they did, they took her, they bound her to the camel, they bound her by a rope and they put her seated (106) The child in her hands

(107) u ṛəbṭu əṣ-ṣəndūq u qāllu l-ž-žməl: baṛṛa, həžžha l-ḍāṛa (108) əl-žməl mša (109) ʕašīya, humma, əl-wlād ka-yāklu wa šāfu əž-žməl ža (110) rqāw hīya qāʕda wa əl-wəld fi-yədda (111) farḥu farḥa kbīra (112) dəxlu lə-ḍ-ḍāṛ, qālūla: aḥkīna šnūwa žāha u šnūwa ʕamlət fīha məṛt būya (113) hīya bdāt tfīq šwīya f-əḍ-ḍāṛ, bəddlət ḥwayžātha u ṣawwbat rūḥa u mšāt l-əšfīšāri, srīt šəmm, xdīt u mšāt l-məṛt būha (114) aaa žīn əl-gumra, bāšu taʕnəqu (115) ma təṭlaʕīš mən hūni kan ma ṭaftṛi (116) hīya mšāt ṭṭəyyəb wa ʕamlət kəškṣu u ḥaṭṭətla šəmm fi-l-žnəbb ntāʕ bənt (117) əl-bənt qālətla: ma žəbtīš l-ma? (118) waqt l-oṃṃa kānət fi-l-kūžīna əl-bənt ḥaṭṭətla šəmm wa l-oṃṃa ma ʕarfətš (119) qālətla: kūl ənti lūla, ənti ḍʕāfa (120) əl-məṛt qālətla: la,la, ənti kbīra (121) l-əkbīra taʕṛəf li ma ʕandhaš šəmm wa əẓ-ẓġīra taʕṛəf li ḥaṭṭətla (122) l-əkbīra xdāt əmġārfa lūla, fīšʕa mātət (123) wəžra əl-kull žāw (124) aš təmma, aš təmma, məṛt bāba mātət (125) nādāw əṣ-ṣəlṭān mən maḥkma, hūwa ža (126) qālla šnu təmmāš? kīfāš? (127) qātlo: bāba taʕṛəf šnu ʕamlətli? (128) ḥkātlo əl-kull (129) qālla: tuwwa təštāhəl (130) ʕanəqa u bāša, fraḥ bāya (131) hīya žābət ṛāẓəlha u xwātu u oṃṃu u šəknu ʕand əṣ-ṣəlṭān u ʕayšu ʕāyša bāhya.

(107) They bound the box and said to the camel: off you go, take her home (108) The camel left (109) In the evening, they, the boys, were eating and saw the camel coming (110) They found her seated with the child in her hands (111) They rejoiced (112) They went home and said to her: tell us what happened to you and what the step-mother did to you (113) She started recovering at home, she changed her clothes, got ready, left and went to the pharmacy, she bought a poisonous substance and went to the step-mother's house (114) O žīn əlgumra, they kissed and hugged (115) You will not leave this place until you eat (116) She went to cook, prepared couscous and put poison on the daughter's side (117) The daughter said to her: will you not bring water? (118) While the mother was in the kitchen, the daughter put poison [in the mother's food], but the mother did not know that (119) She said to her: you eat first, you are so skinny (120) The daughter answered: no, no, you are older (121) The old one knew she did not have any poison and the young one knew she did give her poison (122) The old one took one spoon and died at once (123) All the neighbours came (124) What is the matter? What is the matter? The stepmother has died (125) They called the sultan from the court, he came (126) He said to her: what is the matter? How? (127) She said to him: father do you know what she did to me? (128) She told him everything (129) He said to her: now you deserve (compensation) (130) He hugged her and kissed her, he rejoiced with her (131) She brought her husband and his brothers, and the mother and they lived all together with sultan happily ever after.

5.0. The Tale of the Old Woman

Speaker: Haya Mazouz, age: 76
Place and time of recording: Israel, March 2019

(1) ᴴᴱzūgᴴᴱ yḥabbu baʕdhəm yāsər, ʕarršu, u ma ṭalʕūš mən əd-dāṛ, mən əl-ʕarš ṣahrīn (2) u ḅāḅa ʕandu šəlha (3) hāda dīma yži yʕāwnu u ybīʕu əš-šəlha (4) u ḅāḅa yəbʕaṭlo žwābāt: ya wəldi əži ʕāwni, taʕddāw ṣahrīn, taʕddāw tlāta, u ma žītš tʕāwni (5) ṣahrīn ma žāš, ma ywāžbūš (6) hīya qāmət ənnhāṛ tnəddəf əd-dāṛ (7) məṛtu ḥallət zaṛḅīya u tərqa taḥta žwābāt u qrātham (8) qātlu: šbīk ḅāḅak yəbʕaṭlək kull məṛṛa žwāb, ma trəddluṣ, ma twāžbūš (9) ʕandu šəlha, šəlha wāqfa, bəṛṛa əmši ʕāwnu! (10) ʕandək əl-ḥaqq li ṣahrīn ma mšītš, nəmšīlo (11) lbəš bāhi, u ʕṭātlu mākla u ṭlaʕ (12) waqfət fi-l-balkūn, fi-š-šəbbīk (13) tʕadda wəld ṣəlṭān (14) hūwa ṛāha wa ṭāḥ ʕal ᴴᴱmoxoᴴᴱ (15) mša l-əd-dāṛ mṛīḍ (16) mša l-wāḥda ʕažūža u qālla: aʕmlīli mžīya, əmšī u əxtḅīha (17) qātlu: ya wəldi, hīya mʕarrša b-ṛāzəlha, kīfāš nəmši naxtəḅha (18) bəṛṛa əmši, āna naʕṭīk flūš li tḥabbi (19) l-ʕažūža ma ʕandhaš flūš, hīya mšāt (20) hīya mšāt, ḍaṛbət ʕal bāb qātla: žīt naxtḅək (21) qāltla: ma taḥšmīš? āna mʕarrša b-ṛāzli! (22) ṭayyḥatha mən drūž (23) qātla: hīya mʕarrša, ʕanda ṛāzəlha, šnūwa naʕməllək (24) qālla: bəṛṛa ṛtāḥi wa nšūfu šnūwa naʕmlu

(1) A couple loved each other a lot, they got married and for two months since the wedding have not left their home (2) And the father has stock [to sell] (3) This man always goes to help him sell the stock (4) And the father sends him letters: my son, come and help me, two, three months have passed and you did not come to help me (5) Two months he did not come, did not answer (6) One day she decided (literally: she stood up) to clean the house (7) The wife lifted the carpet and found beneath the letters and read them (8) She said to him: what is the matter with you? Your father sends every day a letter and you do not get back to him, do not answer (9) He has got stock, the stock is stopped, off you go and help him (10) You are right that I have not gone to him for two months, I will go to him now (11) He dressed up properly, she gave him food and he left (12) She was standing on the balcony in the window (13) The son of the sultan was passing by (14) He saw her and lost his mind (15) He came back home sick (16) He went to an old woman and said to her: please do me a favour, go and ask her for her hand (17) She said to him: my child, she is married to her husband, how will I go to ask her hand for you? (18) Please go, I will give you money, whatever you want (19) As the old woman did not have money, she went (20) She went, knocked on the door and said to her: I came to ask for your hand (21) She said to her: are you not ashamed?! I am married to my husband (22) She pushed her from the stairs (23) She said to him: she is married, she has a man, how can I help? (24) He said to her: take a rest and we will see what we will do

(25) baʕd yāmāt hūwa ža wa qālla: baṛṛa əmši ma taʕməllək ḥatta šəyy wa aṭəlbi mənna (26) mšāt, qālla: maṛṛa oxra žīti, šnu thabbi ʕandi? (27) qātla: šəmʕi, əṭləbi ḥwāyž ṣʕāḫ, yšəyyəbni u yšəyybək (28) qātla: šnūwa nqūllu? (29) qātla: qūlīlu yaʕməlli dāmūš, nəṭlʕa mən ḍāṛi bāš ma yšūfni ḥadd u nži l-ʕandu (30) u yaʕməlli qṣaṛṛ: ʕažnāthu hənna u ḥzārthu dhəb, u žābya bi-l-ḥūt u waṛd u moḇīlya bāya, zṛābi (31) wəṣlət, qātlu: šnūwa nqūllək, ʕandi bšāra bāhya: thəbb qṣaṛ u ʕažna hənna, nwāṛ u waṛd u žābya bi-l-ḥūt (32) qālla: ḇṛīma, bāhi (33) l-ʕažūža hablət, ḫāža ṣāyba wa hūwa qāl bāhi? hīya štaʕžbət, ma amnətš (34) mšāt l-mṛa qātla: hūwa ṛḍa (35) qātla: ṛḍa? ṛḍa (36) tʕadda waqt wa hūwa ža l-ʕažūža qālla: qūllīla kull šəyy ḥāḍaṛ (37) hīya štaʕžbət, ḥabbət tšūf kīfāš ʕamlūha (38) dəxlət l-dāmūš wa hūwa mṛīḍ (39) qālla: əzṛi, əzṛi, dawwīni, bnītlək əqqṣaṛ bla mənha, ḥzārthu dhəb wa ʕažnāthu hənna (40) hīya habṭət dəṛža tālya u qālətlo: yəšhdu ʕalīya ənžūm u šma li āna žītək, kān štənnītni tqīqa wa āna dawwītək (41) hīya wəṣlət wa hūwa mīt (42) ḥaṭṭətlo bi-l-ṣəndūq u ʕabbāthu bi-l-məlḥ u kull yūm thall əṣ-ṣəndūq wa təbki (43) u təṭlʕa əl-fūq, l-ḥmāta u tqūlla: šbīk ḍʕāfīti, šbīk mūš ka-tākli, aššbīk təbkīy

(25) After some days he came again and said to her: please go and ask for her hand, she will not do anything to you (26) She went and the woman said to her: you came again? What do you want from me? (27) She said to her: listen, ask impossible things, he will leave you and me in peace (28) She said to her: what am I supposed to tell him? (29) Tell him: tell him to make a channel, I will leave my home (through the channel) so no one can see me and I will go to him (30) And he will build me a castle, its mortar of henna and its bricks of gold, and a pool with fish and roses and nice furniture, carpets (31) She came back and said to him: what can I say, I have good news: she wants a castle with mortar of henna, flowers and roses and a pool of fish (32) He said to her: excellent (33) The old woman lost her mind, such a difficult thing and he said yes? She was shocked, and did not believe it (34) She went to the woman and said to her: he agreed (35) She said to her: agreed? Agreed (36) After some time he went to the old woman and said to her: tell her that everything is ready (37) She was surprised, and went down to see how he did that (38) She entered the channel and found him ill (39) He said to her: come and cure me, I have built you a castle without regrets, its bricks of gold and its mortar henna (40) She went down long stairs and said to him: my witnesses the moon, the stars and the sky that I have come, if you had waited for me one minute more, I would have cured you (41) She arrived and he died (42) She put him in a coffin and filled it with salt and she would open the coffin every day and cry (43) And she would go upstairs and her step-mother would say: how come you have become so slim, you are not eating, why are you crying?

(44) əl-ḥāma qālətla: wīn mšīti, wīn mšīti, ʕalāš ʕīnīk ḥamrīn? (45) ma twāžbāš (46) kull yūm hīya tġīb, təbki, u tži ʕīna nəfxīn (47) ər-ṛāẓəl ža, hūwa bāʕ šəlha u ʕāwən bu (48) ᴴᴱodᴴᴱ šār, ᴴᴱodᴴᴱ ṣahrīn kīf kīf, hīya təmši, təbki u tətḷaʕ (49) žāt om̭m̭u u qātlu: šūf, āna ma naʕrafš šnūwa ʕandha, tġīb šāʕa šāʕtīn u tži (50) ər-ṛāẓəl tġaṣṣaṣ u qāl: yaḷḷa, həžžu ʕaləya mən hunni! (51) hīya mšāt l-ġādi, ʕandha l-mākla, ʕanda kull šəyy, qaʕdət (52) dəxlət l-hāk əḍ-ḍāṛ qaʕdət təbki ʕal əṛ-ṛāẓəl (53) fi-l-lāxər hīya qālət: xālaṣ! (54) ləbšət ḥwāyž taʕ ṛāẓəl, u taʕṛəf ṛāẓəlha qāʕəd fi-l-qahwa (55) ʕamǝlt rūḥa ṛāẓəl, təṣṛəb qāhwa, təṣṛəb te (56) u tṣaḥbat mʕā (57) nhār wāḥəd qātlu: əži l-ḍāṛi (58) ža mʕāha (59) əhbəl ʕal əḍ-ḍāṛ (60) byūt, dhəbb, mobīlya mūš kīf tāʕ kull, zṛābi (61) wa hūwa ṛa žābya mʕa ḥūtāt (62) qālla: aʕṭīni žūž ḥūtāt (63) qālətlu: šūf, naʕṭīk žūž ḥūtāt, naʕṭīk arbaʕ, əṣ-ṣāṛṭ tžībli om̭mək tərqəd mʕāya (64) qālla: ḥāḍar (65) hūwa tḷab žūž ḥūtāt wa hīya ʕṭātlu arbaʕ (66) žābətlo ṣṭaḷḷ, ḥaṭṭətlu arbaʕ, ḥaṭṭətlo l-ma (67) u ža l-om̭m̭u wa qālla: bəṛṛa əmši mʕāya l-ṣāḥbi (68) om̭m̭u žāt mʕāu u šāfət əḍ-ḍāṛ brīma, mūš kīf tāʕ l-ʕbād (69) qaʕdət l-ōm̭, ṣaṛbu qahwa (70) əbn ʕməl laʕba u hrab (71) qātla: wīnhu wəldi? (72) kīfāš mša u xallāni? xallāni mʕa ṛāẓəl? (73) l-ōm̭ tġaṣṣaṭ u tnəfṛž

(44) Her stepmother said to her: where did you go? Where did you go? Why are your eyes red? (45) She would not respond (46) Every day she would disappear, cry and come back with swollen eyes (47) The husband came back, he sold the stock and helped his father (48) Another month, another two months, the same, she would go, cry and leave (49) His mother came and said: look, I do not know what is wrong with her, she disappears for one hour or two and comes back (50) The man got angry and said to her: take her from here! (51) She goes there, she has there food, she has there everything, she sits down (52) She goes into that house, sits down and cries over the man (53) Finally she said: enough! (54) She got dressed as a man and noticed that her husband is sitting in the café (55) She dressed up as a man, having coffee, having tea (56) And she made friends with him (57) One day she said to him: come to my home (58) He went with her (59) He lost his mind with the house (60) Rooms, gold, furniture, carpets (61) And he saw a pool with fish (62) He said to her: give me two fish (63) She said to him: look, I will give you two fish, I will give you even four, on condition that you bring your mother so I can sleep with her (64) He said to her: settled (65) He asked her for two fish and she gave him four (66) She brought him a bucket and put some water [in it] (67) And he went to his mother and said to her: come with me to my friend (68) His mother came with him and saw a marvellous house, not like one of ordinary people (69) The mother sat down, they had some coffee (70) The son played a trick and escaped (71) She said: where is my son? (72) How come he left leaving me with a man? (73) The mother got upset and nervous

(74) qālətla: ma txāfiṣ, āna mūš ṛāẓəl, āna mṛa (75) kīfāš?! (76) qātla: štənni šwīya u tšūfi (77) hīya dəxlət l-ḍ-ḍāṛ wa ləbšət ḥwāyəž ntāḥḥa (78) qatla: šnūwa ənti ᴴᴱkəllāᴴᴱ ntʕāy? (79) qātla: ēy (80) qatla: šūfi, wəldək bāʕ oṃṃu ʕal žūž ḥūtāt (81) əl-bənt ḥkātla əl-aḥkāya ntāḥḥa ʕal ʕažūža li žātha, šnūwa li ṣṛāla (82) qālətla ḥwāyəž ṣʕāb wa hūwa ʕaməlhəm, kīfāš ma nəmši nšūf (83) āna ma wṣəlt hūwa māt (84) xdīt fi-qalbi, ṣaxxafni, qʕadt nəbki (85) qālətla: wəldək ʕal žūž ḥūtāt xalla oṃṃu (86) mən ġadwa əṛ-ṛāẓəl ža bāš yāxəd oṃṃu (87) hīya qātlo: xallītni mʕa ṛāẓəl?! ma taḥšəmš?! (88) āma ʕandək məžžāl, hīya məṛtək, hūwa fraḥ wa ʕayšu fi-l-xīr.

(74) She said to her: fear not, I am not a man, I am a woman (75) How come?! (76) She said to her: wait a minute and you will see (77) She went to her room and put on her regular clothes (78) She said to her: how come? Are you my daughter-in-law? (79) She said to her: yes (80) She said to her: look, your son sold his mother for two fish (81) The daughter told her the story about the old woman who came to her and what happened to her (82) She said to her: (I had asked) hard things and he did them, how I would not go and see them? (83) I barely arrived and he died (84) I took it to my heart, I felt pity, I would sit and cry (85) She said to her: your son for two fish left his mother (86) The next day the man came to pick up his mother (87) She said to him: did you leave me with a man?! Are you not ashamed?! (88) But you are lucky, she is your wife, he rejoiced and they lived happily.

6.0. Ẓaʕfrāna

Speaker: Haya Mazouz, age: 76
Place and time of recording: Israel, March 2019

(1) təmma wāḥəd ṣəlṭān wa ʕandu wəld (2) l-wəld hāda, kull mərra yāxəd əmṛa, bənt, žəmaʕ yəqʕad mʕā u yšəyyəbha (3) kānət wāḥda mṛa, kānət ʕandha bənt wa əl-bənt ʕažīža ʕalīya yāsər, šəmmātha ẓaʕfrāna (4) oṃṃha thəžža l-škūla u tžībha mən škūla (5) ẓaʕfrāna ya bənti, tnādha (6) wəld əṣ-ṣəlṭān hūwa šmaʕ ẓaʕfrāna (7) mša ṭlabha mən oṃṃa wa ʕarrəš mʕā (8) qʕad mʕā žəmaʕ u šəyyəbha l-oṃṃha, yaḷḷa (9) u kull mərra yāxəd bənt u yləwwḥa (10) ẓaʕfrāna, waqt hūwa xdāha, ʕṭāla bəžawonk (11) ʕṭāla wa qālla: kān tžībi bənt, ḥaṭṭīha fi-drāʕ, u kān tžībi wəld, ḥaṭṭīlo fi-fxādu (12) hīya žābət wəld, ḥaṭṭətlo bəžawonk ʕal fxəddu (13) əl-wəld kbar wa yəmši l-škūla (14) təmma wāḥad, yḥabb yəmši l-ḥažž wa ʕandu bənt (15) hūwa mša l-məḍḍəb wa ʕṭāw ṣəndūq mʕa l-ḥwāyž ntāʕu (16) mša l-ʕandu, qāllu: āna māši l-ḥažž, naʕṭīk bənti ṛədd bālək ʕaləya, u naʕṭīk əṣ-ṣəndūq (17) kīf nži nqūllək (18) qāllu: bāhi (19) hādāk mša l-ḥažž u l-āxər xda əl-bənt (20) qālla: ʕarrši mʕāya! (21) ma ḥabbətš wa hūwa ṣakkərha fi-l-ḥīṭ (22) əṛ-ṛāẓəl ržaʕ wa qāllu: aʕṭīni bənti wa aʕṭīni əṣ-ṣəndūq (23) qāllu: la naʕrfək, u la žītni, u la šəftək (24) hūwa bda yəbki, aʕṭīni bərq əl-bənt, qāllu: ma ʕandīš (25) wa hāk əl-bənt yaʕṭīla xabž u žītūn u yəxallīya fi-l-ḥīṭ (26) u yqūlla: ʕarrši mʕāya, wa tqūllu: ma, wa hūwa yqaʕʕadha (27) kull yūm kīf kīf

(1) There is a sultan and he has a son (2) This son, each time he takes a woman, girl, he spends with her one week and leaves her (3) There was a woman and she had a daughter who was very dear to her, her name was Zʕafrāna (4) The mother would walk her to school and back (5) Zʕafrāna, my daughter, she would call her (6) The son of the sultan heard Zʕafrāna (7) He went to the mother to ask for her hand and he married her (8) He spent one week with her and left her with the mother (9) And each time he would take a girl and leave her (10) When he got engaged to Zaʕfrāna, he gave her a bracelet (11) He gave it to her and said to her: if you give birth to a girl, put this bracelet on her arm, and if you give birth to a son, put it on his shin (12) So she gave birth to a son and put the bracelet on his shin (13) The son grew up and went to school (14) There was a man, he wanted to go to Mecca and he had a daughter (15) He went to a trustee and gave him a box with his belongings (16) He went to him and said to him: I am going to Mecca, please pay attention to my daughter and I am giving you the box (17) When I get back I will tell you (18) He said to him: fine (19) He went to Mecca and the other took the girl (20) He said to her: marry me! (21) She did not want to and he locked her in a wall (22) He came back and said to him: give me my daughter and the box back (23) He answered: I do not know you, you have never come to me and I have never seen you! (24) He started crying, give me just my daughter, and he replied: I do not have her (25) And he would give to the daughter bread and olives and leave her in the wall (26) And he would tell her: marry me, and when she replied: no, he would make her stay (in the wall) (27) Every day the same

(28) əl-bāba mša l-ḥākəm (29) qāllu: ʕandək šhūd? (30) qāllu: la (31) qāllu: kīfāš taʕṭi əṣ-ṣəndūq u bəntək bla šhūd? (32) qāllu: ma ʕrafṭṣ (33) ma nnəžmu naʕmlu šəy, ma ʕanduš šhūd (34) əš-šībāni, kādu yāsər ʕal bəntu, yāxəd ʕbar, məllāha bi-l-ma, ḥaṭṭu ʕala kətfu wa yaʕṭi l-zġār fi-škūla yəṣṛəbu l-ma (35) u qāllhəm: ʕal ktāfha ʕawīša bnīti, bəntu šma ʕawīša (36) ža əl-wəld ẓaʕfrāna (37) hādāk əl-wəld fāyq, ʕandu ʕqəl bāhi (38) əl-mīstru ma žāš (39) qāllu: āna ṣəlṭān, nəmši wa nṭallaʕ hāk əṛ-ṛāẓəl (40) bāba əl-wəld, əṣ-ṣəlṭān mʕa wžīru yaʕmlu ḍūra fi-l-blād wa šāfu wəld zġīr wa qālləm: āna naḥkəm! (41) əl-mīstru ža wa qāllum: yaḷḷa, ədxlu l-bīt (42) əṣ-ṣəlṭān qāl l-wəld: əži l-hūni (43) qāllu: šnūwa tḥabb ʕandi? (44) qāllu: qūlli kīfāš taḥqəm bāš ṭṭəḷḷʕa haqq ntaʕ ṛāẓəl (45) qāllu: ma nqūllək kān ma taʕṭīni ət-tāž (46) wəld zġīr yaḥkəm ʕalīna f-ət-tāž (47) qālla: bāhi (48) xūdu, dəxxəlu l-ḥammām, ʕawwmu, bədllūlu wa ḥaṭṭu ət-tažž (49) fi-l-ḥammām rqāw fi-fxəddu əl-bəžawonk (50) qallūlo: ya šəddi ṣəlṭān, hāda wəldu (51) ḥaṭṭlu tažž u qāllu: qūlli šnūwa əl-əḥkūm ntāʕk, šnūwa naʕmlu tuwwa? (52) qāllu: šūf, nḥabb mīya ʕaškri, nəbʕaṭəm u yfərkšu əḍ-ḍār kulla rəkna rəkna (53) baʕṭu əl-ʕāškər, dəxlu wa fərkšu rəkna rəkna (54) wa yəšməʕu bənt: aa... aa...

(28) The father went to the judge (29) He said to him: do you have witnesses? (30) He replied: no (31) He said: how did you give your daughter and the box without witnesses? (32) He said: I do not know (33) We cannot do anything, he does not have witnesses (34) The old man felt pity for her, he took a jug, filled it with water, put it on his shoulders and shared out the water for children in the school (35) And he would say: on the shoulders of my daughter ʕawīša, his daughter's name is ʕawīša (36) The son of Zʕafrāna came (37) That boy was smart, he had a great mind (38) The teacher did not come (39) He said: I am the sultan and I will restore justice for this man (40) The father of the boy, the sultan, was going around the city with his ministers and they saw a little boy saying: I will rule! (41) The teacher came and said to them: go into the classroom (42) The sultan said to the boy: come here! (43) He asked: what do you want? (44) He said: tell me how you will rule in order to restore justice for this man (45) He replied: I will not tell you unless you give me the crown (46) A little boy with the crown will rule over us? (47) He said: fine (48) They took him, put him in the hammam, washed him, changed his clothes and put on his head the crown (49) In the hammam they found on his shin the bracelet (50) They said to him: your majesty, this is your son (51) They put the crown on his head and said to him: come and say what is your ruling, what are we going to do now? (52) He said: look, I need a hundred soldiers, we will send them and they will search the house corner by corner (53) They sent the soldiers, the soldiers entered and searched corner by corner (54) And they heard a girl: aa... aa...

(55) l-ḥāl ntāḥḥa ṣāyəb yāsər (56) qāllu: aʕṭīni nḥall əl-bāb (57) ḥallu əl-bāb wa rqāw bənt, hīya dʕīfa, bəš-šīf tətkəlləm (58) xdāwha fīšʕa l-ṣbīṭāl, ʕawwmūha, nəddfūha, ʕṭāwūla tākəl (59) wa šəddu ər-rāẓəl, qāllu: kəddāb, xdīt əl-bənt xabbītha hūni (60) ḥaṭṭūhu fi-l-ḥabš, qāllu: žīb əṣ-ṣəndūq ntāʕu (61) fīšʕa ʕṭālo əṣ-ṣəndūq (62) wa farḥu bi-l-bənt (63) əl-bənt kabrat, ʕarrəš ʕaləya əl-wəld ṣəlṭān (64) līlətha li ʕarrəš, yaḥləm wāḥad dərbu kəff (65) hūwa qām f-əṣ-ṣbāḥ, qāl: nāxəd kəff fi-l-blād ntāʕy? (66) hrab mən-əl-blād u ṣfāṛ l-blād oxra (67) l-mṛa qāmət, wīn əl-ʕrīš, wīnhu? (68) ma təmmāuš, ma naʕrəfš wīn mša (69) hūwa mša, hbaṭ fi-blād, la ʕandu ḍāṛ, la ʕandu flūš, la ʕandu ḥaṭṭa šəy (70) u ža ʕaməl gīṭūn u qʕad fīhu u yəxdəm mīstru wa yʕalləm zġāṛ (71) yākəl wa yʕīš f-āk əl-gīṭūn (72) təmma ġādi ṣəlṭān, bəntu bāš tʕarrəš (73) ʕaṛḍu əl-mīstru, qāllu: əži əl-ʕarš ntāʕna, bənti bāš tʕarrəš (74) hūwa lābəš ḥwāyəž dərʕlīn (75) kullhəm qāʕdīn fi-l-əbdu wa hūwa qāʕəd fi-l-lāxər (76) ʕamlu l-ʕarəš mākla u šṛāb u kull (77) fi-l-lāxər ža ṛāẓəl bəntu, nšību, mən wāḥad l-wāḥad yqūllu: šnūwa ḥabb taʕṭi rīgālu? (78) wa hūwa yqayyəd fi-žmām (79) wāḥəd yqūl mīya, wāḥad yqūl mīytīn, wāḥad yqūl tlāta, arbaʕ

(55) Her situation was severe (56) They said to him: let me open the door (57) They opened the door and saw a girl, she was skinny and barely spoke (58) They took her immediately to the hospital, they took care of her, washed her (59) And they caught the man, they said to him: liar! You took the girl and hid her in here (60) They took him to the prison and said to him: bring his box (61) He gave him the box at once (62) And they rejoiced over the girl (63) The girl grew up and the sultan's son married her (64) On the night of the wedding he had a dream that someone hit him with the palm of a hand (65) He woke up in the morning and said: how will someone hit me with a palm in my own city? (66) He fled from the town and travelled to another city (67) The woman woke up, where is the groom? Where is he? (68) He is not here, I do not know where he has gone (69) He went away, he escaped the city, he does not have accommodation, he does not have money (70) He made a tent and lived inside and he was working as a teacher and he was teaching children (71) He would eat and live in this tent (72) There was there a sultan and his daughter was about to get married (73) They invited the teacher, they said to him: come to our wedding, my daughter is getting married (74) He wears shabby clothes (75) Everyone was sitting together and he sat at the end (of the table) (76) They have set out the wedding-feast, food, beverages, everything (77) At the end the sultan's son-in-law was going from one person to another asking: what would you like to give as a gift? (78) And he would register in his notebook (79) Someone said one hundred (cattle), someone else two hundred, three, four

(80) ḥatta wəṣlu l-hāda l-ẓāwāli (81) šnūwa taʕṭi ənti? (82) naʕṭi mīyat nāga, hūwa ršəm, mīyat ʕlāləš, hūwa ršəm, ʕašra aḥṣānāt (83) ʕalāš mūš tqayyəd, tqayyəd! (84) yqayyəd, fi-l-lāxər hādāk əṛ-ṛāẓəl tġaṣṣəṣ ʕṭāw wāḥəd kəff (85) qāllu: əršəm əl-yədd li ʕṭāti (ə)l-kəff ṭatqaṣṣ (86) lāžəm tqayyədha u qayyədha (87) ufa əl-ʕarš u mša l-blādu (88) əl-ḅāḅa fraḥ li əl-wəld ža, qāllu: nḥabb mīya ḥāža u mīya hāda u mīya hāda wa əl-ḅāḅa ʕṭālo (89) hūwa rkab ʕal aḥṣān kbīr (90) hūwa wṣəl l-ḅlāṣa u krā (91) u ža l-ṣ-ṣəḷṭān qāllo: āna wəld ṣəḷṭān šmaʕt li yaʕməl ʕarš tāʕ bəntək u ma ʕṛadṭṣ ʕaləya, āna nḥabḅ tuwwa (92) ʕaməl əl-ʕarš mən ždīd (93) hūwa akbar mənhu (94) qāllu: bāhi (95) qāllu: aʕṛaḍ ʕal əl-ʕbād l-kull li kānu (96) qāllu: bāhi (97) ʕamlu əl-ʕarš ntāʕu kīf kīf (98) əl-ʕərš əntāʕu fārəġ (99) qāllu: škūn hūni qāʕəd? (100) qāllu: wāḥad ẓāwāli, ṣəṛṃaṭ (101) qāllu: āna nəqʕad fī (102) qāllu: la, mūš mən qadṛək (103) qāllu: la, āna nəqʕad fī (104) ʕamlu ʕarš mən ždīd kīf maṛṛa lūla (105) wəṣlu l-il-rīgālu (106) bdāw yqayydu ḥatta wəṣlu əl-hūwa (107) qāllu: šnūwa taʕṭi ənti? (108) qāllu: mīyāt nāga (109) dxəllu mīya (110) mīyāt ʕayẓa, dxəllu mīya (111) kāməl ᴴᴱrešīmaᴴᴱ šnūwa məktūb lūṭa hādi? (112) məktūb: li ʕṭa kəff tətqəṣṣ yəddu (113) qāllu: āna li kān hūni, tuwwa qəṣṣu yəddu.

(80) Finally they came to that poor man (81) What will you give? (82) I will give one hundred female camels, he logged, one hundred lambs, he logged, and ten horses (83) Why are you not registering? Register! (84) He registered and at the end, the man got nervous and hit him with a palm (85) Write: the hand that hit me will be cut (86) We have to log it and they logged it (87) The wedding was over and he went back to his city (88) The father was glad that the son came back, he said to him: I want one hundred of this and one hundred of that and the father gave him (89) He rode on a big horse (90) He arrived at a place and rented it (for the animals that he brought) (91) And he went to the sultan and said to him: I am a son of the sultan and I have heard that you held a wedding for your daughter and you did not invite me, I would like now (to attend) (92) They held the wedding again (93) He is more powerful than him (94) He said: fine (95) He said to him: invite all the people that attended the last wedding (96) He said: fine (97) They organised the chairs in exactly the same way (98) His chair was empty (99) They said: who was sitting here? (100) They answered: a poor, shabby man (101) He said to them: I will sit there (102) They said: no, it is beneath your honour (103) He answered: no, I will sit down here (104) They made the wedding like the first time (105) They came to the gifts (106) They started registering until they came to that man (107) They asked: what will you give? (108) He said to him: a hundred female camels (109) They brought them (110) A hundred goats, they brought them (111) He finished the list, what is written beneath? (112) It says: the person who hit with a palm will have his hand cut (113) He said to him: I am the one who was sitting here, now cut his hand.

7.0. The Sultan and the Daughter of a Peasant

Speaker: Lea Maymon, age 81

Place and time of recording: Israel, March 2022

(1) hādi əl-xarrāfa tāʕ nānti ummi žəyma (2) qālət: təmma wāḥda bnīya yšəmmyūha maqṣūfāt šəbʕat šnīn (3) hādīk əl-maqṣūfāt šəbʕat šnīn, nhār bābāha tʕadda u lqā əṣ-ṣəltān (4) qāllu: šnūwa ḥālək wa šnūwa hāda (5) qāllu: naḥəmdu ṛəbbi, la bāš ʕalīna (6) qāllu: nḥabb nəšdək nəšda (7) aaa! aṣ-ṣəltān tʕadda, lqā yəẓṛaʕ fi-l-bṣəl (8) hūwa qāllu: əl-bṣəl hāda, tāklu wəlla yāklək? (9) qāllu: əšmaʕ, tlāta ayyām fi-yəddək tžībli əl-xbār (10) kān la bʕad yəqtlu (11) ḥžīn mša l-əḍ-ḍāṛ, yəndəb ʕal ṛāṣu, əl-ʕamla mšūma li ʕaməltha u yəbki (12) žāt bəntu hādi mšəmmya maqṣūfāt šəbʕa šnīn (13) ḥkāha bābāha, qātlu: bāba ma txāfṣ, nhār tālət əl-yūm āna nqūllək šnūwa twāžbu l-əṣ-ṣəltān (14) nhār tālət əl-yūm, qālətlo: baṛṛa qūllu l-ṣ-ṣəltān: kān ʕašt, nāklu u kān mīt klāni (15) mša l-əṣ-ṣəltān, qāllu: aka aka, wuka wuka (16) āma nḥabbək tqūlli: šnūwa yqūl, əš-šəžwa, kīf ḥaṭṭūha ʕal əl-nāṛ, šnūwa yqūl, kīf yṭəyyəbu əl-qahwa b-əšəžwa, šnūwa yqūl? (17) uuu, qālla, əl-ʕamla mšūma ʕaməltha tuwwa (18) qātlu: bāba ma txāfṣ (19) nhār tālət əl-yūm, qātlu baṛṛa qūllu: āna qahwa wa li yəṣṛəbni šāhwa wa li yətʕalləm bīya təmknu daʕwa (20) əl-ᴴᴱmélexᴴᴱ ṣārlu ʕažəb hādi ḥāža əl-ʕbəd (21) qāllu: tuwwa nḥabbək tqūlli əẓ-zṛāṛa (22) kīf yṭallʕu ṣṭall mən bīr, šnūwa tqūl? (23) qāl: kīfāš naʕməl tuwwa, mša l-bəntu yəbki (24) qatlu: bāba ma txāfṣ

(1) This story is from my grandmother, *ummi žəyma* (2) There was a girl, whom people used to call a 'seven-year-old rascal' (3) This seven-year-old rascal, one day her father was passing and the sultan met him (4) He asked him how are you and so on (5) He said: thank God everything is all right (6) He said to him: I would like to ask you a question (7) Oh! when the sultan was passing by, he found him planting onion (8) He asked him: this onion, you will eat it or it will eat you? (9) He said: listen, you have three days to bring me the answer (10) If not, they would kill him (11) The poor man went home weeping over his head: what a mistake I made (by planting the onion) (12) His daughter came, the one that is called a 'seven-year-old rascal' (13) The father told her (what happened), she said: do not be afraid, father, in three days I will tell you what to answer to the sultan (14) On the third day she said to him: go and tell him 'if I am alive, I will eat it, and if I am dead, it means it ate me' (15) He went to the sultan, he told him this and that (16) But I want you to tell me now: what they would say, a coffee kettle, when they put it on the fire, what does it say? When people prepare coffee in a kettle, what does it say? (17) Oh! he said, what a mistake I made now! (18) She (the daughter) said: father, do not be afraid (19) Three days later, she said to him: go and tell him 'I am coffee, and those who drink me enjoy, and those who get used to me, I become their curse' (20) The king was amazed by this man (21) He said: now I want you to tell me, a water well (22) When people take out a bucket from a well, what does it say? (23) He said: what will I do now? He went to his daughter (24) She said: father, do not be afraid

(25) nhār tālət əl-yūm, qālətlo: qūl l-ṣ-ṣulṭān: āna lūḫ u rīḫti tfūḫ u laḥmi maẓrūḫ (26) qāllu: əḥwāyəž hādu, škūn qāʕəd yfaššərlək fīhəm? (27) qāllu: nḥabbək tuwwa taʕməlli həkka (28) ʕryān u lābəš, yəbki u yəḍḥak, u rākəb u yəmši ʕal rəžlī (29) aḥžīn xāf (30) mša l-bəntu qatlu: bāba ma txāfṣ (31) nhār tālət əl-yūm, qātlu: žībli bhīm (32) bhīm zġīrūn qālətlo, qṣīr (33) ḥaṭṭəthu ʕal əl-bhīm (34) rākəb ʕal əl-bhīm u rəžlī fi-lūṭa (35) u naḥḥātlu ḥwāyəž u ləbšətlu tīla (36) ət-tīla fīha nqāb, wa hādāk ʕryān u lābəš (37) u yəbki wa hādi xdāt ṛāṣ əl-bṣəl u ḥakkətlo ʕal žbīnu (38) ʕadmu habṭīn ʕalī, ḥāltu ḥlīla u rūḥu ṭalʕat (39) u yəḍḥak məyyət mən əḍ-ḍḥak (40) mša l-ᴴᴱmélexᴴᴱ, l-ᴴᴱmélexᴴᴱ qāllu: tuwwa nḥabbək tqūlli škūn hādi li qāʕ tfaššərlək fi-l-ḥwāyəž hādu l-kulla (41) qāllu: ya šəddi ᴴᴱmélexᴴᴱ, hādi bənti (42) qāllu: bəntek hādi āna nḥabb nāxədha (43) ža l-ᴴᴱmélexᴴᴱ, xda tlāta ṣənnaʕ ntāʕu (44) qāl: əmlāw qoffa bi-l-ḥwāyəž bāhīn l-kull, u ffāḥ u ṣabūn u həžžu l-ʕārūṣa (45) wəṣlu l-dāṛ tāʕ əṛ-ṛāžəl, ḍarbu ʕal əl-bāb (46) wa hīya qālət: ʕaqli fi-ḥaẓri, ma nnžəmš nqūm tuwwa (47) rūḥu l-ᴴᴱmélexᴴᴱ (48) qāllu: hādi l-mṛa ənta tāxəd? hīya mahbūla, qālət ʕaqla fi-ḥzarha (49) qāl: əntūm mahbūlīn, ʕaqla fi-ḥzarha hādīk txalləṣ fi-ṣaʕrha u ṣaʕrha wāṣəl ḥatta rəžlīn, kān tqūm txabbər, aržʕu l-ġādi (50) ražʕu, ṭəblu ʕal əl-bāb

(25) Three days later, she said: you will tell him 'I am wood, my smell is pleasant and my body hurts' (26) He said to him: who explains all these things to you? (27) He said: now I want you to do for me this (28) Naked and dressed, cries and laughs, rides and walks on feet (29) The poor man got scared (30) He went to his daughter and she said to him: father, do not be afraid (31) Three days later she said to him: bring me a donkey (32) A small one, she said, a short one (33) She put him on the donkey (34) He rides the donkey with his legs on the floor (35) And she undressed him and put on him a piece of fabric (36) In the fabric there were holes, so he was both dressed and naked (37) And she took an onion and rubbed it on his forehead (38) Tears started dripping from his eyes, his situation was awful and he almost died (39) And he was crying, almost dying of laughter (40) He went to the king, the king said to him: now I want you to tell me who this person is, who explains all those things to you (41) He said: your majesty, it is my daughter (42) He said to him: this daughter, I would like to marry her (43) The king came and took his three servants (44) He said to them: fill up a basket with the best clothes, perfumes and soap and go to the bride (45) They arrived at the man's house and knocked at the door (46) And she said: my mind is on my knees, I cannot stand up now (47) Go to the king (48) They said to him: are you going to marry this woman? She is insane, she said that her mind is on her knees (49) He said to them: you are insane, her mind was on her knees because she was finishing [combing] her hair and her hair reaches her legs, when she stands up she will let you know, go back there! (50) They came back and knocked on the door

(51) qāltəlhəm: ḥaṭṭu ržəlkəm ʕal əl-bənnāy u yədd ʕal ṇəẓẓār u yədd ʕal əl-ḥaddād (52) mšāw l-ᴴᴱmélexᴴ, qāllu: šnūwa əl-ḥwāyəž hādu? (53) xalṭətna moxxna l-m̱ra hādi (54) qālləm: ḥaṭṭu ržəlkəm ʕal ʕaṭba u yədd ʕal əl-bāb u yədd bi-l-ḥalka u təḍərbu bi-l-ḥdīd (55) daxlu, farḥat bīhəm u šāfət əl-qoffa (56) qāltəlhəm: šəlmu l-ᴴᴱmélexᴴᴱ bərša bərša bərša (57) āma qūlūlu, nāqṣīn fi-š-šma tlāta kwākəb u fi-l-bḥar tlāta mrākəb (58) rəwwḥu u qālu: ya ʕrūṣa, ya ʕažīža, u qāblətna u farḥat bīna (59) eee, qāl, ya šəddi ᴴᴱmélexᴴᴱ! qāltənna nāqṣīn fi-š-šma tlāta kwākəb u fi-l-bḥar tlāta mrākəb (60) wa qāləlhəm l-ᴴᴱmélexᴴᴱ hakka: šnūwa xnəbtu mən l-qoffa? (61) ᴴᴱbemétᴴᴱ xənbu tlāta mən kull ḥāža (62) hūwa yḥabb yʕarrəš ʕaləya u bdāw əl-ʕarš (63) qālla: əšmʕi, ʕandi mʕāk ṣəṛṭ wāḥad (64) ən-nhār li nāxdək ma tədwīyəš mʕa əl-nāš (65) ʕarršu, nhār əl-ᴴᴱmélexᴴᴱ tʕadda, māši ʕal əl-bḥar, yərqa, kīfāš? (66) ža wāḥəd əl-ᴴᴱmélexᴴᴱ yəškīlu (67) qāllu šnūwa, qāllu: ya šəddi ᴴᴱmélexᴴᴱ, āna ʕandi farṣa u bəyyətha fi-l-fəndūq u wəldət bʕīr, təmma farṣa tžīb aḥmīr? (68) qāllu: xallīli nətfakkər (69) əl-ʕbəd hāda kān mḥayyər (70) hūwa ka-yəmši fə-ṣəṭṭ əl-bḥar mḥayrān, wa hīya qaʕdət fi-l-balkūn šāfəthu yəmši (71) qatlu: šbīk? (72) qālla: b-ṛāṣək ya m̱ra, xallīni (73) qaltlu: lāžəm taḥkīli

(51) She said to them: put your legs on the bricklayer, one hand on the carpenter and the other hand on the blacksmith (52) They went to the king and said to him: what are those things? (53) This woman has messed with our heads! (54) He said to them: [it means] put your legs on the doorstep, one hand on the door and the other on the lock and knock (55) They went in, she received them with happiness and saw the basket (56) She said to them: give my best regards to the king (57) But tell him: there are three stars missing in the sky and three ships in the sea (58) They went back and said to him: what a dear bride and how she received us! (59) Oh! your majesty, but she said that there are three stars missing in the sky and three ships missing in the sea (60) And the king said to them: what had you stolen from the basket? (61) Indeed, they had stolen three items from each kind (62) He wanted to get married to her so they started the wedding (63) He said to her: listen, I have one condition with you (64) From the day we get married you will not talk to people (65) They got married and one day the king was passing by, walking on the beach and found what? (66) A man came to the king to complain to him (67) He said to him: what happened? He said to him: your majesty, I have a thoroughbred mare and I spent a night with her in an inn and she gave birth to an interbred foal, how come a thoroughbred mare delivers a donkey?! (68) He said to him: let me think about it (69) The man was worried (70) While he was walking worried on the beach, she sat down on the balcony and saw him walking (71) She said to him: what is wrong with you? (72) He said to her: let it go, O woman, leave me in peace (73) She said to him: you have to tell me

(74) qāllu: ʕandi fərṣa u žābət bʕīr u l- ᴴᴱmélexᴴᴱ qāl twaḥmət ʕal bʕīr u hādāk hūwa li žāb (75) qālətlu: ġadwa əl- ᴴᴱmélexᴴᴱ fi-šətta tāʕ ṣbāḥ lāžəm yətmašša ʕal ṣəṭṭ əl-bḥar (76) ənta ġadwa fi-ṣbāḥ xūd šʕīr u əbda aġəršu fi-gəẓẓa tāʕ əl-bḥar (77) tʕadda, l- ᴴᴱmélexᴴᴱ qāllu: ya mahbūl, təzraʕ l-šʕīr fi-ṣəṭṭ əl-bḥar? (78) qāllu: mana təmma fərṣa tžīb l-bʕīr (79) ʕraf əl- ᴴᴱmélexᴴᴱ, qāl: hāda ᴴᴱrakᴴᴱ mərti, ma təmmāš ḥāža oxra (80) ža l-dāṛ qālla: əšmʕi, tuwwa āna ᴴᴱmélexᴴᴱ u ma nḥabbūš fdḥāya (81) līla fi-llīl xūdi li ʕažīž ʕalīk wa trūḥi l-bābāk (82) āna ḥkəmt ʕalīk u ənti ma wqəftīṣ fi-kəlmtək (83) qālətlu: əlli tahkəm yṣīr (84) fi-llīl ḥaṭṭətlu bənṣ, raqdatu rāqda brīma, xdāt əl-frāš ntāʕu, žābət əl-xaddāma ntāha u ḥawwlatu l-ḥūš bābāha (85) qām f-əṣ-ṣbāḥ u lqa l-qaṭṭūṣa tmaʕʕwi u l-ġāǧa tgərgər u hāda qāllu: šnūwa hāda? wən ṣbaḥt? šnūwa naʕməl hūni? (86) qāltlu: mūš ənti ṣ-ṣərt ʕalīya? (87) qālla: ṣəṛt ʕalīk? šnūwa? (88) qālətlu: ḥāža ʕažīža ʕalīya (89) l-ḥāža əlli ʕažīža ʕalīk xūdīha u əmši (90) qātlu: ənti ʕažīž ʕalīya u xdītək (91) qālla: āna, yžīwni fi-nhāṛ u fi-līl nətṣāwər mʕāk u l-maḥkma tṣāṛ bəṛk mən ġadwa, baʕd ma nətṣāwar mʕāk.

(74) He said to her: I have a mare and she gave birth to a donkey and the king told me that she craved a crossbred horse and this is what happened (75) She said to him: tomorrow at seven in the morning the king is supposed to take a stroll on the beach (76) You tomorrow morning take barley and start sowing it in the sand (77) The king was passing by and said to him: are you insane? How come are you sowing barely in the sand? (78) He said to him: and how come the mare delivers a donkey? (79) The king understood and said: only my wife [could have staged that], there is nobody else (80) He went home and said to her: I am a king now and I do not want gaffs (81) Late in the night, take whatever is valuable to you and go back to your father (82) I gave a condition and you did not keep your promise (83) Whatever you decide, will happen (84) At night she gave him sleeping drugs, she put him to sleep, took his bed, brought his servants and moved him to her father's premises (85) He woke up in the morning and found a cat meowing and a hen crowing and he said: what is that? Where did I wake up? What am I doing here? (86) She said to him: aren't you my condition? (87) He said to her: your condition? How? (88) She said to him: a thing that is valuable for me (89) The thing that is valuable for you, take it and leave (90) You are valuable for me so I took you (91) He said to her: they will come to me in the daytime and at night I will consult with you and the court will only happen the day after, after I consult with you.

BIBLIOGRAPHY

Aarts, Bas. 2004. 'Conceptions of Gradience in the History of Language'. *Language Sciences* 26: 343–89.

Adams, J. N. 2003. *Bilingualism and the Latin Language*. Cambridge: Cambridge University Press.

———. 2007. *The Regional Diversification of Latin 200 BC–AD 600*. Cambridge: Cambridge University Press.

Agius, Dionisius, and Amir Harrak. 1987. 'Auxiliary Particles Preceding the Imperfective Aspect in Arabic Dialects'. *Arabica* 34 (2): 164–80.

Aguadé, Jordi. 2012. 'Verbs Reflecting CA Form IV Patterns in Moroccan Arabic'. *Romano-Arabica* 12: 7–15.

———. 2018. 'The Maghrebi Dialects of Arabic'. In *Arabic Historical Dialectology*, edited by Clive Holes, 29–64. Oxford Studies in Diachronic and Historical Linguistics 30. Oxford: Oxford University Press.

Altairi, Hamed, Jason Brown, Catherine Watson, and Bryan Gick. 2017. 'Tongue Retraction in Arabic: An Ultrasound Study'. In *Proceedings of the 2016 Annual Meeting on Phonology*, edited by Karen Jesney, Charlie O'Hara, Caitlin Smith, and Rachel Walker, 12 pages. Washington, DC: Linguistic Society of America.

Anderson, John, and Charles Jones (eds.). 1974. *Historical Linguistics*. Vol. 1, *Syntax, Morphology, Internal and Comparative Reconstruction*. Amsterdam: North Holland.

Archangeli, Diana, and Douglas Pulleybank. 1994. *Grounded Phonology*. Current Studies in Linguistics 25. Cambridge, MA: MIT Press.

Archangeli, Diana. 1999. 'Introducing Optimality Theory'. *Annual Review of Anthropology* 28 (1): 531–52.

Arnold, Werner. 1990. *Das Neuwestaramäische*. Vol. 5, *Grammatik*. Wiesbaden: Harrassowitz.

Bahloul, Maher. 2011. 'Agreement'. In *Encyclopedia of Arabic Language and Linguistics*, online edition, edited by Lutz Edzard and Rudolf de Jong. Leiden: Brill. http://dx.doi.org/10.1163/1570-6699_eall_EALL_COM_0009

Bar-Moshe, Assaf. 2019. *The Arabic Dialect of the Jews of Baghdad: Phonology, Morphology, and Texts*. Wiesbaden: Harrassowitz.

Beaussier, Marcelin. 1931. *Dictionnaire pratique arabe-français*. Rev. ed., edited by M. Mohamed Ben Cheneb. Algiers: Ancienne Maison Bastide-Jourdan, Jules Carbonel.

Behnstedt, Peter. 1998. 'Zum Arabischen von Djerba (Tunesien) I'. *Zeitschrift für arabische Linguistik* 35: 52–83.

———. 1999. 'Zum Arabischen von Djerba (Tunesien) II: Texte'. *Zeitschrift für arabische Linguistik* 36: 32–65.

Behnstedt, Peter, and Manfred Woidich. 2010. *Wortatlas der arabischen Dialekte*. Vol 1. Leiden: Brill.

———. 2018. 'The Formation of the Egyptian Arabic Dialect Area'. In *Arabic Historical Dialectology*, edited by Clive Holes, 64–96. Oxford Studies in Diachronic and Historical Linguistics 30. Oxford: Oxford University Press.

Bekins, Peter. 2014. *Transitivity and Object Marking in Biblical Hebrew: An Investigation of the Object Preposition ʾEt.* Winona Lake, IN: Eisenbrauns.

Belnap, R. Kirk. 1991. 'Grammatical Agreement Variation in Cairene Arabic'. PhD dissertation, University of Pennsylvania.

———. 1999. 'A New Perspective on the History of Arabic Variation in Marking Agreement with Plural Heads'. *Folia Linguistica* 33 (1–2): 169–86.

Belnap, R. Kirk, and John Gee. 1994. 'Classical Arabic in Contact: The Transition to Near-Categorical Agreement Patterns'. In *Perspectives on Arabic Linguistics VI,* edited by Mushira Eid, Vicente Cantarino, and Keith Walters: 121–49. Current Issues in Linguistic Theory 115. Amsterdam: John Benjamins.

Belnap, R. Kirk, and Osama Shabaneh. 1992. 'Variable Agreement and Nonhuman Plurals in Classical and Modern Standard Arabic'. In *Perspectives on Arabic Linguistics IV,* edited by Ellen Broselow, Mushira Eid, and John McCarthy, 245–62. Current Issues in Linguistic Theory 85. Amsterdam: John Benjamins.

Ben-Sasson, Menahem. 1982. 'The Jewish Community of Gabes in the 11th Century: Economic and Residential Patterns'. In *Communautés juives des marges sahariennes du Maghreb,* edited by Michael Abitbol, 264–85. Jerusalem: Ben-Zvi Institute.

Benkato, Adam. 2014. 'The Arabic Dialect of Benghazi, Libya: Historical and Comparative Notes'. *Zeitschrift für arabische Linguistik* 59: 57–102.

Bettega, Simone. 2018. 'Agreement Patterns in Omani Arabic: Sociolinguistic Conditioning and Diachronic Developments'. *Sociolinguistic Studies* 12 (2): 143–63.

Bettega, Simone, and Luca D'Anna. 2023. *Gender and Number Agreement in Arabic*. Leiden: Brill.

Bhat, Darbhe. 2007. *Pronouns*. Oxford: Oxford University Press.

Blau, Joshua. 1951. 'The Numerals in Judeo-Arabic'. *Tarbiz* 23 (1): 27–35. [Hebrew].

———. 1965. *The Emergence and Linguistic Background of Judaeo-Arabic: A Study of the Origins of Middle Arabic*. Oxford: Oxford University Press.

———. 1961. *A Grammar of Mediaeval Judaeo-Arabic*. Jerusalem: Magnes Press. [Hebrew].

———. 2010. *Phonology and Morphology of Biblical Hebrew: An Introduction*. Linguistic Studies in Ancient West Semitic 2. Winona Lake, IN: Eisenbrauns.

Blench, Roger. 2001. 'Types of Language Spread and their Archeological Correlates: The Example of Berber'. *Origini* 23: 169–90.

Binnick, Robert. 1991. *Time and the Verb: A Guide to Tense and Aspect.* Oxford: Oxford University Press.

Brockelmann, Carl. 1908. *Grundriss der vergleichenden Grammatik der semitischen Sprachen*. Vol. 1. Berlin: Wentworth Press.

Brown, Gillian, and George Yule. 1983. *Discourse Analysis*. Cambridge: Cambridge University Press.

Brunot, Louis, and Elie Malka. 1940. *Fès: Glossaire judeo-arabe de Fès*. Rabat: Ecole du Livre.

Brustad, Kristen. 2000. *The Syntax of Spoken Arabic.* Washington, DC: Georgetown University Press.

Bukshaisha, F. A. M. 1985. 'An Experimental Phonetic Study of Some Aspects of Qatari Arabic'. Doctoral dissertation, University of Edinburgh.

Bulliet, Richard. 1979. *Conversion to Islam in the Medieval Period.* Cambridge, MA: Harvard University Press.

Bunis, Ivri. 2018. 'The Morphosyntax of Jewish Palestinian Aramaic from the Byzantine Period'. PhD dissertation, Hebrew University of Jerusalem. [Hebrew].

———. 2020. 'The Morphosyntactic Conservatism of Western Neo-Aramaic Despite Contact with Syrian Arabic'. In *Studies in the Grammar and Lexicon of Neo-Aramaic,* edited by Geoffrey Khan and Paul M. Noorlander, 235–85. Cambridge Semitic Languages and Cultures 5. Cambridge: Open Book Publishers.

Bybee, Joan. 2003. 'Mechanism of Change in Grammaticalization: The Role of Frequency'. In *The Handbook of Historical Linguistics,* edited by Brian Joseph and Richard Janda, 602–23. Oxford: Blackwell.

Bybee, Joan, Revere Perkins, and William Pagliuca. 1994. *The Evolution of Grammar: Tense, Aspect and Modality in the Languages of the World.* Chicago: University of Chicago Press.

Cadi, Kaddour. 1987. *Système verbal rifain: Forme et sens.* Leuven: Peeters.

Cantineau, Jean. 1960. *Cours de phonétique arabe.* Paris: Klincksieck.

Carruthers, Janice. 2012. 'Discourse and Text'. In *The Oxford Handbook of Tense and Aspect*, edited by Robert I. Binnick, 306–34. Oxford: Oxford University Press.

Caubet, Dominique. 1993. *L'arabe marocain*. Études chamito-sémitiques. Leuven: Peeters.

Chetrit, Joseph. 2014. 'Judeo-Arabic Dialects in North Africa as Communal Languages: Lects, Polylects, and Sociolects'. *Journal of Jewish Languages* 2: 202–32.

———. 2015. 'Diversity of Judeo-Arabic Dialects in North Africa: Eqa:l, Wqal, Kjal and ʔal Dialects'. *Journal of Jewish Languages* 4: 1–43.

———. 2017. 'Moroccan Judeo-Arabic'. In *Encyclopedia of Jews in the Islamic World*, online edition, edited by Norman A. Stillman. Leiden: Brill. http://dx.doi.org/10.1163/1878-9781_ejiw_COM_000794

Chtatou, Mohamed. 1997. 'The Influence of the Berber Language on Moroccan Arabic'. *International Journal of the Sociology of Language* 123: 101–18.

Coghill, Eleanor. 2018. 'Information Structure in the Neo-Aramaic Dialect of Telkepe'. In *Information Structure in Lesser-Described Languages: Studies in Prosody and Syntax*, edited by Evangelia Adamou, Katharina Haude, and Martine Vanhove, 297–328. Amsterdam: John Benjamins.

Cohen, Marcel. 1912. *Le parler arabe des Juifs d'Alger*. Paris: Champion.

———. 1924. *Système verbal sémitique et l'expression du temps*. Paris: Leroux.

Cohen, David. 1964–1975. *Le parler arabe des juifs de Tunis*. 2 vols. The Hague: Mouton.

Colin, Georges S. 1926. 'Étymologies magribines'. *Hésperis* 6 (1): 55–82.

Comrie, Bernard. 1976. *Aspect*. Cambridge: Cambridge University Press.

———. 1981. *Language Universals and Linguistic Typology: Syntax and Morphology*. Chicago: Chicago University Press.

Connolly, Magdalen. 2018. 'Linguistic Variation in Egyptian Judaeo-Arabic Folk Tales and Letters from the Ottoman Period'. PhD dissertation, University of Cambridge.

Corbett, Grenville G. 2006. *Inflection*. Cambridge: Cambridge University Press.

Correll, Christoph. 1978. *Untersuchungen zur Syntax der neuwestaramäischen Dialekte des Antilibanon (Maʕlūla, Baḫʕa, Gubb ʕAdīn) mit besonderer Berücksichtigung der Auswirkungen arabischen Adstrateinflusses*. Abhandlungen für die Kunde des Morgenlandes XLIV, 4. Wiesbaden: Steiner.

Corriente, Federico. 2012. *A Descriptive and Comparative Grammar of Andalusi Arabic*. Leiden: Brill.

Cowell, Mark. 1964. *A Reference Grammar of Syrian Arabic*. Washington, DC: Georgetown University Press.

Cristofaro, Sonia. 2003. *Subordination*. Oxford Studies in Typology and Linguistic Theory. Oxford: Oxford University Press.

Cruttenden, Alan. 1997. *Intonation*. Cambridge: Cambridge University Press.

Čech, Radek, and Petr Pajas. 2009. 'Pitfalls of the Transitivity Hypothesis: Transitivity in Conversation and Written Language in Czech'. *Glottotheory* 2: 41–49.

D'Anna, Luca. 2017. 'Agreement with Plural Controllers in Fezzānī Arabic'. *Folia Orientalia* 54: 101–23.

———. 2020. 'Collectives in the Qurʾān Revisited: Another Possibility of Semantic Agreement'. *Journal of Semitic Studies* 65 (1): 147–69.

———. 2021. 'The Judeo-Arabic Dialect of Yefren (Libya): Phonological and Morphological Notes'. *Journal of Jewish Languages* 9 (1): 1–31.

Davis, Stuart. 1995. 'Emphasis Spread in Arabic and Grounded Phonology'. *Linguistic Inquiry* 26: 465–98.

Dayf, Šawqī. 1990. *Taysīrāt luġawiyya*. Cairo: Dār al-Maʕārif.

DeLancey, Scott. 1997. 'Grammaticalization and the Gradience of Categories: Relator Nouns and Postpositions in Tibetan and Burmese'. In *Essays on Language Functions and Language Type*, edited by Joann Bybee, John Haiman, and Sandra Thompson, 51–69. Amsterdam: John Benjamins.

Diem, Werner. 1979. 'Studien zur Frage des Substrats im Arabischen'. *Der Islam* 56: 12–80.

Diessel, Holger. 1999. *Demonstratives: Form, Function, and Grammaticalization*. Amsterdam: John Benjamins.

Dror, Yehudit. 2013. 'Adjectival Agreement in the Qurʾān'. *Bulletin d'études orientales* 62: 51–76.

———. 2016. 'Collective Nouns in the Qurʾān: Their Verbal, Adjectival and Pronominal Agreement'. *Journal of Semitic Studies* 61 (1): 103–37.

Dryer, Matthew S. 2005. 'Order of Relative Clause and Noun'. In *The World Atlas of Language Structures*, edited by Martin Haspelmath, Matthew S. Dryer, David Gil, and Bernard Comrie, 366–69. Oxford: Oxford University Press.

Eisele, John. 1990. 'Time Reference, Tense, and Formal Aspect in Cairene Arabic'. In *Perspectives on Arabic Linguistics I*, edited by Mushira Eid, 173–212. Current Issues in Linguistics Theory, 63. Amsterdam: John Benjamins.

———. 1992. 'Egyptian Arabic Auxiliaries and the Category of AUX'. In *Perspectives on Arabic Linguistics IV*, edited by Ellen Broselow, Mushira Eid, and John McCarthy, 143–65. Current Issues in Linguistic Theory 85. Amsterdam: John Benjamins.

———. 2011. 'Aspect'. In *Encyclopedia of Arabic Language and Linguistics,* online edition, edited by Lutz Edzard and Rudolf de Jong. Leiden: Brill. http://dx.doi.org/10.1163/1570-6699_eall_EALL_COM_0029

Eksell, Kerstin. 1980. 'The Analytic Genitive in the Modern Arabic Dialects'. (= *Orientalia Gothoburgensia* 5). PhD dissertation, University of Göteborg.

———. 2009. 'D/L Particles in Arabic Dialects: A Problem Revisited'. In *Relative Clauses and Genitive Constructions in Semitic*, edited by Janet Watson and Jan Retsö, 35–49. Oxford: Oxford University Press,.

El Aissati, Abderrahman. 2011. 'Berber Loanwords'. In *Encyclopedia of Arabic Language and Linguistics*, online edition, edited by Lutz Edzard and Rudolf de Jong. Leiden: Brill.

http://dx.doi.org/10.1163/1570-6699_eall_EALL_COM_0042

El Hankari, Abdelhak. 2015. 'Tarifit Berber: From VSO to Topic-Initial'. *Brill's Journal of Afroasiatic Languages and Linguistics* 7: 307–30.

El Yasin, Mohammed. 1985. 'Basic Word Order in Classical Arabic and Jordanian Arabic'. *Lingua* 65 (1–2): 107–22.

Feghali, Michel. 1928. *Syntaxe des parlers arabes actuels du Liban*. Paris: Librairie Orientaliste Paul Geuthner.

Ferguson, C. A. 1989. 'Grammatical Agreement in Classical Arabic and the Modern Dialects: A Response to Versteegh's Pidginization Hypothesis'. *Al-ʿArabiyya* 22: 5–17.

Ferrando, Ignacio. 2011. 'Collective'. In *Encyclopedia of Arabic Language and Linguistics,* online edition, edited by Lutz Edzard and Rudolf de Jong. Leiden: Brill. http://dx.doi.org/10.1163/1570-6699_eall_EALL_SIM_0018

Fischer, Wolfdietrich. 2002. *A Grammar of Classical Arabic*. Translated by Jonathan Rodgers. New Haven: Yale University Press.

Foley, William, and R. D. Van Valin, Jr. 1984. *Functional Syntax and Universal Grammar*. Cambridge: Cambridge University Press.

Forsyth, John. 1970. *A Grammar of Aspect.* Cambridge: Cambridge University Press.

Gamaleldin, Saad. 1967. *A Syntactic Study of Colloquial Egyptian Arabic*. Mouton: The Hague.

Gębski, Wiktor. 2022. 'Expressions of Tense and Aspect in the Tunisian Varieties of Arabic: A Comparative Study of Jewish and Muslim Dialects'. *Journal of Jewish Languages* 10: 54–86.

———. 2023a. 'The Phonology of the Judaeo-Arabic Dialect of Gabes'. *Journal of Semitic Studies* 68 (1): 165–97.

———. 2023b. 'The Development of Sibilant Harmony in Maghrebi Arabic from the Perspective of Language Contact in Pre-Islamic Africa'. *Mediterranean Language Review* 30: 155–81.

———. Forthcoming a. 'The Arabic Dialect of the Jews of Wad-Souf (Saharan Algeria): Phonology and Morphology'. *Zeitschrift für arabische Linguistik*.

———. Forthcoming b. 'Between Analogy and Language Contact: A Case Study of Grammatical Change in Maghrebi Judaeo-Arabic Dialects'. *Folia Orientalia*.

Ghazali, Salem. 1977. 'Back Consonants and Back Coarticulation in Arabic'. PhD thesis, University of Austin, Texas.

Givón, Talmy. 1980. 'The Binding Hierarchy and the Typology of Complements'. *Studies in Language* 4: 333–77.

———. 1990. *Syntax: A Functional-Typological Introduction*. Vol. 2. Amsterdam: John Benjamins.

Goldenberg, Gideon. 1995. 'Attribution in Semitic Languages'. *Langues orientales anciennes: Philologie et linguistique* 5–6: 1–20.

Grand'Henry, Jacques. 1972. *Le parler arabe de Cherchell (Algérie)*. Louvain-la-Neuve: Institut Orientaliste.

———. 2011. 'Algeria'. In *Encyclopedia of Arabic Language and Linguistics,* online edition, edited by Lutz Edzard and Rudolf de Jong. Leiden: Brill. http://dx.doi.org/10.1163/1570-6699_eall_EALL_COM_0011

Greenberg, Joseph. 1966. *Universals of Language.* Cambridge, MA: MIT Press.

Grotzfeld, Heinz. 1965. *Syrisch-arabische Grammatik (Dialekt von Damaskus).* Porta Linguarum Orientalium, Neue Serie 8. Wiesbaden: Harrassowitz.

Guerrero, Jairo. 2015. 'Preliminary Notes on the Current Arabic Dialect of Oran (Western Algeria)'. *Romano-Arabica* 15: 219–33.

———. 2021. 'On Interdental Fricatives in the First-Layer Dialects of Maghrebi Arabic'. *Brill's Journal of Afroasiatic Languages and Linguistics* 13: 288–308.

Gundel, Jeanette. 1988. 'Universals of Topic-Comment Structure'. In *Studies in Syntactic Typology,* edited by M. Hammond, 209–39. Amsterdam: John Benjamins.

Gzella, Holger. 2013. 'Animacy'. In *Encyclopedia of Hebrew Language and Linguistics,* online edition, edited by Geoffrey Khan. Leiden: Brill. http://dx.doi.org/10.1163/2212-4241_ehll_EHLL_COM_00000103

———. 2015. *A Cultural History of Aramaic.* Leiden: Brill.

Halliday, Michael, and Ruqaiya Hasan. 1976. *Cohesion in English.* London: Longman.

Hanitsch, Melanie. 2019. *Verbalmodifikatoren in den arabischen Dialekten: Untersuchungen zur Evolution von Aspektsystemen.*

Porta Linguarum Orientalium, Neue Serie 27. Wiesbaden: Harrassowitz.

Harrell, Richard. 1962. *A Short Reference Grammar of Moroccan Arabic.* Washington, DC: Georgetown University Press.

Hary, Benjamin. 2009. *Translating Religion: Linguistic Analysis of Judaeo-Arabic Sacred Texts from Egypt.* Leiden: Brill.

Haspelmath, Martin 2009. 'Lexical Borrowing: Concepts and Issues'. In *Loanwords in the World's Languages: A Comparative Handbook*, edited by Martin Haspelmath and Uri Tadmor, 35–54. Berlin: De Gruyter Mouton.

Hasselbach, Rebecca. 2007. 'Demonstratives in Semitic'. *Journal of the American Oriental Society* 127: 1–27.

———. 2014. 'Agreement and the Development of Gender in Semitic (Part I)'. *Zeitschrift der Deutschen morgenländischen Gesellschaft* 164: 33–64.

Heath, Jeffrey. 1987. *Ablaut and Ambiguity: Phonology of a Moroccan Arabic Dialect.* Albany: State University of New York Press.

———. 2002. *Jewish and Muslim Dialects of Moroccan Arabic.* London: Curzon.

———. 2015. 'D-possessives and the Origin of Moroccan Arabic'. *Diachronica* 32 (1): 1–31.

Heath, Jeffrey, and Moshe Bar-Asher. 1982. 'A Judeo-Arabic Dialect of Tafilalt (South-Eastern Morocco)'. *Zeitschrift für arabische Linguistik* 9: 32–78.

Heine, Bernd. 2003. 'Grammaticalization'. In *The Handbook of Historical Linguistics,* edited by Brian Joseph and Richard Janda, 575–601. Oxford: Oxford University Press.

Henshke, Yehudit. 2007. *Hebrew Elements in Daily Speech: A Grammatical Study and Lexicon of the Hebrew Component of Tunisian Judeo-Arabic.* Jerusalem: Bialik Institute. [Hebrew].

———. 2013. 'Tunisia, Pronunciation Traditions'. In *Encyclopedia of Hebrew Language and Linguistics*, online edition, edited by Geoffrey Khan. Leiden: Brill. http://dx.doi.org/10.1163/2212-4241_ehll_EHLL_COM_00000372

Hirschberg, Haim Zeev. 1974. *A History of the Jews in North Africa: From Antiquity to the Sixteenth Century.* Vol 1. Leiden: Brill.

Hoberman, Robert. 1989. 'Parameters of Emphasis: Autosegmental Analysis of Pharyngealization in Four Languages'. *Journal of Afroasiatic Languages* 2: 73–97.

Holes, Clive. 1990. *Gulf Arabic.* London: Routledge.

———. 1991. 'Kashkasha and the Fronting and Affrication of the Velar Stops Revisited: A Contribution to the Historical Phonology of the Peninsular Arabic Dialects'. In *Semitic Studies in Honor of Wold Leslau,* edited by Alan S. Kaye, 652–78. Wiesbaden: Harrassowitz.

Holmstedt, Robert D. 2011. 'Relative Clause: Biblical Hebrew'. In *Encyclopedia of Hebrew Language and Linguistics*, edited by Geoffrey Khan. Leiden: Brill. http://dx.doi.org/10.1163/2212-4241_ehll_EHLL_COM_00000385

Hopper, Paul. 1979. 'Aspect and Foregrounding in Discourse'. In *Discourse and Syntax,* edited by Talmy Givón, 213–41. New York: Academic Press.

Hopper, Paul, and Sandra Thompson. 1980. 'Transitivity in Grammar and Discourse'. *Language* 56: 251–99.

Hopper, Paul, and Elisabeth Closs Traugott. 2003. *Grammaticalization*. Cambridge: Cambridge University Press.

Horesh, Uri. 2002. 'Tense or Aspect: Is Arabic Past Tense an Implicature?'. Ms., University of Pennsylvania.

———. 2011. 'Tense'. In *Encyclopedia of Arabic Language and Linguistics,* online edition, edited by Lutz Edzard and Rudolf de Jong. Leiden: Brill. http://dx.doi.org/10.1163/1570-6699 _eall_EALL_COM_0340

Huehnergard, John. 2006. 'On the Etymology of the Hebrew Relative šɛ-'. In *Biblical Hebrew in its Northwest Semitic Setting: Typological and Historical Perspectives*, edited by Steven E. Fassberg and Avi Hurvitz, 103–25. Winona Lake, IN: Eisenbrauns.

Ingham, Bruce. 1994. *Najdi Arabic: Central Arabian.* London Oriental and African Language Library 1. Amsterdam: John Benjamins.

Janda, Laura. 1999. 'Whence Virility? The Rise of a New Gender Distinction in the History of Slavic'. In *Slavic Gender Linguistics,* edited by Margaret H. Mills, 201–28. Amsterdam: John Benjamins.

Jongelling, Karel, and Robert Kerr. 2005. *Late Punic Epigraphy.* Tübingen: Mohr Siebeck.

Keenan, Edward, and Bernard Comrie. 1977. 'Noun Phrase Accessibility and Universal Grammar'. *Linguistic Inquiry* 8 (1): 63–99.

Khan, Geoffrey. 1988. *Studies in Semitic Syntax*. Oxford: Oxford University Press.

———. 2016. *The Neo-Aramaic Dialect of the Assyrian Christians of Urmi*. Leiden: Brill.

———. 2018. 'Remarks on the Historical Development and Syntax of the Copula in North-Eastern Neo-Aramaic Dialects'. *Aramaic Studies* 16 (2): 234–69.

———. 2021. 'The Coding of Discourse Dependency in Biblical Hebrew Consecutive Weqaṭal and Wayyiqṭol'. In *New Perspectives in Biblical and Rabbinic Hebrew*, edited by Aaron Hornkohl and Geoffrey Khan, 299–354. Cambridge Semitic Languages and Cultures 7. Cambridge: Open Book Publishers.

Kiparsky, Paul. 2003. 'Syllables and Moras in Arabic'. In *The Syllable in Optimality Theory*, edited by Caroline Féry and Ruben van de Vijver, 147–82. Cambridge: Cambridge University Press.

Kortmann, Bernd. 1997. *Adverbial Subordinators: A Typology and History of Adverbial Subordinators based on European Languages*. Berlin: Mouton de Gruyter.

Kossmann, Maarten. 2009. 'Loanwords in Tarifiyt, a Berber Language of Morocco'. In *Loanwords in the World's Languages: A Comparative Handbook*, edited by Martin Haspelmath and Uri Tadmor, 191–214. Berlin: De Gruyter Mouton.

———. 2013. *The Arabic Influence on Northern Berber*. Leiden: Brill.

Krahmalkov, Charles. 2001. *A Phoenician-Punic Grammar*. Leiden: Brill.

Krifka, Manfred. 1987. 'An Outline of Genericity'. Tübingen: Forschungsberichte des Seminars für natürlich-sprachliche Systeme, Universität Tübingen.

Kuryłowicz, Jerzy. 1947. 'La nature des procès dit analogiques'. *Acta Linguistica* 5: 17–34.

Ladefoged, Peter. 1982. *A Course in Phonetics*. San Diego, CA: Harcourt Brace Jovanovich.

Le Bohec, Yann. 2021. *Les Juifs dans l'Afrique romaine*. Saint Macaire: Memoring Éditions.

Ledgeway, Adam, and Ian G. Roberts. 2017. *The Cambridge Handbook of Historical Syntax*. Cambridge: Cambridge University Press.

Lehmann, Christian. 1988. 'Towards a Typology of Clause Linkage'. In *Clause Combining in Grammar and Discourse*, edited by John Haiman and Sandra A. Thompson, 181–226. Amsterdam: John Benjamins.

Leitner, Bettina, Erik Anonby, Mortaza Taheri-Ardali, Dina El Zarka, and Ali Moqami. 2021. 'A First Description of Arabic on The South Coast of Iran: The Arabic Dialect of Bandar Moqām, Hormozgan'. *Journal of Semitic Studies* 66: 215–61.

Leoug, Tommi, Dimitrios Ntelitheos, and Meera Al Kaabi. 2021. *Emirati Arabic: A Comprehensive Grammar*. London: Routledge.

LeTourneau, Mark. 2011. 'Subordination'. In *Encyclopedia of Arabic Language and Linguistics,* online edition, edited by Lutz Edzard and Rudolf de Jong. Leiden: Brill. http://dx.doi.org/10.1163/1570-6699_eall_EALL_COM_0323

Levi, Yaakov. 2011. 'Agreement: Biblical Hebrew'. In *Encyclopedia of Hebrew Language and Linguistics*, online edition, edited by Geoffrey Khan. Leiden: Brill. http://dx.doi.org/10.1163/2212-4241_ehll_EHLL_COM_00000501

Liddicoat, Mary-Jane, Richard Lennane, and Iman Abdul Rahim. 1998. *Syrian Colloquial Arabic: A Functional Course*. Griffith: M-J Liddicoat and Richard Lennane.

Löbner, Sebastian. 1998. *Understanding Semantics*. London: Arnold Publishers.

Loock, Rudy. 2013. 'Extending Further and Refining Prince's Taxonomy of Given/New Information: A Case Study of Non-Restrictive, Relevance-Oriented Structures'. *Pragmatics* 23 (1): 69–91.

Louali, Naima, and Gérard Philippson. 2004. 'Berber Expansion into and within North-West Africa: A Linguistic Contribution'. *Afrika und Übersee* 87:105–30.

Magidow, Alexander. 2013. 'Towards a Sociohistorical Reconstruction of Pre-Islamic Arabic Dialect Diversity'. PhD dissertation, University of Texas at Austin.

Marçais, Philippe. 1948. 'L'articulation de l'emphase dans un parler maghrebin'. *Annales de l'Institut d'Etudes Orientales* 8: 5–28.

———. 1956. *Le parler arabe de Djidjelli (Nord constantinois Algérie)*. Paris: Librairie d'Amérique et d'Orient.

———. 1957. 'Parlers arabes'. In *Initiation à l'Algérie*, 215–37. Paris: Librairie d'Amérique et d'Orient.

———. 1977. *Esquisse grammatical de l'arabe maghrebin*. Paris: Librairie d'Amérique et d'Orient.

Marçais, William. 1902. *Le dialecte arabe parlé à Tlemcen: Grammaire, textes et glossaire*. Paris: Ernest Leroux.

———. 1950. 'Les parlers arabes et berbères'. In *Initiation à la Tunisie*, 195–219. Paris: Librairie d'Amérique et d'Orient.

Marmorstein, Michal. 2016. *Tense and Text in CA: A Discourse-oriented Study of the CA Tense System*. Studies in Semitic Languages and Linguistics 85. Leiden: Brill.

Matsa, Shay. 2019. 'The Arabic Dialect of the Jews of Damascus: Distinctive Phonological, Morphological and Lexical Features'. PhD dissertation, Hebrew University of Jerusalem. [Hebrew].

McMahon, April. 1994. *Understanding Language Change*. Cambridge: Cambridge University Press.

Naïm, Samia. 2011. 'Possession'. In *Encyclopedia of Arabic Language and Linguistics*, online edition, edited by Lutz Edzard and Rudolf de Jong. Leiden: Brill. http://dx.doi.org/10.1163/1570-6699_eall_EALL_COM_vol3_0266

Napiorkowska, Lidia. 2015. *A Grammar of the Christian Neo-Aramaic Dialect of Diyana-Zariwaw*. Leiden: Brill.

Nebes, Norbert. 1982. *Funktionsanalyse von kāna yafʿalu: Ein Beitrag zur Verbalsyntax des Althocharabischen mit besonderer Berücksichtigung der Tempus- und Aspektproblematik*. Hildesheim: G. Olms.

Noonan, Michael. 2007. 'Complementation'. In *Complex Constructions*, vol. 2 of *Language Typology and Syntactic Description*, edited by Timothy Stophen, 52–150. Cambridge: Cambridge University Press.

Ohala, John. 1992. 'What's Cognitive, What's Not, in Sound Change'. In *Diachrony within Synchrony: Language History and Cognition*, edited by Günter Kellermann and Michael D. Morrissey, 309–55. Frankfurt am Main: Peter Lang Verlag.

Omani, Osama, and Aziz Jaber. 2019. 'Variation in the Acoustic Correlates of Emphasis in Jordanian Arabic: Gender and Social Class'. *Folia Linguistica* 53 (1): 169–200.

Owens, Jonathan. 2018. 'Dialects (Speech Communities), the Apparent Past, and Grammaticalization: Towards an Understanding of the History of Arabic'. In *Arabic Historical Dialectology*, edited by Clive Holes, 206–56. Oxford Studies in Diachronic and Historical Linguistics 30. Oxford: Oxford University Press.

Öpengin, Ergin 2020. 'Kurdish'. In: *Arabic and Contact-Induced Change: A Handbook*, edited by Christopher Lucas and Stefano Manfredi, 459–87. Berlin: Language Science Press.

Palva, Heikki. 2011. 'Dialects: Classification'. In *Encyclopedia of Arabic Language and Linguistics,* online edition, edited by Lutz Edzard and Rudolf de Jong. Leiden: Brill. http://dx.doi.org/10.1163/1570-6699_eall_EALL_COM_0087

Pappas, Panayiotis, and Brian Joseph. 2002. 'On Some Recent Views Concerning the Development of the Greek Future System'. *Byzantine and Modern Greek Studies* 26 (1): 247–73.

Pat-El, Na'ama. 2009. 'The Development of the Definite Article in Semitic: A Syntactic Approach'. *Journal of Semitic Studies* 54 (1): 19–50.

———. 2012. *Studies in the Historical Syntax of Aramaic*. Piscataway, NJ: Gorgias Press.

Pat-El, Na'ama, and Alexander Treiger. 2008. 'On Adnominalization of Prepositional Phrases and Adverbs in Semitic'. *Zeitschrift der deutschen morgenländischen Gesellschaft* 158 (2): 265–83.

Pereira, Christophe. 2010. *Le parler arabe de Tripoli (Libye)*. Zaragoza: Instituto de Estudios Islamicos y del Oriente Próximo.

Prince, Alan, and Paul Smolensky. 2004. *Optimality Theory: Constraint Interaction in Generative Grammar*. Oxford: Blackwell.

Prince, Ellen F. 1981. 'Toward a Taxonomy of Given/New Information'. In *Radical Pragmatics*, edited by Peter Cole, 223–54. New York: Academic Press.

Procházka, Stephan, and Ines Gabsi. 2017. 'Agreement with Plural Heads in Tunisian Arabic: The Urban North'. In *Tunisian and Libyan Arabic Dialects: Common Trends—Recent Developments—Diachronic Aspects*, edited by Veronika Ritt-Benmimoun, 239–60. Zaragoza: Prensas de la Universidad de Zaragoza.

Ratcliffe, Robert R. 1992. 'The Broken Plural Problem in Arabic, Semitic and Afroasiatic: A Solution Based on the Diachronic Application of Prosodic Analysis'. PhD dissertation, Yale University.

———. 1998. *The 'Broken' Plural Problem in Arabic and Comparative Semitic: Allomorphy and Analogy in Non-Concatenative Morphology*. Amsterdam: John Benjamins.

———. 2002. 'The Broken Plural System of Moroccan Arabic: Diachronic and Cognitive Perspectives'. In *Perspectives on Arabic Linguistics XIII–XIV*, edited by Dilworth Parkinson and Elabbas Benmamoun, 87–110. Amsterdam: John Benjamins.

———. 2011. 'Number'. In *Encyclopedia of Arabic Language and Linguistics*, online edition, edited by Lutz Edzard and Rudolf de Jong. Leiden: Brill. http://dx.doi.org/10.1163/1570-6699_eall_EALL_COM_vol3_0237

Reckendorf, Hermann. 1921. *Arabische Syntax*. Heidelberg: Winter.

Reichenbach, Hans. 1947. *Elements of Symbolic Logic*. London: Macmillan.

Retsö, Jan. 2011. 'Classical Arabic'. In *The Semitic Languages: An International Handbook*, edited by Stefan Weninger et al., 782–811. Handbücher zur Sprach- und Kommunikationswissenschaft 36. Berlin: De Gruyter Mouton.

Ritt-Benmimoun, Veronika. 2011. *Texte im arabischen Beduinendialekt der Region Douz (Südtunesien)*. Wiesbaden: Harrassowitz.

———. 2014. *Grammatik des arabischen Beduinendialekts der Region Douz (Südtunesien)*. Wiesbaden: Harrassowitz.

———. 2017. 'Agreement with Plural Heads in Tunisian Arabic: The Bedouin South'. In *Tunisian and Libyan Arabic Dialects: Common Trends—Recent Developments—Diachronic Aspects*, edited by Veronika Ritt-Benmimoun, 261–87. Zaragoza: Prensas de la Universidad de Zaragoza.

———. 2020. 'Conditional Structures in South Tunisian Bedouin Dialects'. *Mediterranean Language Review* 28: 29–60.

Rössler, Otto. 2001 [1958]. 'Die Sprache Numidiens'. In *Gesammelte Schriften zur Semitohamitistik*, collected works of Otto Rössler, 392–418. Münster: Ugarit Verlag.

Rubin, Aaron. 2005. *Studies in Semitic Grammaticalization*. Winona Lake, IN: Eisenbrauns.

Saada, Lucienne. 1958. 'Le parler arabe des Juifs de Sousse (Phonologie et morphologie)'. Unpublished manuscript. Paris.

———. 1963. 'Caractéristiques du parler arabe de l'île de Djerba'. *Comptes rendus du Groupe Linguistique d'Études Chamito-Sémitiques* 10: 15–21.

———. 1984. *Elements de description du parler arabe de Tozeur (Tunisie): Phonologie, morphologie, syntaxe*. Paris: Geuthner.

Saadoun, Haim (ed.). 2006. *Jewish Communities in the East in the Nineteen and Twentieth Centuries: Tunisia*. Tel Aviv: Ben-Zvi Institute. [Hebrew].

Saarikivi, Janne. 2006. *Studies on Finno-Ugarian Substrate in Northern Russian Dialects*. Tartu: Tartu University Press.

Sasse, Hans-Jürgen. 2002. 'Recent Activity in the Theory of Aspect: Accomplishments, Achievements, or Just Non-Progressive State?". *Linguistic Typology* 6 (2): 199–271.

Sebag, Paul. 1991. *Histoire des Juifs de Tunisie: Des origines à nos jours*. Paris: L'Harmattan.

Segert, Stanislav. 1976. *A Grammar of Phoenician and Punic*. Munich: Beck.

Shachmon, Ori. 2022. *Tēmōnit: The Jewish Varieties of Yemeni Arabic*. Semitica Viva 62. Wiesbaden: Harrassowitz.

Shimron, Joseph. 2003. *Language Processing and Acquisition in Languages of Semitic, Root-Based Morphology*. Amsterdam: John Benjamins.

Sibony, Jonas. 2022. 'Phonetical and Phonological Adaptations of Hebrew Loanwords in Moroccan Judeo-Arabic: The Case of Fez'. *Romanica-Arabica* 21: 103–24.

Siewierska, Anna. 1991. *Functional Grammar*. London: Routlege.

Simeone-Senelle, Marie-Claude. 1985–1986. 'Systèmes aspecto-temporels en arabe maghrébin (Tunisie)'. *Matériaux arabes et sudarabiques* 3–4: 63–81.

Singer, Hans-Rudolf. 1984. *Grammatik der arabischen Mundart der Medina von Tunis*. Berlin: Mouton de Gruyter.

Skik, Hichem. 1969. 'Description phonologique du parler arabe de Gabès'. In *Travaux de phonologie*, edited by Taïeb Baccouche, 83–114. Cahiers du C.E.R.E.S., Série Linguistique 2. Tunis: Université de Tunis, Centre d'études et de recherches économiques et sociales.

Souag, Lameen. 2005. 'Notes on the Algerian Arabic Dialect of Dellys'. *Estudios de Dialectología Norteafricana y Andalusí* 9: 151–80.

———. 2017. 'Clitic Doubling and Language Contact in Arabic'. *Zeitschrift für arabische Linguistik* 66: 45–60.

Spitaler, Anton. 1962. 'al-ḥamdu lillāhi lladī und Verwandtes'. *Oriens* 15: 97–115.

Stewart, Devin J. 1998. 'Clitic Reduction in the Formation of Modal Prefixes in the Post-Classical Arabic Dialects and Classical Arabic Sa-/Sawfa'. *Arabica* 45: 104–28.

Stumme, Hans. 1896. *Grammatik des tunisischen Arabisch.* Leipzig: Hinrich.

Taine-Cheikh, Catherine. 1983. 'Le passif en ḥassāniyya'. In *Matériaux arabes et sudarabiques* 1: 61–104.

Talmoudi, Fathi. 1980. *The Arabic dialect of Sūsa (Tunisia).* Göteborg: Acta Universitatis Gothoburgensis.

———. 1986. *A Morphosemantic Study of Romance Verbs in the Arabic Dialects of Tunis, Susa, and Sfax.* Goteborg: Acta Universitatis Gothoburgensis.

Tobi, Tsivia. 2016. *From Bride to Daughter-in-Law: World of Jewish Women in Southern Tunisia and Its Reflection in Popular Literature.* Jerusalem: Yad Izhak Ben-Zwi; Hebrew University of Jerusalem. [Hebrew].

Traugott, Elisabeth Closs, and Graeme Trousdale (eds). 2010. *Gradience, Gradualness and Grammaticalization.* Typological Studies in Language 90. Amsterdam: John Benjamins.

van den Boogert, Nico. 1997. *The Berber Literary Tradition of the Sous.* Leiden: NINO.

Van Valin, Jr., Robert D., and Randy J. LaPolla. 1997. *Syntax: Structure, Meaning and Function.* Cambridge: Cambridge University Press.

Vendler, Zeno. 1957. 'Verbs and Times'. *The Philosophical Review* 66 (2): 143–60.

Vycichl, Werner. 1990. 'Die Palatalisierung von Q im Berberischen'. *Rivista degli Studi Orientali* 63: 39–43.

Wagner, Esther-Miriam. 2010. *Linguistic Variety of Judaeo-Arabic in Letters from the Cairo Genizah.* Leiden: Brill.

———. 2014. 'Subordination in 15th- and 16th-century Judaeo-Arabic'. *Journal of Jewish Languages* 2: 143–64.

Wald, Benji. 1983. 'Referents and Topic within and across Discourse Units: Observations from Current Vernacular English'. In *Discourse Perspectives on Syntax,* edited by Flora Klein-Andreu, 91–116. New York: Academic Press.

Watson, Janet. 1993. *A Syntax of Ṣanʿānī Arabic.* Wiesbaden: Harrassowitz.

———. 1999. 'The Directionality of Emphasis Spread in Arabic'. *Linguistic Enquiry* 30 (2): 289–300.

———. 2007. 'Syllabification Patterns in Arabic Dialects: Long Segments and Shared Moras'. *Phonology* 24: 335–56.

Whittaker, Dick. 2009. 'Ethnic Discourses on the Frontiers of Roman Africa'. In *Ethnic Constructs in Antiquity: The Role of Power and Tradition,* edited by Ton Derks and Nico Roymans, 189–206. Amsterdam: Amsterdam University Press.

Woidich, Manfred. 1975. 'Zur Funktion des aktiven Partizips im Kairenisch-Arabischen'. *Zeitschrift der Deutschen morgenländischen Gesellschaft* 125: 273–93.

Woodhead, D. R., and Wayne Beene (eds). 1969. *A Dictionary of Iraqi Arabic.* Washington, DC: Georgetown University Press.

Wright, William. 2005. *Arabic Grammar: Translated from the German of Caspari and Edited with Numerous Additions and Corrections.* 3rd ed., revised by W. Robertson Smith and M. J. De Goege. Mineola, NY: Dover Publications.

Yoda, Sumikazu. 2005. *The Arabic Dialect of the Jews of Tripoli (Libya): Grammar, Text and Glossary.* Wiesbaden: Harrassowitz.

———. 2006. '"Sifflant" and "Chuintant" in the Arabic Dialect of the Jews of Gabes (South Tunisia)'. *Zeitschrift für arabische Linguistik* 48: 7–25.

Younes, Munther. 1993. 'Emphasis Spread in Two Arabic Dialects'. *Perspectives on Arabic Linguistics V*, edited by Mushira Eid and Clive Holes, 119–45. Current Issues in Linguistic Theory 101. Amsterdam: John Benjamins.

INDEX

A

accessibility, 25 n. 1, 263, 268–69, 278, 281, 319
accusative, 209, 284–85, 305
acoustic, 25–26, 35, 52–53, 69
adjacent, 43, 47, 50–51, 53, 55–56, 58–59, 62, 116, 118, 289
adjective, 104, 139, 148–49, 149 n. 7, 150, 159 n. 25, 163–64, 170–71, 171 n. 44, 172, 175–77, 184, 197, 198 n. 55, 219–20, 226–27, 234, 243–45, 254, 262, 266, 271, 273, 292, 296, 318, 326, 366
adnominal, 270–71, 284, 388
adverb, 284–85, 311, 319, 326, 337, 365, 381–82
adverbial, 261, 279, 281–85, 289, 291–92, 295–98, 318–19, 334, 341, 381, 388, 404
affirmative, 211
affix, 86, 245
affricate, 28
Africa, 7, 7 n. 6, 7 n. 7, 8, 12–14, 14 n. 8, 17, 26, 33, 37–38, 42, 96, 102 n. 12, 247, 271, 339, 343, 349–50, 353, 383, 390, 401
    North Africa, 7, 7 n. 7, 8, 12–14, 14 n. 8, 17, 26, 33, 37–38, 42, 96, 102 n. 12, 247, 339, 343, 349–50, 353, 383, 390, 401
agency, 211, 213–14, 218, 223, 228
agreement, 22, 106, 151, 209, 213, 227, 234, 237, 243–45, 247–59, 259 n. 28, 260, 283, 286, 370, 374, 376, 403–4
Akkadian, 244, 271, 284
Aktionsart, 331
Alambak, 266
Algeria, 3, 19 n. 11, 45, 76, 96, 100, 172, 232, 236–37, 252, 271, 390
alienable, 236–37
alignment, 256, 367–68, 372, 374
allomorph, 175–76, 178–81, 183, 233, 236
allophone, 20, 27 n. 4, 29, 30 n. 6, 40 n. 19, 60, 62, 65–66, 68–69, 72, 74–75, 328

alveolar, 35, 38–39, 41, 110, 129
analogy, 92, 95, 95 n. 7, 99, 101, 110, 188, 243 n. 19, 249, 258–59, 403
analytic, 109, 144–46, 174, 229–31, 234, 236–39, 241–42
anaphora, 214, 216, 227, 242, 375
Anatolia, 232
animacy, 207–10, 212, 218–19, 222, 227–29, 244–45, 247, 249, 259, 259 n. 28
annexation, 230, 233–35, 237–40, 242
antecedent, 279
anteriority, 289, 329
anthropomorphism, 228
apodosis, 294–95, 327
apposition, 273, 298
approximant, 28, 56
Arabian Peninsula, 100, 109 n. 13, 232
Arabic,
  Algerian, 5, 10, 45, 97 n. 11, 98, 132, 364
  Andalusi, 16
  Bedouin, 2, 3 n. 4, 4, 32, 41, 43–44, 44 n. 24, 45, 47, 49 n. 29, 63, 66, 75–76, 84 n.

3, 87, 94, 96, 96 n. 10, 98, 118, 120, 127, 136, 140 n. 1, 142, 146, 176 n. 48, 187–88, 224, 230–32, 237, 248–49, 252–53, 294, 321, 328, 343, 352, 399, 405
  Benghazi, 4, 40, 40 n. 17, 96, 252
  Cairene, 51, 248–49, 329, 352
  Cherchell, 132, 134
  Classical Arabic, 4, 21, 26–27, 29, 32, 32 n. 10, 33–38, 41–45, 45 n. 25, 46–47, 49–50, 50 n. 30, 53, 59, 75–78, 82, 91, 93–95, 102–3, 107, 109, 113, 116–17, 117 n. 17, 118, 121–22, 126, 128–29, 131–32, 134–35, 140–44, 146, 148, 152–55, 155 n. 14, 156–57, 160, 162–64, 170–71, 171 n. 44, 172–75, 179–80, 184, 189, 199, 205, 226, 229, 232, 244–45, 248–50, 265–66, 272, 277, 283–85, 291, 304–5, 319, 329, 333, 364–66, 374–75, 403
  Damascene, 5, 249, 312
  Debdou, 98

Djerba, 1, 3, 3 n. 2, 4, 5 n. 5, 6, 25 n. 2, 26, 44 n. 24, 61, 64–65, 65 n. 35, 68, 75–76, 79, 91, 97–98, 136, 154 n. 13, 155 n. 16, 164, 171–72, 183, 187–88, 201 n. 56, 224, 326, 357–58, 402–3

Djidjelli, 4, 61, 98, 120 n. 19, 128, 132, 134, 188, 232, 266

Douz, 32, 41, 47, 49 n. 29, 84 n. 3, 95 n. 8, 96, 103, 105, 112–13, 117, 127, 130, 132, 134, 140 n. 1, 142, 146, 188, 224, 321, 342–43, 399

Egyptian, 11, 26, 171, 207, 216, 237, 240, 256–57, 281, 323, 364–65, 390

Fes, 99, 400

Ibadite, 97, 326, 358

Iraqi, 11, 85

Jordanian, 26

Judaeo-Arabic, 5–6, 25 n. 1, 227, 230, 232, 243 n. 19, 248–50, 255–60, 277–79, 349–51, 404, 406

Ksar Es-Souk, 98

Kuwaiti, 240, 281, 348, 358, 360, 390, 399

Levantine, 102, 227, 325

Maghrebi, 2, 5–6, 7 n. 6, 8–12, 16, 26–27, 30 n. 8, 36, 47, 52, 61, 61 n. 32, 62, 75, 78, 81, 83, 85, 91, 95, 95 n. 7, 97 n. 11, 100, 103, 123, 134, 136, 145, 157, 162, 170–71, 174, 187, 189, 196, 207, 209, 217, 220, 233, 237, 243 n. 19, 249, 257–58, 352–53, 382, 401, 405

Malakite, 97

Marāzīg, 94, 106, 129, 131, 136, 187

Meknes, 99

Middle Arabic, 249

Moroccan, 3–5, 10–11, 16, 52, 58, 61, 85, 92 n. 33, 97 n. 11, 98–99, 102, 175, 183, 207, 217, 218 n. 6, 220–27, 229, 232–33, 235, 240, 266, 273, 276, 278–79, 281, 312, 323, 327, 342–43, 348, 356–57, 364, 390–91, 397–99, 403

Mzab, 98

North African, 2, 4–6, 9, 11, 16–17, 22, 25–26, 26 n. 3, 27, 38 n. 14, 47, 52, 61, 63, 86, 91, 102, 143, 146, 203, 205, 207, 227, 232, 248–49, 251–52, 276, 296, 333, 342,

349–51, 353, 387, 398, 401, 405
Old Arabic, 95, 97, 100, 249
Omani, 26, 248
Oran, 4, 98
Oujda, 98
Oulad Brahim, 98
Quranic, 248
Rabat, 99
Sūsa, 95, 97, 102–3, 105–6, 112–14, 117, 117 n. 17, 125, 129
Syrian, 207, 234, 240, 281, 312, 348, 358, 360, 390, 399
Tlemcen, 98, 127, 132, 134, 136
Tripoli, 4, 27, 30–31, 31 n. 9, 37 n. 13, 37 n. 12, 39 n. 15, 40, 40 n. 17, 40 n. 18, 42, 44, 47, 50 n. 30, 61–62, 66 n. 37, 78 n. 1, 80, 84 n. 3, 91 n. 1, 93–94, 95 n. 8, 96, 102, 113, 118, 125, 134, 136, 143, 155 n. 14, 159 n. 22, 159 n. 25, 179, 184, 190, 195, 217, 224, 248, 252, 257–58, 296, 321, 324–25, 342, 352, 355, 390, 394, 396

Tunis, 1, 4–5, 16, 27, 30 n. 8, 31–32, 34, 36–37, 37 n. 12, 37 n. 13, 38–39, 40 n. 18, 41–42, 44, 46–48, 51, 59, 61–62, 64, 67, 75–77, 82, 86–87, 91, 93, 95, 97, 103, 105–6, 112, 117–18, 120, 123, 125, 127, 131, 134, 136, 141, 145 n. 4, 149 n. 7, 150, 152, 156 n. 18, 158 n. 21, 159 n. 25, 166 n. 37, 167 n. 38, 171–72, 174, 179, 182, 184, 187–89, 194–95, 199, 201, 218, 238–39, 251, 254–56, 259, 264, 309, 321, 342–43, 346–47, 352, 355, 358, 398–99, 401–4
Tunisian, 3–5, 5 n. 5, 25, 51–52, 68, 75, 87–88, 94, 96–98, 113, 172, 183, 232, 248, 320 n. 33, 321, 334, 343, 364–65, 402
Wad-Souf (El-Oued), 3, 33, 44 n. 24, 45, 67 n. 38, 76, 87, 98, 106, 118, 131, 137, 142 n. 2, 188, 252, 257–58, 390, 397
Yemeni, 5, 26, 266

Aramaic, 8, 233, 243–44, 258, 261, 284, 312, 324, 350–51, 353, 365, 380, 386, 390
   Neo-Aramaic, 8, 244, 312, 324, 351, 380, 390
   Telkepe, 375, 380–82
articulation, 36, 45–47, 50, 79
aspect, 6, 22, 139, 144, 166, 210–11, 241, 262, 277, 281, 283, 289, 292, 299, 304, 311, 319–20, 320 n. 33, 320 n. 34, **321–65**, 389, 402, 405
aspiration, 328
assimilation, 35, 38, 59–60, 80, 98, 128, 143, 323–24, 351
associative, 214, 216, 227, 242
asymmetry, 58, 226
asyndetic, 262, 275, 277–79, 286, 291, 312
atelic, 211–12, 340, 345, 364
attribution, 238, 270–71, 284
Augustine, Saint, 13–14
auxiliary, 78–79, 81, 110, 143, 321–23, 326, 329, 331, 335, 356, 360, 364

B

backgrounding, 363–64, 371–72, 378

balanced, 283
Bantu, 210, 244
Banū Hilāl, 2
Banū Sulaym, 2
Basque, 269
Berber, 8–13, 43, 61 n. 32, 62, 101–2, 102 n. 12, 207, 209, 258, 349, 352–53, 383
   Awjila, 101
   Chleuh, 101
   Figuig, 101
   Kabyle, 101
   Touareg, 101
bilabial, 29, 31, 49
binary, 99, 330, 335
binodal, 368, 373, 375
bipartite, 99, 137, 403
borrowing, 10, 44–45, 66
broken plural, 174, 250

C

Cairo Genizah, 1, 279
causative, 102
Christianity, 15
Chukchee, 212
classificatory, 234–35, 240–42
clause, 195, 211–13, 218, 220, **261–383**, 404
clitic, 209, 322–23, 325–26
close-mid, 75

cluster, 75, 78–83, 86, 95 n. 8, 110, 125, 129, 134, 220, 385
coda, 81–82
collective, 150–52, 159, 163, 209, 252
communal, 6, 15, 334
complement, 30, 261, 264–65, 270, 284, 298–306, 308–20, 372, 404
complementation, 298–99, 304–6, 317, 319, 404
complementiser, 266, 299, 303–5, 308, 316–18
compound, 199, 321, 335, 353
concessive, 297–98, 319
concomitant, 335, 337
concord, **243–60**, 403
conditional, 282–83, 293–94, 327, 355–56
congruence, 243
conjugation, 67, 91 n. 1, 93, 97, 104, 106, 112–14, 117, 117 n. 17, 118, 120–24, 127, 130, 132, 135, 193, 315, 323, 331, 402
conjunctive, 274, 276
consonant, 17, 20, 20 n. 13, 21, 21 n. 14, 25–27, 27 n. 4, 28–29, 29 n. 5, 30 n. 7, 31–36, 38–47, 49–51, 53, 55–59, 62–66, 68, 71, 73–76, 78–83, 85–87, 93, 95 n. 8, 103, 106, 109–10, 113–14, 116–18, 121, 124–25, 127, 129, 134–36, 140–41, 143, 149 n. 5, 152, 156–57, 158 n. 21, 159, 161–65, 167–68, 170, 174–76, 180, 187–91, 193, 323–24, 328, 401–2
construct state, 50 n. 30, 144–46, 152, 226, 230, 270–71, 284, 399
contrastive, 237, 241–42, 328, 372
controller, 243, 245, 247, 249–53, 255–58
coordination, 261, 275–76, 279, 282, 291–93, 297–98, 318–19, 404
coreference, 313
Czech, 212–13

D
Damascus, 249, 312, 351
dative, 193
declarative, 102
definite article, 21, 143, 206, 215–16, 218 n. 6, 220–21, 223, 225–28, 233, 266, 277

definiteness, 22, **205–29**, 239–42, 274, 276–79, 318, 370, 403–4
deflected, 249–59, 403–4
deixis, 241–42, 244, 385–91, 393–99
demonstrative, 139, 161 n. 28, 198–99, 218, 227, 232, 234, 266, 274, **385–400**
dental, 32–33, 129
deontic, 308, 319, 358, 360, 404
deranked, 283
derivation, 326
derived stems, 91, 123, 169
desiderative, 300, 304, 313–14, 320
determination, 207, 243
devoicing, 31–33, 59, 323
diachronic, 6, 8, 10, 12, 77, 140, 156, 203, 247–48, 250, 256, 322, 324, 326, 365, 401, 403
dichotomous, 210
diphthong, 63, 75–76, 87–88, 110, 113, 121, 123, 141, 146, 152, 402
disambiguation, 99
discourse, 207–8, 211–20, 317, 333, 363, 365–67, 371–72, 375, 379, 387, 389–90, 392–93, 395–96, 398, 405
distal, 374, 391, 393, 396–98, 405
disyllabic, 191
dorsum, 31
dual, 91, 145–48, 266, 272
durative, 315, 330, 355–57, 363

E
egocentric, 208, 210
Egypt, 4, 102, 232, 257, 349
  Upper Egypt, 102
elision, 60, 125, 174, 296, 324, 352, 399
ellipsis, 300
embedding, 275–76, 282, 298
emphasis, 21, 26, 26 n. 3, 29–30, 32–33, 35, 41, 50–59, 87, 143, 324, 402
emphatic, 20, 20 n. 13, 25–30, 30 n. 7, 31–42, 49–51, 53, 55–59, 64, 65 n. 36, 66–68, 71, 74, 76, 87, 106–7, 110, 116, 124, 136, 143, 178 n. 49, 324, 402
emphaticisation, 31, 39, 41, 50, 58, 324
endophoric, 388–89

English, 262, 266, 342, 344, 374, 395
epenthetic, 30, 78–79, 83, 85, 93, 95 n. 8, 115 n. 15, 127, 129, 132, 134
epistemic, 303, 308, 319, 358, 360, 404
equi-deletion, 300–301, 371
Ethiopic, 244, 284, 385
etymological, 30 n. 6, 31, 35, 46–47, 76, 120, 173 n. 47, 184 n. 50, 232
exophoric, 388–90
exponent, 229, 231–33, 235–42, 271, 325, 403
expositive, 242
extension, 30, 96, 100–101, 258–59, 385

F
feminine, 10, 78 n. 1, 136, 141–46, 148, 150–51, 154, 155 n. 14, 158–59, 161, 161 n. 28, 162, 165, 171, 176, 182, 184, 187, 187 n. 52, 188, 198–99, 210, 237, 239, 244–45, 249–50, 253–54, 385
folktale, 18, 22, 159 n. 23, 159 n. 24, 214, 257, 377, 396 n. 3

foregrounding, 363, 371, 378
France, 2, 18
French, 5, 36, 39, 81, 99, 173, 268, 301, 335
frequency, 35, 37, 53, 55–56, 103, 232
fricative, 28, 31–32, 38–39, 40 n. 16, 41–42, 45–47, 49, 59, 81, 110, 129
frontal, 36, 42, 69
Functional Grammar, 281
future, 19 n. 11, 99, 294, 303, 305, 314, 317, 335–37, 350–51, 357–60, 365, 405

G
gemination, 21, 29, 29 n. 5, 31–33, 47, 50, 60, 80, 86, 92, 103, 109, 113, 124–25, 127, 133–35, 141, 143, 149, 149 n. 7, 164–65, 180–82
gender, 10, 16, 18, 91, 105, 136, 141–43, 155 n. 14, 161 n. 28, 175, 185, 195, 210, 224, 237, 243–45, 247, 251, 265, 270, 273, 277, 385, 400, 402
generic, 215–16, 221, 240, 251, 254, 277, 330

genitive, 22, 144, 209, **229–42**, 268, 271, 273, 278, 325, 390, 403
Geʕez, 385–86
givenness, 215
glottal stop, 11, 27, 49, 49 n. 29
gradience, 326, 360
grammaticalisation, 244, 284, 322, 325–26, 389
Greek, 31, 171–72, 209, 296, 299, 358
Gumbaynggir, 275
guttural, 76, 79, 93, 106, 110, 116, 124, 136–37

H
habitual, 328–30, 336–37, 356–57, 363
hamza, 49–50, 121–22, 140–41, 152, 155–57, 174, 181–82
Ḥāṛa, 42
harmony, 7 n. 6, 38, 38 n. 14
Hebrew, 5–7, 19, 34–35, 40, 40 n. 16, 46, 49 n. 28, 51, 68, 147, 158 n. 20, 164, 164 n. 33, 173, 173 n. 47, 200, 209, 227, 239, 243–44, 248, 250, 255–59, 266, 269–71, 294–95, 351, 385–86, 403

heteroclisis, 245
historical present, 362
honorific, 210
Hungarian, 212
hybrid, 97, 99
hypotaxis, 292

I
iconicity, 304
identificatory, 234, 241–42, 391–92
imperative, 78 n. 1, 94–95, 102, 105, 109–12, 114–16, 119–33, 135, 299
imperfective, 106, 283, 292, 322, 330–32, 335, 358, 361–62
impersonal, 99, 242, 309, 374
inalienable, 225, 234, 236
inanimate, 208–9, 213, 222, 226, 228, 244, 247, 268
indefinite, 200, 206, 212–13, 216–21, 224, 230, 235–36, 241–42, 262–64, 274–79, 292, 318, 370, 380–81, 393–95, 404
indefiniteness, 207–8, 210, 216, 242
individuation, 208, 211–16, 218, 222, 226–27, 240, 249,

251, 253, 255, 259 n. 28, 274, 276–77, 292, 404
Indo-European, 272–73, 299
inferiority, 210
inflection, 11, 104, 134–35, 190, 193–95, 230, 270, 272–73, 284, 314–15, 388
inner, 91
insertion, 78, 82–83
interactional, 367
interdental, 27, 32–33, 33 n. 11, 34, 253, 401
internal plural, 147–48, 174, 176
intransitive, 93, 212
irrealis, 211, 294, 299, 303
irregular, 100, 108, 122, 132, 143, 173
Islam, 8–9, 15, 350–51
isogloss, 2 n. 1, 16, 87, 96 n. 9, 120, 349, 403, 405
Israel, 2, 3 n. 2, 6, 18, 248
Italian, 31, 31 n. 9, 39, 161, 166, 167 n. 39, 173, 191
Italy, 14
iterative, 312, 330, 339

K
kinesis, 211
kinetic, 363–64, 372
kinship, 209, 236, 239

L
labialisation, 29, 43, 60
labiodental, 32
language contact, 5–6, 7 n. 6, 9–10, 12, 15, 17, 19, 35, 42 n. 21, 45, 62, 95 n. 7, 101, 243 n. 19, 249–50, 258–59, 271, 294, 312, 349, 353, 382–83, 401, 403
lateral, 28, 39
Latin, 8, 13–17, 233, 258, 349
  African Latin, 8, 13–16
  Classical Latin, 15
leftward, 51–52, 54–58
lengthening, 47, 50, 156, 351, 380
lexeme, 75, 339, 348, 401
Libya, 3, 8, 61, 96, 100–101, 217, 232, 237, 252
Libyco-Berber, 13
liquid, 39, 81–83, 116, 167 n. 39
loanword, 16, 66, 349

M
Maltese, 16
manipulative, 301–2, 312–13
marker, 11, 96, 99, 101, 142, 144, 148, 149 n. 5, 151, 161 n. 28, 175, 188, 193, 209–

Index 501

10, 216, 218, 239, 244–45, 276, 283–84, 292, 319, 326–27, 357–58, 360, 365, 380, 386
masculine, 10, 33, 59, 105, 136, 141–44, 148, 151, 155 n. 14, 166 n. 37, 182, 184, 187, 187 n. 52, 188, 198–99, 244, 246, 251, 253–54
matrix, 284, 300–306, 312–14, 316, 319–20, 404
merger, 16, 108, 188, 405
Mesopotamia, 232, 350
mid-close, 75
mismatch, 245, 275, 277, 279
modal, 304, 307, 319, 327, 360
modifier, 259 n. 28, 273, 275
monopartite, 99
monosyllabic, 29, 49, 81, 86, 134, 144, 157, 182
mood, 91, 283, 299, 302–3, 327, 356, 360, 364
mora, 83, 85
morpheme, 16, 97, 99, 110, 172–73, 173 n. 47, 209–10, 266, 271, 385–86
morphology, 4, 16–17, 21–22, 25 n. 2, 57, **89–202**, 286, 296, 299–300, 302, 322, 331–33, 335, 390, 402–3

multiclausal, 261
Muslim, 1–4, 6–7, 25–26, 29, 32–33, 36–37, 37 n. 12, 39 n. 15, 40, 40 n. 18, 42 n. 21, 42 n. 22, 43, 44 n. 24, 46–48, 49 n. 29, 51, 63, 65, 67, 82, 84, 86–87, 91, 93, 95–98, 103, 105–6, 112, 117, 117 n. 17, 118, 120, 131–32, 137, 157 n. 19, 169, 179, 187–89, 195, 201, 247, 249, 251, 255–58, 259 n. 28, 260, 320 n. 33, 321, 334, 342–44, 346–51, 365, 401, 404–6

N

narrative, 19, 242, 254, 327, 360–63, 365–67, 371, 378, 380, 387, 389, 391
nasal, 28, 31, 34
negation, 81, 86, 196, 321–22
neutral, 210
newness, 215, 217
nexus, 261
node, 83, 368, 371, 374, 377, 396 n. 3
nomadic, 100
nominaliser, 292
noun, 10–11, 20, 20 n. 13, 21–22, 49, 68, 81, 83, 99, 102,

139–202, **205–260**, 262–64, 266–80, 284–85, 291–92, 299, 318–19, 366, 370, 388–91, 399–400, 403–4
nucleus, 81
number, 1, 12, 14, 16, 18–19, 22, 36–37, 49, 55, 95–96, 108, 145–46, 150, 159 n. 22, 160, 174, 184–85, 195, 199, 207, 212, 234, 237, 243, 263, 265, 270, 273, 275, 277, 300, 302, 323, 326, 348, 366–67, 371, 386, 391, 401, 403

O

object, 99, 137, 151, 158, 163, 192–93, 196, 209, 211–13, 215, 263–64, 268–69, 277–78, 280–81, 300–301, 309, 314–15, 319–20, 365–66, 368, 372, 398, 403
onset, 7, 43, 43 n. 23, 81, 85, 110, 311, 332, 366
opacity, 51–53, 56, 58

P

palatalisation, 35–36, 38, 42 n. 22, 110
parataxis, 292, 299

participle, 91, 102, 105, 108–9, 111–12, 114, 114 n. 14, 115–16, 119–20, 123–24, 128, 131–33, 135, 148, 149 n. 5, 160, 169, 299, 309, 315, 321–27, 329, 335, 339–48, 350–51, 353–54, 356–57, 360, 405
particle, 21, 81, 86, 187 n. 52, 191–92, 194–97, 199, 207, 209, 230, 232–33, 241, 265, 268, 270–71, 274, 281, 284, 286, 291–99, 301, 308–9, 313, 320–29, 331, 335, 353–54, 356–57, 357 n. 60, 358, 360, 362, 364, 372, 405
passive, 91–92, 92 n. 3, 95–96, 96 n. 9, 97–101, 102 n. 12, 105, 108–9, 112, 114 n. 14, 115, 119, 127–28, 131, 137, 148, 169, 249, 309, 374, 403
pejorative, 210, 393
penultimate, 86, 94, 159 n. 25, 186, 380
periphrastic, 99
pharyngealisation, 29, 43, 51, 53, 58
pharynx, 46, 50, 57
phasal, 310–13, 330

Phoenicians, 12
phonemic, 19–20, 27 n. 4, 29–30, 32, 34, 36, 40, 40 n. 18, 43–44, 44 n. 24, 47, 61–62, 62 n. 33, 63–64, 64 n. 34, 65, 65 n. 36, 67, 70, 87, 117, 143, 401–2
phonetic, 19–20, 39–40, 42, 51, 60, 93, 97, 110, 112, 136, 178 n. 49, 324, 328
phonology, 3–4, 11, 17, 21, **23–88**, 401
phonotactics, 21, 77
phrase, 210, 215, 226–27, 233–34, 236, 239–43, 247, 267–69, 272–73, 276–77, 292, 321, 323, 370, 380, 388
plain, 28, 31, 35–38, 42, 51, 53, 55, 57, 66, 71, 73, 334, 336, 359, 402
plosive, 29–30, 30 n. 8, 31, 33–34, 41, 43, 45, 59, 81, 110, 401
plot, 63, 69, 72, 361, 371–72, 379
plurality, 151, 209, 243
Polish, 209–10, 272
polyfunctionality, 270
possessor, 209
post-dental, 32

postalveolar, 35–36, 110, 129
posteriority, 289
postnominal, 266–67, 399, 404
predetermination, 283, 303, 319, 404
predicate, 243–44, 269, 286–87, 298–306, 311–20, 322, 329, 367–68, 372, 380, 404
prefix, 34, 51, 57, 67, 79–80, 91, 94–95, 95 n. 8, 96–97, 97 n. 11, 98, 100–101, 102 n. 12, 104, 106–7, 110–11, 113–14, 120, 122, 127–32, 134, 169–70, 193, 249, 258, 286, 312, 315, 323–25, 357–58, 363–64, 402
preposition, 20–21, 139, 172, 193, 234–35, 238, 264–65, 267–68, 278, 309, 366, 372, 374
pretonic, 351, 353
preverbal, 21, 292, 321–25, 329, 331, 333, 335, 353–54, 356, 362, 364, 372
progressive, 257, 325, 327–29, 337–38, 345, 405
prominence, 9, 12, 86, 208, 210, 213–15, 218, 220, 226, 228–29, 270, 274, 276, 361, 367–68, 370, 375, 393

pronoun, 16, 20, 22, 30 n. 6,
  50 n. 30, 79, 80, 99, 137,
  139, 155 n. 14, 161 n. 28,
  186, 188, 190–201, 209,
  213, 218, 225, 232–34, 240,
  244, 254, 262, 265–66, 268,
  270, 272–74, 276–81, 284,
  299, 309, 314, 318, 320,
  373–74, **385–400**, 403–5
propositional, 305, 316
prosodic, 19, 78, 175, 375
prosthetic, 83, 102, 129, 131–32
protasis, 294–95, 355
proximal, 218, 374, 391–93,
  397–98, 400, 405
punctual, 211–12, 290–91,
  293, 312, 315, 330, 332,
  363
Punic, 7 n. 7, 8, 12–14, 14 n.
  8, 258, 350, 353
  Late Punic, 12–13
  Latino-Punic, 13
  Neo-Punic, 8, 13

Q
Quran, 251, 271

R
radical, 49, 51, 68, 79, 81–82,
  93, 95 n. 8, 102–3, 111–14,

  115 n. 15, 116–17, 117 n.
  17, 118–20, 120 n. 19, 121–
  22, 124–31, 133–36, 140–
  41, 149–50, 152, 154–58,
  160, 162, 164–65, 170, 177,
  180–82, 189, 192, 365
raising, 43, 45, 296, 300–301,
  304–5, 314, 320
realis, 211
realisation, 20, 27, 29, 31–33,
  35–36, 39–40, 40 n. 16, 42,
  42 n. 21, 43, 45–46, 46 n.
  27, 47, 49, 49 n. 28, 62, 66,
  68, 71, 73–75, 87, 112, 253,
  283, 302, 314, 324, 334,
  401
reanalysis, 326, 360
reciprocal, 80, 196
reconstruction, 8, 96, 266,
  324–25, 385
recoverability, 303
reduction, 12, 26, 61–62, 76,
  78, 82, 93–94, 157, 162,
  174, 283, 301, 303, 322,
  324–25, 351–53
reflex, 20, 33, 68, 103, 116
reflexive, 11, 97, 128, 131–32,
  194
relative, 4, 44 n. 24, 195–96,
  218, 232, 261–63, 265–68,

270–80, 282, 284, 292, 294, 318, 334–35, 383, 404
request, 312–13
restrictive, 262, 267–68, 273, 279, 318, 404
resultative, 330, 339, 341–43, 345, 347
resumption, 273, 277–78, 299, 318, 404
retraction, 31, 50, 73
retroflex, 38
rhotic, 28
rhyme, 254
rightward, 30, 51–52, 54, 56–58
Romance, 14, 16–17, 268, 271, 329
root, 46, 50, 53, 55, 67, 73, 103–5, 109, 117, 121, 123–25, 127–34, 140–41, 143, 146, 152, 154–56, 167, 170–71, 173, 173 n. 47, 190, 308–9, 355
rural, 2, 8, 13–15, 17, 33, 45, 97, 405
Russian, 209, 299, 303

S

Sahara, 98, 231, 299
salience, 208, 210, 221–22

scale, 59, 72, 81, 169, 237, 397
scatter, 69, 72–73, 75
sedentary, 2–3, 17, 42, 63, 75, 87, 91, 96, 96 n. 9, 98, 120, 136, 146, 231–32, 236, 253, 324, 328, 352–53, 401, 405
segment, 30 n. 7, 35, 37, 40, 53, 55–57, 60
semantic, 94, 145–46, 154, 167, 234, 236, 243, 282–83, 298, 302, 305–6, 310, 319, 331, 345, 357, 403–4
semi-vowel, 49, 72, 92, 102, 111–13, 117 n. 17, 135, 149, 177, 180
Semitic, 8, 17, 51, 147, 209–10, 213, 227, 243–45, 259–61, 263, 266, 270–73, 281, 284, 292, 318–19, 320 n. 34, 321, 332, 349–50, 358, 380, 382, 385–87, 403, 405
serialisation, 11, 299, 371
shift, 2, 10, 13, 15, 20 n. 13, 31–36, 39, 43–46, 50 n. 30, 55, 64, 67, 75–76, 80, 87, 101, 110, 117, 126, 149 n. 7, 181, 349, 357, 366
sibilant, 15, 25–26, 37–38, 38 n. 14, 41, 72, 87, 401
singulative, 150, 152, 159

Slavic, 208, 210, 267, 299, 331
sociolinguistic, 57, 210
software, 25, 53, 69
sonority, 81–82
Spain, 1, 344
Spanish, 99, 173, 268–69, 299, 303, 344
spatial, 387, 390, 395
specific, 144–45, 145 n. 4, 151, 167, 194, 206, 208–10, 213, 215–21, 221 n. 8, 239–40, 242, 264, 274–78, 281, 293, 322, 333, 370, 380, 389, 393–94
spreadability, 25, 87, 402
statistical, 254
stem, 6, 19, 32, 44, 50–51, 57, 63, 67–68, 78 n. 1, 79, 91–92, 92 n. 33, 93–95, 95 n. 8, 96–102, 102 n. 12, 103–16, 117 n. 17, 118–37, 148, 169–70, 175, 199, 233, 244, 256, 265, 294–95, 321–24, 329, 333, 335–47, 350, 353, 356–65, 374, 403, 405
stop, 11, 27–28, 43 n. 23, 49, 49 n. 29, 55, 73, 95, 121, 129, 324
stress, 20, 50 n. 30, 80, 85–86, 94, 110, 131, 149 n. 5, 156, 159 n. 25, 186, 189, 325, 351, 375
subject, 9, 99, 126, 143, 209, 243–44, 254, 256, 259 n. 28, 264–65, 268–69, 278, 280–81, 286–87, 300–302, 304–5, 308–10, 313–16, 318–20, 323, 365–68, 370–72, 374, 376, 379–80, 391, 404
subjectivity, 208
subjunctive, 271, 283, 299, 301, 303, 305
subordination, 22, **261–320**, 374, 404
substantive, 139, 148, 160, 166, 184, 273
substrate, 16–17, 25, 259–60, 321, 349, 351–53, 401, 405
suffix, 30 n. 6, 34, 50 n. 30, 57, 67, 79–81, 91, 94, 104–6, 109–10, 112–14, 115 n. 15, 116–18, 120, 125, 127, 130, 132, 134–36, 141–42, 146, 148, 149 n. 6, 149 n. 7, 150, 161 n. 28, 162, 170–74, 180, 182–83, 188–93, 197–98, 230, 245, 271, 284, 314–15, 363, 402
syllable, 20, 22, 50 n. 30, 53, 55–58, 62, 77–78, 78 n. 1,

80–82, 84–86, 94, 110–11, 118, 129, 144, 159 n. 25, 161–62, 164, 167, 174, 183, 190–92, 197, 239, 352–53, 375, 380
syndetic, 277–78, 286, 291
syntax, 4, 17, 21–22, **203–400**, 401, 403, 405
synthetic, 231, 233–40
Syria, 232, 351

T

target, 101, 243, 245, 247, 251, 253–56, 304
taxonomy, 40 n. 17, 175, 237, 263, 282, 289, 306, 319, 325, 404
telic, 211–12, 340, 345, 348
temporal, 271, 282–83, 287–93, 296, 302, 311, 319, 321, 329–36, 338, 364, 381–82, 394, 404–5
tense, 22, 99, 189, 299, 302–3, 305, 315, 319–20, 320 n. 33, 320 n. 34, **321–365**, 404–5
thematic, 67, 106–7, 110–11, 117–18, 377
timbre, 79, 106
topic, 16, 91 n. 2, 174, 203, 214, 216–18, 223, 248, 276, 292, 332, 366–68, 370–81, 387, 392, 396
transactional, 366–67
transcription, 18–19, 19 n. 11, 20–21, 21 n. 14, 27 n. 4, 37 n. 13, 67 n. 39, 94 n. 6, 110, 254, 257, 272, 324–25, 375
transitive, 93, 211
trill, 28, 39–40, 42
Tunisia, 1, 3–4, 8, 12, 19 n. 11, 26, 49, 49 n. 28, 75, 96, 96 n. 9, 96 n. 10, 100, 117–18, 195, 217, 232, 236–37, 252, 294, 321, 350, 401, 403
Turkish, 8, 31, 172–73
typology, 3, 17, 22, 52, 83, 203, 220, 261–62, 266, 275, 282, 298, 318, 344, 366–68, 382, 387

U

Ugaritic, 284
ultimate, 86, 94, 111, 159 n. 25, 186
unaspirated, 43, 324, 328
uninodal, 368
unique, 22, 122, 210, 326, 377
unrounded, 75
unvoiced, 28–29
utterance, 30 n. 6, 302–5, 307, 317, 335, 365–66, 389

uvular, 39, 40 n. 16, 41–42, 42
  n. 21, 43, 45, 59, 64, 71,
  328

V
velar, 28, 34, 40 n. 16, 41–46,
  59, 71, 106, 324
verb, 11, 16–17, 20, 22, 44–
  45, 49–50, 67–68, 79–81,
  83, **91–137**, 160, 169–70,
  188–89, 191–94, 209, 212,
  220, 223, 242, 244, 247,
  254, 256, **261–383**, 403
viewpoint, 322, 331, 336–37,
  339
virility, 208, 210, 223–24, 229
vocalic, 30, 80, 93, 100, 117,
  125–26, 130, 140, 190–91,
  193, 352
voiced, 28–29, 34, 44, 47, 59
voiceless, 31–32, 44, 59
volitive, 300, 357–58, 360
vowel, 11–12, 17, 19–20, 25–
  26, 29–30, 30 n. 7, 39–41,
  47, 49, 49 n. 29, 50–52, 56,
  61–67, 67 n. 38, 67 n. 39,
  68–75, 77–83, 85–87, 92–
  95, 95 n. 8, 102–3, 105–7,
  109–14, 115 n. 15, 116–17,
  117 n. 17, 118, 124–27,
  129–32, 134–37, 143, 149,
152, 156–57, 158 n. 21,
161–62, 164, 171, 174–77,
178 n. 49, 180–81, 187–91,
239, 245, 325, 328, 351–53,
399, 402

W
weakening, 10, 36, 47, 78 n. 1
Welsh, 269
word order, 185, 212, **365–83**,
  405

Y
Yemen, 232

About the Team

Alessandra Tosi was the managing editor for this book and provided quality control.

Anne Burberry performed the copyediting of the book in Word. The main fonts used in this volume are Charis SIL, SBL Hebrew, Scheherazade New, and SBL Greek.

Cameron Craig created all of the editions — paperback, hardback, and PDF. Conversion was performed with open source software freely available on our GitHub page at https://github.com/OpenBookPublishers.

Jeevanjot Kaur Nagpal designed the cover of this book. The cover was produced in InDesign using Fontin and Calibri fonts.

Cambridge Semitic Languages and Cultures

General Editor Geoffrey Khan

www.ingramcontent.com/pod-product-compliance
Lightning Source LLC
Chambersburg PA
CBHW052040220426
43663CB00012B/2384